*Praise for* ANTHONY LEWIS'S
# MAKE NO LAW

"Superb . . . Mr. Lewis . . . vividly demonstrates how serious a threat libel judgments were both to the civil rights movement and to freedom of the press. . . . *Make No Law* is even better than *Gideon's Trumpet*."
—Walter Dellinger,
*The New York Times Book Review*

"Our premier teller of judicial tales for the laity—an eminently readable interpreter of the court's cryptic processes . . . Lewis enriches his tale with an informed review of the evolution of free speech law in this century . . . [and] is in a position to be authoritative where judicial historians often are forced to reconstruct by inference and informed guesses. . . . *Make No Law* tells the story vividly and even magisterially."
—*Washington Post Book World*

"A landmark study of legal protection for freedom of expression . . . Lewis tells the story with a reporter's eye for detail. The vignettes are priceless . . . crisp and illuminating. And Mr. Lewis's access to the Brennan files allows him exceptional insight into the process of creation and compromise that characterizes the Court's deliberations. . . . [The] tale is essential reading—and rereading—for anyone interested in the history of the Court or who cares about free speech."
—Robert D. Sack,
*The New York Times*

"[Lewis's] clarity is a marvel, every step of the way. He . . . helps the reader appreciate the moral as well as the legal problems of adjudication between conflicting 'good's: protecting individuals from malice and defending the public's interest in free discussion of public affairs."
—*The New Yorker*

"Anthony Lewis ably intertwines multiple themes—free speech, racial justice, judicial compromise, and public-versus-private power, for example—in recounting the story of the most important libel ruling in United States history. . . . He does us a distinct service by doing so."
—*Christian Science Monitor*

ALSO BY ANTHONY LEWIS

*Gideon's Trumpet*
*Portrait of a Decade*

# ANTHONY LEWIS

# MAKE NO LAW

Now a columnist for *The New York Times*, Anthony Lewis was the *Times* reporter at the Supreme Court from 1957 to 1964, and one of the cases he covered was *New York Times Co. v. Sullivan*. He also taught the case at the Harvard Law School, where he was a Lecturer on Law from 1974 to 1989. Since 1983 he has been the James Madison Visiting Professor at Columbia University.

Mr. Lewis was born in 1927 in New York City, and attended the Horace Mann School there and Harvard College, from which he received his B.A. in 1948. He spent four years in the Sunday department of the *Times*, then three as a reporter for the *Washington Daily News*, where he won a Pulitzer Prize for articles on the federal loyalty-security program. In 1955 he returned to the *Times* and won a second Pulitzer in 1963 for his reporting on the Supreme Court. In 1956–57 he was a Nieman Fellow at Harvard, studying law. At the end of 1964 he became chief of the *Times* London bureau, remaining in London until 1973. In 1969 he began writing his column.

Mr. Lewis is married and has three children and three grandchildren.

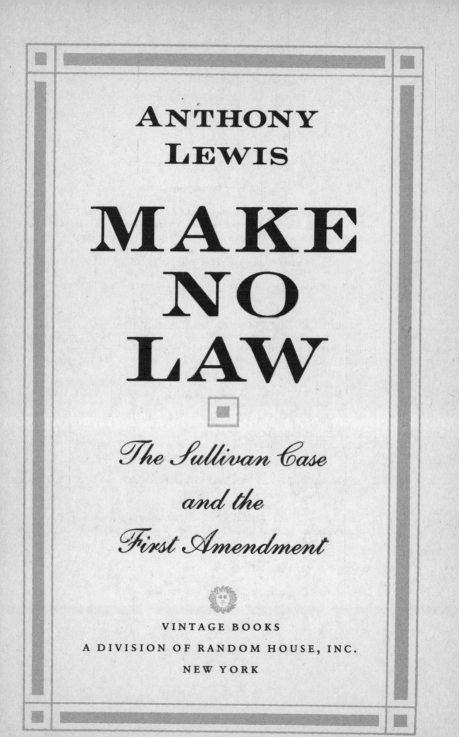

ANTHONY
LEWIS

# MAKE
# NO
# LAW

*The Sullivan Case*

*and the*

*First Amendment*

VINTAGE BOOKS
A DIVISION OF RANDOM HOUSE, INC.
NEW YORK

First Vintage Books Edition, September 1992

*Copyright © 1991 by Anthony Lewis*

All rights reserved under international and Pan-American Copyright
Conventions. Published in the United States by Vintage Books, a division of
Random House, Inc., New York, and simultaneously by Random House of
Canada Limited, Toronto. Originally published in hardcover by
Random House, Inc., New York, in 1991.

Some passages in this book appeared, in a different form,
in *The New Yorker*.
Grateful acknowledgment is made to *The New York Times*
for permission to reprint excerpts from articles by Claude Sitton
from the January 4, 1960, December 5, 1960, July 27, 1962,
and May 13, 1963, issues of *The New York Times* and excerpts
from "Fear and Hatred Grip Birmingham" by Harrison E. Salisbury
from the April 12, 1960, issue of *The New York Times*.
Copyright © 1960, 1962, 1963 by The New York Times Company.
Reprinted by permission.

Library of Congress Cataloging-in-Publication Data
Lewis, Anthony, 1927–
Make no law: the Sullivan case and the First Amendment / Anthony
Lewis. — 1st Vintage Books ed.
p.    cm.
Originally published: New York : Random House, c1991.
Includes bibliographical references and index.
ISBN 0-679-73939-4 (pbk.)
1. Libel and slander—United States.   2. Freedom of the press—
United States.   3. Press law—United States.   4. Sullivan, L. B.—
Trials, litigation, etc. 5. New York Times Company—Trials,
litigation, etc.   I. Title.
[KF1266.L48   1992]
345.73′0256—dc20
[347.305256]          92-50104
CIP

*Book design by Carole Lowenstein*

Manufactured in the United States of America

10 9 8 7 6

*To Margie*

# ACKNOWLEDGMENTS

I owe much to *The New York Times*. Thirty-five years ago James Reston, then the *Times* Washington bureau chief, offered me the chance to cover the Supreme Court. In the years since, the publisher, Arthur Ochs Sulzberger, and many editors have given me great opportunity and great freedom to write, about the law and other things. I have benefited over a long time from conversations with Linda Greenhouse, who now covers the Supreme Court for the *Times*, and from research by Judith Greenfeld and John Motyka of the *Times* research staff.

The Harvard Law School opened my eyes to the law when I spent a year there as a Nieman Fellow. I could never have imagined this book without what I learned then and after from its faculty, and from the students I taught for fifteen years. A former student of mine, Rosemary Reeve, checked the citations in this book and saved me from much grief. I had help from the law school's reference librarians, among them Joan Duckett, Ellen Delaney, Alan Diefenbach, Janet Katz, Heda Kovaly, Beth Radcliffe, Naomi Ronen and Jonathan Thomas. Susan Lewis-Somers of the Yale Law Library was also helpful. Professor Randall Kennedy provided material on Alabama.

Professor Vincent Blasi of the Columbia Law School read the manuscript and gave me the benefit of his deep understanding of the First Amendment. Margaret H. Marshall and Eliza Lewis read it chapter by chapter as it was written, making valuable suggestions and enduring my resistance to them. Herbert and Doris Wechsler were generous in talking with me about the *Sullivan* case over the years. I am also grateful for conversations with other lawyers who participated in the case: Roland Nachman, Marvin Frankel, T. Eric Embry. Professor Alan Brinkley gave me some timely help on history.

My assistant at the *Times*, Susan Crowley-Gerame, kept me going in more ways than I deserved. Mia Lewis made valuable final comments and corrections. Danica Kombol and David Lewis gave support throughout the writing. David Greenway suggested the title.

I acknowledge with gratitude permission from various authors to quote from their works: Taylor Branch for his *Parting the Waters: America in the King Years 1954–63*, Fred Friendly for *Minnesota Rag*, Rod Smolla for *Suing the Press: Libel, the Media and Power*, Richard Polenberg for *Fighting Faiths: the Abrams Case, the Supreme Court and Free Speech*, Leonard W. Levy for *Emergence of a Free Press*, James Morton Smith for *Freedom's Fetters: The Alien and Sedition Acts and American Civil Liberties* and Leonard Garment for his *New Yorker* article, *Annals of Law: The Hill Case*. I should add that Gerald Gunther's superb casebook, *Cases and Materials on Constitutional Law*, helped to guide me through the intricate paths of First Amendment interpretation.

Joseph M. Fox of Random House edited a book of mine long ago. Ever since, he has been encouraging me to lift my eyes from daily journalism again, and I do not think I would have done it for anyone else. His editing hand has lost none of its cunning, his spirit none of its generosity. As copy editor, Sono Rosenberg corrected my lapses and withstood the grinding of teeth. To both, much thanks.

Finally, there is William J. Brennan Jr. What Justice Brennan did for all of us when he wrote the opinion in *New York Times v. Sullivan* needs no further comment. When I decided to write the story, I asked for permission to look at his files on the case. He said yes. In that and so many ways he made it all possible.

# CONTENTS

ACKNOWLEDGMENTS                                                    IX

1   Heed Their Rising Voices                                        5
2   Reaction in Montgomery                                          9
3   Separate and Unequal                                           15
4   The Trial                                                      23
5   Silencing the Press                                            34
6   The Meaning of Freedom                                         46
7   The Sedition Act                                               56
8   World War I                                                    67
9   Holmes and Brandeis, Dissenting                                80
10  "The Vitalizing Liberties"                                     90
11  To the Supreme Court                                          103
12  "There Never Is a Time"                                       113
13  May It Please the Court                                       127
14  "The Central Meaning of the First Amendment"                  140
15  What It Meant                                                 153
16  Inside the Court                                              164
17  Public and Private                                            183
18  "The Dancing Has Stopped"                                     200
19  Back to the Drawing Board?                                    219
20  Envoi                                                         234

APPENDIX 1: First Draft of Justice Brennan's Opinion in
*New York Times Co. v. Sullivan*                    249

APPENDIX 2: Opinions in *New York Times Co. v.
Sullivan* by Justices Brennan, Black
and Goldberg                    275

NOTES                    329

TABLE OF CASES                    341

INDEX                    343

# MAKE NO LAW

*"The growing movement of peaceful mass demonstrations by Negroes is something new in the South, something understandable....*

*Let Congress heed their rising voices, for they will be heard."*

—New York Times editorial
Saturday, March 19, 1960

# Heed Their Rising Voices

As the whole world knows by now, thousands of Southern Negro students are engaged in widespread non-violent demonstrations in positive affirmation of the right to live in human dignity as guaranteed by the U. S. Constitution and the Bill of Rights. In their efforts to uphold these guarantees, they are being met by an unprecedented wave of terror by those who would deny and negate that document which the whole world looks upon as setting the pattern for modern freedom....

In Orangeburg, South Carolina, when 400 students peacefully sought to buy doughnuts and coffee at lunch counters in the business district, they were forcibly ejected, tear-gassed, soaked to the skin in freezing weather with fire hoses, arrested en masse and herded into an open barbed-wire stockade to stand for hours in the bitter cold.

In Montgomery, Alabama, after students sang "My Country, 'Tis of Thee" on the State Capitol steps, their leaders were expelled from school, and truck-

protagonists of democracy. Their courage and amazing restraint have inspired millions and given a new dignity to the cause of freedom.

Small wonder that the Southern violators of the Constitution fear this new, non-violent brand of freedom fighter . . . even as they fear the upswelling right-to-vote movement. Small wonder that they are determined to destroy the one man who, more than any other, symbolizes the new spirit now sweeping the South—the Rev. Dr. Martin Luther King, Jr., world-famous leader of the Montgomery Bus Protest. For it is his doctrine of non-violence which has inspired and guided the students in their widening wave of sit-ins; and it this same Dr. King who founded and is president of the Southern Christian Leadership Conference—the organization which is spearheading the surging right-to-vote movement. Under Dr. King's direction the Leadership Conference conducts Student Workshops and Seminars in the philosophy and technique of non-violent resistance.

of others—look for guidance and support, and thereby to intimidate *all* leaders who may rise in the South. Their strategy is to behead this affirmative movement, and thus to demoralize Negro Americans and weaken their will to struggle. The defense of Martin Luther King, spiritual leader of the student sit-in movement, clearly, therefore, is an integral part of the total struggle for freedom in the South.

Decent-minded Americans cannot help but applaud the creative daring of the students and the quiet heroism of Dr. King. But this is one of those moments in the stormy history of Freedom when men and women of good will must do more than applaud the rising-to-glory of others. The America whose good name hangs in the balance before a watchful world, the America whose heritage of Liberty these Southern Upholders of the Constitution are defending, is *our* America as well as theirs . . .

We must heed their rising voices—yes—but we must add our own.

loads of police armed with shotguns and tear-gas ringed the Alabama State College Campus. When the entire student body protested to state authorities by refusing to re-register, their dining hall was padlocked in an attempt to starve them into submission.

In Tallahassee, Atlanta, Nashville, Savannah, Greensboro, Memphis, Richmond, Charlotte, and a host of other cities in the South, young American teen-agers, in face of the entire weight of official state apparatus and police power, have boldly stepped forth as

Again and again the Southern violators have answered Dr. King's peaceful protests with intimidation and violence. They have bombed his home almost killing his wife and child. They have assaulted his person. They have arrested him seven times—for "speeding," "loitering" and similar "offenses." And now they have charged him with "perjury"—*a felony under which they could imprison him for ten years.* Obviously, their real purpose is to remove him physically as the leader to whom the students and millions

We must raise our selves above and beyond moral support and render the material help so urgently needed by those who are taking the risks, facing jail, and even death in a glorious re-affirmation of our Constitution and its Bill of Rights.

We urge you to join hands with our fellow Americans in the South by supporting, with your dollars, this Combined Appeal for all three needs—the defense of Martin Luther King—the support of the embattled students—and the struggle for the right-to-vote.

# Your Help Is Urgently Needed . . . NOW!!

Stella Adler
Raymond Pace Alexander
Harry Van Arsdale
Harry Belafonte
Julie Belafonte
Dr. Algernon Black
Marc Blitzstein
William Branch
Marlon Brando
Mrs. Ralph Bunche
Diahann Carroll

Dr. Alan Knight Chalmers
Richard Coe
Nat King Cole
Cheryl Crawford
Dorothy Dandridge
Ossie Davis
Sammy Davis, Jr.
Ruby Dee
Dr. Philip Elliott
Dr. Harry Emerson Fosdick

Anthony Franciosa
Lorraine Hansberry
Rev. Donald Harrington
Nat Hentoff
James Hicks
Mary Hinkson
Van Heflin
Langston Hughes
Morris Iushewitz
Mahalia Jackson
Mordecai Johnson

John Killens
Eartha Kitt
Rabbi Edward Klein
Hope Lange
John Lewis
Viveca Lindfors
Carl Murphy
Don Murray
John Murray
A. J. Muste
Frederick O'Neal

L. Joseph Overton
Clarence Pickett
Shad Polier
Sidney Poitier
A. Philip Randolph
John Raitt
Elmer Rice
Jackie Robinson
Mrs. Eleanor Roosevelt
Bayard Rustin
Robert Ryan

Maureen Stapleton
Frank Silvera
Hope Stevens
George Tabori
Rev. Gardner C. Taylor
Norman Thomas
Kenneth Tynan
Charles White
Shelley Winters
Max Youngstein

*We in the south who are struggling daily for dignity and freedom warmly endorse this appeal*

Rev. Ralph D. Abernathy
(Montgomery, Ala.)
Rev. Fred L. Shuttlesworth
(Birmingham, Ala.)
Rev. Kelley Miller Smith
(Nashville, Tenn.)
Rev. W. A. Dennis
(Chattanooga, Tenn.)
Rev. C. K. Steele
(Tallahassee, Fla.)

Rev. Matthew D. McCollom
(Orangeburg, S.C.)
Rev. William Holmes Borders
(Atlanta, Ga.)
Rev. Douglas Moore
(Durham, N.C.)
Rev. Wyatt Tee Walker
(Petersburg, Va.)

Rev. Walter — Hamilton
(Norfolk, V.)
I. S. Levy
(Columbia, S. C.)
Rev. Martin Luther King, Sr.
(Atlanta, G—)
Rev. Henry C. Bunton
(Memphis, Tenn.)
Rev. S. S. Seay, Sr.
(Montgomery, Ala.)
Rev. Samuel W. Williams
(Atlanta, Ga.)

Rev. A. L. Davis
(New Orleans, La.)
Mrs. Katie E. Whickham
(New Orleans, La.)
Rev. W. F. Hal
(Hattiesburg, Miss.)
Rev. J. E. Lowery
(Mobile, Ala.)
Rev. T. J. _emison
(Baton Rouge, La.)

## COMMITTEE TO DEFEND MARTIN LUTHER KING AND THE STRUGGLE FOR FREEDOM IN THE SOUTH

312 West 125th Street, New York 27, N. Y. UNiversity 6-1700

*Chairmen:* A. Philip Randolph, Dr. Gardner C. Taylor; *Chairmen of Cultural Division:* Harry Belafonte, Sidney Poitier; *Treasurer:* Nat King Cole; *Executive Director:* Bayard Rustin; *Chairmen of Church Division:* Father George B. Ford, Rev. Harry Emerson Fosdick, Rev. Thomas Kigore, Jr., Rabbi Edward E. Klein; *Chairman of Labor Division:* Morris Iushewitz

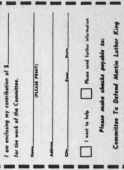

*Please mail this coupon TODAY!*

Committee To Defend Martin Luther King
and
The Struggle For Freedom In The South
312 West 125th Street, New York 27, N. Y.
UNiversity 6-1700

I am enclosing my contribution of $_____
for the work of the Committee.

Name _____

Address _____

City _____ Zone _____ State _____

(PLEASE PRINT)

☐ I want to help    ☐ Please send further information

*Please make checks payable to:*

Committee To Defend Martin Luther King

# 1

■

# HEED THEIR RISING VOICES

I T BEGAN in the most ordinary way. Late in the afternoon of March 23, 1960, John Murray went to *The New York Times* building on West Forty-third Street in New York to make arrangements for an advertisement in the paper. In the advertising department, on the second floor, he was introduced to a salesman named Gershon Aronson.

Aronson had worked for the *Times* for twenty-five years, and he was dedicated to the institution—"reverential," his daughter Judy said. One of his assignments now was to handle ads from organizations advocating some cause—editorial advertisements, as they were called. The *Times* carried a good many of them, some for far-out causes; every year or so Kim Il Sung, the Communist dictator of North Korea, used to take two full pages to praise his "dynamic revolutionary ideology" in small type. Aronson was sometimes tempted to tell people not to bother trying to push extreme views, but he resisted the temptation.

Murray wanted to reserve space, a full page, for an editorial advertisement. It was for an organization called the Committee to Defend Martin Luther King and the Struggle for Freedom in the South. The civil rights movement, with Dr. King as its most important leader, was challenging the rigid racial segregation that in 1960 still existed in the states of the Deep South, enforced by law and by violence. The latest phase of the struggle had begun just the previous month, when four black college students sat down at a Woolworth's lunch counter in Greensboro, North

Carolina, and asked to be served. When they were refused, they kept sitting there—and the sit-in movement spread quickly across the South. Dr. King immediately endorsed what the students were doing. Then, two weeks later, he faced a forbidding legal attack. An Alabama grand jury charged him with committing perjury, a felony, when he signed his 1956 and 1958 state tax returns. It was the first felony tax-evasion charge in Alabama history, and Dr. King feared that state officials were intent on finding some way to put him behind bars.

The committee was set up in New York to raise money for Dr. King and others under pressure in the South. Its officers included union leaders, ministers and such entertainment stars as Harry Belafonte, Sidney Poitier and Nat King Cole. John Murray was a volunteer worker at the committee. A playwright, he had helped to write the advertisement. That day, March 23, he was asked to take it down to the *Times* from the committee's office on 125th Street.

A full-page ad in the *Times* then cost a little over forty-eight hundred dollars. Murray said an advertising agency would handle the payment and send over a written order for the ad, but to save time he wanted the *Times* to go ahead and set the copy in type. He had a letter from the co-chairman of the committee, A. Philip Randolph, a great black leader who was president of the Brotherhood of Sleeping Car Porters, certifying that those shown as signers of the ad had given permission for the use of their names. All this was satisfactory to Aronson. He referred the ad to another Times department, advertising acceptability. The paper had a policy against fraudulent or deceptive advertising, and against "attacks of a personal character." (It was also on guard against smut, and policed movie advertising to keep out suggestive pictures.) The head of advertising acceptability, D. Vincent Redding, looked over the ad and approved it for publication.

The advertisement appeared in the paper of March 29, 1960. The headline, in large type, said "Heed Their Rising Voices." That phrase came from a *Times* editorial of March 19, which was quoted in the top right-hand corner of the ad: "The growing movement of peaceful mass demonstrations by Negroes is something new in the South, something understandable. . . . Let Congress heed their rising voices, for they will be heard." Then came ten paragraphs of text.

"As the whole world knows by now," the ad said, "thousands of Southern Negro students are engaged in widespread non-violent demonstrations in positive affirmation of the right to live in human dignity as guaranteed by the U. S. Constitution. . . . They are being met by an unprecedented wave of terror by those who would deny and negate that document. . . ."

Some examples of racism in the South followed. The third paragraph said: "In Montgomery, Alabama, after students sang 'My Country, 'Tis of Thee' on the State Capitol steps, their leaders were expelled from school, and truckloads of police armed with shotguns and tear-gas ringed the Alabama State College Campus. When the entire student body protested to state authorities by refusing to re-register, their dining hall was padlocked in an attempt to starve them into submission."

The ad did not criticize anyone by name. It spoke, rather, of "Southern violators of the Constitution." It said they were "determined to destroy the one man who, more than any other, symbolizes the new spirit now sweeping the South—the Rev. Dr. Martin Luther King Jr. . . ." The sixth paragraph said: "Again and again the Southern violators have answered Dr. King's peaceful protests with intimidation and violence. They have bombed his home almost killing his wife and child. They have assaulted his person. They have arrested him seven times—for 'speeding,' 'loitering' and similar 'offenses.' And now they have charged him with 'perjury'— a *felony* under which they could imprison him for *ten years*. . . ."

Below the text were the names of sixty-four people, sponsors of the ad, among them Mrs. Eleanor Roosevelt and Jackie Robinson. Then came another list, introduced by the statement "We in the south who are struggling daily for dignity and freedom warmly endorse this appeal," with twenty more names, most of them of black ministers in the South. In the lower right-hand corner of the page there was a coupon for readers to send in with contributions. And readers responded. Within a short time the King defense committee had received contributions totaling many times the cost of the ad.

For John Murray, Gershon Aronson and the others involved in writing and printing the advertisement, that was the end of it. Or so they thought. No one could have guessed then that "Heed Their Rising Voices" would set off a profound struggle on an issue other than that of racial justice. No one could have guessed that the advertisement would test the right of Americans to speak and write freely about the state of their society. No one could have guessed that it would become a landmark of freedom. But that is what happened.

The advertisement was a beginning, not an end: the beginning of a great legal and political conflict. The conflict threatened the existence of *The New York Times*. It threatened the right of the press to report on tense social issues, and the right of the public to be informed about them. In the end, four years later, those threats were dispelled by a transforming judgment from the Supreme Court of the United States. The Court used to the full its extraordinary power to lay down the fundamental rules of our national life. It made clearer than ever that ours is an open society, whose citizens may say what they wish about those who temporarily govern them. The Court drew fresh meaning from those few disarmingly simple words written into the Constitution in 1791, in the First Amendment:

> Congress shall make no law . . . abridging the freedom of speech, or of the press.

# 2

# REACTION IN MONTGOMERY

THE daily circulation of *The New York Times* in 1960 was 650,000. Of that, 394 copies went to subscribers and newsstands in the state of Alabama. One of the subscription papers was mailed to the offices of the Montgomery *Advertiser*, the morning newspaper in Montgomery, and its sister evening paper, the *Alabama Journal*, arriving some days after publication. One reader of the *Times* there—sometimes the only one—was the young city editor of the *Journal*, Ray Jenkins.

"I was fanning through the *Times* one day between our editions," Jenkins recalled years later, "and I saw that ad. I knocked out a story on it." The story appeared in the *Alabama Journal* on April 5, 1960. It began: "Sixty prominent liberals, including Mrs. Eleanor Roosevelt, have signed a full-page advertisement in *The New York Times* appealing for contributions to 'the Committee to Defend Martin Luther King and the Struggle for Freedom in the South.' King, the integration leader and former pastor of the Dexter Avenue Baptist Church here, is scheduled to go on trial in May on two indictments charging him with perjury in filing state tax returns. The Negro Baptist minister is now living in Atlanta. . . ."

Jenkins's story listed some of the signers of the advertisement and quoted parts of the text, including the charge that leaders of the civil rights movement were being subjected to "an unprecedented wave of terror." Then the story said:

"There was one misstatement of fact in the ad, and another statement could not be verified. The ad said Negro student leaders from Alabama State College were expelled 'after students sang "My Country 'Tis of Thee" on the State Capitol steps.' Actually, the students were expelled for leading a sitdown strike at the courthouse grill.

"The ad also states: 'When the entire student body protested (the expulsion) to state authorities by refusing to re-register, their dining hall was padlocked in an attempt to starve them into submission.' Authorities at the college said 'there is not a modicum of truth in the statement.' They pointed out that registration for the spring quarter was only slightly below normal and they deny that the dining hall was padlocked."

When that story appeared in the *Journal*, the editor of the Montgomery *Advertiser*, Grover C. Hall, Jr., "came roaring out into the newsroom and demanded to see the scandalous advertisement," Ray Jenkins said. Jenkins produced it, and Hall went back into his office to read it and fulminate.

Grover Cleveland Hall Jr. was the son of a crusading editor of the Montgomery *Advertiser*. His father won the Pulitzer Prize in 1926 for editorials attacking the Ku Klux Klan. Grover Hall Jr. took a curiously mixed position on issues of race. He passionately defended the South and its racial system, but he condemned extremism and violence in the segregationist cause. There was an example of his attitude a month before the *Times* advertisement. On February 27, 1960, as the sit-in movement spread elsewhere in the South, there were rumors that black students would try to get service at lunch counters in Montgomery. White men carrying small baseball bats roamed the downtown, looking for civil rights protesters. In fact there were none. But a white man smashed a black woman on the head with a bat, and the next day's Montgomery *Advertiser* carried a photograph of the incident with a caption naming the attacker and saying that the police had stood by and done nothing. L. B. Sullivan, a Montgomery city commissioner who was in charge of the police, denounced the *Advertiser* for printing the picture and the caption. Grover Hall replied: "Sullivan's problem is not a photographer with a camera. Sullivan's problem is a white man with a baseball bat." But Hall condemned not only "white thugs" but "rash, misled young Negroes." (Sullivan played a role in the Freedom Rides the next year. He promised to protect a group of Freedom Riders when they reached Montgomery. But when they did, on May 20, 1961, Sullivan's police had left the bus terminal. A white mob set upon the riders with bats and pipes, severely injuring several, including Attorney General Robert F. Kennedy's assistant, John Seigenthaler. Sullivan appeared a little later and told reporters: "All I saw were three men lying in the street. There was two niggers and a white man.")

Dr. King himself praised Hall for an editorial condemning racial bombings in Montgomery. "As I read Hall's strong statement," he wrote in his book *Stride Toward Freedom*, "I could not help admiring this brilliant but complex man who claimed to be a supporter of segregation but could not stomach the excesses performed in its name."

Hall was scornful of the national press for, as he saw it, ignoring racial tensions in Northern cities while sending numbers of reporters to cover the conflict in the South. In 1958 he told a meeting of journalists in Chicago: "A basic reason why the national debate on the race issue is so irrational is the failure of the American press to report strife as eagerly and fully in the North as in the South."

The *Times* advertisement touched that nerve in Grover Hall. He wrote an angry editorial that appeared in the *Advertiser* on April 7. It began: "There are voluntary liars, there are involuntary liars. Both kinds of liars contributed to the crude slanders against Montgomery broadcast in a full-page advertisement in The New York Times March 29." The editorial quoted from the third paragraph of the advertisement's text the statement that students at the State College had been padlocked out of their dining hall. "Lies, lies, lies," the editorial said—"and possibly willful ones on the part of the fund-raising novelist who wrote those lines to prey on the credulity, self-righteousness and misinformation of northern citizens."

Then there was a reference to events a hundred years before: the Civil War and the movement to abolish slavery. "The Republic paid a dear price once for the hysteria and mendacity of abolitionist agitators," Hall wrote. "The author of this ad is a lineal descendant of those abolitionists, and the breed runs true."

City Commissioner Sullivan of Montgomery, who had tangled with Hall about the photograph of the man with the baseball bat, evidently read the editorial. The next day, April 8, he sent a registered letter to *The New York Times*. (It was misdated March 8.) Sullivan said the advertisement charged him with "grave misconduct" and "improper actions and omissions as an official of the City of Montgomery." It demanded that the *Times* publish "a full and fair retraction of the entire false and defamatory matter."

Sullivan sent identical letters that day to four individuals whose names had appeared in the advertisement, on the list of those in the South who endorsed the appeal. The four were black ministers in Alabama: Ralph

D. Abernathy and S. S. Seay Sr. of Montgomery, Fred L. Shuttlesworth of Birmingham and J. E. Lowery of Mobile. They all testified later, without contradiction, that until they received Sullivan's letter they had never heard of the advertisement. Their names had been used without their knowledge or consent.

The New York law firm of Lord, Day & Lord, representing *The New York Times*, replied to Sullivan on April 15. "We . . . are somewhat puzzled," the letter said, "as to how you think the statements [in the ad] reflect on you." Sullivan, after all, was not mentioned in the advertisement. But the letter went on to say that the *Times* had been "investigating the matter." (It had asked for, and received, a quick report from a stringer, or part-time correspondent, in Montgomery, Don McKee.) So far, the letter said, the investigation indicated that the statements in the advertisement were "substantially correct with the sole exception that we find no justification for the statement that the dining hall in the State College was 'padlocked in an attempt to starve them into submission.' " The investigation would continue "because our client, The New York Times, is always desirous of correcting any statements which appear in its paper and which turn out to be erroneous. In the meantime you might, if you desire, let us know in what respect you claim that the statements in the advertisement reflect on you."

Sullivan did not reply, at least not by letter. On April 19 he filed a libel action in the Circuit Court of Montgomery County, an Alabama state court. The suit was brought against The New York Times Company and the four Alabama ministers whose names had appeared in the advertisement. Sullivan asserted that the third paragraph of the ad, mentioning Montgomery, and the sixth paragraph, which spoke of what "Southern violators" had done to Dr. King, libeled him. He asked for damages of $500,000.

On May 9 the governor of Alabama, John Patterson, wrote to *The New York Times* making a virtually identical demand for retraction. He said the ad had charged him with "grave misconduct . . . as Governor of Alabama and Ex-Officio Chairman of the State Board of Education." He pointed to the same two paragraphs of the advertising text that Sullivan did, the third and the sixth. The letter was a plain signal that the governor, too, would sue. Under Alabama law, a public official who brought an action for libel could not recover punitive damages at the trial unless he had asked for a retraction and none was published.

A week later *The New York Times* published a story apologizing to Governor Patterson. The headline was "Times Retracts Statement in Ad." The story described Patterson's objections and then printed this statement by the *Times*:

The advertisement . . . was received by The Times in the regular course of business from and paid by a recognized advertising agency in behalf of a group which included among its subscribers well-known citizens. The publication of an advertisement does not constitute a factual news report by The Times nor does it reflect the judgment or the opinion of the editors of The Times. Since publication of the advertisement, The Times made an investigation and consistent with its policy of retracting and correcting any errors or misstatements which may appear in its columns, hereby retracts the two paragraphs complained of by the Governor. The New York Times never intended to suggest by publication of the advertisement that the Honorable John Patterson, either in his capacity as Governor or as ex-officio chairman of the Board of Education of the State of Alabama, or otherwise, was guilty of "grave misconduct or improper actions or omission." To the extent that anyone can fairly conclude from the statements in the advertisement that any such charge was made, The New York Times hereby apologizes to the Honorable John Patterson therefor.

The same day, May 16, the president of The New York Times Company, Orvil Dryfoos, wrote to Governor Patterson. He enclosed the page of the paper with the retraction story and repeated, "to the extent that anyone could fairly conclude from the advertisement that any charge was made against you, The New York Times apologizes."

Two weeks later Governor Patterson sued, demanding $1 million in damages. He named as defendants *The New York Times* and the four Alabama ministers, as Sullivan had, and added one more: Dr. King. Sullivan and Patterson were joined by three others: Earl James, the mayor of Montgomery; Frank Parks, another city commissioner; and Clyde Sellers, a former commissioner. Each sued the *Times* and the four ministers for $500,000.

The four ministers were named as defendants along with the *Times* in each of the libel suits for a shrewd legal reason. The plaintiffs' lawyers calculated that having the ministers in there would prevent the *Times* from removing the cases from the state court to a federal court. The Constitution authorizes Congress to give the federal courts jurisdiction to hear ordinary civil lawsuits, such as libel cases, when the plaintiff and the defendant are from different states. The idea was that a party from state B might suffer prejudice in the courts of state A, and federal judges would be more neutral. The jurisdictional statutes passed by Congress allow nonresident defendants sued in a state court to remove the case to a federal court. But removal is allowed only when there is complete diversity in the state citizenship of the parties. If an A plaintiff sues a B defendant but also includes a defendant from A, the diversity is incomplete and the case cannot be removed. That is what the Alabama officials did in their libel suits.

As a result of publishing "Heed Their Rising Voices," *The New York Times* now faced libel actions claiming a total of $3 million in damages. That was an enormous sum in those days, and it could not be dismissed by the lawyers or executives of the *Times* as fanciful. In the state courts of Alabama, judges and juries at that time were not likely to be friendly to a Northern newspaper in a case involving the issue of race.

# 3

■

# SEPARATE
# AND
# UNEQUAL

THE Southern Way of Life, it was called. The phrase evoked images of white-columned mansions and gracious white families attended by smiling Negroes. The reality of racial segregation was less idyllic. Dr. King tried to explain it once to a group of whites who thought themselves sympathetic but wanted him to go slow. It was 1963, and he was in jail for leading a protest march in Birmingham, Alabama. Eight local white ministers criticized the march as "untimely." Dr. King wrote them what came to be known as his "Letter from Birmingham Jail."

"It is easy," he wrote, "for those who have never felt the stinging darts of segregation to say, 'Wait.' But when you have seen vicious mobs lynch your mothers and fathers at will . . . ; when you suddenly find your tongue twisted and your speech stammering as you seek to explain to your six-year-old daughter why she can't go to the public amusement park that has just been advertised on television . . . ; when you take a cross-country drive and find it necessary to sleep night after night in the uncomfortable corners of your automobile because no motel will accept you; when you are humiliated day in and day out by nagging signs reading 'white' and 'colored' . . . ; then you will understand why we find it difficult to wait."

Racial discrimination could be found in all parts of the United States. But it was different in the South, and far more virulent, because it had the force of law. State law condemned blacks to a submerged status from cradle to grave, literally. The law segregated hospitals and cemeteries. It confined black children to separate and grossly inferior public schools. Policemen enforced rules that made blacks ride in the back of the bus and excluded them from most hotels and restaurants. And blacks had little or no voice in making the law, for in much of the South they were denied the right to vote.

Officially enforced segregation was not some minor phenomenon found only in remote corners of the South. In the middle of the twentieth century black Americans could not eat in a restaurant or enter a movie theater in downtown Washington, D.C. Public schools were segregated in seventeen Southern and border states and in the District of Columbia: areas with 40 percent of the country's public school enrollment. Through two world wars black men were conscripted to serve in segregated units of the armed forces: a form of federally sanctioned racism that was only ended by President Harry Truman in 1948.

How could segregation by law exist so prominently and tenaciously in a country founded on the premise that "all men are created equal"? The answer lies in history, a very long history. The first ship bringing African slaves to North America landed in Virginia in 1619. Slavery became an important factor in the plantation economies of the Southern colonies, after 1776 the Southern states. Modern historical studies have demonstrated a further ugly truth about the economics of slavery: The breeding and sale of slaves were also highly profitable. By the time of the Constitutional Convention in 1787, the South was so committed to what it called its "peculiar institution" that delegates from the Southern states demanded and obtained provisions to protect the practice of slavery. Article I provided that in counting state populations to apportion seats in the House of Representatives, to "the whole Number of free Persons" there would be added "three fifths of all other Persons." That is, a slave would count as three fifths of a person. The Constitution barred Congress from stopping the international slave trade before the year 1808, although again the text avoided the word "slaves" with a circumlocution: "the Migration or Importation of Such Persons as any of the States now existing shall think proper to admit." Finally, the Constitution required non-slave states to hand over runaway slaves to their owners on demand. In 1857, in the Dred Scott case, Chief Justice Roger B. Taney said that the Constitution regarded persons of African descent as "a subordinate and inferior class of beings" who could not be American citizens.

The Civil War broke that chain of history—or so it seemed at first. Southern states declared their secession from the United States; on February 4, 1861, in Montgomery, Alabama, they organized the Confederate

States of America. The war that followed resulted as much from economic differences as the issue of slavery, but by the end the North was determined to abolish the peculiar institution. In 1863, in the Emancipation Proclamation, President Lincoln freed the Confederacy's slaves. Immediately after the war, in 1865, Congress and the states approved the Thirteenth Amendment to the Constitution, which prohibited slavery.

The South was defeated, but it did not give up its determination to keep Negroes subjugated. Southern states passed what were called Black Codes, regulating the former slaves to the point that they were hardly free. In some places, for example, they had to have a special license to do any kind of work except farming; they were forbidden to own land. Congress responded in 1866 by passing the first Civil Rights Act, designed to overcome the Black Codes. It provided that blacks have the same right as whites "to make and enforce contracts, to sue, be parties and give evidence, to inherit, purchase, lease, sell, hold and convey real and personal property . . . and shall be subject to like punishment, pains and penalties, and to none other, any law, statute, ordinance, regulation or custom to the contrary notwithstanding."

Then, in 1868, the Fourteenth Amendment was added to the Constitution. It provided broad federal authority to protect individuals against state discrimination and other repressive action. The amendment declared that all persons born or naturalized in the United States were citizens, thus overruling Chief Justice Taney's decision in the *Dred Scott* case. The amendment went on in sweeping language: "No State shall . . . deprive any person of life, liberty, or property, without due process of law; nor deny to any person within its jurisdiction the equal protection of the laws."

What did those broad terms mean for Southern laws restricting the rights of blacks? The Supreme Court gave a decisive answer to the question—or, again, one that seemed decisive—in 1880, in the case of *Strauder v. West Virginia*. Blacks were barred by a West Virginia law from serving on juries. The Court held the law unconstitutional. Justice William Strong quoted the language of the Fourteenth Amendment and said: "What is this but declaring that the law in the States shall be the same for the black as for the white? . . . The very fact that colored people are singled out and expressly denied by a statute all right to participate in the administration of the law, as jurors, because of their color, although they are citizens, and may be in other respects fully qualified, is practically a brand upon them, affixed by the law, an assertion of their inferiority, and a stimulant to . . . race prejudice. . . ."

But the *Strauder* case was soon overtaken by political change, and with it went black hopes for justice. When the Ku Klux Klan and others in the South turned to intimidation by violence, Northern politicians realized that equal rights could be secured only by drastic and open-ended intervention, and they shied away from that burden. Their attention now was on the cause of promoting the North's industry. Republicans, dominant in the North, also became disillusioned with the performance of the freed slaves: no doubt a manifestation of racism. Many came to feel that a paternalistic relationship between white and black was the natural order of things, and they increasingly accepted the benign myth of the Old South. In the presidential election of 1876, between Democrat Samuel J. Tilden and Republican Rutherford B. Hayes, the result turned on disputed votes in four states; a special commission with a Republican majority awarded all to Hayes, and he was declared the winner by a single electoral vote. That outcome came to be seen, and perhaps was intended, as an implicit bargain: In return for the victory, Republicans would let the South go its own way in racial matters.

By the late 1880s Southern legislatures were putting blacks down by a device slightly less blatant than the Black Codes but highly effective: Jim Crow laws that segregated railroads and other public facilities. Congress gave up the effort to legislate equal rights. And the Supreme Court, reflecting the dominant political and moral outlook of its time, ratified the new course.

In 1896, in the case of *Plessy v. Ferguson*, the Court held that state-enforced racial segregation did not deny "the equal protection of the laws" commanded by the Fourteenth Amendment. Homer Plessy, in origin one-eighth black, was arrested when he entered a railroad car that Louisiana reserved for whites. He challenged the law as a denial of equal protection, but the Supreme Court upheld its constitutionality by a vote of 7 to 1. Justice Henry Brown, for the majority, said Plessy's argument was fallacious in assuming "that the enforced separation of the two races stamps the colored race with a badge of inferiority. If this be so, it is not by reason of anything found in the act, but solely because the colored race chooses to put that construction upon it." As a reading of the Fourteenth Amendment, and of social reality, this was a long way from the statement in the *Strauder* case that singling out blacks by law was "practically a brand upon them."

In dissent, Justice John Marshall Harlan warned against allowing "the seeds of race hate to be planted under the sanction of law. What can more certainly arouse race hate, what more certainly create and perpetuate a feeling of distrust between these races, than state enactments, which, in fact, proceed on the ground that colored citizens are so inferior and degraded that they cannot be allowed to sit in public coaches occupied by white citizens? That, as all will admit, is the real meaning of such legislation as was enacted in Louisiana. . . . The thin disguise of 'equal' accommodations for passengers in railroad coaches will not mislead any one, nor atone for the wrong this day done."

Segregation, legally anointed by the Supreme Court, had the effect that Justice Harlan predicted. Over the next decades the Southern states excluded blacks from virtually all white public facilities. The notion that equal facilities would be provided for them was, as Justice Harlan said, a pretense to which respect was hardly paid. Blacks died because they were refused admission to white hospitals. Not even the most basic of civil rights, the vote, went untouched. States imposed complex new requirements for registration, such as the ability to expound the meaning of state constitutions, and left it to the subjective judgment of white registrars to say who qualified. The Democratic party in most Southern states excluded blacks from its primaries, which then were the decisive elections.

As the decades of the twentieth century passed, the meaning and the human impact of racism became increasingly hard to deny. The world's experience of the Nazis had a particular significance. After that it was clear that for a society to single out one group for differential treatment was not invidious only if the group chose "to put that construction upon it," as *Plessy v. Ferguson* had theorized, but was in fact designed as an expression of contempt. The idea that Southern racial segregation met the constitutional standard of equal protection became less and less convincing. But the *Plessy* rule remained intact in law, and it had the fervent support of the South's white politicians. And Congress, through mid-century, offered no challenge to the Southern system. There were proposals for civil rights legislation, for one a federal law against lynching. But Southern members used the Senate rules to filibuster and prevent civil rights bills from coming to a vote.

Then, in 1954, the legal foundation for racial segregation was shattered. In the case of *Brown v. Board of Education* a unanimous Supreme Court held that segregation of public schools was unconstitutional. Chief Justice Earl Warren did not say directly that *Plessy v. Ferguson* was wrongly decided in 1896 and must be overruled, but he said the Court could not turn the clock back to that time. "Separate educational facilities," he wrote for the Court, "are inherently unequal."

*Brown v. Board of Education* was a thunderbolt, a decision with as powerful an impact on society as any judgment the Supreme Court—or very likely any court—had ever issued. It aroused furious opposition in the white South. One hundred and one members of the House and Senate from the eleven states of the old Confederacy signed a Southern Manifesto declaring: "The Supreme Court, with no legal basis for such action, undertook to exercise their naked judicial power and substituted their personal political and social ideas for the established law of the land."

But the decision also aroused the blacks of the South. It was as if the voice of the Court, speaking truly at last in terms of equal rights, freed them from the old posture of submission and made them determined to do something about the injustices suffered over generations.

A first manifestation of this new black spirit, as it happened, came in the birthplace of the Confederacy, Montgomery, Alabama. On December 1, 1955, a black seamstress named Rosa Parks got on a bus to go home at the end of the day. She was tired, and she took a seat near the front. The driver ordered her to give that seat to a white man and sit in the back of the bus. Mrs. Parks refused, the police were called and she was arrested and charged with violation of the segregation laws.

In response to the prosecution of Mrs. Parks, the blacks of Montgomery decided to boycott the buses. For more than a year they stayed off the buses, walking miles to and from work or riding in car pools organized by their churches. Ministers led the movement, and first among them was Dr. King. He was then just twenty-seven years old, the pastor of the Dexter Avenue Baptist Church in Montgomery, unknown outside that community. But his leadership of the boycott soon made him a figure in the country and the world. He urged blacks to follow Gandhi's path and offer nonviolent resistance to oppression. "If we are arrested every day," he told his people, "if we are exploited every day, if we are trampled over every day, don't ever let anyone pull you so low as to hate them. We must use the weapon of love. We must have compassion and understanding for those who hate us. We must realize so many people are taught to hate us that they are not totally responsible for their hate. But we stand in life at midnight, we are always on the threshold of a new dawn."

Dr. King's words did not melt racist hostility. He was convicted of conspiring to conduct an illegal boycott. But the boycott went on until the Supreme Court, making clear that the logic of its *Brown* decision was not limited to schools, held bus segregation in Montgomery unconstitutional. On December 21, 1956, blacks and whites rode the buses without segregation.

The School Segregation Case also affected the North, politically. For the first time voters became seriously concerned about the excesses of Southern racism. National newspapers, magazines and broadcasters greatly increased their coverage of racial conflict in the South. In 1957 Congress passed the first Civil Rights Act since 1875. Its provisions were modest, creating a Civil Rights Commission and allowing the Justice

Department to bring suits against violations of voting rights, but passage of the bill signified a large change in the political climate.

But life for blacks in the South did not soon change. White resistance to equal rights became more vocal. White Citizens Councils, organized in many communities, used mass meetings, political endorsements and economic pressure to keep politicians and merchants in line for segregation. Blacks trying to claim the rights that the courts said were theirs faced intimidation and violence. Six years after the School Segregation decision not a single black attended a public school or university with whites in Alabama, Mississippi, Georgia, Louisiana or South Carolina. In those states of the Deep South blacks were assaulted, and some killed, for attempting to vote. As late as 1960 only 4 percent of the Negroes of voting age had managed to register in Mississippi, only 14 percent in Alabama.

Alabama and Mississippi were the most resistant states of all. There was an attempt to desegregate higher education in Alabama in 1956, with a result humiliating to federal authority. Autherine Lucy, a black woman, was admitted to the University of Alabama at the order of a federal court. But when students rioted, the university removed her from the campus. Miss Lucy went back to the courts and asked them to order her reinstatement. University officials then expelled her permanently for making "outrageous" charges against them in her lawsuit. The Eisenhower administration did nothing, and there the case ended.

Not even interstate transportation, a matter plainly within federal control, was immune from segregationist pressure. In the spring of 1961 members of the civil rights movement took buses to Alabama to protest segregation at terminals. The Freedom Riders, as they were called, were assaulted by mobs when they reached Birmingham and Anniston—stomped, slashed with chains. Another group headed for Montgomery. The Kennedy administration, fearing bloodshed, sent a force of five hundred marshals there. Governor John Patterson of Alabama objected, calling the presence of the marshals "a trampling upon and encroachment on the rights of the State of Alabama." When the Freedom Riders reached Montgomery, Dr. King—who had moved to Atlanta—happened to be back on a visit. He was preaching on the subject of nonviolence when a white mob surrounded the church. Only the federal marshals saved Dr. King and his audience from what might have been fatal attacks.

On April 12, 1960, just two weeks after the "Heed Their Rising Voices" advertisement, The New York Times published a news story on page one under the headline "Fear and Hatred Grip Birmingham." The story, by Harrison E. Salisbury, began:

No New Yorker can readily measure the climate of Birmingham today. Whites and blacks still walk the same streets. But the streets, the water supply and the sewer system are about the only public facilities they share. Ball parks and taxicabs are segregated. So are libraries. A book featuring black rabbits and white rabbits was banned. A drive is on to forbid "Negro music" on "white" radio stations. Every channel of communication, every medium of mutual interest, every reasoned approach, every inch of middle ground has been fragmented by the emotional dynamite of racism, reinforced by the whip, the razor, the gun, the bomb, the torch, the club, the knife, the mob, the police and many branches of the state's apparatus.

Harrison Salisbury's reports (a second appeared April 13) brought more libel suits, asking for $3,150,000 in damages from the *Times* and $1,500,000 from Salisbury. The Birmingham newspapers attacked the *Times* as the Montgomery *Advertiser* had over the advertisement, accusing it of "prejudgment, malice and hate."

That was the atmosphere in Alabama as *The New York Times* prepared to defend itself in court in Montgomery against the first libel action, brought by Commissioner Sullivan.

# 4

■

# THE TRIAL

A civil case in the courts, such as a suit for libel damages, is set in motion by what is called service of process: The plaintiff arranges to deliver to the defendant or his agent a paper formally notifying him of the action. But concealed in that simple statement is a bundle of possible legal complexities. Who is a defendant corporation's "agent"? How can the necessary papers be served so that they are legally binding? Can a distant party be forced to answer in the courts of another state at all?

L. B. Sullivan began his libel action against *The New York Times* by having papers served on its Montgomery stringer, Don McKee. McKee worked full time as a journalist for the Montgomery *Advertiser*, and he did very little for the *Times;* in the year 1960 he earned just ninety dollars as a stringer. But Sullivan's lawyers said that was enough to make him a *Times* agent in Alabama. They also served the Alabama secretary of state, who was designated by a state law to receive process on behalf of corporations that did business in the state but had no office or agent there.

Libel suits had not been a serious problem for *The New York Times.* Its policy was never to settle, even for trivial sums, lest it encourage nuisance suits. It lost jury verdicts rarely, and then not for heavy damages. But the paper's lawyer, Louis M. Loeb, realized at once that the *Sullivan* case was different: a serious threat. Loeb was a partner in the Wall Street firm of Lord, Day & Lord, but his time and interest were devoted largely to one client, the *Times*. He came up to the *Times* building most working days, he talked regularly with the top editors and managers, and he was on close personal terms with the publisher, Arthur Hays Sulzberger. Loeb looked a bit like a theatrical British colonel, large and bristly; he was a cultivated man, at home in the world of letters. His wife, Janet, was a sculptor; once they spent a happy day visiting Henry Moore at his home and studio in Much Haddam, England.

Loeb's first move was to retain an Alabama lawyer to represent the *Times* in the *Sullivan* case. This proved far more difficult than he expected. He telephoned a firm in Montgomery that had handled other matters for Lord, Day & Lord, but the partners said they could not take this one on. He tried one of the largest firms in Birmingham; it said no, speaking vaguely of a possible conflict of interest. He finally succeeded with a Birmingham firm that was something of a maverick, Beddow, Embry & Beddow; it had defended a large number of blacks charged with crime. T. Eric Embry agreed to represent the *Times*.

The reason for the difficulty in finding Alabama counsel was of course race. State and local politicians had whipped up outrage against *The New York Times* over the advertisement, denouncing the paper as an interfering Northern agitator. Harrison Salisbury's report on Birmingham made the *Times* even more an object of hatred. In those circumstances fear of association with the *Times* marked even lawyers, who by tradition and ethic are supposed to feel free to represent unpopular clients. Embry never could find a Montgomery lawyer to help him in the *Sullivan* case. When Louis Loeb went down to Alabama to sign Embry on, Embry got him a room in a motel far from Birmingham, under an assumed name.

Embry and his partner, Roderick Beddow, flew up to New York to talk things over not just with lawyers but with the newspaper's executives. "We were there for several days," Embry recalled years later, "and we met with all the top management and editors. They put me through the whole process of how the paper was put together, how the ads were placed. They told me they didn't care what it cost to defend this case, they wouldn't pay anything voluntarily."

As both Loeb and Embry saw the case then, the first best hope of defeating Commissioner Sullivan was to challenge what is called the *in personam* jurisdiction of the Alabama courts: their power to bring *The New York Times* before them. Each of the fifty states in the United States has its own courts and laws. The courts of one state can constitutionally command a party from another state to appear before them only if that distant party has some meaningful connection of business or property or person with the commanding state. A Vermonter who has never had anything to do with Arizona cannot be successfully sued there. But it is perilous to just ignore a distant lawsuit, assuming that another state's courts have no jurisdiction over you. Suppose the Vermonter has some glancing connection with Arizona. He ignores that lawsuit, and the Arizona courts enter a default judgment against him for $100,000 in damages. The Arizona plaintiff now goes to Vermont and asks its courts to enforce that judgment. The Vermonter can argue that he was not subject to Arizona's jurisdiction. But if the Vermont courts find that the little he had to do with Arizona was still enough for jurisdiction there, then the Constitution requires them to give "full faith and credit" to the judgment of the Arizona courts. The Vermonter will have to pay the $100,000 without ever having had a trial on the facts of the case. Hence, it is usually better for a defendant sued in a distant state to have a lawyer there challenge its jurisdiction right at the start.

That is what Embry did. He filed a motion to quash the service of process, on the ground that the *Times* did not do enough business in Alabama to come within the jurisdiction of its courts. Embry argued that the 394 copies of the daily paper, out of a circulation of 650,000, did not amount to a substantial connection with the state. Nor, he said, did the occasional visits to Alabama by *Times* correspondents or the handful of advertisements placed in the paper by Alabama firms: $18,000 worth in the first five months of 1960 out of a total *Times* advertising revenue of $37.5 million.

In challenging the *in personam* jurisdiction of the Alabama courts over the *Times*, Embry had to take care to make what lawyers call a "special appearance," one for that purpose only, since a "general appearance" by a lawyer on behalf of a distant client may itself subject the client to the court's jurisdiction. To make sure he would do it right, he followed the form given in a leading text, *Alabama Pleading and Practice at Law*, by Walter Burgwyn Jones. That should have been safe, because Walter Burgwyn Jones was circuit judge of Montgomery County—and was going to try the Sullivan case. But again, nothing could be assumed in a matter touched by the racial issue.

Judge Jones was a devotee of the Confederacy and the Southern way of life. His father, Thomas Goode Jones, fought in the Confederate army and carried the flag of truce from Lee to Grant at Appomattox; he became governor of Alabama. Judge Jones wrote and published *The Confederate Creed*, which said among other things: "I see in the Stars and Bars, the glorious banner of the Confederacy as it waves in the Southern breeze, a symbol of freedom and devotion to constitutional rights, an emblem of honor and character." On the hundredth anniversary of the founding of the Confederacy, in 1961, Montgomery put on a reenactment of the swearing-in of the Confederate president, Jefferson Davis, and Judge Jones administered the oath of office. Some of the players in the pageant became jurors in a real trial in Judge Jones's court, and he seated them in the jury box wearing their Confederate uniforms.

During the years 1960 and 1961 Judge Jones issued a series of orders to thwart the civil rights movement and the United States government. He forbade the National Association for the Advancement of Colored People to do business in Alabama, barred demonstrations by Freedom Riders against segregation on buses and blocked the U. S. Department of Justice from examining voter-registration records in any county in Alabama. Seating in his courtroom was segregated. During the libel trial after Sullivan's, of the suit brought by Mayor James over the *Times* ad, black spectators took seats among the whites one day. The next day Judge Jones, blaming "recognized rabble-rousers and racial agitators" for what had happened, ordered bailiffs to enforce segregation in the courtroom. The case would be tried, he said, "under the laws of the State of Alabama and not under the Fourteenth Amendment." He praised "white man's justice, a justice born long centuries ago in England, brought over to this country by the Anglo-Saxon race."

Eric Embry believed that Judge Jones actually helped to plan the libel actions by Sullivan and the others. He said, years later, "Grover Hall and some others met in Jones's office and concocted all these lawsuits." But if there had been such a meeting, it was too late to find evidence of it.

Embry's motion to quash the service of process came before Judge Jones in a hearing that started on July 25, 1960. Over several days lawyers argued about the extent of the *Times*'s connections with the State of Alabama: the copies circulated there, the payments to stringers, the advertisements from Alabama. On August 5 Judge Jones ruled that the *Times* did enough business in the state to be subject to the jurisdiction of its courts. And in the event that higher courts said he was wrong about that, he also found jurisdiction on an alternative ground: that Embry had made a mistake in drafting his motion to quash and inadvertently made a "general appearance," thus bringing the *Times* within the reach of the state courts. In order to avoid just that trap Embry had followed Jones on *Alabama Pleading and Practice*, but the judge overruled his own book.

Louis Loeb regarded the loss on the point of jurisdiction as a devastating blow. The *Times* now faced jury trials in the Alabama courts on all the libel actions over "Heed Their Rising Voices." Ironically, the problem that had led supporters of Dr. King to take out the advertisement, his tax perjury prosecution, had disappeared. At a trial in Montgomery in the last week of May the state could produce no convincing evidence for its charge that Dr. King had put to his own use contributions that he said he had passed on to church and civil rights groups, and he was acquitted.

The trial of the Sullivan case in Judge Jones's court took three days, November 1–3. The number of lawyers alone made it clear that this was not a routine libel trial. Sullivan was represented by M. Roland Nachman Jr., Robert E. Steiner III and Calvin Whitesell of Montgomery. Eric Embry had four others to help him speak for the *Times*. Then there were lawyers for the four black Alabama ministers whom Sullivan had named as defendants along with the *Times* because their names appeared at the bottom of the ad. Those lawyers—Fred Gray, Vernon Z. Crawford and S. S. Seay Jr.—were black, and this produced a curious phenomenon. In the stenographic transcript of the trial, printed for the Supreme Court when the case went there and bound in its permanent records, the white lawyers are referred to as "Mr. Nachman," "Mr. Embry" and so on. The blacks are called "Lawyer Gray," "Lawyer Crawford," "Lawyer Seay." The color of their skin denied them the honorific "Mr."

The first step in the trial was to select a jury. Of a panel of thirty-six potential jurors, two were black. Sullivan's lawyers struck them from the list, and a jury of twelve white men was chosen. The *Alabama Journal* published their names and a front-page picture of the twelve in the jury box—a step that *Times* lawyers protested would put the jurors under local pressure to decide in favor of Sullivan. Judge Jones rejected the complaint.

Nachman made the opening statement for Sullivan. He called for damages "to deter these defendants from doing such a thing again and to deter others from doing such a thing." For the *Times*, Embry said the advertisement contained no reference to Sullivan "by the wildest stretch of inference. . . . There is nothing that even remotely refers to him or could possibly refer to him." Gray, for the four ministers, said none of them had even been asked by the committee that placed the ad to let their names be used. "They never gave their consent," he said. "What happened to them could happen to you or anyone else."

The case for Sullivan began with one of his lawyers, Whitesell, reading the advertisement to the jury. When he came to the word "Negro," one of the ministers' lawyers, Crawford, objected that Whitesell was saying "nigger." Judge Jones asked Whitesell if he was indulging in "interpolations" in his reading. Whitesell said he was pronouncing the word as he had "all my life." A reporter for the *Alabama Journal*, Judith Rushin, wrote: "To newsmen, he did not seem to be saying 'nigger,' but something closer to 'nigra' or 'nigro.' "

To make out a case of libel, a plaintiff has to show that (1) the defendant published (2) a defamatory statement (3) about the plaintiff. (Defamatory means tending to lower the plaintiff's reputation.) Sullivan's lawyers necessarily devoted much of their evidence to the third point. Although his name had not appeared anywhere in the *Times* advertisement, they tried to show that the ad nevertheless implicated him, or in lawyers' language was "of and concerning" him. Sullivan was his own principal witness. As one of Montgomery's three city commissioners, he had the particular duties of supervising the Police Department, the Fire Department, the Department of Cemetery and the Department of Scales. He did not manage the police from day to day; there was a chief of police for that. But Sullivan said he felt he was implicated by the mention of "police" in the third paragraph of the advertisement, which read as follows:

> In Montgomery, Alabama, after students sang "My Country 'Tis of Thee" on the State Capitol steps, their leaders were expelled from school, and truckloads of police armed with shotguns and tear-gas ringed the Alabama State College Campus. When the entire student body protested to state authorities by refusing to re-register, their dining hall was padlocked in an attempt to starve them into submission.

Sullivan also objected to this portion of the sixth paragraph:

> Again and again the Southern violators have answered Dr. King's peaceful protests with intimidation and violence. They have bombed his home almost killing his wife and child. They have assaulted his person. They have arrested him seven times—for "speeding," "loitering" and similar "offenses." And now they have charged him with "perjury"—a *felony* under which they could imprison him for *ten years*.

Sullivan maintained that the wrongs attributed to "Southern violators" in that paragraph would be taken as the Montgomery Police Department's doing, and his, because the paragraph mentioned arrests and arrests are a police function. This produced a moment of irony, probably unperceived, when Crawford, one of the ministers' lawyers, was cross-examining Sullivan:

> Q. "Mr. Sullivan, do you consider your police force to be Southern law violators?"
> A. "I certainly do not."

Q. "Then, Mr. Sullivan, do you consider yourself as Police Commissioner a Southern law violator?"
A. "I don't consider myself a violator period, Southern or otherwise."

But Nachman asked his client, "Do you consider that the statements in the advertisement refer to you and are associated with you?" And Sullivan replied, "I certainly do—the statements concerning arrests of people and truckloads of police. I feel they are associated with me."

On the question whether the statements were defamatory, the second point that libel plaintiffs must show, Sullivan testified that the advertisement reflected on his "ability and integrity." He said he had the "feeling" that it reflected "not only on me but on the other commissioners and the community." On cross-examination, Embry suggested that Sullivan's standing in the community had not in fact been affected.

Q. "Have you ever been ridiculed? Do you feel ill at ease walking about the streets of Montgomery?"
A. "I haven't had anyone come up to me personally and say they held me in ridicule because of the ad."
Q. "Have you been shunned by anyone in a public place or at the house of a friend or in any restaurant . . . ?"
A. "I don't recall."

Sullivan's lawyers called six other witnesses to testify on whether the advertisement was "of and concerning" Sullivan and tended to lower his reputation. The first was Grover Hall, the editor of the Montgomery *Advertiser*, who had made his opinion of the *Times* advertisement clear in his stinging editorial attack on it. Hall said he associated the third paragraph of the advertisement, about events at Alabama State College, with the city commissioners because they "are responsible for good order in this community"—and he "would naturally think a little more about the police commissioner." What troubled him in the paragraph was "the phrase about starvation," which "would certainly be indefensible." Asked about his personal relations with Sullivan, Hall said they were not good at the time the advertisement appeared—just after the *Advertiser* photograph of the baseball-bat incident and Hall's biting exchange with Sullivan over that—but had improved.

The other five witnesses were Arnold D. Blackwell, a businessman and member of the Water Works Board; Harry W. Kaminsky, a close friend of Sullivan's who managed a clothing store; H. M. Price Sr., owner of a food equipment business; William M. Parker Jr., a friend and service station owner; and Horace W. White, owner of the P. C. White Truck Line, for which Sullivan had formerly worked as safety director. All said they associated statements in the advertisement with the Montgomery police or Sullivan. If they had believed the statements, they said, they would have thought worse of Sullivan. White, for example, testified that he would be reluctant to rehire Sullivan if he thought Sullivan "had allowed the Police Department to do the things the paper say he did." But on cross-examination all five said that in fact they did not believe the statements and did not think any worse of Sullivan because of the advertisement. Only Grover Hall had actually seen the ad when it was published in the *Times*. White was not sure when he saw it. The other four testified that they first saw the ad when Sullivan's lawyers showed it to them and asked them to testify.

Truth is a defense to libel charges, so Sullivan's lawyers also attempted to show that statements in the advertisement were false—false if the ad meant what they said it did. Their position was that the ad charged the police and Sullivan with bombing Dr. King's home, for example, so they set out to show that Sullivan had not done so. The *Times* was of course taking the position that the advertisement had nothing to do with Sullivan, but its lawyers were unable to stop the trial from proceeding as if Sullivan had been accused of a list of wrongs of which he was innocent. This produced some bizarre moments. Some of the actions described in the advertisement could not have been taken by Sullivan. The perjury indictment, for instance, was brought by Alabama state authorities, and arrangements for registration and dining at the State College were functions of the State Board of Education. But Sullivan's counsel questioned him as if he had been formally charged with the actions, and he solemnly denied those charges and others that nobody had made.

> NACHMAN: "Did you have anything to do with procuring the indictment of Dr. King?"
> SULLIVAN: "Nothing whatever."
> NACHMAN: "I ask you whether the Police Department has during your term of office or at any other time within your knowledge bombed Dr. King's home or been a party to it or condoned such action?"

At that point in the proceedings Embry erupted. "We object to that, Your Honor," he said. "Nobody could read that language and conclude that it imported [implied] that the police bombed his home. This is fantastic, Your Honor—" Judge Jones cut him off to deny the objection. There was other evidence on the issue of falsity. To show that the description of events at Alabama State College in the third paragraph of the advertisement was inaccurate, Sullivan's lawyers introduced a story by Claude Sitton, Southern regional correspondent of *The New York Times*, that had appeared in its issue of March 2, 1960, and a report that Sitton had telephoned to the *Times* lawyers after Sullivan brought his lawsuit. They also introduced the report sent at the lawyers' request by Don McKee, the *Times* stringer in Montgomery. Together, these accounts showed that there were a number of mistaken statements in the third paragraph of the advertisement. The students sang "The Star-Spangled Banner" on the state capitol steps, not "My Country, 'Tis of Thee." Students were expelled not in connection with that episode but after seeking service at a lunch counter in the Montgomery County Court House. The police were deployed near the campus in large numbers, but they did not "ring" the campus. The most serious mistake was the statement about the college dining hall. When *Times* lawyers addressed this point later in their brief to the Supreme Court, they said candidly: "There was . . . no foundation for the charge that the dining hall was padlocked in an effort to starve the students into submission, an allegation that especially aroused resentment in Montgomery." There was also a mistake in the sixth paragraph of the advertisement. Dr. King had been arrested four times, not seven.

That was the plaintiff's case.

For the defense, Embry put on several employees of the *Times*. Gershon Aronson described how the advertisement had come in to the paper. Vincent Redding, manager of the advertising acceptability department, said he had approved it because it was signed "by a number of people who were well known and whose motives I had no reason to question." One executive of the paper testified. Harding Bancroft, secretary of The New York Times Company, said the paper did not think "any of the language in there referred to Mr. Sullivan." Asked why the *Times* had published a retraction at Governor Patterson's demand but not Sullivan's, Bancroft testified: "We did that because we didn't want anything that was published by the Times to be a reflection on the State of Alabama, and the Governor was, as far as we could see, the embodiment of the State of Alabama. . . ."

Finally, there was the case for the four ministers. It was addressed to the first of the three points that a libel plaintiff must prove to make out his case: that the defendant *published* the challenged statement. There was no doubt about publication by defendant New York Times Company. But the ministers were a different story. The four men took the witness stand and testified that they had nothing to do with the advertisement and had not given permission for the use of their names. Then their lawyers called as a witness John Murray, the writer who had helped prepare the ad as a volunteer for the Committee to Defend Martin Luther King. He testified that the twenty Southern endorsers listed near the bottom of the advertisement had not been there when he first brought the copy to the *Times;* they were added later, when Bayard Rustin, the executive director of the committee, said he was not satisfied with the ad. Murray testified that after some discussion Rustin "opened a drawer and pulled out a list of names that was the list of the individual ministers whose churches were affiliated with the Southern Christian Leadership Conference and he then said we can list these names." Murray said he had asked Rustin how the committee could reach all those people to get permission for the use of their names, and Rustin replied that that was not necessary because they were all part of the movement.

Fred Gray, representing the ministers, moved to drop them from the case because there had been no testimony showing that they had had any part in publishing the advertisement. Judge Jones denied the motion. In the closing argument to the jury, Gray asked: "How could these individual defendants retract something—if you'll pardon the expression—they didn't tract?" He called the ministers "the forgotten defendants" who "had no business in the case." But Steiner, for Sullivan, said the inclusion in the ad of the names of two ministers from Montgomery (Ralph D. Abernathy and S. S. Seay Sr.) was "proof positive the ad was talking about Mr. Sullivan." Newspapers, he said, "are very fine things, but newspapers have got to tell the truth. One way to get their attention . . . is to hit them in the pocketbook." Embry said the only substantial error in the ad was the statement about padlocking the dining hall, and that "could not possibly have referred to Sullivan." Indeed, he said, nothing in the ad referred to Sullivan—and he had not been damaged. "Where is the evidence that has shown you that Mr. Sullivan suffered any injury?" Embry asked the jury. "Has Mr. Sullivan suffered or has possibly his standing in the community been enhanced?"

When Judge Jones charged the jury, he removed from its consideration the question whether the advertisement was defamatory. He instructed the jury that the challenged statements in the ad were "libelous per se"— that is, undoubtedly defamatory of anyone they described, because they would tend to injure that person's reputation and business or professional status. Judge Jones went on to remove the issue of falsity from the jury's concern as well. Under Alabama law, he said, a statement that was libelous per se was presumed to be false; the defendant could overcome that presumption only by proving the statement true in all material respects. Since the *Times* had conceded error in the advertisement—in the passage about padlocking the dining hall—it had failed to meet its burden.

Damage was also presumed, so Sullivan did not have to offer any proof of injury. In sum, the case went to the jury with instructions that the advertisement was libelous, false and injurious. Three issues were left for the jury to decide: Had the defendants published the advertisement? Were the statements in it "of and concerning" L. B. Sullivan? And if the jury answered yes to those questions, how much money should be awarded to Sullivan as damages?

It took the jury two hours and twenty minutes to decide. It brought in a verdict for the plaintiff, against both the *Times* and the four ministers, in the full amount Sullivan had demanded: $500,000.

# 5

## ■

# SILENCING
# THE
# PRESS

**M**ONTGOMERY'S evening paper, the *Alabama Journal*, commented
the day after the jury verdict that the $500,000 award to Commissioner Sullivan "could have the effect of causing reckless publishers
of the North . . . to make a re-survey of their habit of permitting anything
detrimental to the South and its people to appear in their columns." The
editorial said the South was "libeled every day"; it was subjected to more
calumnies than it had been "in the days of the New England fanatical
abolitionists, Uncle Tom's Cabin and Simon Legree." Northern publishers had until now "regarded themselves as safe from prosecution for their
offenses because they were far off, and were under the impression that
they could be sued for their derelictions only in the courts of their home
cities." Now the *Sullivan* case had changed the rules, the editorial said.
It gave this warning: "The Times was summoned more than a thousand
miles to Montgomery to answer for its offense. Other newspapers and
magazines face the same prospect. The only way to prevent such long
distance summons is to print the truth."

"To print the truth" sounds straightforward. After the Sullivan trial
it was anything but that. The rules applied by Judge Jones made it forbiddingly difficult to write anything about the realities of Southern racism
in the 1960's without risking heavy damages for libel. Any publication
that sent a correspondent into Alabama, circulated a few copies there or
sold a few ads could be forced into the state courts. An official who was

not named in a news article or advertisement could claim, and easily
persuade a jury, that an account of local conditions inferentially reflected
on him. If the text, read that way, would tend to injure his reputation,
it would be presumed to be false. The newspaper could overcome that
presumption of falsity only by proving that every material part of the
challenged statement was accurate. There would also be an irrebuttable
presumption that the plaintiff had been injured by the publication, even
though there was no evidence that anyone thought the worse of him
because of it. A local jury could award damages in any amount.

With perhaps inadvertent candor, the Montgomery *Advertiser* headlined a story about the libel cases: "State Finds Formidable Legal Club
to Swing at Out-of-State Press." That was the effect, and that was the
purpose. Sullivan and Governor Patterson and the others were out to
transform the traditional libel action, designed to repair the reputation
of a private party, into a state political weapon to intimidate the press.
The aim was to discourage not false but true accounts of life under a
system of white supremacy: stories about men being lynched for trying
to vote, about cynical judges using the law to suppress constitutional
rights, about police chiefs turning attack dogs on men and women who
wanted to drink a Coke at a department-store lunch counter. It was to
scare the national press—newspapers, magazines, the television networks—off the civil rights story.

The strategy was shrewd, because it put the press to a grave financial
risk. The $500,000 awarded to Sullivan was the largest libel judgment
in Alabama history, and enormous by the standards of verdicts anywhere
in the country at the time—and it was just the first of the five suits over
the advertisement. The next, by Mayor James, was tried the following
February and again resulted in a jury verdict for the full amount claimed,
$500,000. The *Times* had to anticipate Alabama judgments in those five
cases for all the damages sought, $3 million. Then there were the suits
over the Salisbury articles on Birmingham. The *Times* was financially
vulnerable in those days. James Goodale, later its general counsel, said
of the 1960 libel cases: "Without a reversal of those verdicts there was
a reasonable question of whether the *Times*, then wracked by strikes and
small profits, could survive."

The files of the Birmingham city government, disclosed years later,
show how the minds of officials turned to libel as a way of repressing
the movement for civil rights. In 1963 a six-page pamphlet was issued
by a group calling itself The Inter-Citizens Committee, Inc.; the Reverend
J. L. Ware was listed as president and the Reverend C. H. Oliver as
secretary. The pamphlet told a horrifying story. Theotis Crymes, a black
man twenty-six years old, said he was driving home to Montevallo,

Alabama, on the night of March 19, 1960, when he was stopped by a police car. As he was standing with his hands on the police car, Crymes said, the police officer shot him in the back. When he asked why, the officer said, "Shut up, nigger." Crymes was paralyzed from the waist down for the rest of his life. The F.B.I. was notified of the incident, investigated and identified the officer as Roy Damron, the police chief of Helena, Alabama. Damron was indicted by a federal grand jury but acquitted by an all-white jury. The pamphlet telling that story was referred to the Birmingham Department of Law. By letter of October 14, 1963, William A. Thompson, assistant city attorney, advised his superiors that the distributors of the pamphlet could be prosecuted for criminal libel for the statements about Chief Damron.

The strategy of intimidation by civil libel suits spread. The Columbia Broadcasting System was sued for $1.5 million for a television program about the difficulties Montgomery blacks had in registering to vote. Officials in the other Southern states copied those in Alabama. By the time the Supreme Court decided the *Sullivan* case, in 1964, Southern officials had brought nearly $300 million in libel actions against the press.

Suppose the strategy had worked. Suppose that Southern judges and juries had had the last word, that the press had had no higher recourse in the American system. Suppose that the Southern officials had collected those hundreds of millions of dollars in damages and that the press, or much of it, had stopped covering the racial story except with anodyne reports. Would it have made a difference in the progress of the civil rights movement? Would it have slowed the political revolution that overtook the South, ending the tradition of enforced white supremacy and bringing blacks into the political process? Would history have been changed? Dr. King's own strategy indicates that the answer to those questions is yes.

Dr. King's model was Mohandas Gandhi, who undermined British colonialism in India by campaigns of nonviolent protest. Gandhi succeeded because he had an audience, the British public, that could be touched by his message and was outraged by the repressive methods used to put his movement down. The Gandhian approach might well not have worked with a more hard-hearted colonial power or one that prevented its public from knowing what it did in the colony. All that was equally true in Dr. King's case. His belief that nonviolent resistance could overthrow white supremacy in the South was premised on the existence of an audience, the American public, whose conscience could be aroused and would be outraged at the brutality used to enforce racial segregation when it was challenged. That belief in turn depended on a press that would tell the story.

When *Brown v. Board of Education* was decided in 1954, most of the country still had a romantic image of the South: *Gone With the Wind*, not sheriffs with attack dogs. But the major newspapers and magazines now devoted increasing resources and space to reporting the reality of white supremacy. American journalism, for all its inadequacies, its short-ness of attention span, can rise to moments of historic change, and this was one. A number of outstanding reporters worked on the Southern story, showing the readers in human terms what it meant to live under a racist system. One of them was the Southern regional correspondent of *The New York Times*, Claude Sitton.

Sitton was a white Southerner himself. He had a deep soft accent, and he might have been mistaken for a Good Ol' Boy until he sat down at the typewriter. There he unflinchingly recorded the scenes of insult and menace that were part of daily life for blacks but were never admitted in the myth of Southern gentility. A powerful example was a story he filed from Sasser, Georgia, on July 26, 1962. It read in part as follows:

"We want our colored people to go on living like they have for the last hundred years," said Sheriff Z. T. Mathews of Terrell County. Then he turned and glanced disapprovingly at the thirty-eight Negroes and two whites gathered in the Mount Olive Baptist Church for a voter-registration rally. "I tell you, cap'n, we're a little fed up with this registration business," he went on.

As the seventy-year-old peace officer spoke, his nephew and chief deputy, M. E. Mathews, swaggered back and forth fingering a hand-tooled black leather cartridge belt and a .38 caliber revolver. Another deputy, R. M. Dunaway, slapped a five-cell flashlight against his left palm again and again. The three officers took turns badgering the participants and warning of what "disturbed white citizens" might do if this and other rallies continued. . . .

The concern of Sheriff Zeke Mathews, "twenty years in office without opposition," is perhaps understandable. Terrell County has 8,209 Negro residents and only 4,533 whites. While 2,894 of the whites are registered to vote, only 51 Negroes are on the rolls, according to the Secretary of State's office. . . .

The sound of voices around the automobiles parked beside the church could be heard as license numbers were called out. And the faces of the audience stiffened with fear. A group of thirteen law officers and roughly dressed whites clumped through the door at this point. One pointed his arm at three newspaper reporters sitting at the front and said: "There they are."

"If God be for us, who can be against us," read Mr. Sherrod. "We are counted as sheep for the slaughter." . . .

Sheriff Mathews, trailed by Deputy Dunaway, burst into the

sanctuary and strode to the front. Standing before the reporters, but looking away from them, he began to address the audience. "I have the greatest respect for any religious organization but my people is getting disturbed about these secret meetings," he said. . . .

Sheriff Mathews then turned to the Negroes, saying that none of them was dissatisfied with life in the county. He asked all from Terrell to stand.

"Are any of you disturbed?"

The reply was a muffled "Yes."

"Can you vote if you are qualified?"

"No."

"Do you need people to come down and tell you what to do?"

"Yes."

"Haven't you been getting along well for a hundred years?"

"No."

The sheriff then said he could not control the local whites and that he wanted to prevent violence. "Terrell County has had too much publicity," he said. "We're not looking for violence."

Chief Deputy Mathews then expressed his viewpoint. "There's not a nigger in Terrell County who wants to make application to vote who has to have someone from Massachusetts or Ohio or New York to come down here and carry them up there to vote." . . .

A long exchange of forceful questions followed. After that, Deputy Mathews turned to the others and told them: "There is a prohibit to register between now and December." . . .

Deputy Mathews turned to Deputy Dunaway and ordered him to take the names of all those present.

"I just want to find out how many here in Terrell County are dissatisfied," explained Sheriff Mathews.

Turning to a local Negro and pointing at Mr. Allen [Ralph Allen, a twenty-two-year-old white college student from Massachusetts helping the registration drive], the chief deputy then said: "He's going to be gone in two weeks, but you'll still be here." . . .

As the sheriff walked away, he said to reporters: "Some of these niggers down here would just as soon vote for Castro and Khrushchev."

The Negroes began humming a song of protest popularized during the sit-in demonstrations, "We Shall Overcome." And as the law officers withdrew to the outside, the song swelled to a crescendo.

The business meeting then got under way. Miss Patch [Penelope Patch, an 18-year-old white student at Swarthmore College]

reported on her work in Lee County. Mr. Allen told of having
been knocked down twice last Saturday, beaten and threatened
with death by men in Dawson, the county seat. . . .
    Shortly after 10 o'clock, the Negroes rose and joined hands
in a circle. Swaying in rhythm, they again sang "We Shall Overcome." . . . [They] filed out the front door past the group of law
officers. "I know you," said one officer to a Negro. "We're going
to get some of you."


Sitton covered lynchings. On April 25, 1959, Mack Charles Parker, a
twenty-three-year-old black accused of raping a white woman, was
dragged from the jail in Poplarville, Mississippi, and murdered. On January 4, 1960, Sitton did an extraordinary report from Poplarville recon-
structing the killing in detail. The facts were common gossip in the town,
he said. The F.B.I. did an intensive investigation of the lynching, wrote
a 378-page report and turned it over to Mississippi authorities. But when
Circuit Judge Sebe Dale impaneled a grand jury in Poplarville to consider
the case, it did not ask for the F.B.I. report and declined to hear F.B.I.
agents who had offered to testify. "In his charge to the jury," Sitton
wrote, "the judge said that recent Supreme Court decisions might have
been responsible for the lynching. He referred to the Court as that 'board
of sociology, sitting in Washington, garbed in judicial robes.' Three days
later the grand jurors went home without action in the Parker case. . . ,
Those questioned in Poplarville last week said that residents generally
agreed with the grand jury's course. They pointed out that there would
have been practically no chance of convicting Parker's murderers had
they been indicted. A trial, they contended, would only have embarrassed
the community. 'You couldn't convict the guilty parties if you had a
sound film of the lynching,' said one official."
    Birmingham, Alabama, was a running story of white intransigence. In
the spring of 1963 blacks began a campaign to desegregate department-
store lunch counters and open jobs as saleswomen to blacks. Sit-ins and
marches were met by the police commissioner, Eugene "Bull" Connor,
with police dogs and mass arrests. Appeals by federal officials, including
President Kennedy, finally persuaded business leaders to sign a desegregation agreement, but two days later bombs hit the black section of
the city, including the home of Dr. King's younger brother, the Reverend
A. D. King. On May 13 Sitton talked with Mayor Arthur J. Hanes, who
along with Commissioner Connor had been voted out in a recent election
but was still holding office during litigation over control of the city
government. "Martin Luther King is a revolutionary," Hanes said. "The
nigger King ought to be investigated by the Attorney General. This nigger

has got the blessing of the Attorney General and the White House." Then, Sitton wrote, Hanes said of Attorney General Robert F. Kennedy: "I hope that every drop of blood that's spilled he tastes in his throat, and I hope he chokes on it."

School desegregation brought violence in a number of cities. In November 1960 four little black girls entered the first grade in white elementary schools in New Orleans—the first desegregation in Louisiana. Sitton reported on the tortuous federal court proceedings needed to overcome successive resistance schemes passed by the state legislature, and then on violent protests. Most white parents withdrew their children from school rather than walk a child through gangs of screaming, spitting women. On December 4 Sitton wrote about an exception:

> One person who braved the gangs was Mrs. Orlando Gabrielle, who knew moments of terror as she made the eight-block round trip from her apartment to the school with her six-year-old daughter, Yolanda. On Tuesday and again on Wednesday, roughly dressed women tagged at the heels of the 42-year-old mother and screamed insults into her ears. Burly policemen broke up attempts to drag her down on two occasions. Before emerging to face her hecklers one sunny afternoon, Daisy Gabrielle told why she had chosen to defy the militant segregationists. . . .
>
> "It isn't the fault of these colored people that they were brought here," she said. "If you uproot a people, there is a penalty for it. This is the penalty the South has to pay. . . ."
>
> Mrs. Gabrielle conceded that at first she feared for the safety of her daughter and herself, "but I decided I could never give in to mob violence." To steel herself in the face of the jeering women, she said she had closed her mind and repeated a part of the Twenty-third Psalm—"Yea, though I walk through the valley of the shadow of death, I will fear no evil." She bears no hatred for her tormentors.
>
> "I have compassion for them," she said. "They are going through the deepest hell. They have been presented with a new idea and they are expected to accept it just like that. They have to grow into it."

The reporting of Claude Sitton and the other correspondents in the South made the meaning of official racism clear to many in the North who had been ignorant or unconcerned about it. Television was even more compelling in its impact as it penetrated more deeply into American life. Professor Alexander M. Bickel of the Yale Law School, writing in

1962 about the confrontations over school desegregation in New Orleans, Little Rock, Arkansas, and elsewhere, said that television coverage had made a decisive difference in national opinion. "Compulsory segregation," he wrote, "like states' rights and like 'The Southern Way of Life,' is an abstraction and, to a good many people, a neutral or sympathetic one. These riots, which were brought instantly, dramatically and literally home to the American people, showed what it means concretely. Here were grown men and women furiously confronting their enemy: two, three, a half dozen scrubbed, starched, scared and incredibly brave colored children. The moral bankruptcy, the shame of the thing, was evident."

The print and broadcast press aroused not only the public but the politicians of the North. The South's political defenses against federal interference with its racial practices were bound to crumble when the rest of the country cared enough to make a serious challenge to racism. And the country and its political leaders did begin to care. That was made dramatically evident after the Birmingham violence in 1963 when President Kennedy, who had seemed reluctant to take bold steps on civil rights, made a nationwide television broadcast on the subject of racial justice, the first ever from the White House:

"This nation was founded by men of many nations and backgrounds. It was founded on the principle that all men are created equal, and that the rights of every man are diminished when the rights of one man are threatened. . . . It ought to be possible, therefore, for American students of any color to attend any public institution they select without having to be backed up by troops. It ought to be possible for American consumers of any color to receive equal service in places of public accommodation, such as hotels and restaurants and theaters and retail stores, without being forced to resort to demonstrations in the street. And it ought to be possible for American citizens of any color to register and to vote in a free election without interference or fear of reprisal. In short, every American ought to have the right to be treated as he would wish to be treated, as one would wish his children to be treated. But this is not the case. . . . We face, therefore, a moral crisis as a country and a people. It cannot be met by repressive police action. It cannot be left to increased demonstrations in the streets. It cannot be quieted by token moves or talk. It is a time to act in the Congress, in your state and local legislative body and, above all, in all of our daily lives. . . ."

President Kennedy called for sweeping federal civil rights legislation. He was assassinated before it could be enacted, but in 1964 the Senate closed off a filibuster on a civil rights bill for the first time ever. Congress passed and President Johnson signed a bill outlawing discrimination in public accommodations, schools and employment. The next year, in the Voting Rights Act, Congress wrote into law provisions so strong that blacks were finally able to vote throughout the South. In the years afterward blacks became mayors and state legislators, and the politics of the region was transformed. Southern senators, counting their constituents, now supported civil rights legislation. A black man, Mike Espy, was elected and reelected to Congress from Mississippi. Another, Douglas Wilder, became governor of Virginia. Thirty years after Sullivan's libel trial, the Alabama Bureau of Tourism and Travel was sending out brochures urging visits to monuments of black history in Montgomery.

In those developments, however belated, the American constitutional system worked exactly as it was meant to work. From the beginning, the Constitutional Convention of 1787, the theory was that the American people would be free to inform themselves about the doings of those who governed them, free to criticize policy and change it. That freedom was guaranteed when the First Amendment was added to the Constitution in 1791, forbidding Congress to abridge the freedom of speech or press. James Madison, a principal figure at the convention and the drafter of the First Amendment, saw plainly the connection between political democracy on the one hand and freedom of expression on the other. If George III had been able to throttle the American press before 1776, Madison said, we might have remained "miserable colonies, groaning under a foreign yoke."

Commissioner Sullivan's real target was the role of the American press as an agent of democratic change. He and the other Southern officials who had sued the *Times* for libel were trying to choke off a process that was educating the country about the nature of racism and was affecting political attitudes on that issue. Thus in the broadest sense the libel suits were a challenge to the principles of the First Amendment. But making a legal argument to that effect faced an enormous obstacle. Libelous utterances had always been regarded as outside the First Amendment, an exception to "the freedom of speech" it guarantees. The Supreme Court had repeatedly said that libelous publications were not protected. In 1952, in *Beauharnais v. Illinois*, the Court upheld an Illinois law that made it a crime to publish material exposing any racial or religious group to "contempt, derision or obloquy." Libel, the Court said, was not "within the area of constitutionally protected speech."

After Commissioner Sullivan's $500,000 jury verdict, *Times Talk*, a monthly journal published by the *Times* for its employees, printed an article on the libel suits the paper faced in Alabama. It was by Ronald Diana, a young associate at Lord, Day & Lord. He listed some arguments that would be advanced on appeal: that "the Times could not be legally sued in Alabama," that the advertisement "did not in fact refer to" Sullivan and that the damage award was "grossly excessive." He did not mention the First Amendment.

Despite the history, lawyers for the *Times* had raised the First Amendment. Embry argued to Judge Jones, unsuccessfully, that allowing Sullivan to recover damages for an advertisement that did not mention him would violate the freedom of the press. Now the lawyers prepared to renew this and other arguments in an effort to get the judgment set aside.

The first step was to move for a new trial. Both the *Times* and the four ministers did so, and Judge Jones scheduled a hearing on the motions for the beginning of February 1961. When the *Times* moved for a continuance, the hearing was put off for a month. Judge Jones then ruled that because the ministers' lawyers had not made a separate motion for continuance, they had forfeited their right to ask for a new trial. This had cruel consequences in Judge Jones's court. He held that because the ministers had no motion pending, their property should be seized and sold to pay the $500,000 judgment against them if and when it became final. A deputy sheriff immediately impounded Ralph Abernathy's five-year-old Buick. Orders were issued to seize any assets he and the other three might have in local civic and savings institutions. The sheriff sold at auction a small plot of land owned by Abernathy. When the *Times* printed a brief report on the sale, its publisher, Arthur Hays Sulzberger, was outraged. In a note to Louis Loeb he said the ministers were suffering: "How and in what way could we legitimately help them?" Loeb replied that something might be done "if their cases and ours were on all fours [that is, exactly the same], but unfortunately they are not because they do not have the question of jurisdiction, which is the main string to our bow for eventually obtaining a reversal." (On Loeb's advice, the *Times* kept its correspondents out of Alabama for a year lest legal process be served on one of them and the paper thereby lose the hope it still cherished of winning the argument that it was not subject to the jurisdiction of the Alabama courts.)

"I am afraid that all I can advise," Loeb wrote to Sulzberger, "is that we cooperate closely with them [the ministers] in the future course of the litigation, which we are doing, that we bend every effort towards the ultimate reversal of these judgments, which I am confident we will succeed in accomplishing, and then lend them every conceivable assistance in recovering the meager assets of which they are being deprived in this heartless and vindictive manner."

Judge Jones denied the *Times*'s motion for a new trial. The next step was appeal to the Supreme Court of Alabama. The prospects there were gloomy for the ministers and the *Times*. The Alabama court at this time was devoted to the maintenance of racial segregation. It played a large part in a legal charade that kept the National Association for the Advancement of Colored People out of the state for eight years. At the state's request in 1956, Judge Jones of Montgomery issued a temporary restraining order against the N.A.A.C.P., without giving it a hearing. Then he held the Association in contempt for not producing membership lists on demand. When the Supreme Court of the United States set the contempt order aside, the Alabama Supreme Court refused to carry out the judgment, saying that the high court had acted on a "mistaken premise." The Supreme Court again decided in favor of the N.A.A.C.P. Now the Alabama court refused to consider the merits of the Association's case on the ground that its brief had wrongly grouped different arguments under single headings. This lame evasion was brushed aside in a third decision by the Supreme Court. Justice John Marshall Harlan, a patient and gentlemanly judge, ended his opinion as follows: "Should we unhappily be mistaken in our belief that the Supreme Court of Alabama will promptly implement this disposition, leave is given the Association to apply to this Court for further appropriate relief." The Alabama court finally obeyed, and the injunction against the N.A.A.C.P. was lifted. (As racial discrimination in Alabama eased in ensuing years, and its politics changed, so did its courts; in 1975 T. Eric Embry, the *Times*'s lawyer in the Sullivan case, was elected to the Alabama Supreme Court—over a candidate on George Wallace's slate.)

On August 30, 1962, the Alabama Supreme Court affirmed the judgments against the *Times* and the ministers. It upheld Judge Jones in all respects, using broad language that made the libel case an even greater threat to reporting on the racial issue. The court agreed with Judge Jones that the statements in the advertisement were "libelous per se," and hence presumptively false and damaging. As to the jury finding that the statements were "of and concerning" Sullivan, the court said: "We think it common knowledge that the average person knows that municipal agents, such as police and firemen and others, are under the control and direction of the city governing body, and more particularly under the direction and control of a single commissioner. In measuring the performance or deficiencies of such groups, praise or criticism is usually attached to the official in complete control of the body." This statement of what "of and concerning" could mean was menacing to the press, and for that matter to individuals or civic groups that discussed government business. It meant that any criticism of public bodies in Alabama, even an inferential mention of "police" for example, could be taken as a personal attack on the official nominally in charge and could justify heavy libel damages for the official.

The Alabama Supreme Court also agreed with Judge Jones that the $500,000 award to Sullivan was not excessive. The *Times* had shown "irresponsibility," it said, because the paper had in its news files material that "would have demonstrated the falsity of the allegations in the advertisement." Failure to check the files justified a large award. So did the *Times*'s failure to retract on Sullivan's demand while it did publish a retraction for Governor Patterson; the statements in the ad were "equally false as to both parties," the court said.

Finally, there was the First Amendment argument. The Alabama court rejected it in a single sentence: "The First Amendment of the U. S. Constitution does not protect libelous publications." As far as any court had held up to that point, the statement was correct.

# 6

◼

# THE
# MEANING OF
# FREEDOM

As originally written at the Philadelphia Convention of 1787, the Constitution of the United States had little to say about what we today call "constitutional rights." It did not mention freedom of religion, due process of law or the other now familiar protections of the individual. It was primarily a structural document, designed to join the thirteen then independent states under a new federal government. The states were in chaotic conflict with each other then. They imposed tariffs on each other's trade. They had different coinages; there was no national currency, no government to issue one. Alexander Hamilton and James Madison planned the convention—"plotted" is not too strong a word—in order to create a central authority. Until the last moment, when General Washington decided to attend, they were not sure enough delegates would turn up to make the convention worthwhile. Against the odds, the delegates wrote a charter for a central government. But they had to reckon with another deep feeling among themselves and their constituents: fear of power. They had made a revolution against a king, and they did not want his concentrated power to reappear in another guise. Their dilemma was that they also wanted effective government.

The convention drafted a plan for a republic in which the citizens would be sovereign. The people would have the ultimate power to pass on the acts of the governors and change the government. But that was not thought to be sufficient assurance against the abuse of official power, so the convention adopted what Madison called "auxiliary precautions." These were structural devices to fragment power and hem it in. First, the states would retain much authority, ceding to the new government only certain specified powers—for example over foreign relations and interstate commerce. Second, the federal government would have three separate branches: legislative, executive and judicial. When one branch drew too much power to itself, the other two would fight back, and this natural competition for power would work against autocracy. Those devices should be enough, the Framers believed, to satisfy Americans that the Constitution would prevent tyranny. They were right about the genius of their structural devices but wrong in their estimate of public feeling.

Today we are in such awe of the Constitution that we tend to assume it was greeted with similar deference by eighteenth-century Americans. Far from it. The proposed Constitution was put to conventions in the thirteen states for ratification, and there were passionate opponents. Such famous voices of liberty as Patrick Henry and George Mason, both of Virginia, argued that a new central government, however hemmed in, would inevitably lead to tyranny. It was only by making a concession to this fear of power that the Constitution won the day. The decisive tests came in the ratifying conventions of three states where opposition was strong—Massachusetts, New York and Virginia. In Massachusetts, John Hancock, the president of the convention, had an ingenious idea to ease the fear of federal power. He proposed that the convention couple a vote for ratification with a call for the first Congress elected under the Constitution to approve specific limitations on the authority of the federal government. His tactic changed enough votes so the Massachusetts convention agreed to ratification, 187 to 168. New York followed, 30 to 27, and then Virginia, 89 to 79. Both called for a set of amendments— a bill of rights—to limit federal power.

The first Congress duly considered amendments to meet the demand of the state conventions. Ten were approved by Congress and the states and became part of the Constitution in 1791, to be known collectively as the Bill of Rights. The first provided:

*Congress shall make no law respecting an establishment of religion, or prohibiting the free exercise thereof; or abridging the freedom of speech, or of the press; or the right of the people peaceably to assemble, and to petition the Government for a redress of grievances.*

What do the free expression clauses of the First Amendment mean? The words seem simple and all-encompassing. There shall be "no law," they say, "abridging the freedom of speech, or of the press." What could be more straightforward? Americans must, then, be free to say or publish anything without fear that a law will penalize them. But that has never been true, and it really cannot be. If it were, blackmail could not be made a crime in the United States, because the blackmailer operates by speaking or writing. Neither could perjury, which is lying under oath.

Then how is the meaning of the speech and press clauses to be decided? Or, first, another question: Who decides? Today the answer is obvious: Interpreting the Constitution is the business of the courts, especially the Supreme Court. But in the beginning it was not so obvious. Some believed that each branch of the government should decide for itself what the Constitution meant. Congress, for example, would consider constitutional objections when it passed a law, and the President would do so when he decided whether to sign it. Enactment would be a final determination that the statute was constitutional, and an individual charged with violating it would not be able to ask the courts to strike it down. If that view had prevailed, the provisions of the Constitution would have been only guides or admonitions, not binding law. But it did not prevail. In 1803, in the case of *Marbury v. Madison*, the Supreme Court decided that the Constitution was law—and, Chief Justice John Marshall wrote, "It is emphatically the province and duty of the judicial department to say what the law is." President Jefferson was highly critical of Marshall's opinion. In claiming the power to decide for all branches of government what was and was not constitutional, he said, the Chief Justice "would make the judiciary a despotic branch." Earlier Jefferson, who was the American Minister in Paris when the Constitution was written and ratified, had urged Madison to add a Bill of Rights because of "the legal check which it puts in the hands of the judiciary." In any event, ever since *Marbury v. Madison* the courts have had the last word on the meaning of the Constitution.

In interpreting the Constitution, the Supreme Court and other courts use the method of the common law: to decide case by case, building on what previous judges have decided. From medieval times, judges in England looked at earlier decisions and applied those precedents to ever-changing facts. In a previous case, say, a man who let a wild beast loose on another's land was made to pay damages; now if in the next case it was a dangerous dog. . . . From the growing body of precedents one could derive legal rules that were, and are, the common law. It is law made by judges from case to case, rooted in experience. Justice Holmes said in his great book *The Common Law* that in Anglo-American societies "the life of the law has not been logic: it has been experience." This method, still followed in all English-speaking countries, contrasts with the Continental practice of legislating a detailed code of laws that judges must apply. (Of course in modern Britain and the United States legislatures enact many statutes that override the common law.)

In keeping with the common-law tradition, courts will not decide in the abstract what a clause of the Constitution means; they do so only when a particular case draws the clause into question. The law gains meaning from factual situations. For example, does the constitutional freedom of speech include the freedom *not* to speak? Stated this way, in the abstract, the question is too broad to answer. But narrow it to a concrete case: May a state require children in public school to salute the flag, and expel any who refuse? Those facts bring out the values and the tensions involved. (In 1942 the Supreme Court considered the case of children who refused to salute, and were expelled, because their religion—they were Jehovah's Witnesses—regarded the salute as the worship of an idol. The Court held that forcing expression of faith in the flag violated their freedom of speech.)

As early as 1793 the Supreme Court decided that it could not give advisory opinions. When President Washington asked the justices for advice on some pressing legal questions, they replied that they could not provide "extrajudicial" opinions—that is, opinions not required by real lawsuits. So the Constitution has not been expounded to order, in a methodical way. It has been interpreted and reinterpreted over the years as the movement of history and legal thought made particular provisions relevant to current human controversies.

It is the regular business of judges to interpret written documents: business contracts, wills, legislation. That is one reason why it fell quite naturally to the courts to expound the Constitution. But doing so is different from construing other documents. Those who framed the Constitution and its most important amendments used spacious phrases—"the freedom of speech," "the equal protection of the laws" and the like—that do not give self-evident answers to concrete questions. The authors of the Fourteenth Amendment, for example, did not say directly whether racial segregation was to be allowable. Instead they guaranteed "equal protection," leaving it to future generations to define what that meant in terms of contemporary awareness. The Framers laid down principles rather than specifics, and they surely did so intentionally. They chose to avoid binding the future with a code of precise instructions. They understood that precision is the enemy of permanence. Detailed rules, which necessarily reflect the limited vision of any age, become obsolete as circumstances change. A rigidly detailed constitution would not last, so the Framers gave us values to protect, in bold strokes: "no law . . . abridging the freedom of speech." They wrote a document whose grandly phrased provisions can be interpreted, faithfully, to deal with new circumstances. Writing in 1819, Chief Justice Marshall put it that the Constitution was "intended to endure for ages to come, and, consequently, to be adapted to the various *crises* of human affairs." The Constitution remains our fundamental law because great judges have read it in that spirit.

The courts will try to find out what they can about the origins of constitutional provisions such as the speech and press clauses, seeking illumination on what the Framers had in mind. With a constitutional clause, as with a statute, a judge will first look at the legislative history: statements by the authors, committee reports in Congress, the record of floor debates. But in the case of the First Amendment those materials are so sparse as to be useless. James Madison, a member of the House from Virginia in the First Congress, made it his responsibility to push—almost alone at first—for the Bill of Rights demanded by several of the state conventions that ratified the Constitution. In his first speech on the subject, on June 8, 1789, he proposed a number of amendments, one of them as follows: "The people shall not be deprived or abridged of their right to speak, write, or to publish their sentiments; and the freedom of the press, as one of the great bulwarks of liberty, shall be inviolable." Without explanation, a House committee changed that to: "The freedom of speech and of the press, and the right of the people peaceably to assemble and consult for their common good, shall not be infringed." The debate on the floor of the House threw no light on what members understood by "the freedom of speech and of the press." The Senate combined the speech, press and assembly guarantees with provisions on religion and petition, in the form that is now the First Amendment. Again, we do not know the reasons for the changes. The Senate kept no record of its debates then; and no one made private notes as Madison had, to the great benefit of historians, at the Constitutional Convention. The House and Senate agreed on September 25, 1789, and submitted twelve amendments to the states. The first two, dealing with the number of representatives from each state and with congressional salaries, were defeated. (What became the First Amendment was the third submitted.) The remaining ten were added to the Constitution on December 15, 1791, when Virginia, the last of the necessary three fourths of the states, ratified them.

If legislative history offers no meaningful clues, the seeker for early understanding will look to contemporaneous use of language similar to the Constitution's in speeches, political documents, newspapers, legal proceedings. And here there is a large amount of material relevant to the free press clause of the First Amendment. Before the phrase appeared in the federal Constitution, nine of the original thirteen states had spoken of the freedom of the press in their own constitutions or other basic documents. The earliest was Virginia's Declaration of Rights of 1776, which said: "The freedom of the press is one of the greatest bulwarks of liberty, and can never be restrained but by despotic Governments." (Only Pennsylvania, in its Declaration of Rights, mentioned freedom of speech.) References to "the freedom of the press" or "the liberty of the press" abound in the documents of late eighteenth-century America. But those who used the phrases—politicians, editors, judges—used them to mean two quite different things.

One conception of press freedom was simply a right to publish something without first obtaining official approval—without prior restraint, as lawyers term control before publication. That definition of the freedom gave the author or publisher no protection *after* publication. He was subject to criminal punishment for criticizing the government: not much of a freedom in modern eyes. The other conception was comprehensive freedom, the right to publish without prior restraint and without fear of subsequent punishment for political criticism. Which of those concepts Americans in 1791 understood as "the freedom of the press" has been much debated. Professor Leonard W. Levy caused a stir with his 1960 book, *Legacy of Suppression*, by arguing that prior to the Constitution state and colonial courts had taken the narrower view. Professor David Anderson countered by noting that before the Revolution *Cato's Letters*, a collection of English essays that praised freedom of speech and press in broad terms, was extremely popular and influential in political thought. If colonial America was largely a repressive society, Professor Anderson added, by the revolutionary period the press "was free, in fact if not in law, to criticize the government seditiously and even licentiously." In a new edition of his book in 1985, Professor Levy conceded that the actual practice of the press, if not the statements of judges, evidenced the broader view of freedom.

The special concern about prior restraint of publication goes back to a phenomenon of English history that left a lasting imprint on both British and American attitudes. This was the practice of licensing the press. King Henry VIII first imposed, in 1538, a requirement that anything to be printed must first obtain the approval of Crown licensers. The device had a twofold purpose: economic, to control the new trade of printing, and political, to prevent the distribution of unwelcome opinions. The royal licensing system remained in force until the Cromwellian revolution overthrew the monarchy—when, in 1643, Parliament enacted its own licensing statute. Licensing was a heavy burden. To publish a book, a pamphlet, a sermon or even a handbill, one had to receive the imprimatur of censors; and there was no appeal in law from their often arbitrary decisions. The licensing system evoked memorable protests, the classic being John Milton's *Areopagitica—A Speech for the Liberty of Unli-*

*censed Printing* in 1644. The system survived the thunderbolts of Milton, finally dying only in 1694, when Parliament decided not to renew the licensing statute.

Milton was in favor of letting anyone publish without prior official approval. But he showed no protectiveness—indeed, no mercy—when it came to punishment after publication of a work found to be disrespectful of the Church, the state or its officials. "Those [works] which otherwise come forth, if they be found mischievous and libelous," he wrote, "the fire and the executioner will be the timeliest and the most effectuall remedy that mans prevention can use." Words could still be a crime. The crime was known as seditious libel. It was a common-law crime, defined by judges, and it was defined so loosely that it could intimidate anyone who thought of publishing dissident political views. Any publication that tended to lower the public's esteem for the government or a public official or institution might be found by a court to be a seditious libel. If you wrote that a royal personage or Crown servant was corrupt, you were not allowed to defend yourself against a charge of seditious libel by producing evidence of the corruption. Truth was no defense because the criminal harm lay in lowering esteem—and truth might do that most effectively. The greater the truth, the greater the libel, as the saying went. There were jury trials, but juries could decide only whether the defendant had published the offending matter and whether it referred to a governmental institution or personage. The judge decided whether the publication was "malicious" and had a "bad tendency," which would make it seditious libel. The rationale for having such a crime was stated by Chief Justice John Holt in 1704: "It is very necessary for all governments that the people should have a good opinion of it. And nothing can be worse to any government than to endeavour to procure animosities, as to the management of it; this has always been looked upon as a crime, and no government can be safe without it be punished."

The term "seditious libel" may sound antique now, but the concept is certainly familiar in the twentieth century. It is the standard practice of tyrannical governments to use the criminal law to insulate themselves from disagreement. The law condemning "anti-Soviet agitation" in the U.S.S.R. before Mikhail Gorbachev introduced glasnost was a species of seditious libel law. Professor Harry Kalven Jr. of the University of Chicago Law School, a notable writer on the law of free speech and press, said the idea of seditious libel was "the hallmark of closed societies throughout the world. Under it criticism of government is viewed as defamation and punished as a crime. The treatment of such speech as criminal is based on an accurate perception of the dangers in it; it is likely to undermine confidence in government policies and in the official incumbents. But political freedom ends when government can use its powers and its courts to silence its critics. In my view, the presence or absence in the law of the concept of seditious libel defines the society. . . . If, however, it makes seditious libel an offense, it is not a free society, no matter what its other characteristics."

Given the repugnant quality of seditious libel to us today, how could Englishmen of the seventeenth and eighteenth centuries—"the liberty-loving English people," as Justice Felix Frankfurter used to call them in his affection for Britain—talk of "freedom of the press" while prosecutions for seditious libel went on? The answer is that the idea of freedom of discourse on public matters grew only slowly among English philosophers and political commentators. Not only factual charges of corruption or malfeasance but even opinions were regarded as dangerous. Milton is revered as a voice of freedom, but on matters of religious opinion he allowed only one truth: the Protestant. He would not permit publication of Roman Catholic or non-Christian doctrines. It was really not until John Stuart Mill that the classic argument for freedom of opinion was made in Britain. In 1859, in *On Liberty*, Mill listed reasons for that freedom:

> First, if any opinion is compelled to silence, that opinion may, for aught we can certainly know, be true. To deny this is to assume our own infallibility. Secondly, though the silenced opinion be in error, it may, and very commonly does, contain a portion of the truth; and since the general or prevailing opinion on any subject is rarely or never the whole truth, it is only by the collision of adverse opinions that the remainder of the truth has any chance of being supplied. Thirdly, even if the received opinion be not only true, but the whole truth; unless it is suffered to be, and actually is, vigorously and earnestly contested, it will, by most of those who receive it, be held in the manner of a prejudice, with little comprehension or feeling of its rational grounds. . . .

The great authority on the common law, revered by lawyers in America as in England, was Sir William Blackstone. In his *Commentaries on the Laws of England*, published from 1765 to 1769, Blackstone said:

> Where blasphemous, immoral, treasonable, schismatical, seditious or scandalous libels are punished by the English law . . . the liberty of the press, properly understood, is by no means infringed or violated. The *liberty of the press* is indeed essential to the nature of a free state; but this consists in laying no *previous*

restraints upon publications, and not in freedom from censure for criminal matter when published. Every freeman has an undoubted right to lay what sentiments he pleases before the public: to forbid this is to destroy the freedom of the press: but if he publishes what is improper, mischievous or illegal, he must take the consequences of his own temerity. . . . To punish (as the law does at present) any dangerous or offensive writings, which, when published, shall on a fair and impartial trial be adjudged of a pernicious tendency, is necessary for the preservation of peace and good order, a government and religion, the only solid foundations of civil liberty.

It should be added that Blackstone's "fair and impartial trial" on a charge of seditious libel was one in which truth was not a defense and the judge alone decided whether the publication was seditious.

Blackstone's *Commentaries* were influential in America after 1776. The states, now independent, continued to follow English common law in their courts, and the *Commentaries* were a convenient compendium of the precedents. State courts regularly referred to Blackstone, and several explicitly adopted his statement on the law of seditious libel. As late as 1803 an editor in Hudson, New York, Harry Croswell, was prosecuted for seditious libel under the common law as formulated by Blackstone. His newspaper, *The Wasp*, had published a story that Thomas Jefferson, while Vice President under John Adams, had paid a journalist named James T. Callender to denounce Adams and former President Washington in colorful terms. (Callender called Washington "a traitor, a robber and a perjurer.") When Croswell was tried, the judge refused to postpone the trial to give Croswell time to call Callender as a witness to testify on whether Jefferson had indeed paid him; the testimony would be irrelevant because the truth was no defense. The judge found the publication seditious, and Croswell was convicted. (A year later the New York Legislature passed a statute that made truth a defense in seditious libel cases; Croswell went free, gave up journalism and became an Episcopal minister.)

On evidence of this kind, Professor Levy found in his 1960 book that the Blackstonian view of seditious libel was widespread in the United States at the time the First Amendment was adopted, so "the freedom of the press" may indeed have meant only freedom from prior restraint. In his revised view, in 1985, he said he had been wrong to look only at legal theory and judicial opinions. The practice in the late eighteenth century was very different from the theory, Levy said he now realized. The press was "habitually scurrilous" then, devoted to roasting politicians. Prosecutions for seditious libel were infrequent, no doubt because governments feared that the public would sympathize with those prosecuted. "The actual freedom of the press had slight relationship to the fact that as a legal concept, freedom of the press was a cluster of constraints. The law threatened repression; the press conducted itself as if the law scarcely existed." In the United States, Levy concluded, "the English common-law definition had become unsuitable, and libertarian theory had not caught up with practice." Freedom of the press in practice meant "a right to engage in rasping, corrosive and offensive discussions on all topics of public interest."

The early American newspapers were certainly filled with calumny. If the politicians who think themselves unfairly treated by the press in the late twentieth century looked back two hundred years, they might feel less sorry for themselves. Who could have been loftier than Washington, more above criticism? Yet when he left the presidency in 1797, the Philadelphia *Aurora* wrote: "The man who is the source of all the misfortunes of our country, is this day reduced to a level with his fellow citizens, and is no longer possessed of power to multiply evils upon the United States. If ever there was a period for rejoicing, this is the moment—every heart in unison with the freedom and happiness of the people ought to beat high, with exultation that the name of Washington from this day ceases to give a currency to political iniquity, and to legalize corruption." Political cartoonists were already at their work of denigration as well, one of them putting Washington's face on an ass.

There the question of seditious libel stood at the time of the First Amendment: the concept still law in the state courts but the press raucously ignoring its existence. Then came an extraordinary episode, one that made the relationship of the First Amendment to the idea of seditious libel a burning political issue. Congress passed a law, the Sedition Act of 1798, that made criticism of the federal government a crime.

# 7

■

# THE
# SEDITION
# ACT

"PERHAPS it is a universal truth that the loss of liberty at home is to be charged to provisions against danger, real or pretended, from abroad."

James Madison made that perceptive observation in a letter to Vice President Jefferson on May 13, 1798. Its truth has been demonstrated again and again in American history as politicians used the fear of foreign ideology and power to justify the suppression of freedom. The fear that prevailed when Madison wrote was fear of France.

France had supported the American colonies in their war with Great Britain. But gratitude for that help gave way to growing alarm as the French Revolution of 1789 was followed by the Terror and the guillotine. Americans, especially those of conservative bent, came to see France as the home of a malevolent ideology that it would try to send across the Atlantic. Then came war between France and Britain. The United States proclaimed its neutrality, but in Jay's Treaty of 1794 it accepted Britain's claim of the right to seize neutral vessels carrying cargo for France. As a result, in 1796 French warships began attacking American merchant ships bound for Britain.

Anti-French feeling was brought to a boil in April 1798 by the XYZ affair. Talleyrand, the French foreign minister, refused to receive a special American diplomatic mission sent to Paris to try to ease relations. Three agents of Talleyrand demanded a large payment as the price of opening negotiations. The Americans rejected the demand and went home, sending a dispatch ahead to President Adams on what had happened. Adams informed Congress of the business in a message that concealed the names of the offending French agents by referring to them as X, Y and Z. Adams quoted Y as saying that France did not fear the U. S. diplomats' breaking off their mission because "the French party in America" would soon repair the breach.

Adams's supporters in Congress and the country used "the French party in America" as a reference to the President's political opponents, Jefferson and his supporters. Political parties were just beginning to be formed then. The Framers of the Constitution had not envisaged this development; they provided for the President to be chosen not by popular election but by an august Electoral College. The first choice, Washington, was inevitable. But thereafter forces began to form behind Washington's Vice President, Adams, and his Secretary of State, Jefferson. The election of 1796, after Washington's two terms, was close, Adams defeating Jefferson by 71 electoral votes to 66. As runner-up, Jefferson became Vice President. (The present system of presidential/vice presidential tickets was introduced by the Twelfth Amendment to the Constitution in 1804.)

The Adams supporters were the Federalist party. The Jeffersonians, ancestors of the modern Democratic party, called themselves Republicans or Democratic Republicans. Two hundred years later, it is not so easy to see why the two parties fought each other so bitterly. Both included signers of the Declaration of Independence and delegates to the Constitutional Convention. Alexander Hamilton, one of the authors of the Federalist Papers, the great exposition of the Constitution, was a Federalist; his principal co-author, Madison, was a Republican. But the differences were passionately felt, as the use of the damning phrase "the French party" indicates. The Federalists tended to be the propertied class, more concerned about order in society; they wanted a strong federal government and felt close to Britain. The Republicans spoke, often in populist voice, for farmers and the less affluent; they were suspicious of federal power. Of course those generalities yielded to circumstance: When Jefferson became president, he was by no means timid in the assertion of federal power. But at the time, each saw the other in exaggerated terms. To Republicans, the Federalists favored centralized authority and English manners so much that they really wanted to introduce a monarchy. To Federalists, Republicans were Jacobins who if they took office would install a French-style terror. Abigail Adams, the President's wife, wrote a friend in 1798 that the French party—the Republicans—were busy all over the country "sowing the seeds of vice, irreligion, corruption and sedition."

It was in this atmosphere of bitterness and suspicion that the Sedition Act of 1798 became law. The Federalists controlled both Houses of Congress as well as the presidency, but they saw the Republicans gaining politically. They believed they could arrest that trend by silencing critics of the government, especially in the Republican press, and they made the suppression of criticism a partisan cause. A sedition bill was proposed by the Senate in June 1798 and was approved by a straight party-line vote on July 4: a date evidently chosen by its backers to identify it as patriotic legislation. The House passed its version on July 10; the Republican members had managed to add a clause providing that the law expire on March 3, 1801, when the President's term of office ended. Adams signed the bill into law on July 14.

The Sedition Act made it a crime, punishable by up to two years in prison and a fine of two thousand dollars, to "write, print, utter or publish . . . any false, scandalous and malicious writing or writings against the government of the United States, or either house of the Congress . . . or the President . . . with intent to defame . . . or to bring them, or either of them, into contempt or disrepute; or to excite against them, or either or any of them, the hatred of the good people of the United States." The act punished abuse of Congress or the President, but it strikingly omitted Vice President Jefferson from its protection.

The act punished political criticism only if it was "false, scandalous and malicious," and only if the author intended to defame. Those provisions were described by the Federalists as ameliorations of the common-law crime of seditious libel, against which truth was no defense. But though they seemed to promise much, in fact they were of little or no use to those who were charged with sedition under the act. The federal courts, its judges all appointed by Federalist presidents, interpreted the requirement of falsity to make the defendant bear the burden of proving the truth; a critical statement was presumed to be false unless the defendant could prove it true in all respects. The courts applied this rigorous requirement even to statements of mere opinion. If an editor wrote that government policy was headed for disaster, he had to prove the prediction true—which of course he could not. Malice was also presumed, and intent to defame was inferred from publication of words that had a "bad tendency"—the ancient test of seditious libel at common law. Another supposedly liberalizing feature of the statute was that it let the jury decide issues of both fact and law. But here again judges charged juries in a way that left them nothing to decide except whether the accused had published the statement complained of. Moreover, modern research suggests that federal judges and marshals packed juries in Sedition Act cases with Federalists.

The Federalists of 1798 were hardly unique in practicing the politics of fear. There have been repeated examples of what Richard Hofstadter called "the paranoid style in American politics." In the twentieth century Congress passed many laws branding as infamous anyone, citizen or would-be visitor to America, who was suspected of the faintest Communist taint; for forty years politicians won votes by charging their opponents with being soft on communism. The Sedition Act was a product of such zealotry and political calculation. Many Federalists probably believed that their opponents were dangerous radicals who would ruin the country, and this belief was compounded by a royalist assumption that those who were in power had a right to remain there. Speaking for the Sedition Bill in the House, Representative John Allen of Connecticut said: "Let gentlemen look at certain papers printed in this city [Philadelphia, then the seat of government] and elsewhere, and ask themselves whether an unwarrantable and dangerous combination does not exist to overturn and ruin the Government by publishing the most shameless falsehoods." Allen said the critical newspapers printed statements that the Government was hostile to the country's welfare and "ought, therefore, to be displaced, and that the people ought to raise an *insurrection* against the Government." Allen slid easily from criticism of the government to insurrection. The Republican papers were certainly hostile in their criticism, but their aim was to displace the Federalist administration not by insurrection but by means of the ballot box.

A Republican from Pennsylvania, Albert Gallatin, who was later Jefferson's brilliant Secretary of the Treasury, told the House: "This bill and its supporters suppose, in fact, that whoever dislikes the measures of [the] Administration and of a temporary majority in Congress, and shall, either by speaking or writing, express his disapprobation and his want of confidence in the men now in power, is seditious, is an enemy, not of [the] Administration, but of the Constitution, and is liable to punishment." Gallatin concluded that the bill was only a weapon used by a party in power in order "to perpetuate their authority and preserve their present places."

At the end of the debate the House turned to the constitutionality of the bill. Republicans argued that it was beyond the power of Congress and therefore unconstitutional for two reasons. First, the original Constitution had granted no power to the federal government over the press. (Some of the Framers had made this point in arguing that a Bill of Rights with protection of the press was unnecessary.) Second, the speech and press clauses of the First Amendment specifically denied Congress the right to pass such legislation. The Federalists replied that a power to prevent seditious attacks in the press was a necessary incident of any government and hence was within the clause of the Constitution enabling Congress to pass all "necessary and proper" measures to carry out its granted authority. Further, relying on Blackstone, they argued that the First Amendment's "freedom of the press" meant only freedom from prior restraints.

Gallatin and Representative John Nicholas made considered speeches against the bill's constitutionality. Gallatin ridiculed the Blackstonian view of press freedom, saying it was "preposterous to say, that to punish a certain act was not an abridgment of the liberty of doing that act." Gallatin made the further ingenious argument that the Blackstone theory was "absurd" as applied to the free speech clause of the First Amendment. If "freedom" meant only freedom from prior restraint, he asked, how could a government apply prior restraints to men speaking? The free speech clause would have to have been designed to deprive Congress of "a power to seal the mouths or to cut the tongues of the citizens of the Union," for those "were the only means by which previous restraints could be laid on the freedom of speech." Nicholas rejected as inconsistent with freedom any attempt to distinguish truth from falsity in speech, or liberty from license—distinctions that the Federalists had emphasized in their defense of the bill. Any vigorous political criticism would be charged with falsehood, Nicholas said, and printers "would be afraid of publishing the truth, as, though true, it might not always be in their power to establish the truth to the satisfaction of a court." In this passage Nicholas anticipated an important element in the theory of free speech as it developed in the twentieth century: that in true freedom there must be room for error.

Early in 1799 Republicans in the House moved to repeal the Sedition Act. The proposal was rejected in committee and by a party-line vote in the House. But John Nicholas wrote a minority committee report that further developed the idea of free speech. The thinking behind the Sedition Act, he said, was derived from Great Britain, which had a very different system of government. "The King is hereditary, and according to the theory of their Government, can do no wrong. Public officers are his representatives, and derive some portion of his inviolability." They therefore receive "a different sort of respect," Nicholas said, "from that which is proper in our Government, where the officers of Government are the servants of the people, are amenable to them, and liable to be turned out of office at periodical elections."

But the most important voice heard in protest of the Sedition Act was Madison's. After passage of the act, he and Jefferson decided to try to arouse opposition to it in the state legislatures. They acted in secret, for fear that they would be prosecuted under the act—a Father of the Constitution and the Vice President of the United States! Jefferson drafted a resolution that went to the Kentucky Legislature and was approved there in November. It made the argument of federalism—that the Constitution reserved to the states any power to legislate on the press. The Virginia legislature approved resolutions drafted by Madison making the argument that freedom of speech and of the press were the essential guardians of a republican political system. The Virginia Resolutions protested against "the palpable and alarming infractions of the Constitution" in the Sedition Act. It exercised, the resolutions said, "a power not delegated by the Constitution, but, on the contrary, expressly and positively forbidden by one of the amendments thereto—a power which, more than any other, ought to produce universal alarm, because it is leveled against the right of freely examining public characters and measures, and of free communication among the people thereon, which has ever been justly deemed the only effectual guardian of every other right."

That phrase of Madison's, "the right of freely examining public characters and measures," echoed down the decades as the premise of the American political system—the Madisonian premise. Madison expanded on the idea in a Report on the Virginia Resolutions that he wrote in late 1799 and that the Virginia legislature approved in January 1800. Under the United States Constitution, he said, "The people, not the government, possess the absolute sovereignty." That was "altogether different" from Britain—the point Nicholas had made. "Is it not natural and necessary, under such different circumstances, that a different degree of freedom in the use of the press should be contemplated?" In America, Madison continued, "the press has exerted a freedom in canvassing the merits and measures of public men, of every description, which has not been confined to the strict limits of the common law. On this footing the freedom of the press has stood; on this foundation it yet stands."

The Virginia Resolutions and Madison's Report are landmarks in the history of free speech and a free press in the United States. But there was another view in Virginia at the time: a "minority address" from the House of Delegates, supporting the Sedition Act. It argued:

> To contend that there does not exist a power to punish writings coming within the description of this [Sedition] law, would be to assert the inability of our nation to preserve its own peace, and to protect themselves from the attempts of wicked citizens, who incapable of quiet themselves, are incessantly employed in devising means to disturb the public repose. Government is instituted and preserved for the general happiness and safety; the people therefore are interested in its preservation, and have a

62

right to adopt measures for its security, as well against secret plots as open hostility. But government cannot be thus secured, if, by falsehood and malicious slander, it is to be deprived of the confidence and affection of the people.

It is in vain to urge that truth will prevail, and that slander, when detected, recoils on the calumniator. The experience of the world, and our own experience, prove that a continued course of defamation will at length sully the fairest reputation, and will throw suspicion on the purest conduct. Although the calumnies of the factious and discontented may not poison the minds of a majority of the citizens, yet they will infect a very considerable number, and prompt them to deeds destructive of the public peace, and dangerous to the general safety. This the people have a right to prevent; and therefore, in all the nations of the earth, where presses are known some corrective of their licentiousness has been deemed indispensable.

According to Albert J. Beveridge, author of the standard life of Chief Justice John Marshall, Marshall wrote that minority address. (He was elected to Congress as a Federalist in April 1799.) More recent scholarship attributes the document to Henry Lee, another Virginia Federalist. Whoever wrote it, the minority address was a fascinating expression of the political premises that underlay the Sedition Act. It saw government as a fragile creature that had to be protected from "wicked citizens." There could hardly be a sharper contrast to Jefferson's belief that democratic government requires the acceptance of risk and change. Or to Madison's view that the people are sovereign and hence entitled to say what they choose about those whom they appoint temporarily to govern. To the minority spokesman, the government was sovereign, and entitled to preserve itself. It was a very English view.

As for the First Amendment, the author of the minority address argued in an ingenious way that the Sedition Act did not violate its guarantee of press freedom. The same First Amendment, he noted, said, "Congress shall make no law respecting an establishment of religion." But when the amendment came to the press, he said, "the word *respecting* is dropt, and Congress is only restrained from passing any law abridging its liberty." Thus, he argued, the establishment clause was an absolute bar; but the press clause merely prohibited abridgment of what was then understood as "the freedom of the press." He went on to define that freedom in extremely narrow terms—as Blackstone had, no more. "In fact," he wrote in the minority report, "the liberty of the press is a term which has a definite signification completely understood. It signifies a liberty to publish, free from previous restraint, . . . but not the liberty of spreading with impunity false and malicious slanders, which may destroy the peace and mangle the reputation of an individual or of a community." (As a reading of the intention of those who framed the First Amendment, the argument about the word "respecting" was dubious. The Framers wanted to bar Congress from either establishing a national church or ordering states that had established churches to disestablish them; the neutral word "respecting" was designed to keep Congress from acting one way or the other.)

The significance of the Sedition Act was made clear by the prosecutions brought under it. The most complete modern account, *Freedom's Fetters*, by James Morton Smith, says fourteen men were charged with violating the act during its brief life. They included the editors and owners of the leading Republican newspapers, the Philadelphia *Aurora*, Boston *Independent Chronicle*, New York *Argus*, Baltimore *American* and Richmond *Examiner*. Two other New York State papers, the *Time Piece* and the Mount Pleasant *Register*, ceased publication because of Sedition Act prosecutions. The New London, Connecticut, *Bee* suspended publication from April to August 1800 because its editor, Charles Holt, was serving a sentence for sedition. Most of the cases came to trial in the year 1800, and that was not an accident. President Adams's Secretary of State, Timothy Pickering, encouraged Sedition Act prosecutions, and he planned cases to silence the important Jeffersonian newspapers during the election contest of 1800 between Adams and Jefferson.

The first Sedition Act prosecution was brought not against an editor but against a Republican member of the House of Representatives, Matthew Lyon of Vermont. He was indicted for writing a letter to the editor that was published by the Vermont *Journal* of Windsor, Vermont. Lyon said he would gladly support a government that worked for the happiness of the people but could not be the "humble advocate" of an executive engaged in "a continual grasp for power, in an unbounded thirst for ridiculous pomp, foolish adulation, and selfish avarice. . . ." The indictment charged that those words were a criminal libel on President Adams, "scurrilous, feigned, false, scandalous, seditious and malicious." At the trial the presiding judge was Justice William Paterson of the Supreme Court. (The justices all did extra duty as trial judges in those days, riding a judicial circuit on horseback.) Justice Paterson charged the jury that all it had to decide was whether Lyon's statement could have been made "with any other intent than that of making odious or contemptible the President and government, and bringing them both into disrepute. If you find such is the case, the offense is made out, and you must render a verdict of guilty." The jury convicted Lyon, and he was sentenced to four months in prison, with a fine of $1,000 and court costs of $60.96. Lyon was reelected to Congress while in prison. His jail term was due to expire on February 9, 1799, but he had no money to pay the fine or court costs, and failing payment would have to remain incarcerated. But leading Republicans around the country contributed to a fund for him, Senator Stevens T. Mason of Virginia brought the money in gold to Vermont, and Lyon was released to a triumphal parade in his honor. He returned to Congress a hero, the prosecution having badly misfired.

An even more extreme example of the uses of the Sedition Act was the prosecution of David Brown, a wandering orator—really a vagabond— who traveled around Massachusetts between 1796 and 1798 denouncing the government for land speculation and, latterly, for the Sedition Act and companion measures against aliens. After he spoke in Dedham in 1798, citizens raised a liberty pole with a sign saying: "No Stamp Act, No Sedition, No Alien Bills, No Land Tax; downfall to the Tyrants of America, peace and retirement to the President, Long Live the Vice-President and the Minority; May moral virtue be the basis of civil government." Brown was charged under the Sedition Act for inspiring the erection of the liberty pole. In a trial before the most infamously partisan Federalist on the bench, Justice Samuel Chase of the Supreme Court, sitting on circuit in Massachusetts, Brown pleaded guilty. Justice Chase sentenced him to eighteen months in prison and a fine of $480, saying he imposed the severe sentence because of Brown's "vicious industry" in circulating "his disorganizing doctrines and impudent falsehoods, and the very alarming and dangerous excesses to which he attempted to incite the uninformed part of the community." When his prison term expired in December 1800, Brown could not pay the fine. He remained in prison until Jefferson became President on March 4, 1801, and pardoned all the victims of the Sedition Act.

James T. Callender, a political pamphleteer whose invective infuriated the Federalists, was indicted for sedition in Virginia. He was accused for passages in a book, published as the campaign of 1800 was getting under way, that called Adams a "hoary headed incendiary" and told voters, "Take your choice, then, between Adams, war and beggary, and Jefferson, peace and competency." (The New York Federalist, Harry Croswell, was prosecuted for common-law seditious libel in 1803 for writing that Jefferson had paid Callender to publish those statements.) Justice Chase presided over the grand jury that indicted Callender, and then over the trial. He baited Callender's lawyers and dismissed their arguments so cavalierly that they resigned from the case. The jury, composed entirely of Federalists, convicted Callender, and Justice Chase sentenced him to a prison term of nine months and a $200 fine. Callender stayed in prison until the Sedition Act expired, but that did not silence him. He wrote articles from prison for Virginia newspapers during the election campaign, and he attacked Justice Chase as a judge who acted like a prosecutor. The Callender case was the most celebrated of the Sedition Act prosecutions, and once again it backfired on the Federalists. Republicans published the transcript of Callender's trial, and it became popular evidence of a Federalist inclination to tyranny.

The constitutionality of the Sedition Act was never tested in the Supreme Court because the law expired before a case could reach there. But it should be noted that three of the six men who sat on the Court in 1800, Justices Chase, Paterson and Bushrod Washington, had presided at Sedition Act trials without intimating any constitutional qualms.

As a political tactic, the Sedition Act was a disaster. It aroused popular outrage, becoming a campaign issue itself in the election of 1800 and contributing to Jefferson's defeat of Adams. The Federalists also lost control of Congress in that election, and they soon disappeared as a party. But the act did make an inadvertent contribution, an important one, to the American system of government. It made large numbers of Americans appreciate the importance of free speech and freedom of the press in a democracy: the Madisonian premise. Whether or not the authors of the First Amendment intended it to eliminate the crime of seditious libel, ten years later the weight of opinion, informed and popular, was that such a crime was inconsistent with the American constitutional system.

Jefferson quickly pardoned all those who had been convicted under the Sedition Act. He gave his reasons in a letter to Abigail Adams in 1804. (Despite their bitter enmity before the election of 1800 Jefferson had a long and happy correspondence with both John and Abigail Adams. The two men were intimate friends until they died—on the same day, July 4, 1826, the fiftieth anniversary of the Declaration of Independence.) Jefferson wrote Mrs. Adams:

> I discharged every person under punishment or prosecution under the Sedition Law, because I considered, and now consider, that law to be a nullity, as absolute and palpable as if Congress had ordered us to fall down and worship a golden image; and that it was as much my duty to arrest its execution in every stage, as it would have been to have rescued from the fiery furnace those who should have been cast into it for refusing to worship the image.

It has often been said that Congress remitted the fines of those convicted under the act, but there was no general repayment. Many years later, in

1840, Congress did vote to refund to the heirs of Representative Matthew Lyon the $1,000 fine and $60.96 in court costs, plus interest. One other refund statute, passed in 1850, repaid with interest a $400 fine imposed on Dr. Thomas Cooper, a Pennsylvania pamphleteer, who before his death in 1839 exacted a promise from his wife to keep demanding repayment.

The vengeful spirit of the Sedition Act was really replaced by a better American tradition when Jefferson gave his inaugural address on March 4, 1801. "We are all Republicans—we are all Federalists," he said. "If there be any among us who wish to dissolve this Union or to change its republican form, let them stand undisturbed as monuments of the safety with which error of opinion may be tolerated where reason is left free to combat it." With that, the time when Americans could be punished for their political opinions was over. Or so it seemed.

# 8

▪

# WORLD WAR I

FOR more than a century after the First Amendment was adopted, its protections of free speech and freedom of the press scarcely figured in the decisions of the Supreme Court. Before World War I only a handful of cases dealt with freedom of expression. Then, suddenly, issues of free speech became profoundly important, and bitterly contested, in the Court. Starting in 1919 and continuing through the decades without end, the justices puzzled out the meaning of the speech and press clauses—those delusively simple clauses—in hundreds of cases. It was an extraordinary process of exploration, informed by counsel and by scholars. And Commissioner Sullivan's libel suit eventually came to play a notable part in it.

That so few cases on freedom of speech and press reached the Supreme Court before 1919 must seem puzzling, but there were reasons. The amendment restrained only the federal government, not the states. That is evident from its words: "*Congress* shall make no law . . ." Madison in fact drafted, and the House approved, an amendment protecting the freedom of speech, press and religion and trial by jury from abridgment by the state governments. Madison thought it "the most valuable" of all his proposals, but it was rejected by the more state-oriented Senate. (Jefferson did not share his great friend's desire to protect the press from state restriction. In his 1804 letter to Abigail Adams about the Sedition Act he said: "Nor does the opinion of the unconstitutionality and consequent nullity of that law remove all restraint from the overwhelming torrent of slander which is confounding all vice and virtue, all truth and falsehood in the US. The power to do that is fully possessed by the several state legislatures.") In 1833 the Supreme Court confirmed, in an opinion by Chief Justice Marshall, that the provisions of the Bill of Rights applied only to the federal government. And there were no federal laws restricting the freedom of speech or of the press. After the Sedition Act of 1798, it was one hundred and nineteen years before Congress ventured into that business again.

In the latter part of the nineteenth century and the early years of the twentieth the Supreme Court focused on protecting the economic interests of business. It found in the Fourteenth Amendment's rule against deprivation of liberty or property without due process of law a "liberty of contract," enforcing this by, for example, holding maximum-hour laws and restrictions on child labor unconstitutional. But when it came to the personal liberties guaranteed by the first ten amendments, the Court took a narrow view. In an 1897 decision it said: "The first ten amendments to the Constitution, commonly known as the Bill of Rights, were not intended to lay down any novel principles of government, but simply to embody certain guaranties and immunities which we had inherited from our English ancestors, and which had from time immemorial been subject to certain well-recognized exceptions arising from the necessities of the case."

The Court addressed freedom of speech and press in that tone: grudgingly. It disposed of cases without even recognizing speech issues. When it did deal with them, it followed the logic of Blackstone and seditious libel, saying that speech with a "bad tendency" could be punished in the interest of society. (In legal terms, speech with a "bad tendency" was speech that might someday have undesirable social consequences. The rule did not define either the time frame or the kind of consequences with any specificity. In practice, what was condemned as having a "bad tendency" was speech that judges thought right-thinking people would consider morally or politically offensive.) In the case of *Patterson v. Colorado* in 1907 an editor was held in contempt of court for criticizing a judge; he was not allowed to plead that his criticism was true, and he argued that that rule denied him due process of law. Justice Oliver Wendell Holmes Jr., following Blackstone, said "the main purpose" of free speech guarantees was to prevent "*previous restraints* upon publications," but "they do not prevent the subsequent punishment of such as may be deemed contrary to the public welfare." Rejecting the editor's claim of a right to plead truth as a defense, Holmes said true statements could be punished if they did social harm—as comments that "tend to

obstruct the administration of justice" might. Under this test freedom of
expression was a shadow right, for virtually anything could be "deemed
contrary to the public welfare." A specialist in this period of judicial
history, Professor David M. Rabban, wrote: "Supreme Court decisions
in the generation before World War One reflected a tradition of pervasive
hostility to the value of free speech."

But a very different view of free speech and the American tradition
was developing in another quarter. A number of respected legal scholars,
starting in the first decade of the twentieth century, published works
arguing that freedom of speech had a far broader meaning in the United
States than it had in England. A 1914 essay by Henry Schofield, *Freedom
of the Press in the United States*, showed that many tracts published in
America before the Revolution would have been seditious at common
law by Blackstone's definition. Schofield concluded that "one of the ob-
jects of the Revolution was to get rid of the English common law on
liberty of speech and of the press." The First Amendment, he said, made
lawful the publication of "truth on . . . a matter of public concern." He
drew a distinction between public or political comments, which should
be protected, and statements about private matters, which should not.
Schofield criticized the Supreme Court and other courts for saying that
the First Amendment was "only declaratory of the anti-republican English
common law of the days of Blackstone." Judges seemed to have forgotten,
he wrote, that the Framers of the Constitution were distinguished not
for "their reception of the English common law" but for their adaptation
of democratic strands in the past "to a new career of popular freedom
and equal justice."

Then in 1917 the United States entered World War I. The mood of
the country turned violently jingoistic. Dissent from the war was not
tolerated. German names were changed; sauerkraut became liberty cab-
bage. In this atmosphere Congress passed a sweeping Espionage Act.
Among many other things the act made it a crime, punishable by up to
twenty years in prison, to "cause or attempt to cause insubordination,
disloyalty, mutiny, or refusal of duty in the military or naval forces"
when the United States was at war, or to "willfully obstruct the recruiting
or enlistment service." Hundreds of people were prosecuted under the
act for merely speaking or writing in negative terms. The most innocuous
criticism of government policy or discussions of pacifism were found to
be violations of the Espionage Act. Judges told juries to convict if they
found that a defendant's words had been "disloyal." It was the Sedition
Act reborn.

One month after the passage of the Espionage Act, the Postmaster
General, Albert Burleson, ordered the magazine *The Masses* excluded

from the mails. *The Masses* described itself as "a monthly revolutionary journal." Burleson said that four articles and four cartoons in the issue of August 1917, attacking the war and the military draft, would violate the act. *The Masses* went to court and asked for an order forbidding its exclusion from the mails. The case came before Learned Hand, then a federal trial judge, later promoted to the U.S. Court of Appeals and for many years one of the most distinguished American judges. Judge Hand decided in favor of *The Masses;* he enjoined the New York postmaster from acting against the magazine. The decision was quickly reversed by the Court of Appeals for the Second Circuit, and it was lost in a tide of cases enforcing the Espionage Act against speakers and publishers. The case was largely forgotten until Professor Gerald Gunther, Judge Hand's biographer, called attention to it in 1970 and after. It was only then that the Hand opinion was seen for the landmark it was: the first significant judicial exposition in this country of the values of free speech and freedom of the press.

The articles and cartoons in *The Masses* constituted, Judge Hand said, "a virulent attack upon the war." They might, "unhappily," encourage disagreement with the war. But, Hand said, "they fall within the scope of that right to criticize either by temperate reasoning, or by immoderate and indecent invective, which is normally the privilege of the individual in countries dependent upon the free expression of opinion as the ultimate source of authority." To suppress statements because they might ultimately change some minds would mean "the suppression of all hostile criticism, and of all opinion except what encouraged and supported the existing policies, or which fell within the range of temperate argument. It would contradict the normal assumption of democratic government that the suppression of hostile criticism does not turn upon the justice of its substance or the decency and propriety of its temper." Judge Hand said the statute should be read to make criminal only direct incitement of mutiny, insubordination and the like, and he found no such direct urging in *The Masses*. "To assimilate agitation, legitimate as such, with direct incitement to violent resistance, is to disregard the tolerance of all methods of political agitation which in normal times is a safeguard of free government. The distinction is not a scholastic subterfuge, but a hard-bought acquisition in the fight for freedom. . . ."

It was a courageous opinion, delivered at a time when pacifism and radical views of any kind were detested. It was also a pathbreaking opinion. Judge Hand turned away from the Blackstonian notion that speech is protected only against prior restraints; he held the subsequent punishment of the Espionage Act to exacting standards. He rejected the traditional view that speech could be penalized if it had a "bad tendency," saying instead that it could be punished only if the words themselves called directly for illegal action. By this standard most of the Espionage Act prosecutions would have failed. An even more profound change, pointed out by Professor Vincent Blasi, was embodied in Hand's statement that freedom of expression, including hostile criticism, is "the ultimate source of authority" in a democracy. Until then judges had treated speech as nothing special but as just one of many claims by individuals to be free of official control—claims that had to yield to the larger interests of society. Now Hand was saying that the larger interest of society *was* free speech. The very criticism that government officials resent is what gives government legitimacy. Free speech, in other words, is an essential component of self-government. In a country where the citizens are sovereign, they cannot be punished for disagreeing with those they temporarily designate to govern them. Judge Hand did not cite Madison, and it is not known whether he had read Madison's Report on the Virginia Resolutions. But his approach was reminiscent of Madison's statements that "the people, not the government, possess the absolute sovereignty," and have the right freely to examine "public characters and measures."

In March 1919 the Supreme Court handed down its first decisions on the Espionage Act. There were three cases, all decided unanimously. Justice Holmes wrote the opinions, and they were far from the libertarian spirit of Judge Hand in *The Masses*. Holmes dealt with the First Amendment in one paragraph of the first case, *Schenck v. United States.* He drew back, with what seemed like reluctance, from his statement in *Patterson v. Colorado* in 1907 that "the freedom of speech" in the First Amendment meant no more than Blackstone's narrow freedom. "It may well be," he now said, "that the prohibition of laws abridging the freedom of speech is not confined to previous [prior] restraints, . . . as intimated in *Patterson v. Colorado*," though stopping prior restraints "may have been the main purpose" of the First Amendment's speech and press clauses. But even if the First Amendment protected some speech from subsequent punishment, that did not help these defendants. They had circulated leaflets, denouncing conscription as slavery, to men called up in the draft. "We admit," Holmes wrote, "that in many places and in ordinary times the defendants in saying all that was said in the circular would have been within their constitutional rights. But the character of every act depends upon the circumstances in which it is done. The most stringent protection of free speech would not protect a man in falsely shouting fire in a theater and causing a panic." (This image of a false cry of fire in a theater became famous, but it was hardly a fair analogy to speech critical of government policy.) "When a nation is at war," Holmes wrote, "many things that might be said in time of peace are such a hindrance to its effort that their utterance will not be endured so long as men fight."

That departed little, if at all, from the tradition of Supreme Court disregard for the value of free speech. There was no hint of Judge Hand's perception that freedom of speech is not merely an individual luxury but a social necessity in a democracy. But there were two sentences in the *Schenck* opinion that proved to be critical in the development of free speech doctrine. "The question in every case," Holmes wrote, "is whether the words used are used in such circumstances and are of such a nature as to create a clear and present danger that they will bring about the substantive evils that Congress has a right to prevent. It is a question of proximity and degree."

"A clear and present danger." Holmes's cryptic phrase tormented later generations of law students—and judges, for that matter. How much protection did speech really have if it could be punished when it presented "a clear and present danger" of a "substantive evil"? What sort of evil does the state have the right to prevent? But when Holmes first used the phrase, he almost certainly had no notion of laying down a rule to protect speech. When he was asked a few years later where the idea had come from, he referred to his own 1881 book, *The Common Law*, and its discussion of attempted crimes. An act can be punished as a criminal attempt, he wrote, when it would have produced a crime if it had had "its natural and probable effect." Professor Rabban argued convincingly that Holmes regarded Schenck's leaflet as an attempt that, if something *more* happened, could cause harm to the war effort. Because that potential harm was so serious, Holmes was ready to punish the act at a point further than usual from realization of the harm—indeed, at a point remote from any actual damage to the war effort.

Just how remote was made clear by the third Espionage Act case decided in March 1919. In it the defendant was Eugene V. Debs, the leader of the Socialist party and five times its candidate for President. Debs was prosecuted for a speech he made in Canton, Ohio, in June 1918. Holmes described it as follows: "The main theme of the speech was socialism, its growth, and a prophecy of its ultimate success. . . . [Debs] began by saying that he had just returned from a visit to the workhouse in the neighborhood where three of their most loyal comrades were paying the penalty for their devotion to the working class—[men] who had been convicted of aiding and abetting another in failing to register for the draft. He said that he had to be prudent and might not be able to say all that he thought, thus intimating to his hearers that they might infer that he meant more, but he did say that those persons were paying the penalty for standing erect and for seeking to pave the way to

better conditions for all mankind. . . . [Debs] addressed the jury himself,
and while contending that his speech did not warrant the charges said 'I
have been accused of obstructing the war. I admit it. Gentlemen, I abhor
war. I would oppose the war if I stood alone.' "

For his Ohio speech, Debs was convicted of obstructing recruitment
to the armed forces in violation of the Espionage Act and sentenced to
ten years in prison. He actually served three years. (Compare what happened fifty years later in the Vietnam war. Opponents of that war used
far harsher words than Debs, but no one was imprisoned for mere speech.)

Counsel for Debs in the Supreme Court, Seymour Stedman of Chicago,
drew a parallel between the Espionage Act, as the Government sought
to apply it to Debs's speech, and the Sedition Act of 1798. The latter's
"fate," he said, "has heretofore been accepted as so decisive a settlement
of the constitutionality of such legislation that our text-writers have dealt
with the crime of seditious libel as obsolete." He cited the recent scholarly
writings on the speech and press clauses of the First Amendment.

Another brief urging the Supreme Court to reverse Debs's conviction
was filed by a prominent civil liberties lawyer, Gilbert E. Roe of New
York, as a friend of the court. Roe relied heavily on the Sedition Act
history. He said Congress had repaid fines imposed under the act. He
quoted the Virginia Resolutions protesting the act, and Madison's Report
on it. He quoted Jefferson's letter to Abigail Adams explaining why he
had pardoned all those convicted under the act. "One other fact remains
to be stated in this connection," Roe said. "The [Madison] Report . . .
was made a campaign document in Mr. Jefferson's election by the people
and the overwhelming defeat of his opponents was a clear declaration
by the people at that time that they approved of his views as to the
unconstitutionality of the [Sedition Act]."

Unusually, the Justice Department filed a special brief in reply to Roe's.
It was written by John Lord O'Brian, who later became a distinguished
Washington lawyer known for his sensitivity to civil liberties, and Alfred
Bettman. As to the Sedition Act, O'Brian and Bettman said it had to be
borne in mind that the Virginia Resolutions, Madison's Report and other
attacks on the act were "made in the heat of the antifederalist election
campaign of 1798 and 1799, and that, after all, these resolutions and
reports have distinctly the character of partisan documents." They then
pointed to a minority report of the Virginia House of Delegates by John
Marshall, which took a narrow view of the First Amendment, and quoted
from it at length. They cited the 1897 Supreme Court opinion saying
that the first ten amendments were no more than assurances of rights
already established in England. By contrast, Roe's brief suggested that
the First Amendment, like other provisions of the Constitution, "was

adopted to destroy British tyranny rather than to perpetuate it." (Roe also had a tart comment on Blackstone's cramped definition of press freedom. Noting that Blackstone also believed in witchcraft, Roe said "there is no more reason for accepting his beliefs about one than about the other as a measure of liberty and freedom in this country today.")

Justice Holmes was unmoved by the constitutional arguments on behalf of Debs. He upheld the conviction in an opinion that did not even discuss the constitutional issues, saying that his *Schenck* opinion that day had "disposed of" them. Following the then dominant view that speech could be punished if it had a "bad tendency," Holmes said there was evidence to "warrant the jury in finding that one purpose of the speech . . . was to oppose not only war in general but this war, and that the opposition was so expressed that its natural and intended effect would be to obstruct recruiting."

Holmes was criticized for his part in the first three Espionage Act decisions, especially the *Debs* case, in circles where he was usually praised. He was a hero to liberals because of his biting, aphoristic dissents from some decisions striking down economic-reform legislation. When Congress passed a law forbidding the interstate shipment of products of child labor, for example, a majority of the Supreme Court held the law to be a violation of state powers. Dissenting, Justice Holmes noted that the Court had upheld Congress's right to restrict trade in alcoholic beverages. "It is not for this Court to pronounce," he wrote, that regulation "is permissible as against strong drink but not as against the product of ruined lives."

In general Holmes believed that the majority must have its way, whether he thought it wise or unwise. He took the same view in these first Espionage Act cases, but critics saw suppression of free speech as very different from the suppression of child labor. Professor Ernst Freund, an early exponent of a more generous view of freedom of speech, criticized the *Debs* opinion in an article in *The New Republic* two months after the decision. He called Holmes's analogy between falsely shouting fire and political speech "manifestly inappropriate." Relying on juries was useless, he said, when unpopular opinion was being suppressed. Free speech was "a precarious gift" if it was "subject to a jury's guessing at motive, tendency and possible effect."

Judge Hand also weighed in, but privately and delicately. He had begun corresponding with Justice Holmes after they met on a train on June 19, 1918. (The correspondence was unearthed and published in 1975 by Professor Gunther.) The two judges evidently talked about freedom of speech, for three days after their train encounter Hand wrote Holmes: "I gave up rather more easily than I now feel disposed about Tolerance.

. . . Here I take my stand. Opinions are at best provisional hypotheses, incompletely tested. The more they are tested, after the tests are well scrutinized, the more assurance we may assume, but they are never absolutes. So we must be tolerant of opposite opinions. . . ." Holmes replied warmly but made his disagreement plain. "Free speech," he wrote, "stands no differently than freedom from vaccination." (In 1905 the Supreme Court, including Holmes, had upheld a Massachusetts compulsory vaccination law, rejecting religious objections.) Shortly after the *Debs* case was decided in 1919, Hand wrote Holmes again. Following his view in *The Masses*, he suggested that speech should be punishable only when "directly an incitement" to illegality. Juries are not to be relied on, he indicated, "since the cases actually occur when men are excited." Letting juries decide whether words have a "tendency" to some bad result "will serve to intimidate—throw a scare into—many a man who might moderate the storms of popular feeling. I know it did in 1918." Holmes replied, "I am afraid that I don't quite get your point."

The most significant commentary in the period after the first Espionage Act decisions was an article by Professor Zechariah Chafee Jr. of the Harvard Law School. Entitled "Freedom of Speech in War Time," it appeared in the June 1919 *Harvard Law Review*. It may have been the best-timed law-review article ever published. Chafee believed deeply in free speech, and he marshaled all possible evidence from history (and perhaps a little beyond the possible) to show that the First Amendment gave broad protection to speech even in the agitated conditions of wartime. Chafee said that those who wrote the amendment intended "to wipe out the common law of sedition, and make further prosecutions for criticism of the government, without any incitement to law-breaking, forever impossible in the United States of America." He described the amendment as "a declaration of national policy in favor of the public discussion of all public questions." The Sedition Act of 1798 was an attempt to revive the doctrine of seditious libel, and it "proved so disastrous" that a century passed without any such law. Chafee said the test of criminality was crucial, and speech could not be free if it was punished for a "tendency" to do harm. "The real issue in every free-speech controversy," he wrote, is "whether the state can punish all words which have some tendency, however remote, to bring about acts in violation of law, or only words which directly incite to acts in violation of law." He was sounding the same theme as Judge Hand.

Given his commitment to freedom of speech and the logic of his argument, Chafee might have been expected to attack the three Espionage Act decisions of March and Justice Holmes's opinions. To the contrary, he praised Holmes for his casual phrase in the *Schenck* opinion, "clear and present danger." Chafee described it as a shrewd and deliberate stroke to protect free speech. Holmes had introduced a doctrine, he said, to make "the punishment of words for their bad tendency impossible." Chafee recognized that Holmes had taken the phrase from the law of criminal attempts, but he said Holmes meant that an attempt "must come dangerously near success" to be punished. Chafee did criticize the *Debs* decision, but did so on the ground that it had not followed the true meaning of "clear and present danger." The jury convicted Debs because it "thought his speech had a tendency to bring about resistance to the draft," but it should have been allowed to convict only on proof that Debs's words created a "clear and present danger" of illegal actions. Chafee surely took liberties with Holmes's thought when he concluded that Holmes, in his *Schenck* opinion, "substantially agrees with the conclusion reached by Judge Hand, by Schofield [the scholar who wrote the 1914 paper on freedom of the press], and by investigation of the history and political purpose of the First Amendment."

In October 1919 the Supreme Court heard argument in another Espionage Act case, *Abrams v. United States*. It was a prosecution brought under amendments to the act that Congress had passed in 1918. The amendments, approved in an atmosphere of wartime hysteria about traitors and revolutionaries, amounted to a new Sedition Act. They made it a crime to "utter, print, write, or publish any disloyal, profane, scurrilous, or abusive language" about the Constitution, the armed forces, military uniforms or the flag, or to "advocate any curtailment of production" of things "necessary or essential to the prosecution of the war." The maximum penalty for violation was increased to twenty years in prison and a $10,000 fine.

The defendants in the *Abrams* case were four refugees from the pogroms and tyranny of Czarist Russia, three of them anarchists and the fourth a socialist, who were outraged at President Wilson's decision to send American troops into Russia after the Bolshevik Revolution. On the evening of August 22, 1918, copies of two leaflets they had prepared—though not signed—were thrown from the roof of a building on New York's Lower East Side. The leaflets, one in English and the other in Yiddish, attacked Wilson's intervention. The Yiddish version, translated, was headed "Workers—Wake Up!!" It began: "The preparatory work for Russia's emancipation is brought to an end by his majesty, Mr. Wilson, and the rest of the gang; dogs of all colors!" The leaflets urged a general strike in protest against intervention in Russia. The four defendants were charged with an attempt to harm American prosecution of the war against Germany. All were convicted, and three were sentenced to twenty years in prison; the fourth, Mollie Steimer, twenty years old at the time, was given fifteen years. (The full story of the defendants and the case was told by Professor Richard Polenberg in his book *Fighting Faiths*. The four defendants were released from prison in 1921 on condition that they go to the Soviet Union. There Mollie Steimer and Jacob Abrams tangled with the new tyranny and left for Mexico. Hyman Lachowsky and Samuel Lipman stayed in the U.S.S.R. and became victims, one of Stalin's terror, the other of the Nazis.)

The Supreme Court decided the case in November 1919. The opinion of the Court, by Justice John H. Clarke, said the purpose of the defendants may have been to help the Russian Revolution, which was not a crime. But the language of their leaflets had the effect of interfering with the war with Germany, and the defendants were "accountable for the effects which their acts were likely to produce." The Court affirmed the convictions. This was hardly unexpected, given the decisions of the previous March. But there was a surprise in the *Abrams* case: Justice Holmes, joined by Justice Louis D. Brandeis, dissented.

Holmes stood by his opinions of the previous March—or at least he said he did. "I never have seen any reason to doubt," he wrote, "that the questions of law that alone were before this Court" in the earlier cases "were rightly decided." The United States has the power to "punish speech that produces or is intended to produce a clear and imminent danger that it will bring about forthwith certain substantive evils. . . ." But in restating his "clear and present danger" formula, Holmes had toughened it with two new adjectives, "imminent" and "forthwith." And then he continued with an explanation that gave the phrase more concreteness:

It is only the present danger of immediate evil or an intent to bring it about that warrants Congress in setting a limit to the expression of opinion where private rights are not concerned. Congress certainly cannot forbid all effort to change the mind of the country. Now nobody can suppose that the surreptitious publishing of a silly leaflet by an unknown man, without more, would present any immediate danger that its opinions would hinder the success of the government arms or have any appreciable tendency to do so. . . . In this case sentences of twenty years imprisonment have been imposed for the publishing of two leaflets that I believe the defendants had as much right to publish as the Government has to publish the Constitution of the United States now vainly invoked by them. Even if I am technically wrong and enough can be squeezed from these poor and puny anonymities [the leaflets] to turn the color of legal litmus paper . . . , the most nominal punishment seems to me all that possibly could be inflicted, unless the defendants are to be made to suffer not for what the indictment alleges but for the creed that they avow—a creed that I believe to be the creed of ignorance and immaturity when honestly held, as I see no reason to doubt that it was held here, but which, although made the subject of examination at the trial, no one has a right even to consider in dealing with the charges before the Court.

If Justice Holmes had stopped there, his dissent would have been memorable. He had made the case, with passion, that savage sentences had been imposed for the publishing of words that only wartime zealotry could stretch into harm of the war effort. But Holmes did not stop there. He expounded on his implied suggestion that Abrams and the others were really being tried for their anarchist and socialist beliefs, ending his opinion with a passage that must be given in full:

Persecution for the expression of opinions seems to me perfectly logical. If you have no doubt of your premises or your power and want a certain result with all your heart you naturally express your wishes in law and sweep away all opposition. To allow opposition by speech seems to indicate that you think the speech impotent, as when a man says that he has squared the circle, or that you do not care whole-heartedly for the result, or that you doubt either your power or your premises.

But when men have realized that time has upset many fighting faiths, they may come to believe even more than they believe the very foundations of their own conduct that the ultimate good desired is better reached by free trade in ideas—that the best test of truth is the power of the thought to get itself accepted in the competition of the market, and that truth is the only ground upon which their wishes safely can be carried out.

That at any rate is the theory of our Constitution. It is an experiment, as all life is an experiment. Every year if not every day we have to wager our salvation upon some prophecy based upon imperfect knowledge. While that experiment is part of our system I think that we should be eternally vigilant against attempts to check the expression of opinions that we loathe and believe to be fraught with death, unless they so imminently threaten immediate interference with the lawful and pressing purposes of the law that an immediate check is required to save the country.

I wholly disagree with the argument of the Government that the First Amendment left the common law as to seditious libel in force. History seems to me against the notion. I had conceived that the United States through many years had shown its repentance for the Sedition Act of 1798, by repaying fines that it imposed.

Only the emergency that makes it immediately dangerous to leave the correction of evil counsels to time warrants making any exception to the sweeping command, "Congress shall make no law . . . abridging the freedom of speech." Of course I am speaking only of expressions of opinion and exhortations, which were all that were uttered here, but I regret that I cannot put into more impressive words my belief that in their conviction upon this indictment the defendants were deprived of their rights under the Constitution of the United States.

# 9

■

# HOLMES AND BRANDEIS, DISSENTING

THE Supreme Court's recognition of freedom of expression as a paramount constitutional value began with Justice Holmes's dissent in *Abrams v. United States*. And what a beginning. Holmes boldly asserted, as no judge had before him, that the First Amendment had wiped out the common-law crime of seditious libel. In his statement that truth was best tested in the marketplace of ideas, he made legal doctrine of John Stuart Mill's argument for the value of contrary opinions. His language approached poetry in its rhetorical power. ". . . opinions that we loathe and believe to be fraught with death. . . ." "It is an experiment, as all life is an experiment." Reading Holmes's peroration aloud, one feels the hair rise at the back of the neck.

The question is, Where did that opinion come from? Only eight months earlier Holmes had upheld convictions under the Espionage Act in dry, almost perfunctory opinions. He threw in the phrase "clear and present danger," using it, a commentator said, as an apology for repression. Now he had turned the phrase into a sword to protect freedom of speech, and wielded it with a passion that could not possibly have allowed him to sustain the conviction of Eugene Debs. What had happened?

There are some clues about the influences on Holmes in the months between *Debs* and *Abrams*. He was aware that he had disappointed his admirers by upholding the Espionage Act convictions in March, and he was sensitive about it. He wrote a letter to the editor of *The New Re-*

*public,* Herbert Croly, replying to Ernst Freund's criticism of *Debs.* He decided not to mail it but sent a copy to his young friend Harold Laski, an English socialist. He told Laski that he thought the law constitutional but "hated to have to write the *Debs* case and still more those of the other poor devils before us. . . . I could not see the wisdom of pressing the cases, especially when the fighting was over and I think it quite possible that if I had been on the jury I should have been for acquittal." He also told Laski that he hoped President Wilson "might do some pardoning."

Judge Hand's letter about the March decisions may have continued to work on Holmes's mind, despite his response that he didn't quite get the point. So may Gilbert Roe's brief in the *Debs* case, with its argument that the Jeffersonian victory in the election of 1800 ratified the view that the Sedition Act was unconstitutional. What was surely influential was Professor Chafee's article in the *Harvard Law Review.* Holmes had read it that summer. In a letter to Chafee in 1922 he said he had been "taught" by Chafee about the historical roots of the First Amendment. Professor Polenberg traced other reading by Holmes in the summer of 1919 and found that much of it touched on issues of freedom. He read a book on the Civil War that criticized Lincoln for suppressing freedom of speech and press during the war. He read a new book of Laski's, *Authority in the Modern State,* that argued for "absolute" freedom of thought. He read the *Two Treatises on Civil Government* by John Locke, the seventeenth-century English philosopher of freedom. It is fair to conclude that Holmes spent much of that summer thinking the problem of free speech through again.

The result, his dissenting opinion in *Abrams,* had a great impact. Holmes had enormous prestige. Moreover, the whole Court had joined the *Schenck* opinion, and it was argued that the phrase "clear and present danger" therefore had the weight of an agreed precedent, with the expanded meaning that Holmes now gave it. Professor Chafee wrote about Holmes's *Abrams* opinion: "Although a dissenting opinion, it must carry great weight as an interpretation of the First Amendment, because it is only an elaboration of the principle of 'clear and present danger' laid down by him with the backing of a unanimous Court in *Schenck v. United States.*" Looking back at the episode decades later, Professor Kalven commented dryly: "The strategy is thus to read the burst of eloquence at the end of the *Abrams* dissent into the casual *Schenck* dictum [clear and present danger] and then to claim that it was there all the time, that it was this intense commitment to a stringent test for freedom of speech that the whole Court underwrote in *Schenck.*"

One other factor made Holmes's dissent in *Abrams* so potent: the fact that it was joined by Justice Brandeis. It was the beginning of an association that came to have a particular significance in the public mind: Holmes and Brandeis (or Brandeis and Holmes) dissenting from the decisions of an insensitive Court. The two men became close as colleagues and friends, which was remarkable in a way, so different were they in background and temperament.

Oliver Wendell Holmes Jr. was a cavalier, a lover of wine and women, the son of a famous poet and essayist from an old Boston family. He fought in the Civil War and was gravely wounded three times; he knew the terrors of war but thought it noble to fight. He was sixty-one years old when appointed to the Court in 1902 by Republican Theodore Roosevelt, seventy-eight when *Abrams* was decided, but with flowing white mustache was still dashingly handsome. He was a skeptic who thought that movements for social reform were mostly futile—but that judges must let them be tried.

Louis Dembitz Brandeis, appointed by Democrat Woodrow Wilson in 1916, was sixty-three at the time of *Abrams*. He was the first Jew to sit on the Supreme Court, from a Kentucky family of German origins. Like Holmes, he was a graduate of the Harvard Law School, where his record was said to have been the most brilliant ever. But where Holmes made his mark as a scholar (*The Common Law*) and judge of the Supreme Judicial Court of Massachusetts, Brandeis first had a highly successful law practice in Boston. He became deeply engaged in social reform, working for amelioration of labor-management conflicts and against agglomerations of financial and industrial power; one of his books was called *The Curse of Bigness*. He was a Zionist, a leader of the movement for a Jewish national home in Palestine; his nomination to the Court drew bitter opposition from conservative leaders of the bar, some of it thinly disguised anti-Semitism. Holmes favored brief, often cryptic opinions; Brandeis wrote long essays analyzing social problems. He was a puritan who allowed no alcohol or tobacco in his home. Several of his law clerks told of working all night on a memorandum for the justice, slipping it under his apartment door at sunrise and feeling it pulled in from the other side—without comment. Holmes and Brandeis really had different views on free speech, too, but they almost always joined in dissent from the repressive majority opinions of the age.

The Supreme Court upheld the use of the Espionage Act in three more cases in 1920 and 1921, Holmes and Brandeis dissenting. Brandeis wrote the dissenting opinions for both in two of the cases; in the third each wrote a separate dissent. The majority simply ignored their argument that the facts in each case did not add up to a clear and present danger. The conflict about the meaning of free speech went on through the

1920s, Holmes and Brandeis persisting in their view and expressing it in strongly worded dissents. In one sense it was a curious performance by the two of them, for each had a deep commitment to the Supreme Court as an institution and thought that division among the justices should be avoided when possible. Holmes gave an explanation in a dissent for Brandeis and himself in 1925 in the case of *Gitlow v. New York.* "The criterion sanctioned by the full Court in *Schenck v. United States* applies," he said—that is, clear and present danger. Then he added: "It is true that in my opinion this criterion was departed from in *Abrams v. United States,* but the convictions that I expressed in that case are too deep for it to be possible for me as yet to believe that it . . . settled the law."

The majority opinion in the *Gitlow* case, by Justice Edward T. Sanford, did produce one significant gain for freedom of expression. For the first time the Court held that the Constitution protected freedom of speech and press from *state* infringement. The Bill of Rights, as mentioned earlier, applied only to federal action. The Fourteenth Amendment, adopted after the Civil War, forbade the states to deprive any person of "liberty" without "due process of law." The Supreme Court had said that this provision protected "fundamental" liberties, but so far had ranked only economic rights, not speech, as fundamental. Now, abruptly, the Court changed its mind. Justice Sanford said: "For present purposes we may and do assume that freedom of speech and of the press—which are protected by the First Amendment from abridgement by Congress—are among the fundamental personal rights and 'liberties' protected by the due process clause of the Fourteenth Amendment from impairment by the states." This change made a great difference in the development of the principles of free expression. From 1925 on, cases testing those issues poured in to the Supreme Court from the states, and it was in these cases that the Court largely worked out the meaning of free speech and a free press.

The *Gitlow* case was a product of the Red Scare of 1919–20 and after, a phenomenon that recurred in the United States from time to time over the next seventy years. The Bolshevik Revolution in Russia, and then the creation of the Comintern to operate internationally, agitated Americans about the threat of communism and radicalism of any kind. President Wilson's Attorney General, A. Mitchell Palmer, scoured the country for subversive aliens in the well-publicized Palmer raids. The New York State Legislature tried to expel from its ranks duly elected Socialists. (They were successfully defended by Charles Evans Hughes, who in 1930 would become Chief Justice of the United States.) Conservative graduates of the Harvard Law School tried to hound Professor Chafee out of the school; but Harvard's president, A. Lawrence Lowell, though a staunch conservative himself, stood by the principle that professors should not be subject to outside retribution.

Benjamin Gitlow was prosecuted for helping to publish the manifesto of a Socialist party splinter group that decried democracy and advocated mass action to achieve a "revolutionary dictatorship of the proletariat." He was convicted of violating a New York law against advocacy of "the criminal anarchy doctrine"—doctrine alone, without any call for immediate violence or revolution. Holmes's dissent was on the ground that there was "no present danger of an attempt to overthrow the government by force on the part of the admittedly small minority who shared the defendant's views." It continued:

> It is said that this manifesto was more than a theory, that it was an incitement. Every idea is an incitement. It offers itself for belief and if believed it is acted on unless some other belief outweighs it or some failure of energy stifles the movement at its birth. The only difference between the expression of an opinion and an incitement in the narrower sense is the speaker's enthusiasm for the result. Eloquence may set fire to reason. But whatever may be thought of the redundant discourse before us it had no chance of starting a present conflagration. If in the long run the beliefs expressed in proletarian dictatorship are destined to be accepted by the dominant forces of the community, the only meaning of free speech is that they should be given their chance and have their way.

What "extraordinary prose to find in a judicial opinion," Professor Kalven commented. Yes, and characteristic of Holmes. So is the cryptic ambiguity of its moral. On the one hand, Holmes dismisses Gitlow's manifesto as a "redundant discourse," as if to say that a harmless crank utterance can be indulged its freedom. On the other, he says with a detachment approaching fatalism that we citizens of a democracy must be prepared to let it fall to proletarian dictatorship if "the dominant forces in the community" so ordain.

Brandeis was not a fatalist. He believed that human beings could improve themselves and their societies by means of reason, and that the exercise of reason depended on freedom of thought and expression. He believed, too, that freedom of speech was crucial to individual fulfillment. All this—the affirmative view of speech, the idealism—came together in one great statement: Brandeis's opinion in the case of *Whitney v. California*.

Anita Whitney was prosecuted under a California law against "criminal syndicalism," defined as advocating force and violence to bring about "a change in industrial ownership" or "any political change." The statute, similar to laws adopted by many other states after 1917, was aimed at the Industrial Workers of the World—the Wobblies, as they were called, a trade union that used radical rhetoric and was hated by the business community. A member of a socially prominent family, Ms. Whitney had helped to found the Communist Labor party of California. Its program praised the Wobblies for their struggles in the class war and urged a "revolutionary working class movement." Ms. Whitney was convicted of membership in an organization advocating criminal syndicalism and sentenced to one to fourteen years in San Quentin. In 1927 the Supreme Court upheld her conviction. Writing for the majority, Justice Sanford followed the logic of his opinion in *Gitlow*. Justice Brandeis wrote a separate opinion for himself and Justice Holmes. It was not a dissent, because Justice Brandeis found that Ms. Whitney's lawyers had failed to raise in the California courts the crucial constitutional question: whether her membership in the Communist Labor party raised a clear and present danger of injury to the state. Brandeis wrote a concurring opinion, agreeing that the appeal had to be dismissed but setting out the constitutional principles of free speech more completely than either he or Holmes ever had before.

The Court had not yet defined when a danger was "clear," Brandeis said, "how remote the danger may be and yet be deemed present," or how substantial an evil must be "to justify resort to abridgement of free speech" to prevent it. "To reach sound conclusions on these matters, we must bear in mind why a State is, ordinarily, denied the power to prohibit dissemination of social, economic and political doctrine which a vast majority of its citizens believes to be false and fraught with evil consequence." Brandeis then gave his reasons, in an extended passage that is the most profound statement ever made about the premises of the First Amendment in protecting the freedom of speech. He wrote:

Those who won our independence believed that the final end of the state was to make men free to develop their faculties; and that in its government the deliberative forces should prevail over the arbitrary. They valued liberty both as an end and as a means. They believed liberty to be the secret of happiness and courage to be the secret of liberty. They believed that freedom to think as you will and to speak as you think are means indispensable to the discovery and spread of political truth; that without free speech and assembly discussion would be futile; that with them, discussion affords ordinarily adequate protection against the dissemination of noxious doctrine; that the greatest menace to freedom is an inert people; that public discussion is a political duty; and that this should be a fundamental principle of the American government. They recognized the risks to which all human institutions are subject. But they knew that order cannot be secured merely through fear of punishment for its infraction; that it is hazardous to discourage thought, hope and imagination; that fear breeds repression; that repression breeds hate; that hate menaces stable government; that the path of safety lies in the opportunity to discuss freely supposed grievances and proposed remedies; and that the fitting remedy for evil counsels is good ones. Believing in the power of reason as applied through public discussion, they eschewed silence coerced by law—the argument of force in its worst form. Recognizing the occasional tyrannies of governing majorities, they amended the Constitution so that free speech and assembly should be guaranteed.

Fear of serious injury alone cannot justify suppression of free speech and assembly. Men feared witches and burnt women. It is the function of speech to free men from the bondage of irrational fears. To justify suppression of free speech there must be reasonable ground to fear that serious evil will result if free speech is practiced. There must be reasonable ground to believe that the danger apprehended is imminent. . . .

Those who won our independence by revolution were not cowards. They did not fear political change. They did not exalt order at the cost of liberty. To courageous, self-reliant men, with confidence in the power of free and fearless reasoning applied through the processes of popular government, no danger flowing from speech can be deemed clear and present, unless the incidence of the evil apprehended is so imminent that it may befall before there is opportunity for full discussion. If there be time to expose through discussion the falsehood and fallacies, to avert the evil by the processes of education, the remedy to be applied is more speech, not enforced silence. Only an emergency can justify repression. Such must be the rule if authority is to be reconciled with freedom. Such, in my opinion, is the command of the Constitution. It is therefore always open to Americans to challenge a law abridging free speech and assembly by showing that there was no emergency justifying it.

The persistent theme of this astonishing passage is civic courage. Brandeis was convinced, Professor Blasi said, that courage was "the paramount virtue in a democracy." His repeated rejection of fear as the basis for political action—"Men feared witches and burnt women"—gave hope to Americans in the dark times that descended on the country in later years. The image of witch-burning was not far from the reality of the period after World War II when Senator Joseph McCarthy won headlines by accusing war heroes of treason, and politicians generally vied with each other to see who could invent the most vindictive—and pointless—legislation against "Communism." There was comfort then in hearing Brandeis's voice evoke a better American tradition.

As with Holmes's *Abrams* opinion, one wonders about the sources of Brandeis's rhetoric in *Whitney*. He cited Hand's opinion in *The Masses*, Professor Chafee's 1920 book *Freedom of Speech* and an article by the historian Charles Beard on the American tradition of political liberty. But the roots were deeper. Professor Paul A. Freund identified the words of Pericles, the great Athenian, as the source of Brandeis's statement that those who won American independence "believed liberty to be the secret of happiness and courage to be the secret of liberty." In a biography of Brandeis, Professor Philippa Strum showed that he admired and identified with the Athenians of the fifth century B.C. His favorite book was Alfred Zimmern's *The Greek Commonwealth*, which described Pericles' Funeral Oration as the highest point of democracy. Brandeis made ancient Athens his model because in that small state citizens took responsibility for governing and accepted, as he wrote in *Whitney*, that "public discussion is a political duty."

Brandeis's words in *Whitney* were for the ages, but they also helped Anita Whitney. A month after the Supreme Court turned down her appeal, the governor of California, C. C. Young, pardoned her. In his message he quoted the Brandeis opinion at length.

One more dissenting opinion of the 1920s still has the power to move us. It was in the case of *United States v. Schwimmer*, decided by the Supreme Court in 1929. Rosika Schwimmer was a pacifist who came to the United States from Hungary and in time applied for citizenship. Asked whether she would take up arms to defend the United States, she said she would not. For that answer she was denied the right to become a citizen. The Supreme Court upheld the denial. Holmes was far from being a pacifist himself. He once described war as "inevitable and rational," and he often spoke of willingness to fight as the highest test of a man's character. But he dissented in the *Schwimmer* case, joined once more by Brandeis and this time, perhaps surprisingly, by the author of the majority opinions in *Gitlow* and *Whitney*, Justice Sanford. Holmes, now eighty-eight years old, wrote:

> The applicant seems to be a woman of superior character and intelligence, obviously more than ordinarily desirable as a citizen of the United States. It is agreed that she is qualified for citizen-

ship except so far as the views set forth in a statement of facts "may show that the applicant . . . cannot take the oath of allegiance without a mental reservation." The views referred to are an extreme opinion in favor of pacifism and a statement that she would not bear arms to defend the Constitution. So far as the adequacy of her oath is concerned I hardly can see how that is affected by the statement, as she is a woman over fifty years of age, and would not be allowed to bear arms if she wanted to. And as to the opinion, the whole examination of the applicant shows that she holds none of the now-dreaded creeds but thoroughly believes in organized government and prefers that of the United States to any other in the world. Surely it cannot show lack of attachment to the principles of the Constitution that she thinks it can be improved. I suppose that most intelligent people think that it might be. Her particular improvement looking to the abolition of war seems to me not materially different in its bearing on this case from a wish to establish cabinet government as in England, or a single house, or one term of seven years for the President. To touch a more burning question, only a judge mad with partisanship would exclude because the applicant thought the Eighteenth Amendment [imposing Prohibition, which Holmes detested] should be repealed. . . .

She is an optimist and states in strong and, I do not doubt, sincere words her belief that war will disappear and that the impending destiny of mankind is to unite in peaceful leagues. I do not share that optimism nor do I think that a philosophic view of the world would regard war as absurd. But most people who have known it regard it with horror, as a last resort, and even if not yet ready for cosmopolitan efforts, would welcome any practicable combinations that would increase the power on the side of peace. . . .

Some of her answers might excite popular prejudice, but if there is any principle of the Constitution that more imperatively calls for attachment than any other it is the principle of free thought—not free thought for those who agree with us but freedom for the thought that we hate. I think that we should adhere to that principle with regard to admission into, as well as to life within this country. And recurring to the opinion that bars this applicant's way, I would suggest that the Quakers have done their share to make the country what it is, that many citizens agree with the applicant's belief and that I had not supposed hitherto that we regretted our inability to expel them because they believe more than some of us do in the teachings of the Sermon on the Mount.

If the words of Holmes and Brandeis were no more than beautifully expressed protests against the intolerance of their day, they would not be remembered except perhaps as literary exercises. But they were much more. To an extent exceptional in our constitutional history, those dissents became the law. The Holmes-Brandeis views of free speech persuaded the country and, in time, the Court. The *Schwimmer* decision was overruled by the Court seventeen years later. Brandeis's words in *Whitney* and Holmes's in *Abrams* gradually wove their way into the Court's definition of "the freedom of speech, and of the press" guaranteed by the First Amendment.

Holmes and Brandeis had no political or judicial power beyond their votes on the Supreme Court, two of nine. Their power was in their rhetoric. And that tells us something about the extraordinary role of the Supreme Court in the American system of government. The Framers of the Constitution expected the Court to be weak. It had neither sword nor purse, Alexander Hamilton observed. The Court had only the power to persuade. But that has proved enough to defeat Presidents and Congresses, enough to give the Supreme Court the last word in much of American life. Its obligation is to explain its judgments to the country's sovereign citizens. When it has failed to do so convincingly, its decisions have come under question. Congress has often passed statutes to correct the Supreme Court's interpretation of earlier legislation—tax provisions, for example, and civil rights laws. Even constitutional decisions have been overruled in time: by the Supreme Court itself, as in the School Segregation Case, or by a constitutional amendment, as occurred when the Court held that the government could not levy an income tax. When the Supreme Court finds a legislative or executive act unconstitutional, it must justify that thwarting of the political will by persuading us that it speaks for values more permanent than a passing majority's wishes; values that underlie our existence as a nation. Holmes and Brandeis taught the country, and persuaded it, that freedom of speech, broadly understood, was such a value.

# 10

■

# "THE
VITALIZING
LIBERTIES"

A s the Supreme Court struggled from 1919 on to define "the freedom of speech" protected by the First Amendment, it left unexplored the parallel guarantee of press freedom. The majority in the *Gitlow* case included freedom of the press along with freedom of speech as a fundamental liberty protected against state abridgment as well as federal. But as late as 1930 the Court had not decided a case in which a newspaper or magazine or book had been subjected to restrictions that would test the freedom of the press in a concrete way.

Then, in 1931, the Court had its first great press case, *Near v. Minnesota*. Just ten years later there came *Bridges v. California*, a decision important to the press and to free speech. In both cases the Court divided 5 to 4, and in both the claims of freedom won. Despite the narrow majorities the two decisions became accepted landmarks of constitutional law. They gave freedom of expression a value that was significant when *The New York Times* looked to the First Amendment for protection from Commissioner Sullivan's libel suit.

Jay M. Near, the subject of *Near v. Minnesota*, was a muckraking journalist of dubious character. In a book on the case, *Minnesota Rag*, Fred W. Friendly described Near as "anti-Catholic, anti-Semitic, anti-black and antilabor." In 1927 he started a weekly newspaper in Minneapolis, *The Saturday Press*. It was viciously anti-Semitic, charging that "Jew gangsters" were "practically ruling Minneapolis" in league with a corrupt police chief. Near seemed an altogether unsavory figure. And yet, Friendly discovered, he did perform the critical function of a free press: challenging authority.

While Friendly was working on the book, he discussed it at lunch one day in the dining room of the Ford Foundation in New York. He was overheard at a nearby table by Irving Shapiro, the chairman of E. I. du Pont de Nemours & Company. "Are you talking about the *Near* case?" Shapiro asked. "I knew Mr. Near." Shapiro's father, Sam, owned a dry-cleaning store in Minneapolis. A local gangster, Big Mose Barnett, demanded that he stop doing his own dry cleaning and instead send the clothes to the Twin Cities Cleaners and Dyers Association. When Shapiro refused, four of Big Mose's men came to the store and sprayed the customers' clothes with sulfuric acid. Irving Shapiro, then eleven years old, watched from behind a partition. The established newspapers reported the attack without mentioning Barnett and his threats; the authorities did nothing. But Jay Near got the story from Sam Shapiro and printed the full details in *The Saturday Press*. He described Barnett's threats and charged that other newspapers were afraid to mention the gangster's name. After the story in *The Saturday Press*, Barnett was indicted for the attack on Sam Shapiro's store and eventually convicted on the testimony of, among others, Irving Shapiro.

Near was not always so apt in his choice of targets. One of the officials he regularly attacked was Floyd B. Olson, the county attorney of Hennepin County, which includes Minneapolis. Olson was a liberal reformer who went on to become a three-term governor of Minnesota. But stung by Near's nasty words, he took an illiberal action that he later came to regret. He invoked against *The Saturday Press* a curious state statute called the Public Nuisance Law. A nuisance, in legal terms, is something that spoils the neighborhood: a garbage pile, a noisy club. But this law declared that anyone running "a malicious, scandalous and defamatory newspaper" was "guilty of nuisance." Judges were authorized to enjoin the publication of such nuisances—shut them permanently. The legislation, passed in 1925, was aimed at an earlier muckraking paper, *The Duluth Rip-saw*. It had no opposition from the state's established papers, which disdained what they considered the blackmailing press. Now, in November 1927, Floyd Olson asked a judge to close *The Saturday Press* under the Public Nuisance Law. The judge granted the order. After just nine issues, *The Saturday Press* was out of business.

Near appealed to the Minnesota Supreme Court. His lawyer argued that the Public Nuisance Law violated both the Fourteenth Amendment and a free press clause of the state constitution, but the court brusquely rejected the claim. Its unanimous opinion said: "Our constitution was never intended to protect malice, scandal and defamation when untrue or published with bad motives or without justifiable ends. It is a shield for the honest, careful and conscientious press. Liberty of the press does not mean that an evil-minded person may publish just anything any more than the constitutional right of assembly authorizes and legalizes unlawful assemblies and riots." In this statement one can hear echoes of the Federalist argument for the Sedition Act of 1798. Like that Act, the Minnesota law allowed the defense that what the challenged newspaper had said was true, but only if it was "published with good motives and for justifiable ends." This amounted to freedom for those who agree with us, as Holmes put it in the *Schwimmer* case.

That might well have been the end of the *Near* case. Jay Near had no money to try to appeal to the Supreme Court of the United States. But he asked for help and got it from two highly disparate sources, the American Civil Liberties Union and the eccentric right-wing publisher of the *Chicago Tribune*, Robert Rutherford McCormick. Colonel McCormick was not often on the same side of an issue as the A.C.L.U., but he was a zealous advocate of the freedom of the press and thought it was threatened by the Minnesota Public Nuisance Law. His own lawyer, Weymouth Kirkland, took the case over from the Civil Liberties Union. Colonel McCormick lobbied his hitherto uninterested colleagues in the American Newspaper Publishers Association until they finally passed a resolution deploring the Minnesota law as "one of the gravest assaults upon the liberties of the people."

The Supreme Court heard argument in the *Near* case in January 1931. Weymouth Kirkland, representing Near, told the justices that publication of defamatory articles about public persons could not constitutionally be a reason to suppress a newspaper: "So long as men do evil, so long will newspapers publish defamation." Kirkland said that Boss Tweed, the infamous New York politician exposed by *The New York Times* in the nineteenth century, "would have invoked a law such as this against the newspapers that exposed the corruption of his regime."

When Deputy Attorney General James E. Markham took up the argument for the State of Minnesota, Justice Brandeis returned to the question of corruption. Brandeis had been studying the case, even reading the nine issues of The *Saturday Press*. Now he said to Markham: "In these articles the editors state that they seek to expose combinations between criminals and public officials in conducting and profiting from gambling halls. They name the chief of police and other officials. . . . We do not know whether these allegations are true or false, but we do know that just such criminal combinations exist to the shame of some of our cities. What these men did seems like an effort to expose such a com-

bination. Now is that not a privileged communication if there ever was
one? How else can a community secure protection from that sort of thing
if people are not allowed to engage in free discussion of such matters?
Of course there was defamation; you cannot disclose evil without naming
the doers of evil. It is difficult to see how one can have a free press and
the protection it affords in the democratic community without the privilege this act seems to limit. . . . What sort of matter could be more
privileged?"

Markham's strategy in defending the Minnesota law was to rely on
the old Blackstone view that freedom of the press meant only freedom
from prior restraint, and to argue that the Public Nuisance Law did not
impose prior restraints. His point was that the Minnesota law did not
require anyone to get approval from a bureaucrat before printing something, as the English licensing laws condemned by Milton did. Only after
a newspaper had been published and found to be scandalous could future
issues be suppressed, and then only by a judge. The burden of acting was
not on the publisher, as in the licensing laws, but on the state. Arguing
that the First Amendment adopted Blackstone's view of press freedom
as only freedom from prior restraint, Markham referred to Justice
Holmes's 1907 opinion in *Patterson v. Colorado*, which said the amendment was intended to prevent "previous restraints upon publications."
Holmes, now nearing his ninetieth birthday, remarked from the bench,
"I was much younger when I wrote that opinion than I am now, Mr.
Markham. . . . I now have a different view."

Chief Justice Hughes wrote the opinion of the Court in *Near v. Minnesota*. It included the Supreme Court's first comments on the function
of the press in the American system of government. Hughes quoted Madison's Report on the Virginia Resolutions, the protest against the Sedition
Act of 1798. "Some degree of abuse is inseparable from the proper use
of everything," Madison wrote, "and in no instance is this more true
than in that of the press. It has accordingly been decided by the practice
of the States, that it is better to leave a few of its noxious branches to
their luxuriant growth, than, by pruning them away, to injure the vigour
of those yielding the proper fruits. And can the wisdom of this policy be
doubted by any who reflect that to the press alone, chequered as it is
with abuses, the world is indebted for all the triumphs which have been
gained by reason and humanity over error and oppression . . . ?"

After quoting Madison, Hughes offered his own appraisal of the press's
contemporary role:

> While reckless assaults upon public men, and efforts to bring
> obloquy upon those who are endeavoring faithfully to discharge

official duties, exert a baleful influence and deserve the severest condemnation in public opinion, it cannot be said that this abuse is greater, and it is believed to be less, than that which characterized the period in which our institutions took shape. Meanwhile, the administration of government has become more complex, the opportunities for malfeasance and corruption have multiplied, crime has grown to most serious proportions, and the danger of its protection by unfaithful officials and of the impairment of the fundamental security of life and property by criminal alliances and official neglect, emphasizes the primary need of a vigilant and courageous press, especially in great cities.

In that passage one can sense the influence of Brandeis's exchange with Markham at the argument, which Hughes must have recalled. The Chief Justice could have gone on in his opinion to the further point made by Brandeis, that defamation is inevitable if the press does its job of scrutinizing official performance. He could also have found that the press freedom protected by the First Amendment included a right to criticize public officials in the course of its scrutiny. But instead, Hughes rested his opinion on the conclusion that Minnesota had imposed a forbidden system of prior restraints. The "chief purpose" of the First Amendment's press clause, he said, was "to prevent previous restraints upon publication." He quoted Blackstone, and he quoted Holmes's opinion in *Patterson v. Colorado*. Hughes said that Minnesota officials who had been abused by critics like Near could sue them for libel, but he took care to leave open the question of whether and how the First Amendment protected the press from penalties after publication. Blackstone had been criticized as a guide to the First Amendment's freedom, he said, not because "immunity from previous restraint upon publication has not been regarded as deserving of special emphasis, but chiefly because that immunity cannot be deemed to exhaust the conception of the liberty. . . ."

Joining Hughes in the majority were Holmes, Brandeis and the two newest associate justices, Harlan F. Stone and Owen Roberts. The dissenters were the Court's four staunchest conservatives, Pierce Butler, Willis Van Devanter, James C. McReynolds and George Sutherland. Butler wrote the dissent, which argued, with a good deal of historical justification, that the Minnesota law did not impose prior restraints of the kind that Blackstone meant—that is, requiring the prior approval of an administrative licenser for every publication.

*Near v. Minnesota* established one of the basic propositions of press law in the United States: that prior restraints are suspect under the First Amendment. Suspect, not absolutely barred, for Hughes indicated some exceptions. In wartime, he said, "no one would question but that a government might prevent . . . the publication of the sailing dates of transports or the number and location of troops." But in ordinary circumstances the decision ruled out prior restraints, defining them broadly to include not only administrative censorship but judicial injunctions. Because of *Near*, judges in this country almost automatically turn down requests for prior restraints on the press.

Commentators have argued about whether prior restraints are really more damaging to freedom of the press than subsequent penalties. If editors had a choice between, on the one hand, submitting articles on government secrets for clearance before publication and, on the other, a system that made publication of secrets punishable by a $10 million fine, which would they prefer? The threat of severe punishment can cause editors and writers to censor themselves; it can be as heavy a deterrent to free expression as a formal legal restraint. But there are respects in which prior restraint does seem to be more repressive than most subsequent penalties. A request for an injunction against publication is decided by a judge alone, while a criminal prosecution is tried by a jury. Moreover, a party seeking to stop something before publication is free to speculate at large to the judge on all the horrors that might occur if it was published, while in a lawsuit after publication people may see that in fact there has been no damage.

In 1971, forty years after *Near v. Minnesota*, the United States government tried to stop *The New York Times* and *The Washington Post* from publishing secret official documents on the origins of the Vietnam war. It was a prior restraint case, the most important since *Near*. But the *Times* had published extended excerpts from the documents for three days before the government moved, so the lawyer for the *Times*, Alexander M. Bickel, was able to say to the trial judge, "The Republic still stands." The judge, Murray Gurfein, rejected the government's request for an injunction. The case went on to the Supreme Court, where a 6–3 majority—relying in good part on the *Near* precedent—agreed that there should be no injunction. If the government had gone to court before the newspapers had printed any of the documents, its lawyers would surely have warned in the most alarming terms about the damage that would be done to the country if anything appeared. The judges and the public might well have been more impressed by such warnings in the absence of a chance to observe the actual effects—in this case nonexistent—of newspaper publication. The Pentagon Papers case showed that prior restraint is a more dangerous procedure than subsequent punishment in one other respect. The government considered bringing a criminal prosecution against *Times* editors and executives but decided that that would be politically embarrassing. Proceeding by injunction was easier. But it never should be easy to silence the press. The political constraints on prosecuting editors and publishers are wise.

Whatever the balance of those arguments, prior restraints are extremely rare in the United States. That is in sharp contrast with Britain, where judges regularly prohibit the publication of articles or even books because it is claimed that they may libel someone or damage some official interest. For years British judges prohibited the publication of *Spycatcher*, a book by a former British counterespionage official, but it appeared without challenge in the United States. At the request of the Israeli government in 1990, Canadian courts enjoined a similar memoir by a former Israeli secret agent; but when a New York judge granted an injunction against the book, appellate judges quickly threw it out.

The *Near* case should be remembered also for what it said about the function of the press. Colonel McCormick had carved in marble in the lobby of the *Chicago Tribune* building Chief Justice Hughes's words about "the primary need of a vigilant and courageous press, especially in great cities." Hughes was the first to sound a theme that others took up after him, perhaps most passionately Justice Hugo L. Black. In the Pentagon Papers case he wrote a concurring opinion—his last opinion before a sudden illness, retirement and death—that included this passage:

> The press was protected [in the First Amendment] so that it could bare the secrets of government and inform the people. Only a free and unrestrained press can effectively expose deception in government. And paramount among the responsibilities of a free press is the duty to prevent any part of the government from deceiving the people and sending them off to distant lands to die of foreign fevers and foreign shot and shell. In my view, far from deserving condemnation for their courageous reporting, The New York Times, The Washington Post and other newspapers should be commended for serving the purpose that the Founding Fathers saw so clearly. In revealing the workings of government that led to the Vietnam War, the newspapers nobly did precisely that which the Founders hoped and trusted they would do.

Jay M. Near, that often sordid journalist, had established a principle serving larger ends than his: noble ones, in Justice Black's view. But then great victories for civil liberty are frequently won in the cases of unappealing people.

A unanimous Supreme Court cited the *Near* decision approvingly in a press case five years later. Huey Long, the tyrannical populist governor

of Louisiana, put through his tame legislature a newspaper tax that fell
mainly on papers opposed to the Long regime. The Court found the tax
a violation of the First Amendment (as applied to the states by the Fourteenth). Justice Sutherland, one of the dissenters in *Near*, wrote the opinion in Madisonian terms. The people are entitled to "full information in
respect of the doings or misdoings of their government," he said; "informed public opinion is the most potent of all restraints upon misgov-
ernment." As to the idea that only prior restraints were barred by the
First Amendment, Sutherland said that was "impossible to concede," for
censorship had "permanently disappeared from English practice" by the
time of the First Amendment's adoption. These statements by a conservative judge showed how far the Supreme Court had come in its understanding of the press's function, and the First Amendment's, in
maintaining democratic government.


*Near v. Minnesota* liberated American expression from a confining English practice, the ready use of prior restraints on publication. In 1941
*Bridges v. California* did the same thing for contempt of court. Judges
had long had the power to jail or fine people for contempt on the ground
that they had (1) violated a court order, (2) created a disturbance in the
courtroom, or (3) said something outside the court that threatened the
integrity of the judicial process. It was the third category that was involved
in the *Bridges* case. To this day the English courts take a very strict view
of outside comments that may have some effect on what goes on inside
a court. For example, if a newspaper publishes the past criminal record
of a man about to go on trial, the editor may be summarily sent to prison
or fined. A paper may even be in contempt for publishing articles about
a pending *civil* case. *The Sunday Times* of London was enjoined from
printing a series about a tranquilizer, thalidomide, that turned out to
cause horrible birth defects in children, because pending civil-damage
actions against the drug company might be affected. *Bridges v. California*
saw to it that there would be no such use of the contempt power in the
United States.

*Bridges* was a remarkable case in many ways, not least in the conflict
it evoked between two members of the Supreme Court appointed by
President Franklin Roosevelt, Hugo Black and Felix Frankfurter. Black
was a senator from Alabama when he was appointed in 1937, a Jeffersonian populist who may well have been the most radical Southerner to
sit in the Senate. He taught himself constitutional history, spending long
nights reading Madison and the great British dissenters. He prized the
First Amendment over all else in the Constitution, and he read its com-

mands as "absolutes." The words "no law," he used to say, meant "no law." Frankfurter, appointed in 1939, came to the United States as a boy from Vienna, and he loved America with the special joy of an immigrant. As a Harvard Law School professor he had been a prime critic of the old Supreme Court for holding economic-reform legislation unconstitutional. Now he argued that the Supreme Court should be cautious in using its power to protect more appealing liberties, such as freedom of speech. He had many English friends and a high regard for English tradition.

The *Bridges* decision actually covered two cases in which California judges had imposed contempt-of-court sentences for statements made outside the court about pending cases. Harry Bridges, the leader of the West Coast longshoremen's union, was fined for contempt when he sent a telegram to the U.S. Secretary of Labor criticizing a judge's decision in a California lawsuit between his union and another. In the second case the *Los Angeles Times*, a paper that was then highly critical of labor unions, was fined for publishing three editorials about cases in court. The most objectionable of the editorials was headed "Probation for Gorillas?" It said a judge would make a serious mistake if he granted probation to two members of the Teamsters Union who had been convicted of assault; the community, it said, needed "the example of their assignment to the jute mill." Bridges and the *Times* asked the Supreme Court to set aside their convictions as infringements of their rights to free expression under the First Amendment.

The cases were argued in October 1940. At the private conference that the justices have after each week of argument—no one but the nine is ever admitted—they voted 6 to 3 to uphold the contempt convictions. In the majority were Chief Justice Hughes and Justices McReynolds, Stone, Roberts, Frankfurter and Frank Murphy, who had been appointed by President Roosevelt earlier that year. Dissenting were Black and two other Roosevelt appointees, Stanley Reed and William O. Douglas. The Chief Justice assigns the opinions when he is in the majority, and Hughes asked Frankfurter to write one for the *Bridges* and *Los Angeles Times* cases. After some time Frankfurter circulated among his colleagues a draft that relied heavily on history, both English and American. "The power exerted" by the California courts, he wrote, "is deeply rooted in history. It is part and parcel of the Anglo-American system of administering justice. . . . It is believed that the judicatures of the English-speaking world, including the United States Courts and the courts of the forty-eight states, have from time to time recognized and exercised the power now challenged." In all the years since 1791 the First Amendment had never been invoked to upset a finding that someone's utterance was in contempt of court.

Justice Black dictated a dissent that survives in the manuscript collection of the Library of Congress, typed but with pages of his handwritten inserts. (Justice Black ordered his son Hugo Jr. to burn his private Supreme Court papers, and it was widely believed that all had been destroyed. But apparently the only ones burned were his notes on the Court's conferences, which he thought should remain forever confidential; the rest are held by the Library of Congress.) The dissent began: "First in the catalogue of human liberties essential to the life and growth of a government of, for, and by the people are those liberties written into the First Amendment to our Constitution. They are the pillars upon which popular government rests. . . ." Justice Black said "the first and perhaps the basic fallacy of the Court's opinion is the assumption that the vitalizing liberties of the First Amendment can be abridged in whole or in part by reference to English judicial practices. . . . In my judgment, to measure the scope of the liberties guaranteed by the First Amendment by the limitations that exist or have existed throughout the English speaking world is to obtain a result directly opposite to that which the framers of the Amendment intended. . . . Perhaps no single purpose emerges more clearly from the history of our Constitution and Bill of Rights than that of giving far more security to the people of the United States with respect to freedom of religion, conscience, expression, assembly, petition and press than the people of Great Britain had ever enjoyed."

On February 1, 1941, Justice McReynolds retired. This left a majority of 5 to 3 for affirming the California courts in their contempt actions. Then at some point that spring—the date is uncertain—Justice Murphy changed his mind. He wrote Justice Frankfurter: "The still-new robe never hangs heavier than when my conscience confronts me. Months of reflection and study compel me to give it voice. And so I have advised the Chief Justice and Justice Black that my vote . . . must be in reversal." The Court was now equally divided on the contempt cases, 4 to 4, and they were put over to the following October for reargument. By then Chief Justice Hughes had retired, explaining to his regretful colleagues, "I never want to be here under the illusion of adequacy." The vote was now 4 to reverse the contempt convictions, 3 to affirm. Roosevelt appointed Stone as Chief Justice and named two new associate justices to replace McReynolds and Stone. Those two divided, Robert H. Jackson to reverse the contempt convictions, James F. Byrnes to affirm. Justice Black had a 5–4 majority for reversal.

The decision came down on December 8, 1941, the day after the

Japanese attacked Pearl Harbor and the United States was plunged into World War II. Justice Black had drastically revised his opinion now that it was to speak for the Court, removing much of its personal tone. But in the opinion of the Court and what was now Justice Frankfurter's dissent, the essence of their disagreement remained. Frankfurter regarded the First Amendment—as indeed he regarded the whole Constitution—as a natural development of English traditions. Black saw the First Amendment as something new and distinctively American. "It is a prized American privilege," he wrote, "to speak one's mind, although not always with perfect good taste, on all public institutions." Here he inserted a footnote quoting a letter of Thomas Jefferson's: "I deplore . . . the putrid state into which our newspapers have passed, and the malignity, the vulgarity, and mendacious spirit of those who write them. . . . These ordures are rapidly depraving the public taste. It is however an evil for which there is no remedy, our liberty depends on the freedom of the press, and that cannot be limited without being lost." Black was not troubled by hostile criticism of judges. In a comment reminiscent of Brandeis's warning in *Whitney* against "silence coerced by law," he said "an enforced silence, however limited, solely in the name of preserving the dignity of the bench, would probably engender resentment, suspicion, and contempt much more than it would enhance respect."

Justice Black did agree that comment outside a courtroom could sometimes endanger the fairness of a trial. "Legal trials," he said, "are not like elections, to be won through the use of the meeting-hall, the radio, and the newspaper." To deal with this problem and still protect free speech, he said that outside comment on the judicial process could not be punished as contempt unless it raised a "clear and present danger" of producing "unfair administration of justice." He imported into the new issue of contempt the formula that Holmes and Brandeis had developed for subversive or dangerous speech. In the fourteen years since *Whitney v. California*, that kind of speech had begun to receive some protection from the Supreme Court. In 1930, in the case of *Stromberg v. California*, Chief Justice Hughes wrote an opinion holding unconstitutional a California law that prohibited display of a red flag "as a sign, symbol or emblem of opposition to organized government." In 1937 Hughes wrote again, for a unanimous Court, in *DeJonge v. Oregon*, reversing the conviction under Oregon's Criminal Syndicalism Law of a man who attended a meeting that was sponsored by the Communist party but at which no unlawful conduct was advocated. In that same year a 5–4 decision reversed the Georgia conviction of Angelo Herndon, a black Communist party organizer, for attempting to "incite insurrection." For the majority, Justice Roberts said the Georgia law was "a dragnet which may enmesh anyone who agitates for a change of government if a jury can be persuaded that he ought to have foreseen his words would have some effect in the future conduct of others." None of those decisions, or any others, adopted the "clear and present danger" rule as Brandeis had finally stated it in *Whitney*. But now Black gave it the most forceful expression he could summon up. He wrote:

> What finally emerges from the "clear and present danger" cases is a working principle that the substantive evil must be extremely serious and the degree of imminence extremely high before utterances can be punished. Those cases do not purport to mark the furthermost constitutional boundaries of protected expression, nor do we here. They do no more than recognize a minimum compulsion of the Bill of Rights. For the First Amendment does not speak equivocally. It prohibits any law "abridging the freedom of speech, or of the press." It must be taken as a command of the broadest scope that explicit language, read in the context of a liberty-loving society, will allow.

In truth, Justice Black was not comfortable with the formula of clear and present danger. He may have used it in the *Bridges* case because it made possible the agreement of a majority of the Court. But he thought that the formula was too elastic and that other judges, less committed to freedom of speech than he was, would use it to suppress unpopular utterances. His forebodings proved correct. Ten years after *Bridges*, in 1951, the Supreme Court upheld the convictions of the leaders of the Communist party for conspiring to teach and advocate the violent overthrow of the United States government. By then the party was a remnant, thoroughly infiltrated by the F.B.I., and posed no measurable threat to the government. Nevertheless the Supreme Court held that the prosecution had met the test of clear and present danger, which it defined as follows: "In each case [courts] must ask whether the gravity of the 'evil,' discounted by its improbability, justifies such invasion of free speech as is necessary to avoid the danger." (This phrasing had been used in the U.S. Court of Appeals by Learned Hand, a judge who never liked Holmes's test.) Dissenting, Justice Black said: "Public opinion being what it is now, few will protest the conviction of these Communist petitioners. There is hope, however, that in calmer times, when present pressures, passions and fears subside, this or some later Court will restore the First Amendment liberties to the high preferred place where they belong in a free society."

But Justice Black's treatment of contempt of court in *Bridges v. Cal-*

*ifornia* proved to be a powerful and lasting precedent. He found that neither Harry Bridges nor the *Los Angeles Times* could constitutionally be held in contempt for what they had said. In the years following, more contempt cases came to the Supreme Court, and not once did the justices uphold a conviction for statements made outside the court. The power of courts to punish for contempt was effectively limited to those who violate a court order or who disrupt a courtroom.

The *Bridges* case had broader implications, ones that bore on the Alabama libel judgment and the hopes of *The New York Times* and the ministers to upset it. The decision suggested that the First Amendment was not limited by English tradition but, rather, was a declaration of independence from that tradition. And it showed that no category of expression could be considered outside the command that no law abridge "the freedom of speech, or of the press."

# 11

# TO THE
# SUPREME
# COURT

WHEN the Alabama Supreme Court upheld Commissioner Sullivan's libel judgment on August 30, 1962, *The New York Times* and the four ministers had one last chance to avoid owing $500,000 to Sullivan—and millions more to other Alabama libel plaintiffs. This was to ask the Supreme Court of the United States to hear the case and reverse the judgment. Persuading the Supreme Court may look easy now. The Alabama courts had awarded large damages to a public official because of incidental errors in a newspaper advertisement that did not mention his name, and without any showing that he had suffered financial injury. The sense of unfairness was intensified by the context of racial hostility. But in 1962 the task was anything but easy. The Supreme Court has no power to correct a state court's decision on matters of state law. No matter how unjust such a decision may seem, the Supreme Court can review it only if it presents an issue under the federal Constitution or laws. And libel had always been entirely a matter of state law. No award of damages for libel, however grotesque the sum or outlandish the legal theory underlying it, had ever been held to violate the First Amendment or any other provision of the Constitution.

For the job of persuading the Supreme Court, the *Times* chose a scholar. Herbert Wechsler was a professor at the Columbia Law School, a specialist on the Constitution and the Court. Fifty-two years old, he was a man of formidable intellect and formidable presence. There was a gravity about him, a sense of sureness about the law, an unwillingness to compromise with what he regarded as false doctrine. His colleague Marvin E. Frankel, who revered him as one of the great teachers of law, described Wechsler as "unyieldingly rigorous. He's the kind of person who takes a thought wherever it leads him, refusing to be deflected by where it is going." An example of this habit of mind was the Holmes Lecture that Wechsler gave at the Harvard Law School in 1959. Entitled "Toward Neutral Principles of Constitutional Law," it argued that judges have the obligation to decide constitutional issues on principles that hold true generally, not just for the facts of the present case. The argument led him to say that although he considered racial segregation reprehensible, the Supreme Court had not written an opinion that adequately justified holding it unconstitutional in the *Brown* case and subsequent decisions. That position naturally troubled a good many people; he expected this but was not moved to stop short of the hard, but for him inescapable, example of what might otherwise have been a relatively uncontroversial argument in favor of neutral principles.

Wechsler was known as an expert on a subject relevant to the Sullivan libel case: federalism, the relationship between state and federal law in our complex system. He was the co-author, with Professor Henry M. Hart Jr. of the Harvard Law School, of what was generally considered the most profound and original American legal casebook, *The Federal Courts and the Federal System*. He was also an authority on criminal law, and his life had not been limited to the academy. He was an Assistant Attorney General of the United States from 1944 to 1946, he had done legal work for New York City and State, and he had worked on many cases in the Supreme Court. In 1932–33 he was law secretary (law clerk, as the position later became known) to Justice Harlan Stone. He helped to write the winning brief in *Herndon v. Lowry*, the 1937 case in which the Supreme Court set aside the Georgia conviction of a Communist party organizer for attempting to incite "insurrection."

By 1962 Wechsler had argued perhaps a dozen cases in the Supreme Court. The most important—very important—was the 1941 case of *United States v. Classic*, a prosecution, under federal civil rights laws, of Louisiana election commissioners for falsifying the results of a Democratic congressional primary election. For the prosecution to succeed, Wechsler had to persuade the Supreme Court that federal power over congressional elections extended to primaries in the Louisiana situation. But there was another issue, trickier and even more significant. Until then the Supreme Court had upheld the use of the civil rights laws against state officials only when they were carrying out a policy expressly commanded by state law—and this was almost never the case. Officials would exclude blacks from sitting on juries, for example, by quietly rigging the jury lists. In the *Classic* case no Louisiana statute commanded the election commissioners to miscount ballots. But the civil rights laws condemned wrongful acts when done "under color of law," and Wechsler argued that that language applied whenever an official used his authority for a purpose forbidden by the Constitution or federal law, whether or not he was told to do so by a state statute. The Supreme Court, in an opinion by Justice Stone, adopted this construction of the civil rights acts. The idea was crucial in reviving the almost unused civil rights laws, making them a weapon not only in criminal prosecutions but in civil suits against the police and other officials, North and South, for abuse of their power.

It was Louis Loeb, the *Times*'s regular counsel, who enlisted Wechsler in the libel case. Loeb was an alumnus of the Columbia Law School; he knew Wechsler there and at the Association of the Bar of the City of New York, of which Loeb later became president. In 1960, when the *Times* faced libel suits in Alabama over the Harrison Salisbury articles on Birmingham as well as the "Heed Their Rising Voices" advertisement, Loeb asked Wechsler to advise. Wechsler worked on several briefs, including the appeal of Sullivan's libel judgment to the Alabama Supreme Court, but he did not have primary responsibility until the time came when there was no recourse left except the Supreme Court of the United States.

The first step was to ask the Supreme Court to hear the case. In a very limited category of cases at that time there was a statutory right of appeal to the Supreme Court, but apart from those the Court had the discretion to choose the cases it wished to hear. The procedure in seeking review of a lower-court decision is to file what is called a petition for a writ of certiorari—a writ that goes to the lower court and brings the judgment up for review. The Supreme Court grants only a small percentage of the thousands of such petitions that come before it each year, selecting the few because the legal issue is important or because the lower courts are divided on it.

The *Times* and the ministers had three months from the date of the Alabama Supreme Court decision to file petitions for certiorari. Wechsler could call on Loeb's firm, Lord, Day & Lord, for help, but he told Loeb that he would like to have someone whom he knew and who was close at hand. The choice was Marvin Frankel, who had been a student of Wechsler's at Columbia, graduating in 1948, and returned to the law school in 1962 as a professor. In between he had served brilliantly in the office of the Solicitor General of the United States, who represents the government in the Supreme Court, and then had six years in private practice in New York. (Frankel became a federal District Judge in 1965, remaining on the bench until he returned to practice in 1978.)

As Wechsler began work, he soon came to a disappointing realization. The law of libel in other states, and the common law in England, were not much different from Alabama's. The burden was on the defendant to prove the truth of a defamatory statement; falsity was presumed, as in Alabama. Damages were also presumed in libel, unlike other torts, where medical or other evidence of the extent of an injury was always required. (As a historical matter, the rule was probably different in libel because injury to reputation is harder to measure than, say, the cost of a broken leg.) The law had been stretched very far to fit the facts of Sullivan's case. Other state courts, for example, had approved the award of libel damages to persons whose names had not been mentioned if they were members of a small, identifiable group defamed in a statement, but it was questionable whether other cases had found a statement to be "of and concerning" someone on facts so tenuous.

"Before the case I really didn't know much about libel law," Wechsler said years later. "I remember it came as a shock to me in doing the background reading to realize the nature of the burden put on the defendant. If you didn't know that, or had forgotten it and suddenly came upon it, it seemed to me a terribly disconcerting discovery. And it had to lead you to believe that libel law as it stood on the books was not really enforced in those terms in this country, probably because juries moderated it in practice."

To get this case into the Supreme Court on First Amendment grounds— that is, to get the Court's attention in a petition for review—Wechsler had to argue convincingly that the old rules of libel could violate the constitutional freedom of speech and press if pushed to extremes for the benefit of a public official like Sullivan. Wechsler thought the trend of First Amendment decisions over the previous thirty years was encouraging. The Court had given real protection to unpopular speech and publications, and extended the protection to new areas, such as contempt of court in the *Bridges* case. Then Frankel came up with another way of looking at the First Amendment question. In a memorandum to Wechsler, he said the ordinary law of libel, if used as Alabama had used it in this case, would be as repressive of free expression as the concept of seditious libel had been in the eighteenth century—and that concept, embraced in the Sedition Act of 1798, had been regarded by many as a violation of the First Amendment.

Wechsler was putting these ideas together when a curious episode occurred. He was invited to a meeting with *Times* executives to discuss the case. He thought he would be asked about the strategy to be used in the Supreme Court, and the prospects there. Instead, he found doubts about whether to take the case to the Supreme Court at all. "I was surprised to find," he recalled later, "that I was being asked to show cause why I should file a petition for certiorari. I found myself defending the legal position I was advancing in defense of the *Times*—that the First Amendment applied to libel cases. To my amazement, the Madisonian and Jeffersonian doctrines had not penetrated to the upper reaches of *The New York Times*. People were asking why it wasn't enough for the *Times* to 'stick to our established position that we never settle libel cases, we publish the truth, if there's an occasional error we lose and that's one of the vicissitudes of life'—that at a time when, I was told, the paper was barely making a profit and these judgments were mounting up. As soon as I realized what was involved, my reaction was, first, to give them a sense of how the scope of the First Amendment had been progressively expanded by the Supreme Court in recent years, so that every one of the old shibboleths had gone—the idea that contempt isn't covered by the First Amendment, unlawful advocacy isn't covered—and libel would logically follow. Second, I said that if the *Times* didn't make this argument, in what was overall a very sympathetic case, who could be expected to make it? I did tell them there was a substantial chance that the Court would decide the case on its individual facts rather than by a broad rule, but I pointed out that even to hold that factual shortcomings in a libel case could be a federal constitutional matter would have large implications."

By then Orvil Dryfoos had become publisher of the *Times*, succeeding his father-in-law, Arthur Hays Sulzberger, on Sulzberger's retirement. He was at the meeting, and Wechsler recalled that Dryfoos was "sympathetic to the idea of making the constitutional argument." Soon afterward Louis Loeb, who had also attended the meeting and agreed with Wechsler on taking the case to the Supreme Court, telephoned him and told him to proceed.

The *Times*'s petition for certiorari was filed on November 21, 1962. It was concise, as the Supreme Court's rules required—a printed pamphlet of thirty-one pages. Ten pages were given to recounting the facts of the case: the circumstances of the advertisement, the evidence at the trial, the Alabama legal rulings. Then came a section headed "Reasons for Granting the Writ." This was the legal argument. It began as follows:

> The decision of the Supreme Court of Alabama gives a scope and application to the law of libel so restrictive of the right to protest and to criticize official conduct that it abridges the free-

dom of the press, as that freedom has been defined by the decisions of this Court. It transforms the action for defamation from a method of protecting private reputation to a device for insulating government against attack. If the judgment stands, its impact will be grave—not only upon the press but also upon those whose welfare may depend on the ability and willingness of publications to give voice to grievances against the agencies of governmental power. The issues are momentous and call urgently for the consideration and determination of this Court.

The rule laid down by the Alabama court, the *Times* petition said, was that a public official was entitled to recover presumed damages for a statement critical of an agency under his general supervision if the statement tended to injure his reputation, unless the publisher could prove it entirely true. Such a rule was "indistinguishable in its function and effect from the proscription of seditious libel, which the verdict of history has long deemed inconsistent with the First Amendment." As evidence of this historical judgment, the petition cited Holmes's statement in his *Abrams* dissent that the common law of seditious libel had not survived the First Amendment, and Professor Chafee's writings to the same effect.

The petition then sketched a First Amendment argument that Wechsler had just begun to shape in his own mind; full expression could await the brief to be filed if the Supreme Court agreed to hear the case. Unlimited libel damages awarded on a basis like that in Alabama, the petition said, could stifle the "free political discussion" that the Court had called "the security of the Republic, the very foundation of constitutional government." The quotation was from Chief Justice Hughes's opinion in the 1937 Oregon Criminal Syndicalism case, *DeJonge v. Oregon*. The premise of the Court's rulings on freedom of the press, the petition continued, was that "one of the prime objectives of the First Amendment is to protect the right to criticize 'all public institutions.' " The last phrase was from Justice Black's opinion in *Bridges v. California*, and the petition went on to draw support from that contempt decision. "Concern for the dignity and reputation of the bench," it said, "does not sustain the punishment as a contempt of criticism of the judge or his decision. . . . We do not see how comparable criticism of an elected, political official may consistently be punished as libel on the ground that it diminishes his reputation." Then, quoting one of the contempt cases after *Bridges*, the petition said: "The supposition that judges are 'men of fortitude, able to thrive in a hardy climate' must extend to commissioners as well."

Wechsler felt that he had to address directly the Alabama Supreme Court's statement that "the First Amendment . . . does not protect libelous publications." He conceded that the Supreme Court had often said as much, and he cited six cases, beginning with *Near v. Minnesota*. But with one exception, the petition said, such comments by the Court did no more than note that freedom of expression "is not an absolute; they did not signify advance approval of whatever standards state courts might employ in the repression of expression as libel." The more difficult case was *Beauharnais v. Illinois*, the 1952 decision in which the Court upheld an Illinois law against libel of racial or religious groups. But in that case, the petition said, the racist statements for which Beauharnais had been convicted under the law were found by the state courts to be "liable to cause violence and disorder"; and in upholding the law the Supreme Court had observed that if the occasion arose it could "nullify action which encroaches on freedom of utterance under the guise of punishing libel."

A second section of the petition's statement of reasons for granting review made the alternative argument that Louis Loeb had thought was "the main string to our bow," the jurisdictional argument. Usually jurisdictional points are put first in legal documents, but after much consideration Wechsler had decided that the First Amendment claim was more compelling. Now, in the second part of the reasons for review, the petition maintained that in asserting jurisdiction over *The New York Times*, the Alabama courts had violated due process of law and imposed "a forbidden burden" on the freedom of the press and interstate commerce. As for Judge Jones's ruling that the *Times*'s lawyers had inadvertently waived the claim before trial in Montgomery, the petition said the ruling could be disregarded as unfair because it had no support in Alabama law.

The *Times* petition did not emphasize the racial issue that formed the context of the libel action. It described the Committee to Defend Dr. King and the other aspects of the case that touched on race in neutral, almost detached language. The petition came closest to drama on the point in one brief passage: "This is not a time when it would serve the values enshrined in the Constitution to force the press to curtail its attention to the racial tensions of the country or to forego dissemination of its publications in the areas where tension is extreme. Here, too, the law of libel must confront and be subordinated to the Constitution. The occasion for that confrontation is at hand."

The four Alabama ministers filed their own petition for certiorari. They were represented by new lawyers, headed by I. H. Wachtel of Washington, D.C., a high-powered business lawyer whose conscience had been touched by Dr. King. He volunteered to help the King cause, and preparing this petition was a first contribution. Not surprisingly, Wachtel and his colleagues gave far more attention to the racial aspects of the case. Their petition noted that the trial in Montgomery had been held in a segregated courtroom, and that the black lawyers had been referred to not as "Mr." but as "Lawyer." The statement of reasons for granting review began:

> This case cries for review. The grave constitutional issues involved here and the impact of this decision on civil rights and the desegregation movement—burning issues of national and international importance—are clear and indisputable. What has happened here is further evidence of Alabama's pattern of massive racial segregation and discrimination and its attempt to prevent its Negro citizens from achieving full civil rights under our Constitution.

The ministers' petition told the Court that eight years after *Brown v. Board of Education* the public schools in Alabama still had not been desegregated. In addition, it said, Alabama had systematically excluded blacks from voting and from juries.

> [The state] now strikes at the rights of free speech and press— roots of our democracy. To silence people from criticizing and speaking out against its wrongful segregation activities, Alabama officials now utilize civil libel. . . . The result of all this, together with a trial of white against Negro, before an all-white jury, and an all-white judiciary (since Negroes are disenfranchised) is readily predictable as the judgment below shows. . . . If this case stands unreviewed and unreversed, not only will the struggles of Southern Negroes towards civil rights be impeded, but Alabama will have been given permission to place a curtain of silence over its wrongful activities. This curtain of silence will soon spread to other Southern States in their similar attempts to resist civil rights and desegregation. For fear of libel and defamation actions in these States, people will fear to speak out against oppression; ministers will fear to assist the civil rights struggle which they did heretofore as part of their religious belief; national newspapers will no longer report the activities in the South.

When a party that has lost in the lower courts seeks review in the Supreme Court, the winning side ordinarily tells the Court that the case does not merit its attention (though occasionally the Solicitor General, representing the government, will agree that a case won by the government in the lower courts deserves review). The usual filing is called a brief for respondent in opposition. This one was prepared for Commissioner Sullivan by M. Roland Nachman, Jr., of Montgomery, who along with others had represented Sullivan at the trial.

Nachman, thirty-eight years old, was a graduate of Harvard College and Law School. Immediately after law school he went to work for the office of the Alabama Attorney General. He argued a case for that office in the Supreme Court at the very young age of twenty-seven. In fact, he had been a member of the bar for less than the three years required by the Supreme Court's rules for admission to its bar, but the Court waived its rule to let him argue the case. As he rose to begin his argument, he heard Justice Frankfurter murmur to a colleague, "I don't know why we have these rules if we aren't going to enforce them." Nevertheless, Nachman won the case, *Alabama Public Service Commission v. Southern Railway*, a landmark decision holding that federal courts should ordinarily abstain from deciding constitutional claims when a state administrative proceeding has begun on the issue and it can be reviewed by the state courts. After six years in the attorney general's office, Nachman went into private practice in Montgomery. Among his clients were the local newspapers, the Montgomery *Advertiser* and the *Alabama Journal*. He defended them against libel suits, and he therefore thought he should ask their permission before representing a libel plaintiff, Sullivan. They had no objection. Nachman subscribed to *The New York Times*—one of the 394 buyers in Alabama—so he had actually seen the advertisement before the uproar over it. He was consulted about possible libel actions by all three Montgomery commissioners, and his firm agreed to represent them. Nachman advised that Sullivan sue first. He thought Sullivan had the best claim that the advertisement referred to him because it mentioned police action and he was the commissioner in charge of the police.

Not surprisingly, the brief in opposition put a very different cast on the facts. "This lawsuit arose," it said, "because of a wilful, deliberate and reckless attempt to portray in a full-page newspaper advertisement, for which The Times charged and was paid almost $5,000, rampant, vicious, terroristic and criminal police action in Montgomery, Alabama, to a nationwide public of 650,000. The goal was money-raising. Truth, accuracy and long-accepted standards of journalism were not criteria. . . ." The *Times* had departed from the standards of its own advertising acceptability department, the brief went on. "To be as charitable as possible, it is remarkable that no person connected with The Times investigated" the text before publication. "The New York Times, perhaps the nation's most influential newspaper, stooped to circulate a paid advertisement . . . which libeled respondent [Sullivan] with violent, inflammatory and devastating language."

As to the law, the brief in opposition made with force the argument plainly open to it: "Libelous utterances have never been protected by the Federal Constitution. Throughout its entire history, this Court has never held that private damage suits for common law libel in state courts involved constitutional questions." The brief quoted Jefferson's words about state libel power in his 1804 letter to Abigail Adams giving his reasons for opposing the Sedition Act of 1798: "Nor does the opinion of the unconstitutionality and consequent nullity of that law remove all restraint from the overwhelming torrent of slander which is confounding all vice and virtue, all truth and falsehood in the U.S. The power to do that is fully possessed by the several state legislatures."

By way of example, a telling one, the brief in opposition made the point that the press is not always the sympathetic hero of libel disputes. It mentioned the case of John Henry Faulk, a radio performer who lost his job and could find no work for years after he was smeared as pro-Communist in a publication called *Red Channels*. He sued the publisher for libel, and a New York jury gave him a verdict of $3.5 million. A *New York Times* editorial, the brief noted, praised the verdict as likely to have a "healthy effect." (Faulk's damages were reduced to $500,000 on appeal, and the publishers of *Red Channels*, pleading poverty, paid only $175,000.) The brief ended by speaking of the "enormity" of the wrong done to Sullivan by the *Times*. "Hopefully," it said, "the decision below will impel adherence by this immensely powerful newspaper to high standards of responsible journalism commensurate with its size."

That brief was filed on December 15, 1962. Two days later Nachman filed his brief in opposition to the ministers' petition. The cases were now ready for action by the justices. Their practice was to consider petitions for review in their private conference soon after all the papers were filed, and to make known on the following Monday their decisions about whether to grant review. On Monday, January 7, 1963, a clerk posted a list of numerous petitions denied and of seven granted. Among those granted were the petitions for certiorari in *The New York Times Company v. L. B. Sullivan* and *Abernathy et al. v. Sullivan*. A *Times* reporter at the Supreme Court telephoned the news to Wechsler: The Court was going to hear the case.

## 12

# "THERE
# NEVER
# IS A TIME"

**B**Y THE TIME the Supreme Court granted certiorari in the Alabama libel cases, its calendar for the spring of 1963 was full, the hours of argument all scheduled. That meant that the cases would be heard in the next term, starting in October. The lawyers would have until September to write and file their briefs. Preparing a Supreme Court brief is a formidable job if it is taken as seriously as it should be. A brief is really a small book, setting out the facts and arguing the law in detail. It uses the apparatus of the law, the citations of cases and the sometimes arcane terms. But a skillful brief is readable; it should tell a story, sweeping the reader along to a desired end. Supreme Court justices are just as easily bored, just as much put off by unnecessary legalese as the rest of us—perhaps more so, given the amount they have to read.

Herbert Wechsler took the writing of the brief in *New York Times v. Sullivan* very seriously. The responsibility was his in an intensely private way. There was none of the great machinery of the modern law firm grinding out drafts, there was only Wechsler writing in pencil on yellow pads. Assisting him were Marvin Frankel and Wechsler's wife, Doris; they did research, wrote memoranda and reviewed what Wechsler wrote. Ronald Diana, the young associate at Lord, Day & Lord who had written about the case for *Times Talk*, did some research on the question of the Alabama courts' jurisdiction. Wechsler talked with Louis Loeb and showed the draft brief to the firm's senior partner, Herbert Brownell Jr., but they let him get on with it. By coincidence, Wechsler was on sabbatical from Columbia that spring, so he could devote full time to the brief. (At the same time he was offered the job of executive director of the American Law Institute, the most distinguished of the country's legal organizations, devoted to reform of the law; he put the institute off until the *Times* case was done, then served for twenty years as its director while continuing to teach.)

"Between us I think we read everything ever published on the issues," Marvin Frankel said years afterward. "Ten years of *The Alabama Lawyer*!" Doris Wechsler made a comment that shed some light on her husband's demanding qualities as a lawyer. "I know how it is working with Herb in a way," she said. "I worked on the jurisdictional question. I tried to draft part of that section of the brief. Herb broke my heart; no, I shouldn't say that, but he had some very clear ideas about how it should be handled and did it his way, which was much better than anything I had attempted. Mine was more pedestrian."

There is a measured tone to the *Times* brief, an avoidance of hyperbole, that is the essence of Wechsler's style. "I have my own view about Supreme Court briefs, which almost no other lawyer shares," he explained. "My sense of a Supreme Court brief is that it should be a document that a Supreme Court justice can use in writing an opinion favorable to the briefer."

Wechsler faced one daunting historical obstacle: the fact that libel had always been treated as outside the rules of the First Amendment. Courts do not like to make sudden breaks from history. A lawyer presenting a case to the Supreme Court is well advised to offer implicit assurance that he is asking for something easy, something that follows naturally from precedent. How was Wechsler to do that?

One way to approach the First Amendment would have been to urge the Court to apply the "clear and present danger" formula to libel. The Holmes-Brandeis view of the importance of free speech had become increasingly accepted since the 1920s. After 1937, with the Roosevelt appointments, the Supreme Court largely withdrew from economic issues and gave greater weight to the rights of political liberty, notably freedom of speech. The omens generally were favorable—"the case came at a propitious moment for First Amendment law," Wechsler said. But the specific Holmes-Brandeis doctrine of clear and present danger had not fared well over the years, and it was in some disrepute after the way it had been used in the case of the Communist party leaders to justify repression. In any event, Wechsler found it hard to see how the formula would work in libel cases. The "danger" would be injury to reputation, and this would almost always be "present"—that is, imminent—if a stinging comment was published. Wechsler had actually thought about the idea of applying the clear and present danger doctrine to libel law years earlier, at the New York State constitutional convention of 1938, where he was counsel to the minority leader, but he ended up thinking it was "a misfit."

Instead, Wechsler decided to meet the challenge of history by building on history of another kind: the story of the Sedition Act of 1798. He decided to argue that the resistance to the act, and its ultimate public and political rejection, showed that the freedom of speech and press had to include a broad right to criticize government, and that the way libel law was being used in Alabama put the right in jeopardy. "Madison had laid the whole case out" in his remonstrances against the Sedition Act, Wechsler said later—"that defamation is intrinsic in the criticism of public officials, the discussion of public affairs." So the struggle over seditious libel one hundred sixty years earlier became the focus of the brief. "None of us knew very much about seditious libel then," Wechsler said. No Supreme Court decision had dealt with the concept in any detail, or with the Sedition Act controversy. The three lawyers—Wechsler, Frankel and Doris Wechsler—plunged into eighteenth-century history to learn about seditious libel and the Sedition Act.

Through the summer of 1963 Wechsler wrote away. "Herb is very slow starting," Mrs. Wechsler said. "He reads and reads, digests, reads. I'm always wondering when I'm going to see words on that first piece of yellow paper." The Wechslers missed their usual vacation in Wellfleet, Cape Cod. "It was a hot summer," Frankel recalled. "Herb was a very severe senior partner, but it was marvelous. Finally there came a night when Herb and Doris and I were working, I believe in their apartment, and Herb said, 'That's it. All we need now is the cite checking.' " This was the checking of citations to cases and other sources referred to in the brief, a tedious job usually given to law clerks or young associates. Frankel suggested that a young lawyer at Lord, Day & Lord could do it, "but Herb said, 'I'm not going to trust that to anyone else.' So he took it on. I thought that was a great thing."

The brief was filed on September 6, 1963. It was ninety-five printed pages, twenty-five detailing the facts and the rest making the legal arguments. The argument began by dealing at somewhat greater length than had the petition for certiorari with the past Supreme Court statements that the First Amendment did not protect libelous publications. None of those decisions, the brief said, had "sustained the repression as a libel of expression critical of governmental action." That was what was at stake here—criticism of government—and its repression had to be judged as such, not overlooked because of the "mere label" of libel. Libel had no "talismanic insulation" from the First Amendment, the brief said. The Court had looked past such labels as "contempt" and "sedition" and "breach of the peace," and libel similarly must be "defined and judged in terms that satisfy the First Amendment. The law of libel has no more immunity than other law from the supremacy of its command." Then came a section headed "Seditious Libel and the Constitution." It said the country had a "national commitment" to free political debate, "affirmed repeatedly by the decisions of this Court." The brief quoted Justice Black's statement in the *Bridges* case about the "prized American privilege to speak one's mind, although not always with perfect good taste." It quoted one of Judge Hand's elegant aphorisms on free speech: The First Amendment "pre-supposes that right conclusions are more likely to be gathered out of a multitude of tongues, than through any kind of authoritative selection. To many this is, and always will be, folly; but we have staked upon it our all." Then it made its first particular claim: that political speech cannot, constitutionally, be punished because it is false. "It is clear," the brief said, that political debate "is not delimited by any test of truth, to be administered by juries, courts or by executive officials, not to speak of a test which puts the burden of establishing the truth upon the writer." The last clause was an attack on the common-law rule, and the rule in Alabama, that libel defendants have the burden of proving that their challenged statements are true.

For the point that false political speech cannot be punished, the brief relied especially on a 1940 decision, *Cantwell v. Connecticut*, reversing the breach-of-the-peace conviction of a Jehovah's Witness preacher who went around a Catholic neighborhood denouncing the Catholic Church. The brief quoted a moving passage from the opinion of the Court by Justice Roberts:

> In the realm of religious faith, and in that of political belief, sharp differences arise. In both fields the tenets of one man may seem the rankest error to his neighbor. To persuade others to his own point of view, the pleader, as we know, at times, resorts to exaggeration, to vilification of men who have been, or are, prominent in church or state, and even to false statement. But the people of this nation have ordained in the light of history, that, in spite of the probability of excesses and abuses, these liberties are, in the long view, essential to enlightened opinion and right conduct on the part of the citizens of a democracy.

If truth was not a test, the brief continued, neither could political speech be penalized because it damaged official reputations. If it could, then

nothing "safely could be uttered that was anything but praise." Here
Wechsler quoted Madison's Report on the Virginia Resolutions: ". . . it
is manifestly impossible to punish the intent to bring those who administer the government into disrepute or contempt, without striking at the
right of freely discussing public characters and measures." Now the brief
moved to the crux of the argument: "If criticism of official conduct may
not be repressed upon the ground that it is false or that it tends to harm
official reputation, the inadequacy of these separate grounds is not sur-
mounted by their combination. This was the basic lesson of the great
assault on the short-lived Sedition Act of 1798, which first crystallized
a national awareness of the central meaning of the First Amendment."
In that last sentence, about how the Sedition Act controversy had made
clear "the central meaning of the First Amendment," Wechsler carefully
avoided the debate about whether the First Amendment was "intended"
to abolish the law of seditious libel. Whatever the intention in 1791, he
was saying, the protest against the Sedition Act between 1798 and 1800
produced a consensus that under the First Amendment Americans could
not be punished for criticizing public officials.

The brief described the Sedition Act and the political struggle. It quoted
from the Virginia Resolutions and Madison's Report, including Madison's observation that if sedition laws had been enforced against the
American press before 1776, might not the United States still be "miserable colonies, groaning under a foreign yoke"? It quoted the two most
eloquent opponents of the act in the House of Representatives, Albert
Gallatin and John Nicholas, including Nicholas's warning that although
the act punished only false criticism, men "would be afraid of publishing
the truth, as, though true, it might not always be in their power to
establish truth to the satisfaction of a court of justice."

"Though the Sedition Act was never passed on by this Court," the
brief said, "the verdict of history surely sustains the view that it was
inconsistent with the First Amendment. Fines levied in its prosecutions
were repaid by Act of Congress on this ground." (Here the brief mentioned the 1840 statute repaying the heirs of Congressman Matthew
Lyon.) It cited statements by Justice Holmes and others that the Sedition
Act violated the First Amendment and said "these assumptions reflect a
broad consensus that, we have no doubt, is part of present law."

The brief said the *Times* advertisement was as much a political document as those punished under the Sedition Act. "It was a recital of
grievances and protest against claimed abuses dealing squarely with the
major issue of our time." And the libel rules applied by the Alabama
courts were in fact "more repressive" in their effect than the Sedition Act
was. Falsity was presumed, and so was injury to reputation. The plaintiff

did not have to prove his case beyond a reasonable doubt, as a prosecutor in a criminal case would. The criminal law's protection against double jeopardy did not apply; the same advertisement could lead to many civil libel actions, as indeed this one had. The jury could award damages without limit. Worse yet was the Alabama Supreme Court's declaration that criticism of a government body "attached to the official in complete control of the body," so that he could recover libel damages for the criticism even though it did not name him. If so, "the most impersonal denunciation of an agency of government" may be treated, the brief said, as "defamation of the hierarchy of officials." It said, "Such a concept transforms the law of defamation from a method of protecting private reputation to a device for insulating government against attack."

Forty years earlier, Chicago officials had tried to stop attacks on them in the *Chicago Tribune* by having the city sue the *Tribune* for libel. The gambit failed in the Illinois Supreme Court, which said: "No court of last resort in this country has ever held, or even suggested, that prosecutions for libel on government have any place in the American system of jurisprudence." The brief quoted those words and said: "That answer applies as well to converting 'libel on government' into libel of the officials of whom it must be composed. . . . If this were not the case, the daily dialogue of politics would become utterly impossible."

The boldness of Wechsler's strategy may be hard to appreciate now, because the argument made in his brief has become part of the common understanding of constitutional law. But in 1963 hardly anyone was familiar with the history of the Sedition Act of 1798, and the constitutional-law texts of the time drew no lessons from that episode for the meaning of the First Amendment. The argument had been made in the *Debs* case in 1919, as Wechsler was aware, but it was rejected by the Supreme Court and then forgotten. It was a striking insight now to equate the civil libel judgment won by Commissioner Sullivan with the punishment of "sedition." In formal legal terms the two are quite different, one civil damages for injury to individual reputation, the other criminal punishment for an attack on the state. But by its history and analysis the brief attempted to show that the two were much alike in their practical effect, their impact on freedom.

This main line of argument was fortified by reference to another area of law, the immunity given to officials from libel suits for what they say in the course of their duties. The Supreme Court had dealt with that question just a few years earlier, in the case of a federal official who was sued for libel for a comment he had made about a private individual. The Court held that anything said by public officials "within the outer perimeter" of their duties was absolutely privileged—that is, it could not be the basis of a lawsuit no matter how false and damaging it might be. The Court relied on a statement by Judge Hand that making officials subject to libel actions "would dampen the ardor of all but the most resolute, or the most irresponsible, in the unflinching discharge of their duties." The *Times* brief argued that citizens should "enjoy a fair equivalent" of that immunity, for they have the "political duty" of "public discussion," as Brandeis put it in *Whitney v. California*. The threat of libel suits, the brief said, is surely "no less of a deterrent to the private individual" who wants to speak out on public matters than it is to the official.

So far the brief advocated an absolute freedom to criticize officials. Madison's view was certainly to this effect. After all, he had denounced a Sedition Act that punished only *false* criticism of government. If the civil law of libel was used for the same purpose as the Sedition Act, then on his logic officials should have no right to sue. The brief quoted Madison's statement in the House of Representatives in 1794 that in the American system "the censorial power is in the people over the Government, and not in the Government over the people."

But Wechsler understood that such an absolute argument would have a hard time winning a majority in the Supreme Court. Reputation was a value deserving of respect, too, and over many years the law had respected it despite the First Amendment's strong commitment to free speech. After the McCarthy era especially, even some judges devoted to freedom of expression might be hesitant to strip public officials of all means of redeeming their good names from, say, deliberate lies. Moreover, the cases cited in the brief as showing that "falsity" could not justify punishing speech were concerned with opinions and doctrines—socialism, anarchism and the like. Such ideologies were what Holmes had in mind when he spoke of "freedom for the thought that we hate." But *false facts*, which the Alabama courts had found in Commissioner Sullivan's case, are different. To say that an American has every right to stand on a street corner and advocate socialism is different from saying he has every right to say falsely that politician X took a bribe on the night of October 10.

The *Times* brief therefore offered the Court alternative arguments for legal rules that would bar the Alabama libel judgment but still respect the interest of reputation. A first possibility was for the Court to say that officials could win only what lawyers call "special damages" for libel— damages in the amount of proved financial loss. For example, someone who proved that he lost his job because of a false charge could recover the amount of the lost salary. The common-law rule that damages are presumed would be reversed, and there would be no payment for such speculative matters as injury to reputation and suffering. The Court of Appeals for the District of Columbia had adopted this position in 1942, limiting libel recoveries by public officials to special damages. It said that "discussion will be discouraged, and the public interest in public knowledge of important facts will be poorly defended, if error subjects its author to a libel suit without even a showing of economic loss."

A second proposal in the brief to accommodate both free speech and official reputation was to let officials win libel damages only if they proved "actual malice," a term meaning that a damaging statement was "known to be unfounded." That is, the author or publisher knew it to be false at the time he made the statement. The effect of this rule would be to reverse the common-law presumption of falsity, for the libel plaintiff would now have to prove falsity of a particular kind. A number of states, though not the majority, followed this approach. A footnote in the brief listed eleven state cases and some approving comments by scholars. It cited as a leading case *Coleman v. MacLennan*, decided by the Kansas Supreme Court in 1908, which said that statements made "in good faith" about candidates for office could not be the basis of libel suits even if the statements turned out to be incorrect.

These two alternative rules showed, the brief said, that "if there is scope for the protection of official reputation against criticism of official conduct, measures of liability far less destructive of the freedom of expression are available." If the Supreme Court found that the First Amendment required either of them, Commissioner Sullivan's judgment must fall, for the Alabama libel law made no attempt to balance the interests of speech and reputation but totally subordinated the first.

A third part of the brief offered still another approach to the First Amendment argument. Even if the libel law of Alabama was constitutional on its face, it said, the law had been applied unconstitutionally to the facts of this case. The record showed that the advertisement was not about L. B. Sullivan, and in stretching the law to say that it was about him the Alabama courts had violated the First Amendment. And there was nothing in the record to suggest that Sullivan's reputation had been injured by the advertisement, so the finding that it was of a kind that threatened his reputation was unconstitutional.

Those arguments raised a subtle and interesting question: Did the Supreme Court have the power to read the record of the Sullivan trial itself and find that record inadequate—constitutionally inadequate—on the facts? After all, the Supreme Court has no power to decide issues of state law, and in ordinary circumstances it cannot upset findings of fact by a state judge or jury. But the Supreme Court is entitled to make its own appraisal of the facts when a state court has found the facts in a way that threatens constitutional values. So Wechsler argued, and this was an issue of federalism with which he was intimately familiar. He cited the case of *Fiske v. Kansas*, decided in 1927. Fiske was an organizer for the Industrial Workers of the World (the Wobblies) who was convicted under the Kansas Criminal Syndicalism Act for handing out copies of the preamble to the I.W.W. constitution. The Kansas courts found as a fact that the preamble advocated violent revolution. But the Supreme Court, reading the preamble itself, found in it no language calling for violence and held Fiske's conviction unconstitutional. It was the first time a proponent of radical doctrines had won a decision in the Supreme Court.

On the basis of the *Fiske* approach, the *Times* brief argued that the Supreme Court could decide for itself whether the advertisement was of and concerning Sullivan—whether it could constitutionally be read that way, or as a threat to his reputation. A copy of "Heed Their Rising Voices" was in the record. If the justices read it, the brief said, they would find the advertisement to be "a totally impersonal attack upon conditions, groups and institutions, not a personal assault of any kind." Sullivan maintained, and the Alabama courts had found, that the mentions of "police" in the advertisement referred to him. But there were only two erroneous statements about the police: first, that Dr. King had been arrested seven times, when in fact there had been only four arrests, and, second, that police had "ringed" the Alabama State College campus, when they had merely been deployed there "in large numbers." The brief said: "That the exaggerations or inaccuracies in these statements cannot rationally be regarded as tending to injure [Sullivan's] reputation is, we submit, entirely clear." There were other mistakes in the advertisement— notably, the statement that college students had been locked out of the dining hall in an attempt to starve them into submission—but that had nothing to do with the police, as Sullivan had conceded at the trial, or with Sullivan himself. The brief concluded that the record left "no room" for believing that the advertisement made a statement about Sullivan or "injured or jeopardized his reputation in a way that forfeited constitutional protection."

Finally, the brief argued that the size of the damage award to Sullivan alone, "this monstrous judgment" of $500,000, was "so shockingly excessive that it violates the Constitution." The jury had made the award without saying how much of it was compensatory damages and how much punitive. (The *Times* lawyers had asked Judge Jones to instruct the jury to state the amounts separately, but he refused.) Punitive damages are awarded in tort cases, including libel, not to compensate the plaintiff for his injury but to deter others from injurious conduct. They are like a fine in a criminal sentence, but they are imposed by juries without any of the safeguards of criminal cases: the requirement of proof beyond a reasonable doubt and so on. The whole idea of punitive damages in civil cases might therefore seem constitutionally doubtful, but very early in its history the Supreme Court had rejected an argument that imposing punitive damages without the safeguards of criminal procedure was unconstitutional. For this reason Wechsler decided not to attempt an attack on punitive damages in libel. The brief said merely that even if there were a basis in the record for finding that Sullivan's reputation had been harmed, which it disputed, "there was no rational relationship between the gravity of the offense and the size of the penalty imposed." Lack of such a rational relationship would violate the clause of the Fourteenth Amendment forbidding the states to deprive anyone of property "without due process of law." The brief warned that damages so large, "upon facts such as these," would have a "repressive influence" far beyond the parties in this case.

Then the brief took what had been the most intense passage in the petition for certiorari and restated it in even stronger form: "This is not a time—there never is a time—when it would serve the values enshrined in the Constitution to force the press to curtail its attention to the tensest issues that confront the country or to forego the dissemination of its publications in the areas where tension is extreme."

There followed a section devoted to the *Times*'s argument that the Alabama courts had asserted jurisdiction over the paper unconstitutionally. Then came the Conclusion, always short in Supreme Court briefs: "For the foregoing reasons, the judgment of the Supreme Court of Alabama should be reversed, with direction to dismiss the action." Usually, when the Supreme Court reverses a state-court judgment, the opinion of the Court ends by sending the case back for "proceedings not inconsistent with this opinion"—a polite nod to the state court. But given the hostility in the Alabama courts, Wechsler was suggesting that the Supreme Court bring the libel case to an end without any possibility of further proceedings.

The brief was signed by three lawyers for the *Times*, in order of seniority: Herbert Brownell, senior partner in Lord, Day & Lord; Thomas F. Daly, a partner who had been in the libel case from the beginning, going often to Alabama, and Herbert Wechsler. Listed as "of counsel" were Louis Loeb, T. Eric Embry (the trial counsel in Montgomery), Marvin Frankel, Ronald S. Diana and Doris Wechsler.

. . .

Next came the brief for the four Alabama ministers, signed by Wachtel and eleven other lawyers. Like the ministers' petition for certiorari, it emphasized the particular unfairness of the Alabama proceedings toward them. The ministers' "first knowledge of the Times ad came," the brief said, "when they received in the mail respondent Sullivan's identical letters. . . . These letters did not contain a copy of the ad, but merely quoted out of context the two paragraphs on which Sullivan based his complaint, and demanded that each petitioner 'publish in as prominent and public a manner' as the Times ad, 'a full and fair retraction of the entire false and defamatory matter.' Petitioners could not possibly comply with this demand; and, before they could consult counsel or even receive appropriate advice in regard thereto, suit was instituted."

A section of the ministers' brief was devoted to arguing that the trial before Judge Jones in Montgomery was "a race trial, in which they were from first to last placed in a patently inferior position because of the color of their skins." Throughout the trial, "the jury had before it an eloquent assertion of the inequality of the Negro in the segregation of the one room, of all rooms, where men should find equality before the law": the courtroom. "Where Sullivan, a white public official, sued Negro petitioners represented by Negro counsel before an all-white jury, in Montgomery, Alabama, on an advertisement seeking to aid the cause of integration, the impact of courtroom segregation could only denote the inferiority of Negroes and taint and infect all proceedings." Wachtel picked out as especially prejudicial a remark allegedly made (the closing arguments were not officially transcribed) by one of Sullivan's lawyers, Robert E. Steiner III: "In other words, all of these things that happened did not happen in Russia where the police run everything, they did not happen in the Congo where they still eat them, they happened in Montgomery, Alabama, a law-abiding community."

The brief for Sullivan, written largely by Roland Nachman and signed also by Steiner, Sam Rice Baker and Calvin Whitesell of Montgomery, took the same basic position as the brief in opposition to the petition for certiorari. This was that *The New York Times*, having savaged Alabama officials, was now sanctimoniously claiming that an ordinary libel action was a massive assault on freedom. The brief said:

> It is fantasy [for the *Times*] to argue that the ad which falsely charged respondent, as police commissioner, with responsibility for the criminal and rampant "unprecedented wave of terror" is

"the daily dialogue of politics" and mere "political criticism" and "political expression." If The Times prevails, any false statement about any public official comes within this protected category. The absolute immunity would cover false statements that the Secretary of State had given military secrets to the enemy; that the Secretary of the Treasury had embezzled public funds; that the Governor of a state poisoned his wife; that the head of the public health service polluted water with germs; that the mayor and city council are corrupt; that named judges confer favorable opinions on the highest bidder; and that a police commissioner conducted activities so barbaric as to constitute a wave of terror.

The Supreme Court had said many times that libel was outside the protection of the First Amendment, the brief noted, most recently in 1961. In the last decade alone the Court had refused to review forty-four libel cases that lawyers had sought to bring before it. The brief said that Professor Chafee, "an old and close friend of free speech and press, also disagrees with the Times' law and history." It cited a 1949 book review in which Chafee said: "The phrase 'freedom of the press' was viewed against a background of familiar legal limitations which men of 1791 did not regard as objectionable, such as damage suits for libel." The brief continued:

The Times and its powerful corporate newspaper friends obviously realize that history and precedent support the holding below that this libelous advertisement is not constitutionally protected. They assert, therefore, at least for themselves and others who conduct the business of mass communication, an absolute privilege to defame all public officials—even in paid advertisements; even when the defamation renders the classic defenses of truth, fair comment and privilege unavailable; even when there is no retraction to show good faith. They urge this Court to write such a fancied immunity into the Constitution—at least for themselves, for they are silent on whether this new constitutional protection is to extend to ordinary speakers and writers.

This sally at the Times's "corporate newspaper friends" was aimed at two newspapers that had filed briefs as amici curiae, friends of the court, urging the Supreme Court to reverse the Alabama judgment. An amicus brief can be filed by anyone who asserts an interest in the outcome of a case if he gets the permission of the parties to the case—or, failing that permission, gets the approval of the Court itself. The Chicago Tribune and *The Washington Post* had asked permission to file in the *Times* case; the *Times* agreed, but Sullivan's lawyers refused. Each newspaper then asked the Court for leave to file. Sullivan's lawyers opposed the motion, saying that such a brief would be merely "a vehicle for a propaganda effort." But the Court said yes.

The *Chicago Tribune* brief gave examples of attempts by American politicians to silence critical newspapers by means of libel actions. One was the Chicago case that Wechsler had mentioned, *City of Chicago v. Tribune Company.* "There," the *Tribune* brief said, "the mayor of Chicago, William Hale Thompson, whose administration was marked by graft and corruption, sought to silence this *amicus*, his bitterest and most vocal critic." The brief also described in sickening detail the cruel punishments inflicted on printers condemned for seditious libel in seventeenth-century England: noses slit, ears cut off, hanging, drawing and quartering. . . . It said the Alabama judgment was "a reincarnation of the law of seditious libel."

The *Tribune* brief was filed by Howard Ellis, Keith Masters and Don H. Reuben of Chicago. *The Washington Post*'s bore the names of William P. Rogers, a former U.S. attorney general, Gerald W. Siegel and Stanley Godofsky. It gave more extended and emphatic treatment to one of Wechsler's less absolute alternative arguments. It urged that "utterances highly critical of the conduct of public official capacities," possibly defamatory "because of overstatement or exaggeration," be given First Amendment protection "at least where honestly made in the belief that they are true." In other words, criticism should be protected unless, as the *Times* brief put it, it was "known to be unfounded" when uttered. As a precedent, the *Post* brief cited a 1959 case, *Smith v. California*, in which a bookshop owner had been prosecuted for having an obscene book in his store. The Supreme Court upset the conviction because there had been no evidence that Smith knew the book was obscene. A requirement of knowledge was just as important in the libel situation, the *Post* said, for these reasons:

> In the heat of controversy on political matters, particularly on issues and personalities where strong emotions are aroused, charges and countercharges are often made on the basis of information which, though honestly believed, later turns out to have been incomplete, inaccurate or misleading. On the other hand, it frequently occurs that charges, based upon strong and logically well founded but unprovable suspicions, or upon unconfirmable "inside information," result in ultimate exposure of public incompetence, error or even misconduct. . . . To limit, by

threat of a libel suit for honest error of fact or judgment, publication of criticism of officials to that which is absolutely confirmable in every detail would, as a practical matter, stifle virtually all criticism of the government and its personnel.

In that argument *The Washington Post* might have been anticipating the events of Watergate ten years later, when *Post* reporters, relying on "Deep Throat" and other unnameable and unconfirmable sources, began the disclosure of criminal cover-up that led eventually to the resignation of President Nixon.

There was one more *amicus* brief, filed with the permission of both sides by the American Civil Liberties Union and the New York Civil Liberties Union. It was signed by Edward S. Greenbaum, Harriet F. Pilpel, Melvin L. Wulf, Nanette Dembitz and Nancy F. Wechsler, who was Herbert's sister-in-law. While Sullivan's lawyers suggested that a paid advertisement was less deserving of constitutional protection than other forms of expression, the Civil Liberties Union brief argued that the penalizing of this advertisement would have especially grave effects on political freedom. Assuming that there was any libel at all, the brief said, the *Times* was being heavily penalized "for a concealed 'libel' in a political advertisement. If newspapers are to be liable without fault to heavy damages for unwitting libels on public officials in political advertisements, the freedom of dissenting groups to secure publication of their views on public affairs and to seek support for their causes will be greatly diminished."

# 13

◼

# MAY IT
# PLEASE
# THE COURT

A few days after the Supreme Court agreed to review the *Sullivan* case, in January 1963, Louis Loeb met with Harding Bancroft of the *Times* to discuss who should make the oral argument for the paper. Loeb strongly recommended his senior partner, Herbert Brownell. But Bancroft said he had already discussed that possibility with the *Times* publisher, Orvil E. Dryfoos, and they felt the choice of Brownell would be "unwise." As Attorney General in the Eisenhower administration, Brownell had played a large part in the appointment of three members of the present Court, Chief Justice Earl Warren and Associate Justices John Marshall Harlan and William J. Brennan Jr. As Bancroft summarized his conversation with Loeb in a memorandum for the files, "I said it was our feeling that The Times should bend over backwards so as not to create the appearance that we were using a person who had had a relationship with the Court during the Eisenhower Administration and might be regarded by some as having been responsible for the appointment of certain of the justices. I said that perhaps we were being overpunctilious, but that was the way we felt." Dryfoos may also have felt that Wechsler, whose petition had persuaded the Court to take the case and who was developing the First Amendment argument, would be far more familiar with the case and better able to argue it. Loeb sounded out an eminent judge and a highly respected New York lawyer, and they also thought Wechsler the better choice. He got the assignment.

(Eight years later Brownell and Wechsler were again, fleetingly, involved in a question of legal representation for the *Times*. When the Nixon administration moved to stop the *Times*'s publication of the Pentagon Papers, on the evening after the second day's articles, the firm of Lord, Day & Lord refused to represent the paper. It explained that Brownell had a conflict of interest because he had drafted the executive order under which the Vietnam documents were classified. To many at the *Times*, the real reason appeared to be that Brownell disapproved of the decision to publish or did not want to offend the current administration. The *Times* was due in court the following morning, so its need for a lawyer was urgent. Harding Bancroft telephoned Wechsler and asked whether he would represent the *Times*. He said with great regret that he could not, because he was about to leave for a teaching commitment in Europe. Bancroft then asked him about Professor Alexander M. Bickel of the Yale Law School. Shortly after midnight Bickel was reached and agreed to take the case on.)

Oral argument does not play the part in the work of the Supreme Court that it did in the nineteenth century, when Daniel Webster would argue a case for days, or that it still does in the House of Lords, Britain's highest court, where counsel may go on for a week or more. The modern Supreme Court limits oral argument severely; at the time of the *Sullivan* case it was usually one hour for each side, since then reduced to half an hour. But argument still has an important function. It is the one chance the justices have to emerge from their cloister, the secluded chambers in that marble palace on Capitol Hill, and grapple directly with the lawyers who represent the clashing interests before them. It is also a rare opportunity for the public to gain insights into the minds of those who actually make the decisions. More than any other officials in Washington, the justices still do their own work, assisted only by a handful of young law clerks. To observe them as they question counsel in the courtroom is to see an extraordinarily open process, unaffected, human. In a capital puffed up with bureaucracy and public relations, the Court seems old-fashioned, small, personal. For the lawyers, oral argument is a direct opportunity to reach those nine minds—with an idea, a phrase, a fact. Not many cases are won at argument, but they can be lost if a lawyer is unable or unwilling to answer a justice's question.

The lawyer arguing a case stands at a rostrum below the raised bench in the pillared courtroom. The justices are seated behind the bench with the Chief at the center, the others arranged around him by seniority: the most senior on the Chief Justice's right hand, the next on his left, and so on. At the time of the *Sullivan* case, as a lawyer saw the justices from left to right, at the far left was Byron R. White of Colorado, Rhodes Scholar, football star, Attorney General Robert Kennedy's deputy who went to the South with federal marshals to protect the Freedom Riders, then President Kennedy's choice for the Court, where he had taken a centrist position. Next to him was William J. Brennan Jr., a justice of the New Jersey Supreme Court when President Eisenhower appointed him, a strong supporter of free speech and minority rights but with a nondoctrinaire skill for bringing majorities together. Next, Tom C. Clark, the only remaining Truman appointee, a Texan and former Attorney General, on the conservative side of the Court. Then Hugo Black of Alabama, the longest-serving justice, seventy-seven years old but with his faith undimmed in what he called the absolute commands of the First Amendment. At the center sat the large figure of Chief Justice Earl Warren, who had commanded California politics for years, the first person to be elected governor three times; he was chosen by Eisenhower as a moderate Republican but soon made clear that on constitutional issues he was a committed libertarian. To Warren's right, as a lawyer faced them, was William O. Douglas, Westerner, law professor, mountain climber, who nearly became Franklin Roosevelt's vice presidential nominee in 1944 instead of Harry Truman; he and Black were the remaining Roosevelt appointees, and they were almost always together on issues of free speech. Next to him was John Marshall Harlan, grandson of a justice of the same name, a Wall Street lawyer appointed by Eisenhower, sensitive to claims of freedom but carrying on the recently retired Justice Frankfurter's concern that the Court not overreach and intrude on the rights of the states. Then Potter Stewart of Ohio, a fourth Eisenhower appointee, a centrist promoted from the U. S. Court of Appeals. At the far right Arthur Goldberg, Kennedy's Secretary of Labor, who had replaced Frankfurter and quickly emerged as an activist judge.

The two libel cases were scheduled for argument on January 6, 1964. When the time came that afternoon, Chief Justice Warren read out the title of the first, "Number 39, New York Times Company, Petitioner, versus L. B. Sullivan, Respondent." Wechsler rose from his chair, the Chief Justice said, "Mr. Wechsler?" and the argument began.

"Mr. Chief Justice, may it please the Court, this case is here together with Number 40 on writ of certiorari granted a year ago to the Supreme Court of Alabama." So Wechsler began, in the routine formal style. But in the next sentence he set out to establish that this was not a routine case: "It summons for review a judgment of that court which poses, in our submission, hazards to the freedom of the press of a dimension not confronted since the early days of the Republic." Justice Brennan interrupted to say, "I am sorry; I am having difficulty hearing you." This was unusual, and perhaps a sign of unusual attentiveness to this case. Wechsler repeated his statement.

Wechsler spent half of his allotted hour talking about the facts of the case. He discussed the advertisement. "Since in my submission," he said, "the case not only begins with the publication but ends there as well, I respectfully invite the Court's attention to the text." After reading from it at some length he said: "I suggest, therefore, that the text was thus a statement of protest, an encomium, interwoven, to be sure, with a re-citation of events. But it names no names but Dr. King's, and plainly makes no personal attack on any individual."

Sometimes during arguments the justices take a great interest in factual details, which are less familiar to them than most legal arguments, and which can be crucial. This day they asked Wechsler innumerable questions about the facts. Justice White wanted to know whether Alabama State College was located within the city limits of Montgomery. "I believe it is," Wechsler replied. Justice Brennan asked whether the only inac-curacy Wechsler conceded in the sixth paragraph of the advertisement was the statement that Dr. King had been arrested *seven* times—"the word 'seven.'" "Exactly, sir," Wechsler said. Justice Harlan asked how long the Montgomery jury took to reach its verdict. Two hours and a few minutes, Wechsler replied. As he concluded his description of what had happened in the case so far, he used a homely example to demonstrate the scope of the Alabama Supreme Court ruling that criticism of any government body attaches to the person in charge of it. That was, Wechs-ler said, "a kind of presumption that if you talk about the police you're talking about the commissioner. I can't say that the New York police tap wires, for example, though I believe they do, without giving Com-missioner [Patrick V.] Murphy an action against me, since it's illegal for them to do it without a court order."

When he came to the legal issues, Wechsler said the rule applied by the Alabama courts in this case would inhibit "criticism of official con-duct, which we submit is what the First Amendment . . . I would not say was exclusively about, but was primarily about. And we are actually making . . . the same argument that James Madison made and that Thomas Jefferson made with respect to the validity of the Sedition Act of 1798."

Then came these exchanges:

JUSTICE BRENNAN: "How far does this go, Mr. Wechsler? As long as the criticism is addressed to official conduct?"
WECHSLER: "Yes."

JUSTICE BRENNAN: "Are there any limits whatever which take it outside the protection of the First Amendment?"

WECHSLER: "Well, if I take my instruction from James Madison, I would have to say that within any references that Madison made I can see no toying with limits or with exclusions."

JUSTICE BRENNAN: "You say, then, the First Amendment gives it, in effect, an absolute privilege to criticize . . ."

WECHSLER: "The proposition is that the First Amendment was precisely designed to do away with seditious libel, and seditious libel was the punishment of criticism of the Government and criticism of officials."

JUSTICE GOLDBERG: "And this applies not only to newspapers but to anybody?"

WECHSLER: "Exactly; of course."

JUSTICE GOLDBERG: "In other words, you are not arguing here for a special rule that applies to newspapers?"

WECHSLER: "Certainly not . . ."

JUSTICE STEWART: "Your argument would be the same . . . if The New York Times or anybody else had accused this official of taking a bribe?"

WECHSLER: "Certainly."

JUSTICE STEWART: "Or buying his office?"

WECHSLER: "Certainly. Of course, in the historic period in which Madison was writing, charges of bribery were common, and it was this type of press freedom that he saw in the First Amendment."

JUSTICE WHITE: "Mr. Wechsler, we don't have here a case of deliberate falsehood."

WECHSLER: "No."

Justice White's comment was highly suggestive. It indicated that White might be thinking about the possibility of holding that false criticism of public officials was protected by the First Amendment unless it was knowingly false. This was one of the less than absolute alternatives that Wechsler had offered the Court in his brief. After answering Justice White, he told the Court that the thought brought him to the second part of his legal argument, but before he could get to it the justices had many more questions. Justice Goldberg brought Wechsler back to his claim of absolute immunity. Was he saying, Goldberg asked, that "no public official can sue for libel constitutionally and get a verdict with respect to any type of false or malicious statement made concerning his conduct, his official conduct?" Wechsler replied, "That is the broadest statement that I make. But I wish in my remaining time to indicate what the lesser submissions are, because there are many that I think must produce a reversal." Wechsler's time was running out, and he was concerned that he not appear to be asking the Court for too much.

But Justice Goldberg was not finished. "So to follow this through," he asked, ". . . a citizen would have the right under that broad proposition to state falsely, knowingly and maliciously that his mayor, his governor, had accepted a bribe of $1,000,000 to commit an official act, and . . . the mayor could not sue for libel?" "That's right," Wechsler replied. "What he would have to do is to make a speech, using his official privilege as mayor to make a speech answering this charge. And that, of course, is what most mayors do."

Wechsler finally managed to make a brief statement about the narrower alternatives to absolute immunity for critics of official conduct. One was his argument "that there was in this record no evidence sufficient to support a finding that these particular statements in this particular advertisement threatened this particular respondent's reputation in any tangible way." This touched Justice Harlan's sensitivity about Supreme Court intrusion on state power. "Are we entitled to review the evidence here . . . ?" he asked. "Yes, I think very definitely, Mr. Justice . . ." Wechsler replied. "This Court has the responsibility and the duty to satisfy itself that the record sustains the basis on which the constitutional right asserted has been held to be untenable." The Court had done just that in *Fiske v. Kansas*, he said—and in *Bridges v. California*, where the Court looked at what Bridges and the *Los Angeles Times* had said and held that the statements could not, constitutionally, support the findings of contempt of court.

Justice Brennan asked, "Is the size of the award peculiarly important?" Wechsler said that this was part of the *Times*'s argument on the evidence. "We say there was no evidence for a finding of threat or injury. But we add to that that surely there wasn't any evidence to sustain a judgment of this sort, which is a death penalty for any newspaper if multiplied."

As his time ran out, Wechsler had said nothing about the other point that took up much of his brief, the jurisdiction of the Alabama courts. He had brought with him a copy of Judge Jones's book on Alabama practice, so he could read from it and show the Court that Jones had overruled his own book in holding that the *Times*'s lawyers had inadvertently waived their objection to the jurisdiction. But there was no time. "I should just say in closing," Wechsler said, "that there is a separate submission on the jurisdictional point. I must submit that on the brief." But he was still not finished, because the justices had more questions.

Justice White returned to the point about deliberate falsehood. What did the record in the case show, he asked, "about whether The Times knew these statements were true or false?" The Alabama Supreme Court,

Wechsler replied, said the *Times* had material in its files when it accepted the advertisement showing that some of the text was false, "but the record does not sustain that statement." Justice White: "Then if you accept the Supreme Court of Alabama's version, we must deal with your broader first ground?" In other words, if the *Times* had printed the advertisement knowing that there were falsehoods in it, the libel judgment must stand unless the First Amendment gave absolute immunity to all criticism of government, even knowingly false criticism? Wechsler answered yes, but then he added, "But you have to accept the Supreme Court of Alabama's version also, Mr. Justice, on the 'of and concerning' point." By this he meant that there were two ways the *Times* could win the case short of absolute immunity: first, if the Court held that the advertisement could not constitutionally be read to refer to Sullivan, or, second, if the Court found that the *Times* had published the advertisement unaware of any errors in it, and held that inadvertent falsehood in criticism of government was protected by the First Amendment.

Now Justice Black asked what seemed, on the surface, a surprising series of questions. He took issue with Wechsler's position that the advertisement could not be read as an attack on Sullivan. Wasn't the fact that Sullivan "had charge of the police" and "was responsible for their actions" enough, he asked, "to justify a jury in finding that the charge that the police acted in a terribly bad manner . . . was a charge against Sullivan?" These exchanges followed:

> WECHSLER: "In this case, on this statement, I most vigorously submit that the answer to that question is that they [the jurors] could not."
> JUSTICE BLACK: "Why?"
> WECHSLER: ". . . Because the record shows there were 175 policemen, that there was a police chief in addition to the Commissioner, and there is not the slightest bit of a suggestion here, in my submission, that what the police did they were ordered to do by Commissioner Sullivan."
> JUSTICE BLACK: "Wouldn't the jury have the right to determine that if the police of a city, who were armed with shotguns and tear gas bombs, go around and throw their weight around with all that, and it's shown that the chief of police, the man acted as chief of police, the Commissioner, wouldn't that be enough for a judge or jury reasonably to find that the head of the department was responsible for it . . . ?"

Why would Justice Black, the member of the Court most passionately committed to freedom of speech, be pressing Wechsler to concede that there was good reason for the Montgomery jury to find that the advertisement was an attack on L. B. Sullivan? Justice Black was a great believer in juries; he had been a skillful trial lawyer himself, and on the Court he often urged respect for what juries decided. But he had a deeper purpose here; he wanted the Court to have to confront Wechsler's broader argument. He wanted this case to be treated as if it arose from a direct attack on a public official. He wanted the Court to hold that such an attack was protected by the First Amendment.

Suppose, Justice Black said, that the advertisement charged "by innuendo" that "the police department joined with a bunch of bad people to permit what I would call the offenses that are charged here." Wouldn't that innuendo attach to Sullivan?

Wechsler said it would not. "I think most courts would rule that this document could not be libelous" of Sullivan under common law. The only statements in the ad that could be connected to him were references to the police, and 175 police officers were "too large a group" to permit the ad to be read as an attack on any individual, including Sullivan.

"What difference would it make," Justice Black continued, "if he was one of the group and there are 175 or 200? Do you accept *Beauharnais?*" That was the 1952 group libel decision, upholding an Illinois law that made it a crime to denigrate any racial or religious group. The question put Wechsler in a difficult situation. Justice Black had vigorously dissented from *Beauharnais*, as had Justice Douglas, so they would like Wechsler to say that the decision was wrong, but Justice Clark had joined the majority. Wechsler did not want to alienate anyone, but he had to follow his convictions where they led. He did not duck the question. *Beauharnais* was different, he replied, because it did not involve criticism of officials. "But if you ask me beyond that, Mr. Justice, whether I think *Beauharnais* should be followed and was correctly decided, I do not."

(In 1978 the U.S. Court of Appeals for the Seventh Circuit held that, while the Supreme Court had never formally overruled its *Beauharnais* decision, its recent cases protecting hateful speech had effectively done so. The Court of Appeals therefore held unconstitutional local ordinances designed to block a march by American Nazis through Skokie, Illinois, a village in which many Jewish survivors of the Nazi Holocaust lived.)

Justice White now turned the question of the *Times*'s knowledge of falsity in the advertising copy another way. He asked whether Judge Jones had instructed the jury that it must find deliberate falsehood in order to award punitive damages. Wechsler replied that the jury had been told the purpose of punitive damages (to punish the perpetrator of a libel and to deter others), but had not been instructed about a requirement of deliberate falsehood. And the jury had brought in its verdict without saying whether any part of the $500,000 was punitive.

There was one last exchange before Wechsler sat down.

> JUSTICE GOLDBERG: "You don't argue at law that punitive damages are unconstitutional in that they impose a penalty in a civil proceeding without the burden of proof and safeguards surrounding the criminal proceedings, and because the purpose of punitive damages is, as you have said, to punish; you don't argue that?"
>
> WECHSLER: "No, we have not made that point, Mr. Justice."

Now Roland Nachman argued the case for Sullivan. Like Wechsler, he began with the facts, restating them from the viewpoint of the plaintiff. "We say there was ample and, indeed, overwhelming evidence to support the jury verdict," he said.

Further, this was not a case like *Bridges v. California*, where the findings of contempt were made by judges. "We're here after a jury trial, with all that that means in terms of the Seventh Amendment." (The Seventh Amendment reads: "In Suits at common law, where the value in controversy shall exceed twenty dollars, the right of trial by jury shall be preserved, and no fact tried by a jury, shall be otherwise re-examined in any Court of the United States, than according to the rules of the common law.") Like the other amendments in the Bill of Rights, the Seventh was designed to apply only to the federal government—federal courts, in this instance. So Nachman's reference to it raised an immediate judicial eyebrow.

> JUSTICE GOLDBERG: "I don't want to disturb you, but you made a rather provocative statement I would like to ask you about. You said a jury trial in terms of the Seventh Amendment."
>
> NACHMAN: "Yes, sir."
>
> JUSTICE GOLDBERG: "Is it your idea the Seventh Amendment applies to the states by the Fourteenth? Is that part of your argument?"
>
> NACHMAN: ". . . That was the point that I had in mind, sir, yes, sir."

Nachman argued that the advertisement was "completely false, and there was no attempt by the *Times* to say that any of this was true." Again Justice Goldberg was startled. "Are you arguing to us," he asked, that "the case went to the jury on the posture that this ad was from beginning to end totally false?" Nachman replied, "Yes, sir." "You are?" Justice Goldberg said. Nachman repeated that he was, and he argued that the Supreme Court had no right to upset the jury verdict unless there was "no reasonable basis for it whatsoever."

After ten minutes or so Nachman had not yet made what had to be his strongest legal argument, that historically libel had been treated as outside the First Amendment. Justice White asked: "I suppose if it's your assertion—which I gather it is—that libel falls outside the protection of the First Amendment, that someone has to finally decide what libel is that falls outside the protection of the First Amendment?" The question drew an implicit parallel with the Court's treatment of obscenity. In a 1957 opinion by Justice Brennan, the Court held that obscenity was outside the protection of the First Amendment. But the courts must decide what is obscene, the opinion said, and it then defined obscenity so narrowly that for years most state actions against the supposedly obscene were upset. Nachman answered Justice White's question, "Yes, sir," and these exchanges followed:

> JUSTICE WHITE: "The jury isn't the final answer on that, I suppose?"
> NACHMAN: "You mean the characterization of the ad as libelous? . . . We say that that is a question of state law."
> JUSTICE BRENNAN: "That we can't reexamine here as a constitutional question?"
> NACHMAN: "Your honor, I would answer that in two ways. Up to now, as we read the cases, the Court has left the characterization of publications as libelous or not libelous to the states. Now, we would certainly concede that if a statement was made that somebody had blond hair and a state court held that this statement was libelous *per se*, well, of course this Court could review it. But, adverting to some of Mr. Justice Black's observations, in his questions, we say that when this kind of conduct is charged, this is within the normal, usual rubric and framework of libel. It charges [the plaintiffs] with criminal offenses, charges which would certainly hold them up to contempt and ridicule and disapproval, and we think we're well within the classic definition of libel."

As Nachman continued analyzing the facts of the case, Justice Goldberg, who had evidently been reading the record, asked about the advertisement's use of the phrase "Southern violators." Sullivan had testified that the ad libeled the entire community, Justice Goldberg said. "Since there are many law-abiding citizens in the South as well as some who are not law-abiding, as in all sections of the country, what would prevent, under your theory of the case, any citizen in the South saying that 'I am libeled by this ad of the *Times*,' and by innuendo then to allege and go to the jury on the assumption that I am a Southern citizen, this refers to Southern violators, the 'they' means that I bombed, that I did all these things?" Nachman was not fazed by the question. "The thing that would prevent it in Alabama, your honor," he said, "is Alabama jurisprudence, which requires that a group be sufficiently small that the identification can readily be made."

In time, Nachman took up Justice White's question to Wechsler about deliberate falsehood. "On the question of malice and deliberateness," he said, "we submit, sir, that there was plenty from which the jury could find deliberateness." He mentioned the retraction for Governor Patterson when none was made for Sullivan, the failure to apologize to Sullivan after the *Times* had investigated the statements in the advertisement and found some of them to be inaccurate, and the failure of *Times* advertising people to apply in this case "a very rigorous set of advertising accept ability standards."

"I gather," Justice White said, "that under the Alabama law it's the same as knowing the statement is false at the outset if you refuse to retract after you know it is false."

"Yes, sir."

"So you are saying," Justice White continued, that "this case unavoidably presents the question of whether or not a person may tell a deliberate lie about a public official. Is that the issue?" Nachman answered: "We think that the defendant, in order to succeed, must convince this Court that a newspaper corporation has an absolute immunity from anything it publishes. And, in answer to one, I believe, of Mr. Justice Stewart's questions . . . if a newspaper charges, say, a mayor or police commissioner with taking a bribe, that there is absolute immunity against a libel suit in that regard. And we think that's something brand new in our jurisprudence. We think that it would have a devastating effect on this nation."

That was as close as Nachman came to confronting directly Wechsler's argument that the libel award to Sullivan had the same effect as the Sedition Act in suppressing criticism of government and hence violated the First Amendment. It was as close as he came to warning the Supreme Court that deciding in favor of the *Times* would mean bringing the Constitution and the Court into a vast new field of law, libel, with consequences difficult to foresee.

As Nachman concluded, the time for that day's argument session was over. The *Abernathy* case had to wait until the next morning.

Two lawyers spoke for the Alabama ministers: William P. Rogers, the former Attorney General who had filed the *amicus* brief for *The Washington Post*, and Samuel R. Pierce Jr., a former New York judge who had been on the team for the ministers' brief with Wachtel. (Pierce was later Secretary of Housing and Urban Development in President Reagan's Administration.)

Rogers called Sullivan's libel suit a "perversion of the judicial process" and said the Alabama judgment was the "most serious threat to freedom of the press in this century." He pointed out that Alabama had a criminal libel statute with a maximum fine of $500, one one-thousandth of the damages awarded in this case. He also told the Court that a newspaper cannot possibly check on everything it publishes, a point made in the *Washington Post* brief. He said this case was "a frontal attack, under the guise of a civil libel suit, on freedom of the press, freedom of speech and freedom of assembly." If the Alabama judgment was allowed to stand, he warned, "it will be a mild forerunner of what will follow."

Justice Goldberg asked when the four ministers had received the letters from Sullivan demanding a retraction of the ad—an ad of which they had never heard until then. "Eight days" before Sullivan brought his suit, Rogers replied. He added that Judge Jones had instructed the jury that the ministers' failure to respond to Sullivan's letter before he sued could be taken as evidence that they were responsible for the use of their names in the advertisement.

Pierce emphasized the racial aspects of the trial. He said Sullivan's suit was one of several whose "sole purpose" was to "suppress and punish the voices for racial equality," and that the case was tried in an atmosphere of "racial bias and passion." Noting the fact that the black lawyers for the ministers were not addressed as "Mr." in the trial, Pierce argued that it was hard to find equal protection of the laws in a judicial process where there was "not even an equality of courtesy."

Then Nachman argued again in response to Rogers and Pierce. Early on, Justice Harlan asked him whether "the basic constitutional question we're being asked to decide is one common to both cases." Nachman said it was. Justice Black asked whether there was evidence from which the jury could find that the ministers were responsible for the appearance of their names in the ad. Nachman said yes, there was: The ministers' names were there, and thereafter they had failed to answer Sullivan's retraction letter. Under Alabama law, he said, a "failure to break silence indicates they did what we say they did." Justice Goldberg said: "I get a lot of mail every day that I don't answer. Without a prior relationship between the parties, I can't conceive a rule of law that says you must reply."

Now Chief Justice Warren, who had been the subject of foul denunciations in the South because he wrote the Opinion of the Court in *Brown v. Board of Education*, the School Segregation case, entered the discussion. "It is not unknown to at least one member of this Court," he said, "that he has received letters from various parts of the country accusing him of making libelous statements. If he has made no such statements, must he reply or suffer a one-half million dollar libel judgment?"

Nachman: "I'm not familiar with the contents of the letters."

Warren: "They're far worse than this one."

Nachman: "When it becomes important later in a lawsuit, then we submit his failure to reply may be evidence that he made it."

At midday on January 7, 1964, the two cases were in the hands of the justices. There was nothing more for the lawyers to do except wait and wonder what the outcome would be. But a month or so later Doris Wechsler got what she thought was a clue, a happy one. She and her husband went to Washington for a meeting of the American Law Institute. "While Herb was at that," Mrs. Wechsler said years later, "I decided to go to the Supreme Court and listen to whatever was being argued. I sat in the lawyers' section. Justice Brennan saw me, and I thought he smiled. Somehow I knew."

# 14

■

# "THE CENTRAL MEANING OF THE FIRST AMENDMENT"

O N the morning of March 9, 1964, Herbert Wechsler was teaching a class in one of the large lecture rooms at the Columbia Law School when his secretary, Rhoda L. Bauch, came in. He paused, and she walked down the aisle and handed him a note. "The class knew what must be happening," Wechsler said many years later. "With all those quizzical faces before me, I just read them the note: 'Judgment reversed. Decision unanimous.' They burst into applause. I still remember—it was quite exciting." But the note could hardly suggest the scope of what the Supreme Court had done.

Justice Brennan wrote the Opinion of the Court, and in the first sentence he made clear that he was doing what the modern Court rarely does: taking a fresh look at an entire area of the law. "We are required in this case," he said, "to determine for the first time the extent to which the constitutional protections for speech and press limit a State's power to award damages in a libel action brought by a public official against critics of his official conduct." To those listening as he announced the decision in the courtroom that morning, it had the sense of a great occasion. In the printed volumes of Supreme Court opinions, it still does.

After that opening signal of large intentions, Justice Brennan described the facts of the cases in extended detail. He identified L. B. Sullivan and those whom Sullivan had sued for libel, the four Alabama ministers and "the New York Times Company, a New York corporation which publishes the New York Times, a daily newspaper." (The opinion was entitled *New York Times Co. v. Sullivan*, but a footnote said it also covered the companion case, *Abernathy et al. v. Sullivan*.) Justice Brennan described the advertisement, "Heed Their Rising Voices," and attached a full-sized reproduction of it to the opinion as an appendix, folded up to fit in the bound volumes. The opinion quoted the portions of the ad, in its third and sixth paragraphs, that Sullivan complained of. It stated his theory that he was implicated by the word "police" and the mention of arrests, and hence that the advertisement accused him of intimidating Dr. King, bombing his home and charging him with perjury.

Then, in a dry tone, Justice Brennan recited the mistakes in the advertisement. "It is uncontroverted that some of the statements contained in the two paragraphs were not accurate descriptions of events which occurred in Montgomery," he said. "Although Negro students staged a demonstration on the State Capitol steps, they sang the National Anthem and not 'My Country, 'Tis of Thee.' Although nine students were expelled by the State Board of Education, this was not for leading the demonstration at the Capitol, but for demanding service at a lunch counter in the Montgomery County Courthouse on another day. . . . The campus dining hall was not padlocked on any occasion. . . . Although the police were deployed near the campus in large numbers on three occasions, they did not at any time 'ring' the campus. . . . Dr. King had not been arrested seven times, but only four, . . ."

The trial judge and the Alabama Supreme Court had held, the opinion said, that these mistakes barred the *Times* and the ministers from offering a defense of truth to the libel charge. Under Alabama law, it was their burden to show that libelous statements were true "in all their particulars." Damages were presumed, and the jury could award them in any amount. The award here was not excessive, the Alabama Supreme Court had said, because the jury could infer "malice" from such things as the *Times*'s failure to retract for Sullivan while doing so for Governor Patterson, and its "irresponsibility" in printing the advertisement when it had articles in its files "which would have demonstrated the falsity" of the ad. Finally, and significantly, Justice Brennan noted the Alabama Supreme Court's ruling that the jury could find that the advertisement was "of and concerning" Sullivan because criticism of any governmental body such as the police "is usually attached to the official in complete control of the body."

After describing what had happened in Alabama, Justice Brennan said: "We reverse the judgment. We hold that the rule of law applied by the Alabama courts is constitutionally deficient for failure to provide the safeguards for freedom of speech and of the press that are required by the First and Fourteenth Amendments in a libel action brought by a public official against critics of his official conduct." This bare statement of the result was followed by twenty-eight explanatory pages: a fascinating tour through history and the meaning of the First Amendment.

(In a footnote, Justice Brennan disposed of all the legal issues other than the First Amendment claims. "We do not decide" some of the other questions presented, he said, among them the contention of the ministers that they were denied the equal protection of the laws "by racial segregation and racial bias in the courtroom." But the footnote rejected the *Times*'s claim that the Alabama courts had improperly asserted jurisdiction over it. That argument, Justice Brennan said, "is foreclosed from our review by the ruling of the Alabama courts that The Times . . . waived its jurisdictional objection; we cannot say that this ruling lacks 'fair or substantial support' in prior Alabama decisions." This brusque rejection of the jurisdictional claim disappointed the lawyers who had worked on it for the *Times*, including Doris Wechsler; but it was a fleeting disappointment, given the rest of the opinion.)

The legal argument for Sullivan, Justice Brennan said, relied "on statements of this Court to the effect that the Constitution does not protect libelous publications." A footnote listed seven earlier cases in which such statements were made, going back to *Near v. Minnesota*. But "none of the cases sustained the use of libel laws to impose sanctions upon expression critical of the official conduct of public officials," the opinion said. It discussed the *Beauharnais* case in particular. Beauharnais was punished for circulating a leaflet that was found not only defamatory of a racial group but "liable to cause violence and disorder." Moreover, even in sustaining that group libel law, Justice Brennan said, the Court "was careful to note that it 'retains and exercises authority to nullify action which encroaches on freedom of utterance under the guise of punishing libel.' "

Justice Brennan concluded: "In deciding the question now, we are compelled by neither precedent nor policy to give any more weight to the epithet 'libel' than we have to other 'mere labels' of state law. Like insurrection, contempt, advocacy of unlawful acts, breach of the peace, obscenity, solicitation of legal business and the various other formulae for the repression of expression that have been challenged in this Court, libel can claim no talismanic immunity from constitutional limitations. It must be measured by standards that satisfy the First Amendment."

To each of those "labels" Justice Brennan attached a footnote citing a case in which the Supreme Court had looked past the label in order to apply the First Amendment. To cover "insurrection," for example, there was the decision reversing Georgia's conviction of Angelo Herndon, the

Communist organizer. In this way Justice Brennan disposed of the obstacle that had once seemed so formidable to *Times* lawyers—the historic assumption that libel was outside the protection of the First Amendment. He did so by the analysis suggested in the *Times* brief.

Throughout the Brennan opinion there were threads from the briefs and oral argument: ideas, cases, phrases. The opinion started from the premise argued by Wechsler, that this advertisement was a form of speech about public issues. And now Justice Brennan dealt with the right of such expression to the protection of the First Amendment, saying that had "long been settled by our decisions." He quoted Chief Justice Hughes in *Stromberg v. California:*— "The maintenance of the opportunity for free political discussion to the end that government may be responsive to the will of the people and that changes may be made by lawful means, an opportunity essential to the security of the Republic, is a fundamental principle of our constitutional system." He quoted Justice Black in *Bridges v. California* on the "prized American privilege to speak one's mind, although not always with perfect good taste, on all public institutions." He quoted Judge Hand. And he quoted at length from the Brandeis opinion in *Whitney v. California*, which he called the "classic formulation."

From all those precedents Justice Brennan drew his conclusion:

> Thus we consider this case against the background of a profound national commitment to the principle that debate on public issues should be uninhibited, robust, and wide-open, and that it may well include vehement, caustic, and sometimes unpleasantly sharp attacks on government and public officials. . . . The present advertisement, as an expression of grievance and protest on one of the major public issues of our time, would seem clearly to qualify for the constitutional protection.

Justice Brennan's characterization of American freedom—the commitment to uninhibited, even caustic debate—turned out to be the most frequently quoted passage of the opinion in *New York Times v. Sullivan*. But it was not enough, alone, to win the case for the *Times*. There was still the question, Justice Brennan said, whether the advertisement forfeited constitutional protection because, first, it contained some factual statements that were false and, second, it allegedly defamed Sullivan. He dealt with each of those in turn.

"Authoritative interpretations of the First Amendment guarantees," the opinion said, "have consistently refused to recognize an exception for any test of truth—whether administered by judges, juries, or administrative officials—and especially one that puts the burden of proving truth on the speaker." Quoting an opinion of his own in a case voiding a Virginia ban on "solicitation of . . . legal business" by the National Association for the Advancement of Colored People, Justice Brennan said the constitutional protection "does not turn upon 'the truth, popularity, or social utility of the ideas and beliefs which are offered.' " He cited Madison's statement in his Report on the Virginia Resolutions: "Some degree of abuse is inseparable from the proper use of every thing; and in no instance is this more true than in that of the press." He quoted the passage from Justice Roberts's opinion in *Cantwell v. Connecticut* that Wechsler had used in his brief, ending with the moving statement that speakers may use vilification and false statement, but that "the people have ordained in the light of history that . . . these liberties are, in the long view, essential to enlightened opinion and right conduct on the part of citizens of a democracy." On this point, Justice Brennan's conclusion was that "erroneous statement is inevitable in free debate, and that it must be protected if the freedoms of expression are to have the 'breathing space' that they 'need . . . to survive.' " The quoted words were from his N.A.A.C.P. opinion.

On the next question, whether defamatory words take criticism of officials outside the protected category, the opinion said: "Injury to official reputation affords no more warrant for repressing speech that would otherwise be free than does factual error." In the *Bridges* case, the Court had held that "concern for the dignity and reputation of the courts does not justify the punishment as criminal contempt of criticism of the judge or his decision." Quoting the same phrase that Wechsler had used from a subsequent contempt case, Brennan added, "If judges are to be treated as 'men of fortitude, able to thrive in a hardy climate,' surely the same must be true of other government officials, such as elected city commissioners."

Now Brennan combined these themes with history: the history of the Sedition Act. "If neither factual error nor defamatory content suffices to remove the constitutional shield from criticism of official conduct, the combination of the two is no less inadequate. This is the lesson to be drawn from the great controversy over the Sedition Act of 1798, which first crystallized a national awareness of the central meaning of the First Amendment."

The opinion described the Sedition Act and the opposition it aroused, including that of Jefferson and Madison. It quoted the telling passage in the Virginia Resolutions protesting that the act "ought to produce universal alarm, because it is levelled against the right of freely examining public characters and measures, and of free communication among the people thereon, which has ever been justly deemed the only effectual guardian of every other right." Then, over two pages, it gave Madison's views. The American system was "altogether different" from the British because "the people, not the government, possess the absolute sovereignty." Or as Madison had said earlier in the House, "the censorial power is in the people over the Government, and not in the Government over the people." Madison's Report attacking the Sedition Act, Brennan said, showed that in his view "free public discussion of the stewardship of public officials was . . . a fundamental principle of the American form of government." And now Justice Brennan and the Court decided that the First Amendment had to be read as Madison read it.

"Although the Sedition Act was never tested in this Court," Justice Brennan said, "the attack upon its validity has carried the day in the court of history." Congress had repaid fines imposed on those convicted under the act, he said, citing the 1840 statute that repaid the heirs of Matthew Lyon. Jefferson had pardoned all those convicted, saying (in his letter to Abigail Adams) that he considered the Sedition law "a nullity, as absolute and palpable as if Congress had ordered us to fall down and worship a golden image." Justice Holmes, joined by Justice Brandeis in his *Abrams* dissent, had assumed the invalidity of seditious libel law under the First Amendment. Chafee and other scholars had said the same thing.

In that passage, Justice Brennan did something quite extraordinary: He held unconstitutional an act of Congress that had expired one hundred and sixty-three years before. He put the imprimatur of the Supreme Court—of the Constitution—on the arguments not only of Jefferson and Madison but of Gallatin and Nicholas and all the other Republicans who had resisted the Sedition Act. How little could they have expected that the drama of their resistance would be played out again, six generations later, in a constitutional decision of the Supreme Court.

The opinion rejected Nachman's argument that, as Justice Brennan put it, "the constitutional limitations implicit in the history of the Sedition Act apply only to Congress and not to the States." It was true that the First Amendment originally applied only to federal action, and that Jefferson in his letter to Abigail Adams said that the states retained power to "controul the freedom of the press" while Congress had none. "But this distinction was eliminated with the adoption of the Fourteenth Amendment and the application to the States of the First Amendment's restrictions," Justice Brennan said. He cited *Gitlow v. New York*, which first applied the speech and press clauses to state action, and other cases.

There remained the question of how the constitutional flaws of the Sedition Act affected ordinary civil libel law. Justice Brennan's answer was that the latter could be just as chilling to freedom of expression if used as Alabama had used it. "The fear of damage awards under a rule such as that invoked by the Alabama courts here," he said, "may be markedly more inhibiting than the fear of prosecution under a criminal statute." The damages awarded in this case were one hundred times the maximum fine under the Sedition Act of 1798, and one thousand times the maximum under Alabama's criminal libel law. Civil suits did not have the procedural protections of the criminal law, such as the rule against double jeopardy, so this was not the only judgment the *Times* and the ministers might face over the advertisement. A footnote said that four other suits had been filed, one already tried with a jury award of $500,000, the other three claiming a further $2 million. "Whether or not a newspaper can survive a succession of such judgments," Justice Brennan said, "the pall of fear and timidity imposed upon those who would give voice to public criticism is an atmosphere in which the First Amendment freedoms cannot survive."

Nor was the Alabama libel law saved by its allowance of the defense of truth, Justice Brennan said. Some allowance for error was as important here as the "requirement of guilty knowledge" demanded by the Court in *Smith v. California*, the case mentioned in *The Washington Post's* brief, in which a bookseller had been prosecuted for possessing an obscene book. That opinion was by Justice Brennan too, and it said that allowing the conviction of booksellers for books of which they had no knowledge would lead them to practice "self-censorship." "A rule compelling the critic of official conduct to guarantee the truth of all his factual assertions—and to do so on pain of libel judgments virtually unlimited in amount—leads to a comparable 'self-censorship.' Allowance of the defense of truth, with the burden of proving it on the defendant, does not mean that only false speech is deterred. . . . Would-be critics of official conduct may be deterred from voicing their criticism, even though it is believed to be true and even though it is in fact true, because of doubt whether it can be proved in court or fear of the expense of having to do so." The last comment echoed what John Nicholas had said in the House of Representatives in 1798 as he opposed the Sedition Bill; printers "would be afraid of publishing the truth, as, though true, it might not always be in their power to establish the truth to the satisfaction of a court."

Up to this point, Justice Brennan's opinion seemed to be heading toward an absolute immunity for criticism of officials, however false the criticism and however harsh. That was Madison's position, as Wechsler had urged at the oral argument: that the Sedition Act was palpably unconstitutional even though it allowed truth as a defense.

But suddenly Justice Brennan turned away from the absolute. He said that what was needed was immunity from libel suits for "erroneous statements honestly made." He laid down this formula: "The constitutional guarantees require, we think, a Federal rule that prohibits a public official from recovering damages for a defamatory falsehood relating to his official conduct unless he proves that the statement was made with 'actual malice'—that is, with knowledge that it was false or with reckless disregard of whether it was false or not."

For libel, this was the crux—the rule of the *Sullivan* case, as lawyers call it. The phrase "actual malice" led to some early and indeed persisting misconceptions. The rule laid down by the opinion had nothing to do with "malice" in the ordinary dictionary sense, meaning ill will. "Actual malice" was defined in the latter part of Justice Brennan's statement as knowing or reckless falsehood. The opinion noted that some state courts had followed a similar approach, allowing a privilege for criticism of public officials when made in good faith, even though it turned out to be untrue. To make his point, Justice Brennan quoted from *Coleman v. MacLennan*, the leading Kansas case.

Now the opinion adopted another argument made by Wechsler, the one based on the case of *Barr v. Matteo*, which made officials immune from libel suits for what they said. The reason for that privilege, Justice Brennan said, was that the threat of lawsuits would otherwise inhibit officials from fearless performance of their duties. "Analogous considerations support the privilege for the citizen-critic of government. It is as much his duty to criticize as it is the official's duty to administer." These two sentences were a powerful statement of the American constitutional premise. They adopted Madison's view that in the United States the citizen is sovereign. They followed Justice Brandeis in holding ancient Athens up as the model of good citizenship. Justice Brennan cited the Brandeis opinion in *Whitney v. California*, at the point where Brandeis said: "Those who won our independence believed . . . that public discussion is a political duty. . . ."

There the opinion paused, in a sense—and then went on to a further remarkable section. Having established fundamental new rules to limit libel actions against critics of official conduct, Justice Brennan now proceeded to examine the evidence in the Sullivan trial to see whether it met these new tests. This was highly unusual; ordinarily the Supreme Court sends a case back to a state court or lower federal court on reversing one of their judgments, and leaves it to them to apply the rules now spelled out. Why the exceptional course in this case? Justice Brennan explained:

Since respondent [Sullivan] may seek a new trial, we deem that considerations of effective judicial administration require us to review the evidence in the present record to determine whether it could constitutionally support a judgment for respondent. The Court's duty is not limited to the elaboration of constitutional principles; we must also in proper cases review the evidence to make certain that those principles have been constitutionally applied. This is such a case. . . . We must "make an independent examination of the whole record" [quoting another First Amendment case] so as to assure ourselves that the judgment does not constitute a forbidden intrusion on the field of free expression.

With this statement, the opinion added another bulwark to the protection of public critics from chilling libel suits: the promise that appellate courts, including the Supreme Court itself, would in appropriate cases review the record themselves to make sure that juries had not gone astray in imposing damages. Applying the new constitutional standards, Justice Brennan said, "We consider that the proof presented to show actual malice lacks the convincing clarity which the constitutional standard demands." The phrase "convincing clarity" was still another safeguard, for in civil cases it is ordinarily enough for the plaintiff to win if he meets the much lower standard of a preponderance of the evidence.

Why did the evidence in the Montgomery trial fail to show knowing or reckless falsehood? The case of the ministers required "little discussion," Justice Brennan said. "Even assuming that they could constitutionally be found to have authorized the use of their names on the advertisement, there was no evidence whatever that they were aware of any erroneous statements or were in any way reckless in that regard. The judgment against them is thus without constitutional support."

As for the case against the *Times*, the Alabama Supreme Court had found evidence of bad faith in the paper's failure to retract for Sullivan when it did for Governor Patterson. But the *Times* had replied to Sullivan's demand with a good-faith letter asking how he thought the advertisement referred to him, Justice Brennan said, and he had not replied. And the reason given by the *Times* for treating the governor differently, as the embodiment of the state, "was a reasonable one, the good faith of which was not impeached." There was also the Alabama court's point that the paper had published the advertisement without checking its own files to measure the ad's accuracy. But the presence of stories in the files, Justice Brennan said, would not establish that the *Times* "knew" the advertisement was false; the state of mind required for constitutional malice would have to be brought home to the *Times* personnel responsible for publishing the advertisement. In this case *Times* employees had relied on the good reputation of A. Philip Randolph and other signers of the advertisement; at most this showed negligence, not "the recklessness that is required for a finding of actual malice." With that, the opinion did something else important for the press and for interest groups; it made clear that the press does not have an obligation to check the accuracy of the advocacy advertising submitted by all kinds of organizations.

There was one more surprising turn in the opinion. "We also think," Justice Brennan wrote, that "the evidence was constitutionally defective in another respect: it was incapable of supporting the jury's finding that the allegedly libelous statements were made 'of and concerning' respondent." The opinion examined the evidence offered by Sullivan to show that he would be regarded as a target of the advertisement: its mention of police and arrests, and the testimony of six local witnesses that when shown the ad, they connected its critical statements about Southern racial practices with Sullivan. The witnesses based their view, Justice Brennan said, not on any evidence that Sullivan had in fact been involved in the episodes mentioned in the advertisement "but solely on the unsupported assumption that, because of his official position, he must have been." And then the Supreme Court of Alabama had laid down the proposition that criticism of the performance of any official body amounted to an attack on the person in charge of it. "This proposition has disquieting implications for criticism of governmental conduct," Justice Brennan said. "For good reason, 'no court of last resort in this country has ever held, or even suggested, that prosecutions for libel on government have any place in the American system of jurisprudence.'" The quoted words were from the decision of the Illinois Supreme Court in the case of *City of Chicago v. Tribune Co.*, which Wechsler had cited. Commissioner Sullivan's argument, Justice Brennan said, "would sidestep this obstacle by transmuting criticism of government, however impersonal it may seem on its face, into personal criticism, and hence potential libel, of the officials of whom the government is composed. There is no legal alchemy by which a State may thus create the cause of action that would otherwise be denied for a publication which, as [Sullivan] himself said of the advertisement, 'reflects not only on me but on the other Commissioners and the community.'"

Justice Brennan had gone far to protect the *Times* and the four ministers from further legal harassment when the case returned to Alabama. That was plainly his intention in taking the unusual step of examining the evidence and declaring it insufficient, even though he ascribed his course to "considerations of effective judicial administration" in case Sullivan sought a new trial. But Justice Brennan did not accept Wechsler's suggestion that the Supreme Court order the suit dismissed. His opinion ended with the customary formulation: "The judgment of the Supreme Court of Alabama is reversed and the case is remanded to that court for further proceedings not inconsistent with this opinion."

Brennan did not speak for the entire Court. The note that Wechsler got in the classroom was a bit misleading in saying that the decision was unanimous. All nine justices agreed that the Alabama judgment must be reversed, but Justice Brennan was joined by only five others in his Opinion of the Court. Justices Black, Douglas and Goldberg took the view that the First Amendment required an absolute privilege for critics of official conduct, even if their criticism was intentionally false. The line of disagreement was the one intimated at the argument of the case when Justice White tried to establish that any falsehood in the advertisement was unintentional and Justice Black maintained that the jury had the right to find intentional falsehood. There were two opinions taking the broader ground: one by Justice Black, joined by Justice Douglas, the other by Justice Goldberg, also joined by Douglas. Justice Goldberg said that all comments on the official actions of public officials should be privileged. Justice Black came to the same conclusion, but his opinion was more pungent, drawing on his personal awareness of attitudes in Alabama, his native state. Justice Black was widely reviled in Alabama then because of his association with *Brown v. Board of Education* and other decisions against racial segregation; his son, who practiced law in Birmingham, left the state in 1962 because of the antagonism. It was not until after Hugo Black's death that he was recognized in Alabama as one of the greatest figures the state had ever produced.

In his opinion Justice Black addressed himself directly to the racial issue, as Justice Brennan had not. He wrote:

One of the acute and highly emotional issues in this country arises out of efforts of many people, even including some public officials, to continue state-commanded segregation of races in the public schools and other public places, despite our several holdings that such a state practice is forbidden by the Fourteenth Amendment. Montgomery is one of the localities in which widespread hostility to desegregation has been manifested. This hostility has sometimes extended itself to persons who favor desegregation, particularly to so-called "outside agitators," a term which can be made to fit papers like the Times, which is published in New York. The scarcity of testimony to show that Commissioner Sullivan suffered any actual damages at all suggests that these feelings of hostility had at least as much to do with rendition of this half-million-dollar verdict as did an appraisal of damages. Viewed realistically, this record lends support to an inference that instead of being damaged Commissioner Sullivan's political, social, and financial prestige has likely been enhanced by the Times's publication.

No doubt Justice Brennan and those who joined his opinion of the Court were also aware of those realities. But the writer of a concurring or dissenting opinion can always be more personal than a justice who is writing for the Court, and Justice Black spoke of his region with deadly knowledge.

A second $500,000 verdict based on the advertisement had already been awarded to another Montgomery commissioner, Justice Black noted, and "briefs before us show that in Alabama there are now pending eleven libel suits by local and state officials against the Times seeking $5,600,000, and five such suits against the Columbia Broadcasting System seeking $1,700,000. Moreover, this technique for harassing and punishing a free press—now that it has been shown to be possible—is by no means limited to cases with racial overtones; it can be used in other fields where public feelings may make local as well as out-of-state newspapers easy prey for libel verdict seekers."

In his opinions as in his comments from the bench Justice Black had a directness that could be mistaken by the uninformed as a kind of naïveté. His soft Southern accent and homely examples did seem alien to Washington sophistication at times, but he had a powerfully clear sense of realities that was anything but innocent. With his knowledge of Alabama juries, he scoffed at Justice Brennan's doctrine of "actual malice." Even as Brennan carefully defined it, Black said, malice was "an elusive, abstract concept, hard to prove and hard to disprove." He doubted that the verdict would have been any different in Sullivan's trial "whatever the court had charged the jury about 'malice,' 'truth,' 'good motives,' 'justifiable ends' or any other legal formulas which in theory would protect the press." The Constitution, he said, "has dealt with this deadly danger to the press in the only way possible . . . by granting the press an absolute immunity for criticism of the way public officials do their public duty."

Justice Black agreed with Justice Brennan's exposition of the Sedition Act episode, and his conclusion that it was unconstitutional, but for Black this meant that no discussion of government business could be penalized by libel suits. "This Nation, I suspect," he wrote, "can live in peace without libel suits based on public discussions of public affairs and public officials. But I doubt that a country can live in freedom where its people can be made to suffer physically or financially for criticizing their government. . . . An unconditional right to say what one pleases about public affairs is what I consider to be the minimum guarantee of the First Amendment. I regret that the Court has stopped short of this holding indispensable to preserve our free press from destruction."

Reading that opinion, one would have thought that Justice Black was distressed at what the majority of his colleagues had done. But when Justice Black sent a draft of his separate concurring opinion around to the other justices, on February 26, he sent Justice Brennan a handwritten note on the Court's four-by-six-inch memorandum paper. He said: "You know of course that despite my position & what I write I think you are doing a wonderful job in the Times case and however it finally comes out it is bound to be a very long step towards preserving the right to communicate ideas."

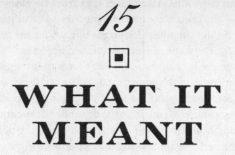

# 15

# WHAT IT MEANT

THE DECISION in *New York Times Co. v. Sullivan* was a striking demonstration of a paradox inherent in the American constitutional system. We live under a written Constitution, and we rely on its unchanging character to give stability to our turbulent society. But the Constitution continues to have meaning and life only because judges apply it in fresh ways to challenges unforeseen by its creators.

Those who drafted and ratified the First Amendment almost certainly did not have civil libel suits in mind. Such private lawsuits presented no threat to the right of citizens to speak and write freely about what Madison called public characters and measures. For nearly one hundred seventy years the law of libel went on in its familiar path, redeeming wounded private reputation. Then Southern officials, juries and judges distorted libel law for a political end, to suppress criticism of the regime of racial segregation. The Supreme Court was forced—"required for the first time," as Justice Brennan put it in the first sentence of his opinion—to consider the relationship of libel to freedom of expression. In doing so, the Court reexamined the premises of the First Amendment, the values of free speech and a free press that the amendment set out to protect.

Justice Brennan's opinion took the libertarian arguments of Brandeis, Holmes and others and wove the threads into the first full statement by the Supreme Court as a whole of an American theory of free speech: the Madisonian theory. The opinion adopted Madison's view that the citizens are sovereign in the United States, and that their freedom to criticize the government is "the central meaning of the First Amendment." It treated free speech as not just an individual right but a political necessity. It held the Sedition Act of 1798 unconstitutional, and approved Justice Holmes's dissenting statement in *Abrams v. United States* that the idea of seditious libel was inconsistent with the First Amendment.

For First Amendment scholars it was a stunning decision. It evoked the views of Alexander Meiklejohn, philosopher and educator, who for many years had argued that the Constitution made the people their own governors—and hence that anything they said in their governing capacity was immune from penalties. Harry Kalven, the scholar who said that no society is free "if it makes seditious libel an offense," found Meiklejohn's influence especially clear in the passage of Justice Brennan's opinion saying that "the citizen-critic of government" needed a privilege like the one officials have, for "it is as much his duty to criticize as it is the official's duty to administer." Kalven said that statement "almost literally incorporated Alexander Meiklejohn's thesis that in a democracy the citizen as ruler is our most important public official." Some time after the *Sullivan* decision was announced, Kalven talked with Meiklejohn, who was then ninety-two years old, and asked him what he thought about it. Meiklejohn replied, "It is an occasion for dancing in the streets."

But Justice Brennan and the majority of the Court did not go as far as Meiklejohn, and Madison, would probably have favored. They did not provide absolute immunity for any speech that relates to the business of governing. Instead they gave immunity to all but knowing or reckless falsehood. And that rule was really a way of balancing the interest of free expression with another interest, reputation, that also has weight in our system of values. Reputation is an aspect of our sense of self; to injure it is almost to violate one's physical integrity. People feel so strongly about reputation that libel and slander once were met by challenges to a duel, or by less gentlemanly assaults. Lawsuits for damages took the place of such attacks. An especially thoughtful federal judge, Harold Leventhal, wrote in 1966: "The rule that permits satisfaction of the deep-seated need for vindication of honor is not a mere historic relic, but promotes the law's civilizing function of providing an acceptable substitute for violence in the settlement of disputes."

In a case that followed closely on *Sullivan, Garrison v. Louisiana,* Justice Brennan indicated why he had struck the balance as he had. Jim Garrison, district attorney of Orleans Parish, Louisiana, charged that local judges were subject to "racketeer influences." He was prosecuted for criminal libel and convicted. The Supreme Court reversed the conviction, holding that statements about public officials may not be "the subject of either civil or criminal sanctions" unless made with knowing or reckless falsity, and deciding that the test had not been met in Garrison's case. "Speech concerning public affairs is more than self-expression," Justice Brennan wrote for the Court; "it is the essence of self-government." (The next year, 1965, Justice Brennan, delivering the annual Meiklejohn Lecture at Brown University, pointed to that sentence and said "doubtless some of you may think" it echoed Meiklejohn.) But then why should "speech concerning public affairs" be punishable if it is knowingly or recklessly false? After all, the victim of a falsehood feels the pain whether it was deliberate or not. Justice Brennan explained:

> At the time the First Amendment was adopted, as today, there were those unscrupulous enough and skillful enough to use the deliberate or reckless falsehood as an effective political tool to unseat the public servant or even topple an administration. . . . That speech is used as a tool for political ends does not automatically bring it under the protective mantle of the Constitution. For the use of the known lie as a tool is at once at odds with the premises of democratic government and with the orderly manner in which economic, social or political change is to be effected. Calculated falsehood falls into that class of utterances which "are no essential part of any exposition of ideas, and are of such slight social value as a step to truth that any benefit that may be derived from them is clearly outweighed by the social interest in order and morality."

We may wonder whether Justice Brennan's concern about the "unscrupulous" using lies even to "topple an administration" had been aroused by the recent phenomenon of Senator Joseph McCarthy.

The manner of the *Sullivan* opinion was as striking as its substance. It was written in the grand style, reordering a whole area of the law as few modern Supreme Court opinions do—or can, really. On most subjects generations of decisions confront the Court, and respect for precedent is a normal instinct in judges. Respect is commanded by what is called the doctrine of *stare decisis*, which means: let the decision stand. The reason is that even if an earlier decision was faulty, society has come to rely on it, and overruling it years later would upset too many expectations. Justice Brandeis put it, "In most matters it is more important that the applicable rule of law be settled than that it be settled right." We can readily understand this in matters of finance and business, where contracts have been made in reliance on rules of law and it would seem unfair to change the rules. But when it comes to constitutional law, the Supreme Court has not followed the doctrine of *stare decisis* strictly. "The Court bows to the lessons of experience and the force of better reasoning," Brandeis said; because constitutional decisions cannot be corrected by legislation, the Court is readier to make such corrections itself. But reexamining a whole area of the law is still a rare event in the Supreme Court. Individual justices may do so, for it is easier to be bold in dissent, but opinions of the Court do not often display a pioneering spirit.

The opinion in *Times v. Sullivan* owed much, of course, to the analytical power of Herbert Wechsler. He addressed history and precedent in a way that made it seem natural and right for the Supreme Court to take the bold steps it did. His brief had turned out to be what he hoped, "a document that a Supreme Court justice can use in writing the opinion favorable to the briefer." Much of the opinion's structure was taken from the brief, including the emphasis on the Sedition Act and the finding that the controversy over it "crystallized a national awareness of the central meaning of the First Amendment." To recognize this is not to diminish Justice Brennan's achievement in building a majority on the Court to rethink an important area of the law, and holding that majority together behind an opinion with distinctive literary and historical qualities: an opinion so rich in its observations on freedom of expression and libel that on repeated readings one keeps discovering new meanings.

"It was a majestic opinion," Floyd Abrams, a leading First Amendment lawyer, said at a twentieth-anniversary discussion of *New York Times Co. v. Sullivan* in 1984. "It had a command of American history that is rare in a judicial opinion. It reminded us of how young we are as a country."

For libel law it was a revolutionary decision. In 1931, in *Near v. Minnesota*, the Supreme Court had broken with the British practice by deciding that the First Amendment usually did not allow injunctions against publication. In 1941, in *Bridges v. California*, it abandoned the British tradition of punishing critical comment on the courts as contempt. Now, in 1964, it completed the First Amendment revolution from Britain. The Court held that libel proceedings were subject to the First Amendment whenever they involved public officials. And in those cases the common law of libel, which in most states was still largely the law inherited from Britain, would have to be drastically changed. Justice Brennan spelled out the changes required to meet the demands of the First Amendment.

A first and principal result of the *Sullivan* decision was to shift the burden of proof in libel cases. A second was to introduce an element of what lawyers call "fault." In all other tort law a plaintiff claiming damages for injury has to show that the defendant has done something wrong and done so with a degree of fault on his part. In an automobile accident case, for example, the plaintiff cannot win damages from the defendant just because their cars were in a collision, but has to show that the collision was caused by the defendant's negligence—his fault. In English libel law, and until 1964 the libel law of most American states, the plaintiff was entitled to damages if a false and damaging statement was made about him, even though the defendant published the falsehood innocently. The defendant could defeat a libel action only by bearing the burden of proving a defamatory statement true. "I thought that was uncivilized law," Wechsler said later, "and against the usual rule in torts requiring a plaintiff to show fault on the defendant's part. In libel, in the majority of states, there was no escape by requiring the plaintiff to prove bad intent. That set of strict concepts grew up in the eighteenth-century effort to maintain royal immunity. Hence the sharp Madisonian reaction against the Sedition Act."

The *Sullivan* rule changed both these aspects of the common law of libel. Now the plaintiff had to show that the defendant had published a falsehood with a high degree of fault—namely knowingly or recklessly. It necessarily followed that the plaintiff first had to show that there was something false in the publication, so the burden shifted to him. This can make all the difference in the result of libel suits. In Britain, newspapers that go to court to defend against a libel suit instead of settling lose almost every time, and a major reason is that they have the burden of proving that the challenged story is true.

The Court also held that freedom requires an allowance for some falsity, some erroneous statements. Giving truth protection was not enough, it said, because fear of getting something wrong might lead citizen-critics of government to hold back. To prevent self-censorship there has to be "breathing room" for error. Hence the allowance for honest mistakes. Here again, British law is quite different. It does not require officials to show deliberate falsehood, or indeed any kind of fault, in order to recover libel damages for a published misstatement; any mistake, however innocent, justifies a judgment for the plaintiff if it materially injures his or her reputation. And British politicians do not hesitate to sue. While he was Prime Minister in the 1960s, Harold Wilson sued for libel over a postcard printed by a pop group, and won.

Another significant result of the *Sullivan* decision was to make clear that the First Amendment protects statements of fact as well as doctrines or political opinions. This may seem obvious, but historically it was not. The great tests of free speech beginning with World War I were about the right to advocate beliefs: socialism, pacifism and the like. The anarchists and socialists involved in the 1919 case of *Abrams v. United States* were prosecuted for pamphlets that opposed President Wilson's intervention against the Bolshevik government in Russia on ideological grounds. Holmes's dissent on their behalf warned against "attempts to check the expression of *opinions* that we loathe and believe to be fraught with death" (emphasis added). In the *Schwimmer* case in 1928 no facts were at issue; Rosika Schwimmer was denied the right to become a citizen because she was a pacifist. Dissenting, Holmes demanded "freedom for the thought that we hate." In 1951 it was the ideology of the Communist party that led to its leaders' imprisonment. But L. B. Sullivan's complaint was that the advertisement in the *Times* had got the *facts* wrong, and the Supreme Court held that honest errors of fact did not lose the First Amendment's protection for criticism of public officials.

This aspect of the decision proved to have major importance for American journalism. Beginning in the late 1960s, the press increasingly tried to look behind the self-serving statements of government officials about their policies and accomplishments. The prime example was coverage of the Vietnam war. Through the earlier years of the Cold War, Washington reporters from the major newspapers, magazines and broadcasting services wrote about national security issues within boundaries generally set by the government. They deferred to officials, believing in their good faith and superior knowledge. But in the Vietnam war, the press discovered that political and military leaders were not necessarily well informed or truthful, and journalists began publishing unauthorized versions of the facts. "The naturally symbiotic relationship between politicians and the press," as one study put it, was frayed. Seymour Hersh challenged official truth by writing about the Mylai massacre. Bob Woodward and Carl Bernstein peeled away layers of official deceit about Watergate in their stories for *The Washington Post*. The rise of such investigative journalism would not have been possible if the old law of libel had still shielded officials from criticism. Reporters and editors would have held back from many stories if critical articles had been sure of escaping libel suits only when they were "absolutely confirmable in every detail," as *The Washington Post*'s *amicus* brief in the *Sullivan* case had warned.

The allowance of room for honest mistakes of fact encouraged the press, in particular, to challenge official truth on two subjects so hidden by government secrecy, Vietnam and Watergate, that no unauthorized story could ever have been "absolutely confirmable." In the Pentagon Papers case in 1971, the federal judge who handled the trial in New York, Murray Gurfein, understood the importance of facts. The government had not tried to stifle editorial opinion, he said. But "it is not merely the opinion of the editorial writer or of the columnist which is protected by the First Amendment. It is the free flow of information so that the public will be informed about the Government and its actions."

The protection given by the *Sullivan* decision for honest mistakes of fact was buttressed by two further elements in the opinion. First, Justice Brennan said the evidence that someone published a statement with knowledge of its falsity or in reckless disregard of the truth must have "convincing clarity." This is a far higher standard than the usual "preponderance of the evidence" required for someone to win a civil case. He also said that if a trial jury found knowing or reckless falsehood and awarded damages to a libel plaintiff, appellate courts would review the facts to make sure that the high standard of proof had been met. This was most unusual. Ordinarily, in civil cases, factual findings by a trial judge or jury are not reexamined by higher courts on appeal. The usual function of the appellate court is to see whether the law has been correctly stated. Justice Brennan's promise of close appellate scrutiny no doubt reflected the context of the *Sullivan* case; he and the Court were concerned that Southern juries and judges would decide in favor of white officials in libel suits whatever the constitutional test was, as Justice Black had warned they would. Former Attorney General Rogers, who argued the case for the Alabama ministers, said at the twentieth-anniversary seminar: "The Court took pains to make sure the actual malice test was not then used further to harass these defendants." But the promise that higher courts would review factual findings to assure observance of the constitutional rule was not limited to the racial context; in later years the Supreme Court maintained the promise in cases far removed from the South and the racial issue.

The opinion intimated a still further constitutional protection. Toward the end, in discussing the evidence produced at the trial, Justice Brennan said the Alabama courts had found falsehood in the advertisement's statements that Dr. King had been arrested seven times, when the correct figure was four, and that the police "ringed" the state college campus when they had merely been deployed near it. Then Justice Brennan said: "The ruling that these discrepancies between what was true and what was asserted were sufficient to injure [Sullivan's] reputation may itself raise constitutional problems, but we need not consider them here." He seemed to be suggesting that, constitutionally, falsities must be substantial enough to injure a libel plaintiff. That is, an insignificant untruth could not justify a libel suit.

The Court also recognized that published statements may be entitled to constitutional protection even though they appear in advertisements. Sullivan's lawyers had argued that the "speech" here was not protected by the First Amendment because it was in a "commercial" advertisement for which the *Times* was paid. But the ad, Justice Brennan said, "communicated information, expressed opinion, recited grievances . . . on behalf of a movement whose existence and objectives are matters of the highest public interest and concern." That the *Times* was paid for the ad, he said, "is as immaterial in this connection as is the fact that newspapers and books are sold. . . . Any other conclusion would discourage newspapers from carrying 'editorial advertisements' of this type, and so might shut off an important outlet for the promulgation of information and ideas by persons who do not themselves have access to publishing facilities—who wish to exercise their freedom of speech even though they are not members of the press." Buttressing that protection for editorial advertisements was the opinion's statement that a newspaper cannot be found culpable of knowing or reckless falsification if its advertising department failed to check statements in the ad copy against news files.

Finally, there was Justice Brennan's important statement that in American law there is no such thing as "libel on government," and that impersonal criticism of government cannot be converted by "legal alchemy" into "libel of the officials of whom government is composed." On this basis, Justice Brennan examined the evidence offered by Sullivan to show that he was a target of the advertisement, and found it "constitutionally defective." The point that no legal alchemy can convert impersonal criticism into libel of officials may seem self-evident, but it was not so in 1964, and still is not in countries with traditions less protective of free speech.

This very issue was raised in South Africa before the fall of the apartheid system. Two men, one white and one black, together committed a murder. They were both convicted and sentenced to death. The white man was reprieved, but the black was hanged. A newspaper article quoted a professor as calling the case an example of racial bias in capital punishment. The article named no names; but the Minister of Justice, whose duties include recommending commutations of sentence, sued for libel, complaining that the article portrayed him as a racist. Counsel for the newspaper referred the court to the American case of *New York Times Co. v. Sullivan* and quoted the part of Justice Brennan's opinion about "libel on government," but the Appellate Division of the South African Supreme Court upheld the Minister's right to sue.

In all these ways the decision in *Times v. Sullivan* transformed American libel law. In cases involving public officials as plaintiffs, lawyers would now have to look to supervening federal law, the law of the First Amendment. And before long the Supreme Court would extend the doctrine of the *Sullivan* case so that nearly all libel suits would be subject, one way or another, to constitutional rules.

For the parties in the *Sullivan* case itself, the decision turned out to be the end of the road. Contrary to the fears expressed by Justice Black and others, Sullivan's lawyers did not seek a new trial in the hope of producing more evidence of actual malice or of a connection between the advertisement and Sullivan. They abandoned the lawsuit after making one more move in the Supreme Court. The Court routinely imposes on the losing side the cost of printing and certain modest fees. In this case the total sum was about thirteen thousand dollars. Sullivan asked the Supreme Court to divide those costs between him and the *Times*, but the Court denied the motion. The other libel actions based on the advertisement soon fell away, too. And in time other courts dismissed the suits against the *Times* over the Harrison Salisbury stories on Birmingham.

Roland Nachman, Sullivan's principal lawyer, was philosophical when he talked about the case in later years. "At the time I thought the law and the facts were with us," he said, "but the surrounding circumstances made it a hard case. There were a great many plaintiffs who came after us. That was one of the problems we had, to put it mildly." The number of Southern libel suits against the *Times* and other press organizations had certainly sent a signal to the Supreme Court; so had the amount of the damages awarded to Sullivan, $500,000, and the same amount awarded in the next libel trial over the advertisement.

Commentators have wondered whether the *Sullivan* case would ever have reached the Supreme Court, and the First Amendment been so strikingly reinterpreted, if Commissioner Sullivan had been more modest in his claim for damages. Would the case then have had the urgency that led the Supreme Court to review it? Would the *Times* have carried it beyond the Alabama courts? At the twentieth-anniversary discussion of the decision, T. Eric Embry, who represented the *Times* at the trial, kidded Nachman about the damage claim. "Roland was a great help in getting to the Supreme Court," he said, "by asking for five hundred thousand dollars. If he'd asked for fifty thousand dollars, we'd never have got there."

Nachman replied, "I didn't want to sue for more than one hundred thousand dollars, but the lawyer who'd brought me into the case wanted one million dollars, so we compromised on five hundred thousand dollars."

Nachman was surprised when the *Times* first made a First Amendment argument, at the beginning of the lawsuit. "I didn't conceive that it would be a winning argument," he said years later. "It never entered my head that the case would come out the way it did." But he added: "Extrinsic circumstances over which the lawyers in the case had no control—including the amount of the verdict, the unfortunate social and political climate and the proliferation of contemporaneous lawsuits brought by others—made this a very hard case for the plaintiff."

For the four ministers whose names had been used in the advertisement without their knowledge, the Supreme Court decision ended four years of legal torment in lives already beset by jailings and other pressures in the civil rights struggle. The ministers had been forced to spend much time raising money for their defense in the libel case. Three of them, Ralph Abernathy, Joseph E. Lowery and Fred L. Shuttlesworth, had had their cars seized and sold at auction by Alabama authorities to help satisfy the libel judgment if it was eventually upheld; and a piece of real estate owned by Abernathy had been seized and sold for $4,350. In his masterly book on Dr. King and his times, *Parting the Waters*, Taylor Branch said some of the ministers in fact had substantial other property that they were afraid would be taken. Fear of further harassment in the lawsuit was a factor in Shuttlesworth's decision in 1961 to leave Alabama for a ministry in Cincinnati. But after the Supreme Court decision the state had to disgorge the seized assets.

Joseph Lowery told the story years afterward. "They sold my car at auction for eight hundred dollars," he said. "It was a 1958 Chrysler. But one of the members of my church in Mobile bought it and then sold it back to my wife for a dollar. In the case of the other two cars, they were just sold and gone. But Abernathy and Shuttlesworth got new cars; their people rallied around and bought them new cars.

"When the Supreme Court vindicated us, the state had to return the money that it got for the cars. I offered it back to the member who'd helped me, but he wouldn't take it. The money went into the movement. Abernathy's real estate in Marengo County was sold, but it was really held in a state of suspense. They couldn't dispose of it because it was tied up among ten or twelve family members. After the Supreme Court decision the property was returned to the family. My sister and I had some property up in north Alabama, but they didn't discover that. Because I was living in Mobile, they weren't smart enough to look in north Alabama, where I grew up."

Fred Shuttlesworth won a double victory on the day the libel case was decided, March 9, 1964. For on the same day the Supreme Court reversed his criminal conviction in another case. It was a case that demonstrated the racial atmosphere in Alabama and how it tainted justice in the state courts. It arose from the Freedom Rides. On May 17, 1961, a group of eighteen people from the civil rights movement went to the Greyhound Terminal in Birmingham to take a bus to Montgomery. Like other Freedom Riders, they were protesting segregation in bus terminals. But before they could board the bus, Birmingham police took the eighteen into what the police called "protective custody." Shuttlesworth, who was there watching, came up and said he should be arrested if they were; for a few moments he stood between the police chief and the Freedom Riders. For doing that—nothing more—he was convicted of violating a Birmingham ordinance against interfering with the police and was sentenced to one hundred eighty days in jail. He appealed to the Alabama Court of Appeals, which did not find a violation of the city ordinance but upheld the conviction and sentence anyway because, it said, Shuttlesworth "could have been clearly convicted" of simple assault. When Shuttlesworth sought review in the Alabama Supreme Court, that court dismissed his petition because it had been filed on paper smaller than the size specified in the court's rules.

When a state court rejects an appeal because its rules of procedure have not been followed, that ordinarily bars review in the U.S. Supreme Court. But in a 1955 decision the Supreme Court said there could be no such bar to its considering a case if the state court had invoked a procedural rule that it had waived in other instances—as the Alabama Supreme Court had waived its rule on paper size. In reversing Shuttlesworth's conviction, the Supreme Court cited that 1955 case and one other, a 1948 decision that an appellate court may not uphold a person's conviction on a ground other than the one on which he was tried. The Supreme Court decided the Shuttlesworth case just eleven days after hearing argument on it, in a three-line unsigned opinion simply citing these two earlier decisions. The swiftness and curtness of the decision made plain what the Court thought about the proceedings against Fred Shuttlesworth.

Orvil E. Dryfoos, *The New York Times* publisher who decided to take the case on to the Supreme Court and make the First Amendment argument, did not live to see the outcome. He died of a heart ailment on May 25, 1963. His successor, Arthur Ochs Sulzberger, sent telegrams to Eric Embry and Herbert Wechsler when the decision came down. The message to Wechsler read: "Warmest congratulations for the great contribution that you made in bringing about the significant decision handed down by the United States Supreme Court today that is of such fundamental importance not only for The Times but for all newspapers and other news media. We were proud to have you argue the case on The Times's behalf and are proud of the result that you achieved."

# 16

■

# INSIDE
# THE COURT

I<small>T WAS</small> just two months and three days from the argument of *New York Times Co. v. Sullivan* to the decision. This was a short time to decide an important case, and to do so in a way that broke so much new ground. Justice Brennan had had to win the agreement of colleagues with very different legal philosophies. It was especially noteworthy—remarkable, some observers thought—that his opinion was joined without qualification by Justice Harlan, whose concern for state powers in our federal system might have been expected to make him wary of imposing national constitutional rules on the law of libel. But there was no sign of discord among the six who joined the opinion of the Court. It appeared that Justice Brennan's account of history and legal analysis had readily persuaded a majority to join him.

The facts were otherwise. Justice Brennan had great difficulty marshaling a majority and holding it. He wrote eight different drafts of his opinion. Until the last moment there was a real possibility, even a probability, that it would not command a majority. Not until the evening of March 8, the night before Justice Brennan announced the decision, did Justice Harlan agree to join him without reservations.

What happened between the argument and the decision emerges in Justice Brennan's papers. His Court files—drafts of opinions, comments received from other justices and so on—are in the manuscript division of the Library of Congress. There is another important source. During

Justice Brennan's thirty-four years on the Court, his law clerks each term wrote accounts of the process of decision in each case in which he was significantly involved—as the writer of the Court's opinion or a dissent, for example. The report on the *Sullivan* case was written by Stephen R. Barnett, one of his two law clerks at the time, later a professor of law at the University of California, Berkeley. His account tells the story in considerable detail. By following the changes from draft to draft one gets a rare insight into the process of opinion writing on the Supreme Court. Ideas were added and subtracted, and language made more compelling, as Justice Brennan reordered his own thoughts and sought to gather a majority.

The justices' practice was and is to discuss argued cases in their conference at the end of each week of argument. *Times v. Sullivan* was discussed on January 10, 1964. In his description of the decisional process, Barnett wrote: "At the oral argument . . . Professor Wechsler, for The Times, had based his argument for reversal on virtually the broadest possible ground—that *all* libel suits by public officials based on statements concerning their official conduct were barred by the First Amendment." This comment overlooked Wechsler's efforts at the argument, frustrated by questions from the justices, to move on to his alternative narrower grounds.

In any event, Barnett's account reported that at their conference all nine justices were in favor of reversing the Alabama judgment, but that most of them were inclined to do so on an extremely narrow ground. This was that when a public official sued a critic of his official conduct, the First Amendment required clear proof of every element in the libel action—and in this case there was insufficient proof either that the advertisement was about Sullivan or that it defamed him. This approach would not have disturbed any of the traditional elements in the common law of libel. It would not, for example, have shifted the burden of proving falsity to the plaintiff, or made him or her show that a falsehood had been published with actual malice. It would merely have required stronger evidence of the matters traditionally left to the plaintiff to prove.

Justice Brennan suggested that for the higher standard of proof the Court rely on the precedent of *Nishikawa v. Dulles*, an expatriation case decided in 1958. Nishikawa, born in California, went to Japan in 1939 and was drafted into the Japanese army. American law provided that anyone who served voluntarily in a foreign army lost his U. S. citizenship. The legal issue was whether Nishikawa had to prove that his service was involuntary in order to retain his citizenship, or whether the government had the burden of proving it voluntary in order to denationalize him. The Supreme Court held, in an opinion by Chief Justice Warren, that the government must prove voluntariness by "clear, convincing and un-equivocal evidence." Justice Brennan's proposal was that an official who sues for libel be required to meet such a demanding test in order to preserve First Amendment values. This ground of decision would have introduced a constitutional rule into the law of libel for the first time, but a very limited one.

By long tradition the Chief Justice decides who will write the opinion of the Court in each argued case in which he is in the majority, assigning it to himself or another member of the Court. (When the Chief is going to dissent, the senior associate justice in the majority makes the assignment.) It is the Chief Justice's one distinct power, for his choice of the opinion writer may influence the character of the decision, or even determine whether a narrow majority will be given a ground on which it can hold together. Soon after the conference at which *Times v. Sullivan* was discussed, Chief Justice Warren sent Justice Brennan a note asking him to write the opinion. Over the years Warren had often chosen Brennan for cases in which it might be difficult to write an opinion that commanded a majority. An outstanding example was the 1962 case, *Baker v. Carr*, in which the Supreme Court for the first time held that federal courts could examine the fairness of political districting—a decision that led to the drawing of new district lines for most state legislatures in the country.

Like most members of the Court, Justice Brennan often asked his law clerks to draft opinions. In this case he did not. He wrote the first draft himself, completing it toward the end of January. The reflection involved in writing an opinion may lead a justice to depart from the views he expressed at conference, and that was what happened in this instance. Justice Brennan went much further than the limited constitutional rule he had suggested in the conference on January 10. He proposed something like the actual malice requirement that in the end became the rule of the *Sullivan* case, but he phrased the test more loosely. He wrote:

> It was suggested on oral argument of the instant case that under Madison's view the First Amendment bars sanctions against defamatory criticism of public officials reflecting upon their official conduct even when tainted with express malice. We do not think that the Amendment reaches so far. . . . The line may surely be drawn to exclude from constitutional protection the statement which is not criticism, or intended as such, but, in the guise of criticism, is deliberate, malevolent and knowing falsity, or utterance reckless of the truth, voiced from vindictive motives to destroy the reputation of a public official.

This last phrase, with its echoes of the McCarthy period's vindictive efforts to destroy public officials, introduced the idea of ill will—malice in its dictionary sense—that was not present in the final version of the rule. The first draft differed in another interesting respect as well. After telling the reader that Wechsler's oral argument for the *Times* had urged adoption of Madison's absolute view, it sought to justify departure from that position. Apparently feeling at this stage that he had to defend his choice of a less than absolute rule, Justice Brennan went on to draw an analogy to what he had said in a well-known obscenity case, *Roth v. United States*. "We have held," he said, "that obscene speech has no constitutional protection because it is 'utterly without redeeming social importance.' This may be also said of the unscrupulous defamers and traducers of reputation." The final opinion made no such attempt to justify the actual malice rule; it simply said, "The constitutional guarantees require, we think, a federal rule that . . ." But in *Garrison v. Louisiana* later in 1964 Justice Brennan did give reasons for not protecting deliberate or reckless falsehoods. And the next year, in his Meiklejohn Lecture, he used the analogy with the *Roth* case to explain why the Court had chosen to balance the interests of free speech and reputation as it did in *Sullivan*.

The first draft went on, like the ultimate opinion, to discuss the Kansas case of *Coleman v. MacLennan*, which it said "well defined" the necessary limits of libel actions by public officials. "Erroneous statement is inevitable in the give-and-take of free discussion," the draft said. "To limit the speaker to the defense of truth must often mean that while his statements are true in fact, his defense must fail. . . . Defendants must be armed with more than the defense of truth if they are not to be made timid about discussing public matters from fear of being mulcted in heavy damages." Moreover, the draft said, there must be a high standard of proof. It cited the case that Justice Brennan had mentioned at conference, *Nishikawa v. Dulles*, and said officials who sue for libel must produce "clear, convincing and unequivocal evidence" of "every element" necessary to win the case under the new constitutional rules. The final version of the *Sullivan* opinion omitted this discussion, merely saying that the proof of knowing or reckless falsehood must have "convincing clarity."

In a last section of the draft, Justice Brennan examined the evidence produced at the trial by Sullivan's lawyers to see whether it met the required standards of proof. First he considered and rejected Nachman's argument that the Seventh Amendment forbade the Supreme Court to review the jury's findings. He relied on *Fiske v. Kansas*, the 1927 decision in which the Court held that the Kansas courts had convicted Fiske of criminal syndicalism only by misreading the document he distributed;

the Court said then that it would "analyze the facts" found by a state court when a constitutional issue was "intermingled" with the facts. (In the final opinion Justice Brennan's discussion of the Seventh Amendment argument was relegated to a footnote.)

Next the draft considered whether the portions of the advertisement to which Sullivan objected had a defamatory meaning. The passages were part of "a recitation of abuses" in the South, Justice Brennan said. Sullivan's own evidence showed that such abuses had occurred: Dr. King's home had been bombed, he had been arrested, student leaders had been expelled. "The discrepancies in the description of those events in the advertisement could hardly be said to be serious. . . . We hold that the statements complained of by respondent are not capable of bearing a defamatory meaning either on their face or when read in the light of the proofs. The statements as part of the advertisement fell well within constitutionally-protected commentary upon a serious contemporary domestic problem."

Then came the question whether the advertisement was "of and concerning" Sullivan. The reference in the text to "Southern violators" could not be read "rationally," the draft said, to impute to Sullivan the bombing of the King home and so on. Further, the testimony of Sullivan himself and his six witnesses that they read the passages in the advertisement as references to him "does not satisfy the standard of clear, convincing and unequivocal evidence of that fact."

Finally the draft considered whether the evidence showed the malice that was now being made a constitutional requirement. Earlier the draft had used the phrase "express malice." Now, in the last paragraph, it used the term that survived in the rule of the *Sullivan* case, "actual malice." Justice Brennan wrote: "The proofs were utterly barren of any evidence that the statements were made by the petitioners with actual malice, that is in bad faith, deliberately, maliciously, and knowing of, or reckless of, their falsity, and out of ill-will toward the respondent, from vindictive motives unrelated to comment upon public affairs." Again, unlike the ultimate rule, Justice Brennan had combined an element of ill will or vindictiveness with knowing or reckless falsity.

In sum, the last section of the draft held that the Alabama libel judgment failed for three reasons: Sullivan had not adequately proved that the advertisement was defamatory, that it was about him or that falsehoods had been published knowingly or recklessly. The opinion ended without any statement about remanding the case to the Alabama courts for further proceedings. At the bottom it had just one italicized word: *Reversed*. Without actually saying that there could not be a new trial, Justice Brennan was trying to foreclose that possibility.

Some of the important features of the final opinion were missing from this first draft. There was no discussion of the idea of "libel on government." The draft did not draw the parallel between the immunity given to government officials for what they say and that needed by "the citizen-critic of government." Madison's statements against the Sedition Act were quoted at length, but the controversy over the act was not described dramatically as pointing to "the central meaning of the First Amendment." Rather, after citing some of the precedents for free speech on public matters—Brandeis, Hand and others—the draft said: "This concept of the basic objective of the First Amendment draws powerful support from James Madison, the Architect of the Bill of Rights. His agreement with this view was made clear in his uncompromising opposition to the ill-starred Sedition Act of 1798. . . ."

Throughout the draft, the rhetoric was less forceful, less assured than in the final version. The opening sentence, for example, was awkwardly phrased: "We decide for the first time in this case the question of the extent that the protections for speech and press of the First and Fourteenth Amendments delimit a State's power to apply its law of civil libel in an action in its courts by a public official against critics of his official conduct."

But the essential structure of the final opinion was there: a first section on the facts, a second on the meaning of the First Amendment, a third measuring the evidence in this case against First Amendment requirements. Justice Brennan also attached a copy of the advertisement, an effective device that remained in the published opinion.

The first draft was not circulated to the other justices. Justice Brennan showed it to his law clerks, and a few days later a second draft was produced. On February 6, 1964, it was circulated to the rest of the Court. There were minor changes in wording throughout, from the beginning of the first sentence: "In this case we are required for the first time to decide the extent that the protections for speech and press . . ."

From the second draft Justice Brennan dropped the long definition of critical speech not protected by the First Amendment: "malevolent and knowing falsity . . . voiced from vindictive motives." He also excised the defensive passage justifying the decision to adopt a less than absolute rule. The second draft introduced the idea of a privilege for critics similar to that given to officials, though again the decisive statement was less compelling than the one in the final version. "It would give public officials a preference unwarranted in a free society," the draft said, "if critics of their official conduct did not enjoy a fair equivalent of that immunity."

The third section of the opinion, applying the newly defined constitutional principles to the facts of the case, was radically changed in the second draft. It omitted the analysis concluding that the advertisement had not been shown to be either defamatory or about Sullivan, as well as the passage citing *Nishikawa v. Dulles* and declaring that the evidence must be "clear, convincing and unequivocal." Instead, the second draft said "we may assume" that there were "no problems of constitutional dimensions" in the Alabama courts' findings that the advertisement could be read as referring to Sullivan and that its mistakes injured his reputation. But even on this assumption, the draft said, the evidence did not meet the test of actual malice, and therefore the Alabama judgment could not stand. But unlike the first, the second draft did not stop there. It dealt explicitly with the possibility of a new trial, saying: "We think, moreover, that a new trial under the correct rule would not be warranted in this case since the evidence submitted was insufficient to establish actual malice." This effort to foreclose the possibility of further harassment of the *Times* and the four ministers was exceptional. But the account of the case by Barnett pointed out that it still left a loophole. The reference to "the evidence submitted" avoided the question whether a new trial would be barred if Sullivan offered to produce additional evidence. Like the first draft, this one ended with the single word "*Reversed.*"

Eleven days later, on February 17, Justice Brennan circulated a third draft among his colleagues. It included many stylistic changes, bringing the form and rhetoric of the opinion significantly closer to its final version. The first sentence was almost in its final form: "We are required for the first time in this case to determine the extent to which the constitutional protections for speech and press limit a State's power to award damages in a libel action brought by a public official against critics of his official conduct." The second draft's pedestrian statement that "the national commitment to freedom of speech . . . cannot be foreclosed by 'mere labels' " was transformed in the third to one of the most arresting passages in the final opinion: "Thus we consider this case against the background of a profound national commitment to the principle that debate on public issues should be uninhibited, robust, and wide-open, and that it may well include vehement, caustic, and sometimes unpleasantly sharp attacks on government and public officials."

In the third draft Justice Brennan also introduced and rejected the idea of "libel on government," quoting the case of *City of Chicago v. Tribune Co.* This draft still said flatly that a new trial "would not be warranted." And it still ended with the single word "*Reversed.*"

When a justice writing an opinion of the Court circulates a draft, he waits anxiously for what are called "returns"—notes from the other justices saying whether they will join his opinion. Justice Brennan got

the first such note on February 13 from Chief Justice Warren. He said
he would join the Brennan opinion. Justice White also agreed, on February 21. But then came less happy news: word from Justices Black,
Douglas and Goldberg that they favored absolute immunity for criticism
of public officials in the performance of their duties and hence would
not join Justice Brennan. Justice Goldberg circulated his separate opinion
on February 25, Justice Black on February 26.

Justice Brennan's opinion now had just three votes, from Chief Justice
Warren, Justice White and Brennan himself. Justices Harlan, Clark and
Stewart were still to be heard from. For a majority, Justice Brennan would
have to have two of those three. The most important of them was Justice
Harlan, the intellectual leader of the relatively conservative wing of the
Court at that time and a deep believer in federalism.

Federalism, the division of powers between the states and the national
government, is an essential element in the American political structure.
The Constitution could not have been agreed at the Philadelphia Convention in 1787, or ratified afterward, if it had not preserved substantial
authority for the state governments. Over the years power drifted to
Washington, especially with the New Deal in the 1930s and World War
II. President Roosevelt and Congress adopted national economic measures to meet a national Depression, and after the Roosevelt appointments
that began in 1937 the Supreme Court held the measures constitutional.
The result was to have the federal government doing all kinds of things
it had never done before: regulating working hours and labor relations,
limiting the acreage planted by farmers, providing welfare payments and
so on. For a time the states were widely scorned as inefficient relics. But
some, in particular Justice Frankfurter and Justice Harlan, continued to
see a strong case for preserving a degree of independent authority in the
states. One reason was that such a division of power reduces the danger
of abuse of power at the center. State courts can and do supplement the
federal Constitution's protections against autocracy by enforcing their
own state constitutions. Another reason is that the existence of separate
state governments allows one or another to try new ideas. Justice Brandeis, a liberal and a reformer, was an eloquent advocate of federalism
for this reason among others. He wrote in 1932: "It is one of the happy
incidents of the federal system that a single courageous State may, if its
citizens choose, serve as a laboratory; and try novel social and economic
experiments without risk to the rest of the country." By the 1960s the
cost of centralizing power in Washington was becoming apparent in
deadening bureaucracy and rigid policy. Justice Harlan was on guard
against further diminishing of state responsibilities.

At this point in the process of decision Barnett's account said, "The reaction of Justice Harlan was awaited with trepidation." The reaction came on February 26, in a letter to Justice Brennan that read as follows:

> Subject to a minor reservation, I agree entirely with parts I and II of your opinion. The reservation is that I would like to see a footnote at some appropriate point to the effect that we are not called upon to delineate at this stage how far down the line of public officials this new constitutional doctrine would reach. I would not want to foreclose a cop, a clerk or some other minor public official from ordinary libel suits without a great deal more thought.
>
> While I agree that there should not be a new trial, I would not feel able to join part III of your opinion as presently written without writing something in addition by way of elaboration. Since I would much prefer not to write separately, I venture to submit the enclosed revision of part III for your consideration. If this, or something like it, commends itself to you, this would enable me to join your opinion without separate writing, which I would very much prefer doing.
>
> You will, I hope, not consider me out of bounds in making these suggestions about an opinion which I realize has been a difficult job, and with whose correctness I am in principle in full agreement.

Three weeks after Justice Brennan first circulated his opinion, he learned for the first time that Justice Harlan had reservations—and had prepared his own draft of the last section. The Harlan letter thus demonstrated an aspect of the Supreme Court that is not generally understood: It functions largely as nine separate small law offices, not as a collaborative institution. The justices meet as a group in conference once a week when the Court is in session. Otherwise each works "largely in isolation," as Justice Robert H. Jackson once said.

The first paragraph of Justice Harlan's letter presented no problem. Justice Brennan incorporated in his opinion the suggested footnote leaving open for future decision what level of officials would be covered by the new constitutional libel rule. But the proposal on the last section raised substantial difficulty. It was also a great surprise. John Harlan, the cautious judge, the judge respectful of state power, wanted to be more explicit in ruling out the possibility of a new trial of Sullivan's libel claim. He wanted to forbid a new trial even if Sullivan's lawyers offered new evidence of actual malice and of the advertisement's connection to Sullivan.

The Harlan proposal for Part III of the opinion "did not evoke much enthusiasm in Justice Brennan's chambers," Barnett wrote, but "the support of Justice Harlan and those who might follow him was deemed indispensable." Justice Brennan therefore redid the last part of his opinion to include most of the Harlan draft and circulated the revised opinion on February 28. This fourth draft included some stylistic changes that survived in the final version, including the statement that the proof presented at the trial lacked "the convincing clarity which the constitutional standard demands." Like the third draft, it examined and found inadequate the trial evidence of a connection between the advertisement and Sullivan and the evidence of actual malice. But it went on to this radically different conclusion:

> Nor do we believe that a new trial would be warranted on the basis that respondent [Sullivan] would be afforded an opportunity to adduce further and sufficient evidence. The alleged connection between the advertisement and him was a hotly disputed issue at the trial, and respondent was amply apprised of petitioners' contention as to the insufficiency of his proof on the issue. We may reasonably assume therefore that he had no evidence of different and more substantial quality to offer. While the absence of proof of connection is itself a sufficient reason for denying a new trial, we note further that there is little likelihood of additional, constitutionally sufficient proof of actual malice. Although we now hold for the first time that proof of actual malice is constitutionally necessary to justify an award of any damages in cases of this kind, it must not be overlooked that Alabama required such proof as a basis for the recovery of punitive damages, and it is manifest from the record that the respondent undertook to make such proof. In short, we conclude that the reasons favoring a retrial are unreal. Exercising our powers under 28 U.S.C. 2106, we decide that a new trial should not be had as to any of the petitioners.

Justice Harlan's proposal was an extraordinary one. The Constitution allows each of the states to maintain its own laws and courts, subject only to overarching federal guarantees. State judges and politicians deeply resent any intrusion on how their courts function. In the early days of the United States there was even resistance to the idea that the Supreme Court could review the judgments of state high courts that involved issues of federal law. When the Supreme Court in 1813 reversed a Virginia decision on the ownership of lands, holding that treaties with Britain required a different outcome, the Virginia Court of Appeals simply refused to carry out the Supreme Court's mandate. The Virginia court held that the congressional statute giving the Supreme Court power to review state decisions on matters of federal law such as a treaty was an unconstitutional intrusion on state power. In 1816, in the great case of *Martin v. Hunter's Lessee*, the Supreme Court considered the matter again. It held that the congressional statute was valid, and that it did have the power to review state judgments in civil cases. Five years later, the case of *Cohens v. Virginia* established the same Supreme Court power of review in state criminal cases. By 1964 the issue of the ultimate power of the Supreme Court was long since settled, but to forbid even an attempt by a litigant in a state court to try to meet new constitutional standards was a novel and intrusive step.

The statute cited at the end of Justice Harlan's paragraph forbidding a new trial, Title 28 of the United States Code, section 2106, authorized federal appellate courts—the Supreme Court and the Courts of Appeals—to "direct the entry of such appropriate judgment, decree, or order, or require such further proceedings to be had as may be just under the circumstances." It was in this language that Justice Harlan found the authority to take the step of directing a state court not to allow a new trial. But no sooner had Justice Brennan incorporated the Harlan proposal than doubts began arising about using Section 2106 as the basis for such an order. Some quick research suggested that the section had never been used in a case coming from a state court to the Supreme Court; its function had been purely to let federal appellate courts direct proceedings in *federal* trial courts. To apply the statute to a state court might raise constitutional problems; it would surely raise state hackles.

Justice Brennan saw the problem when he circulated the new draft. He sent it to Justice Harlan with a letter saying: "Here is the revision marrying your suggestions with my original Part III. I hope it is a satisfactory union. Just one question: Do you have any concern that our use of 28 U.S.C. 2106 disregards the possibility that someone might make a plausible argument that that statute is unconstitutional as applied to deny a state the right to apply its law governing new trials? . . . I thought at least I should raise this since apparently it breaks new ground to tell a state court that it can't give the parties a new trial." Justice Brennan then mentioned the cases of *Martin v. Hunter's Lessee* and *Cohens v. Virginia*. He said those decisions probably settled the issue of judicial power, but he sounded concerned.

At this point Justice Black offered some advice in another of his handwritten notes to Brennan. Black was at the other end of the spectrum from Harlan in judicial philosophy, but he tried to see the problem through Harlan's eyes. "I have given more thought," he wrote, "to John's

suggestion to you about disposing of your case 'as justice may require'—
I do not see how John could possibly adhere to that position on more
mature reflection. I could think of few things that could more violently
clash with his ideas of 'federalism.' My belief is that your method would
be stronger than John's. Construing the statute as authorizing our Court
to *overrule* state laws as to a right to new trial would undoubtedly raise
constitutional questions, some of which as I recall were discussed in the
famous *cause çelebre* Cohens v. Virginia."

Here Hugo Black, who so often disagreed with John Harlan's ideas
on federalism and state power, was acting out of concern for the integrity
of his colleague's position. Justice Black had a reputation for ruthlessness
in maintaining his views. He was certainly determined; he fought on
when he was in the minority, and he lived to see many of his dissents
become the law. But this little episode showed something more. He had
great affection for Justice Harlan. He believed that they were distantly
related, through common ancestors in Kentucky, and happily told people
so. Justice Harlan returned this personal respect. When the two justices
became fatally ill in the summer of 1971, shortly after the decision of
the Pentagon Papers case, both were taken to the Bethesda Naval Hos-
pital. After a time Justice Harlan asked Hugo Black Jr. to visit him. He
asked Hugo Jr. when his father planned to retire. Harlan said that he
must soon retire himself, but he did not want to do so until Justice Black
had made his announcement and received the public recognition due to
"one of the all-time greats of our Court."

(Justice Black sent another, undated note that is found in Justice Brennan's files, making a prediction that did not come true but that shed
some interesting light on his premises as a judge. He wrote: "I did not
and do not see how John can ever agree that this court can say there
shall be no new trial in a state court without a complete reversal of his
views about 'our federalism.' I do think, however, that in getting him to
agree to your opinion as it is you have done a great service to the freedoms
of the First Amendment. For your opinion I believe will inevitably lead
to a later holding that people have complete immunity from having to
pay damages for criticism of Government or its officials in the performance of their public duties. Most inventions even of legal principles
come out of urgent needs. The need to protect speech in this area is so
great that it will be recognized and acted upon sooner or later. The
rationalization for it is not important; the result is what counts, & your
opinion I think will be the point from which this result will be achieved.")

In addition to the questions about section 2106 as a basis for forbidding
a new trial, questions were put to Justice Harlan about his factual assumption that Sullivan's lawyers would be unable to produce meaningful

new evidence at a further trial. For example, the fourth draft of the opinion (incorporating the Harlan proposal) said the witnesses who connected the advertisement with Sullivan based their opinion on his office, "not on any evidence that he had in fact" ordered or approved instances of police misconduct. But suppose witnesses testified at a new trial that Sullivan had taken part in those police actions. In his account Barnett said: "Justice Harlan reportedly conceded that, if such evidence was offered, he did not know how the State could be precluded from granting a new trial."

On Monday, March 2, Justice Brennan met with Justice Harlan to discuss the problem. According to the Barnett account, "Justice Harlan now completely retracted his proposal for explicitly forbidding a new trial. In its stead, he embraced the quite contrary view that, since a new trial upon additional evidence could not be absolutely prohibited, and since reversal was required in any event because the Alabama courts had not applied the rule requiring actual malice, there was no reason for the Court to concern itself at all with the sufficiency of the evidence submitted." In short, Justice Harlan wanted to eliminate virtually all of the last part of the Brennan opinion.

Justice Brennan agreed to drop the language saying that a new trial would not be warranted, simply omitting any reference to that possibility, but that was the limit of his agreement. Later that same day he wrote Justice Harlan: "Upon further reflection I do not think that I should delete Part III beyond the omission of everything which suggests that the respondent is not entitled to a new trial. I think we should retain the analysis of the constitutional insufficiency of the proofs of actual malice and connection even if this has the effect of 'chilling' the possibility of a new trial. I think we are justified in doing this on two counts: (a) the profession should be apprised now that we are going to examine evidence in this area as we have in others, and (b) because the analysis of the proofs to demonstrate their insufficiency will be both illustrative of how we do this and also informative to the parties in this case of a void in the proofs that would have to be filled if a new trial is had. . . . I think I've now come to rest with the problem. I'll try to get it to the printer in the morning with the view to a circulation tomorrow."

On March 3, Justice Brennan circulated a fifth draft of his opinion. It dropped all the strictures against a new trial, made a few further stylistic changes and came to this conclusion: "The judgment of the Supreme Court of Alabama is reversed and the case is remanded to that court for further proceedings not inconsistent with this opinion. *Reversed and remanded.*" With this draft he circulated an explanatory memorandum to his colleagues, which said in part:

John Harlan and I have concluded after much discussion and thought that, even assuming constitutional power to deny a state the right to apply its new trial rules, it would not be wise to use this case as a vehicle for saying so for the first time. John also has misgivings whether the opinion should include any discussion of the sufficiency of the evidence, since the judgment must in any event be reversed. . . . He therefore has advised me that he is filing a short separate memorandum joining the opinion except for its discussion of the evidence. I am convinced, however, that the analysis of the evidence to show its insufficiency under the constitutional rule we lay down is essential to the opinion. Since Sullivan did undertake to prove actual malice as a predicate for punitive damages, we of necessity must demonstrate the insufficiency of his evidence under the constitutional evidence of actual malice. Moreover, if Alabama should give Sullivan a new trial the parties should know that the evidence in this record will not support a judgment—that there is a large void to be filled. If we said nothing and later overturned another judgment entered on this record, we might be rightly accused of having second thoughts because of the implication from our silence here that the application of the valid rule to this evidence would be sustained. Finally, there are a number of other libel suits pending in Montgomery and in Birmingham and those concerned should know what to expect in the way of judicial superintendence from this Court over those proceedings.

This Brennan memorandum made plain the concern he felt about what might happen in Alabama after the decision of this case. Officials might press this and other libel suits, confident of being able to persuade juries that they had proved actual malice, as Justice Black in his separate opinion was warning that they would. But Justice Harlan was unmoved—so far. Later the same day, March 3, he wrote to Justice Brennan:

I was sorry to get your note last night, for I had thought that your idea of simply making a specific reference to the "application" question in the part II discussion of constitutional principles was a happy solution of this bothersome problem. The present version of Part III seems to me to add up to the same thing as the earlier one, which I am now satisfied did not wash, minus however the element of frankness which the earlier version at least possessed. I am sorry therefore to say that I shall not be able to go along with the new version and plan to circulate this afternoon a short Separate Memorandum, joining your opinion except for its discussion of the evidence.

Justice Harlan's memorandum, two short paragraphs, began with a warm endorsement of the main thrust of Justice Brennan's opinion. "I am in full accord with and join the Court's opinion" in its statement of constitutional principles, Harlan said. "I also agree that the Court's responsibility in cases of this kind does not end with the establishment of constitutional ground rules but includes also an obligation to scrutinize the record to ensure that such rules have been constitutionally applied." But, he said, "I do not consider it appropriate for the Court to examine the sufficiency of the evidence at this stage."

The Harlan letter and memorandum were gloomy news for Justice Brennan. He feared that others would join in Justice Harlan's reservations, and then he would no longer speak for a majority. Justice Stewart relieved part of this concern. On the day the Harlan memorandum was circulated, March 3, he sent Justice Brennan a note agreeing to join his opinion. On the same day Chief Justice Warren, in a note, said it was right to keep Part III in the opinion, for otherwise "we will merely be going through a meaningless exercise. The case would be remanded, another improvisation would be devised and it would be back to us in a more difficult posture." But according to the Barnett account, there was reason to worry about Justice Clark. He had sent in a note of agreement on February 28, but now he was moved by Justice Harlan's argument. And Justice White might also be wavering.

On March 4 Justice Brennan went to Clark's chambers to discuss the case. Justice Clark handed him a separate opinion, printed but not yet circulated. "Having demolished respondent's theory of the case," it said, "it appears to me that we should not go further and condemn respondent's evidence." It continued in language that was hyperbolic compared with Justice Harlan's restrained memorandum:

> The action of the Court is a departure from a long-established—and, I dare say, never deviating—rule. It may be that the evidence of malice or reckless disregard for the truth is insufficient; however, this Court should not now measure the old record by a new standard not available at the trial. By so doing the Court forecasts, for all practical purposes, the result of a new trial and thereby forecloses respondent's right to a jury trial. I would leave the state courts free to first determine whether the evidence on a retrial is sufficient.
>
> Prejudging the factual basis of the case places an insurmountable burden upon respondent on remand. In so doing the Court departs from its appellate character and thereby invades the province of Alabama's courts to initially pass upon the facts. And, unfortunately, by thus impugning the integrity of our dual fed-

eralism, the Court fails to reflect that fairness which has always been the hallmark of our judicial processes.

Coming out of the blue as it did, Justice Clark's plan to file a separate opinion was a heavy blow to Justice Brennan. He no longer had a majority for Part III of his opinion. Without a majority, he would be unable to do what he intended in Part III: demonstrate to Alabama officials now, and others later, that the Supreme Court was determined to enforce the new constitutional law of libel by closely examining the facts of cases in which juries awarded damages to public officials for criticism of their official conduct. Far more serious, the lack of a majority for part of the opinion would rob the whole of its air of authority. Unanimity or near-unanimity is crucial to the effect of especially important Supreme Court decisions: what might be called occasions of state. That was why Chief Justice Warren worked with such patience to achieve a unanimous Court in the School Segregation Case. The magisterial quality of Justice Brennan's opinion in *Times v. Sullivan* would have been destroyed by a splintered Court.

With the case now in a position in which no single opinion commanded a majority, Justices Douglas and Goldberg tried to help. They favored an absolute privilege for critics of official conduct, but they much preferred to go along with Justice Brennan's qualified rule as a statement of the full Court than to have a fragmented Court. On March 4, the same day as Justice Clark's bombshell, Justice Douglas wrote a letter suggesting that Justice Brennan append a footnote to Part II of his opinion stating: "Mr. Justice Douglas, while believing that the evidence in question is constitutionally inadmissible because presence or absence of malice is immaterial, would agree that even by the lesser standard prescribed by this opinion the evidence is deficient." With this minor addition Justice Brennan could say that he had the support of five for Part III: himself, Chief Justice Warren and Justices Stewart, White and Douglas. In a note to Justice Brennan, Justice Goldberg sought the same end through a somewhat more generous device. He wrote: "As you know I am enthusiastic about your opinion which I regard to be the most outstanding of the term. You know my view that your evidence [Justice Goldberg meant historical evidence] warrants the rule of an absolute privilege for comment on official conduct. . . . I don't know about Hugo but I am certainly agreeable to joining your excellent opinion and then writing very briefly that I would go beyond to the extent that I have indicated. You can count on my vote for your opinion. It would be very bad if you didn't get a Court."

Justice Black would have none of these maneuvers. He sent Justice

Brennan a note saying that if "malice" were to be the constitutional test, "I think that under the definition you give malice the evidence (so far as I have read it) would prove malice." He therefore could not endorse Part III. He added that he thought the review of the evidence, finding it insufficient, "will have little, if any effect on the course that these litigants will follow hereafter."

Now Justice White suggested a different justification for reviewing the evidence at the Montgomery trial. While the jury had not been required by Judge Jones to specify what part of its award was for general damages and what part for punitive, the award might possibly be entirely punitive. Under Alabama law, punitive damages required a showing of malice in the publication of a falsehood. So if the jury had awarded all punitive damages, it must have found malice—and its judgment on that point had to be affirmed unless its finding of malice was erroneous on the facts. Hence the Supreme Court had to review the facts. This was the logic Justice White proposed. Justice Brennan thought the argument was flawed, because the jury might just as easily have intended to award all general damages and no punitive, in which case no malice need have been found. But he agreed to try the White approach in the hope that it would win over Justice Harlan. It did not. On March 4 Justice Brennan circulated a sixth draft of his opinion, amended to reflect Justice White's proposal. Neither Justice Harlan nor Justice Clark was persuaded.

But the next morning, March 5, Justice Clark sprang another surprise. He told Justice Brennan that he would join the entire opinion if Brennan introduced Part III by saying that a review of the evidence was required by "effective judicial administration." Justice Brennan immediately wrote a note to his law clerks, Barnett and Stephen J. Friedman, saying: "Justice Clark will join if we make the changes shown at pages 29 & 30 [of the latest draft]. He thinks this may even be persuasive to Justice Harlan. The basis of course is 'effective judicial administration' rather than Justice White's—namely, that this verdict is really punitive damages. Incidentally, Justice Black is opposed to the Douglas & Goldberg solution & is urging me & them not to do it. All in all, I think we should accept this compromise with Justice Clark. Please send it to the printer so that we can get a distribution this afternoon."

On the afternoon of March 5 a seventh draft was circulated. Part III said: "Since respondent may seek a new trial, we deem that considerations of effective judicial administration require us to review the evidence in the present record to determine whether it could constitutionally support a judgment for respondent." This statement, retained in the final opinion, has always puzzled commentators. What exactly were the "considerations of effective judicial administration?" Barnett permitted himself a wry comment in recording this phase of the decisional process in the *Sullivan* case. "For reasons that are less than clear," he wrote, the phrase "effective judicial administration" seemed to have "a talismanic significance" in that particular Supreme Court term, "being employed in several difficult situations as a sort of judicial wonder-drug." He cited two other examples of opinions using variants of the phrase.

March 6 was a Friday, the day of the Court's conference. The opinion in *New York Times v. Sullivan* was discussed, and for the occasion Justice Brennan had produced an eighth and final draft. It made a few stylistic changes from the version circulated the day before. The passage about the Sedition Act and "the central meaning of the First Amendment" was finally inserted. In this form, with Justice Clark's tribute to "effective judicial administration," the opinion was approved by a majority for announcement on the following Monday, March 9. It had the votes of Chief Justice Warren and Justices Clark, Brennan, Stewart and White.

Justice Harlan still disagreed with Part III. He had a new version of his brief separate memorandum, which added the statement: "Whatever one may think of this libel action, its ultimate resolution should follow normal adjudicatory processes. The Court's anticipatory assessment of the evidence is an unprecedented step which in my opinion does disservice in the long run to the great national interests which underlie this litigation." The next day, Saturday, Justice Harlan circulated still another version of his memorandum, changing the last phrase to read: ". . . disservice in the long run to the basic constitutional concerns out of which this litigation arose." An undated handwritten note from Justice Harlan to Justice Brennan says: "Dear Bill, I have now looked at your bench note and changes in N.Y. Times, and I'm sorry to say that I remain of the same view—i.e. as per my separate concurrence."

Then, on Sunday evening, March 8, Justice Harlan telephoned Justice Brennan at home. He had decided, he said, to withdraw his separate memorandum and join Brennan's opinion without qualification.

Why did Justice Harlan change his mind at the last moment? There can be no certain answer to the question, but some reasons can be suggested. Justice Brennan had extraordinarily good relations with all his colleagues, whatever their conflicts on legal issues. However sharp his differences, he never allowed a tone of personal attack into his opinions— as Justice Frankfurter had, for example. For his part, Harlan cared greatly about the Court as an institution. He would not have wanted to do anything that detracted from a great occasion for the Court, or for Justice Brennan. Of course those feelings would not have stopped Justice Harlan from expressing deeply felt differences. But he agreed with the basic principles of the Brennan opinion, its recitation of history and its definition of "the central meaning of the First Amendment." Perhaps in the end he decided, after what looks to have been much agonizing, that to disagree on a subsidiary point was putting himself before the occasion. There was no Supreme Court justice more impressive in his modesty than John Marshall Harlan. Finally, Justice Harlan must have been reassured by Herbert Wechsler's role as counsel for the *Times*. Wechsler was an authority on issues of federalism, a scholar of integrity and stature. Justice Harlan knew that Wechsler would not urge a decision that he considered inconsistent with the demands of American federalism.

Over the weekend a few last changes were made in the Brennan opinion. Early Monday morning Justice Harlan circulated this letter to his colleagues:

> Dear Brethren:
> I have advised Brother Brennan, and I wish the other Brethren to know, that I am withdrawing my Separate Memorandum in this case, and am unreservedly joining the majority opinion.

At ten o'clock that morning the justices took their seats on the bench. A few minutes later Chief Justice Warren glanced down the bench at Justice Brennan, and Brennan said, "I have for announcement the opinion and judgment of the Court in number 39, *New York Times Co. v. L. B. Sullivan.*" The audience of lawyers and reporters and tourists and judicial friends could not know the drama of the last week as they heard him read: "We are required in this case to determine for the first time the extent to which the constitutional protections for speech and press limit a State's power to award damages in a libel action brought by a public official against critics of his official conduct. . . ."

# PUBLIC
# AND
# PRIVATE

**N**ew York Times Co. v. Sullivan was a beginning, not an end. For years, for decades, the Supreme Court and other courts have worked out the implications of the decision for different factual situations. Justice Brennan's opinion turned out to bristle with questions. What kind of behavior, for example, amounted to "reckless disregard" for the truth? How could the victim of a false statement discover whether its author had known the truth and recklessly disregarded it? And so on. That the questions were not all settled in 1964 was hardly surprising. "One could not fairly ask the Court," Herbert Wechsler said, "to foresee in one opinion all the problems that would evolve from this demarche in constitutional law." Libel, a subject that used to be outside the purview of the Supreme Court, was now on the docket year after year. Libel cases proved to be richly illustrative of the process by which the justices elaborate constitutional law.

One question proved especially difficult to resolve: how to draw a line between the public and the private spheres of life in the constitutional law of libel. Professor Meiklejohn, a great advocate of free speech in public matters, said that "private defamation"—libel unrelated to "the business of governing"—should have no First Amendment protection at all. At first the Supreme Court seemed to take the Meiklejohn approach. The *Sullivan* decision was based on the special importance of speech about government: Assuring its freedom, Justice Brennan said, was "the central meaning of the First Amendment." The next libel case decided by the Court, the criminal case of *Garrison v. Louisiana*, rested on the same premise. But then came the puzzling case of *Time Inc. v. Hill*.

On September 11, 1952, three escaped convicts took over a home in Whitemarsh, a suburb of Philadelphia. For nineteen hours they held hostage the family that lived there, James J. Hill, his wife Elizabeth and their five children. The convicts did them no harm, as the Hills made clear when the episode was over; but the story got a lot of coverage in the press, some of it sensationalized. The Hill family, especially Mrs. Hill, found the publicity, the exposure, hard to bear. They moved to Connecticut to avoid it, and they rejected all requests for interviews. The family faded from public view—until *Life* magazine, in February 1955, published an article about a new play, *The Desperate Hours*, that portrayed the ordeal of a family held hostage by escaped convicts. *Life* described the play as a reenactment of the Hills' experience, and it photographed the actors in the Hills' former home in Whitemarsh. The impression thus created was false. The playwright, Joseph Hayes, had in fact not based his work specifically on the Hills' experience; and in his drama, unlike theirs, the convicts acted brutally, beating up the father and sexually menacing a daughter. The *Life* article and photographs presented such scenes as if they had actually happened to the Hill family. To the Hills, the notoriety once again thrust upon them, in distorted form, was deeply wounding. They decided to take legal action.

Hill sued for invasion of privacy. By wrongly associating the brutalities in *The Desperate Hours* with his family's experience, he claimed, *Life* had put him in a false light and violated the privacy protected by a New York law. In Justice Brandeis's phrase, he had lost "the right to be let alone." (The legal concept of privacy was first suggested in an 1890 *Harvard Law Review* article by Brandeis and his law partner, Samuel Warren, "The Right to Privacy.") Hill's suit wound through the courts of New York for ten years. Finally a jury awarded him $30,000 in compensatory damages, and the New York courts upheld the judgment. Time Inc., the publisher of *Life*, took the case to the Supreme Court, arguing that the article was protected by the First Amendment. In 1965, the year after the *Sullivan* decision, the Court agreed to hear *Time Inc. v. Hill*.

What could possibly connect the story of James Hill and his family with the *Sullivan* case? There was no great public issue here, like the racial struggle that was the subject of the disputed advertisement in *The Times;* there was only an obscure family brought briefly and involuntarily to public attention. The case did not engage the right to criticize government or its officials. Yet *Time v. Hill* proved to be the occasion for a next large step by the Court in applying the *Sullivan* rule. It was also the occasion for bitter conflict within the Court.

The case was argued in April 1966. A majority of the justices voted to affirm Hill's judgment, rejecting *Life*'s First Amendment claim. Chief Justice Warren assigned the opinion to Justice Abe Fortas, recently appointed to replace Justice Goldberg, who had resigned at President Johnson's urging to become ambassador to the United Nations. Fortas wrote a draft that used exceptionally strong language in condemning *Life*'s behavior:

> Needless, heedless, wanton and deliberate injury of the sort inflicted by Life's picture story is not an essential instrument of responsible journalism. Magazine writers and editors are not, by reason of their high office, relieved of the common obligation to avoid deliberately inflicting wanton and unnecessary injury. . . . The deliberate, callous invasion of the Hills' right to be let alone—this appropriation of a family's right not to be molested or to have its name exploited and quiet existence invaded— cannot be defended on the ground that it is within the purview of a constitutional guarantee designed to protect the free exchange of ideas and opinions. This is exploitation, undertaken to titillate and excite, for commercial purposes.

Those words are not to be found in the official volumes of Supreme Court opinions. Justice Fortas's draft opinion and the story of what happened to it appeared in 1985 in a book by Professor Bernard Schwartz, *The Unpublished Opinions of the Warren Court*. Just why Justice Fortas felt so outraged by the *Life* story is not clear. Despite his years of public activity as a lawyer, judge and adviser to Lyndon Johnson, he was a very private man, and perhaps he had experienced invasive journalism at some point. He and his law firm had also represented some victims of Communist-hunting in the McCarthy years, and that could have made him especially sensitive to the destructive potential of lies. Whatever the reason, the strong language of his draft opinion proved to be counterproductive. It aroused Justice Black, the member of the Court most devoted to freedom of speech and press. Black denounced the Fortas draft, and other members of the Court were troubled. As a result, the case was put over for reargument the following October. The day before the second argument Justice Black circulated among his colleagues a memorandum warning in dire terms against allowing Hill's $30,000 judgment to stand. It concluded: "One does not have to be a prophet, I think, to foresee that judgments like the one in this case can frighten and punish the press so much that publishers will cease trying to report news in a lively and readable fashion as long as there is—and there always will be—doubt as to the complete accuracy of the newsworthy facts."

The Supreme Court decided the *Hill* case in January 1967. Justice Fortas had lost his majority, and James Hill lost his judgment. The opinion of the Court was by Justice Brennan, and he applied the formula that he had fashioned in *Times v. Sullivan*. He said the New York privacy statute could not be used to award damages for "false reports of matters of public interest in the absence of proof that the defendant published the report with knowledge of its falsity or in reckless disregard of the truth."

Why should a test laid down by the Court to protect criticism of government be used to protect a magazine's false picture of the Hill family? Justice Brennan explained:

> The guarantees for speech and press are not the preserve of political expression or comment upon public affairs, essential as those are to healthy government. One need only pick up any newspaper or magazine to comprehend the vast range of published matter which exposes persons to public view, both private citizens and public officials. Exposure of the self to others in varying degrees is a concomitant of life in a civilized community. The risk of this exposure is an essential incident of life in a society which places a primary value on freedom of speech and of press. . . . We create a grave risk of serious impairment of the indispensable service of a free press in a free society if we saddle the press with the impossible burden of verifying to a certainty the facts associated in news articles with a person's name, picture or portrait.

The decision in the *Hill* case raised philosophical doubts. Requiring the press to verify facts would no doubt make its life more difficult, as Justice Brennan said. But the question was whether that burden was socially justified to protect the privacy—or in a libel case the reputation— of a private person, one who had not volunteered for the rough-and-tumble of public life. American society does place a primary value on freedom of speech, but does it follow that the society should demand "exposure of the self to others"? The experience of the twentieth century with totalitarian regimes that kept the innermost lives of their citizens under surveillance suggests otherwise. So George Orwell believed when he made the ever-present eye of Big Brother one of the most oppressive features of life in *1984*.

The application of the *Sullivan* rule to the very different facts of the

*Hill* case shattered the Court's unanimity. The vote to reverse the judgment was 5 to 4. Justice Fortas dissented in an opinion joined by Chief Justice Warren and Justice Clark. He toned down the angry words of his earlier draft, but he ended his dissent with a powerful warning: "For this Court totally to immunize the press—whether forthrightly or by subtle indirection—in areas far beyond the needs of news, comment on public persons and events, discussion of public issues and the like would be no service to freedom of the press, but an invitation to public hostility to that freedom."

Justice Harlan also dissented, in a notable opinion that anticipated problems with which the Court would wrestle in future. There seemed to him two reasons, he said, why speech should not lose its constitutional protection solely because it was false. First, some error is inevitable in free debate. Second, in many areas "'truth' is not a readily identifiable concept, and putting to the pre-existing prejudices of a jury the determination of what is 'true' may effectively institute a system of censorship. Any nation which counts the *Scopes* trial as part of its heritage cannot so readily expose ideas to sanctions on a jury finding of falsity." (The trial of John T. Scopes, a Tennessee schoolteacher, was one of the great legal and cultural clashes of the 1920s. Tennessee had a law making it a crime to teach any theory of man's origin except the Bible's account of creation. Scopes was prosecuted for teaching the Darwinian theory of evolution. Clarence Darrow, a great civil liberties lawyer, represented him; William Jennings Bryan, a fundamentalist Christian who had three times been the Democratic nominee for President, was on the prosecution team. The jury convicted Scopes.)

Justice Harlan said "the marketplace of ideas" was the best place to test the truth where it worked, but in a case like Hill's it did not. Hill would have a hard time finding a platform from which to refute *Life*, so the case presented "the dangers of unchallengeable untruth." Moreover, the *Sullivan* opinion said public officials had to be a hardy breed, but that could not be expected of a James Hill. For those reasons, Justice Harlan said, a person like Hill should be able to recover damages for a falsehood that was not reckless but merely negligent. And it was negligent if the press failed to make "a reasonable investigation" before publishing. Justice Harlan ended his opinion with a warning not unlike Fortas's: "A constitutional doctrine which relieves the press of even this minimal responsibility in cases of this sort seems to me unnecessary and ultimately harmful to the permanent good health of the press itself."

An interesting aspect of *Time v. Hill* was that Hill was represented in the Supreme Court by Richard M. Nixon, who was practicing law in New York while waiting to make his second, successful run for the presidency in 1968. The *Hill* case made a surprising appearance in one of the White House tapes that led to President Nixon's downfall in the Watergate affair. He was talking with his counsel, John Dean, on February 28, 1973. According to a transcript made by the House Judiciary Committee in its impeachment inquiry, Dean said that the threat of a libel suit had had "a very sobering effect on several of the national magazines," making them think again before printing "this Watergate junk." These exchanges followed:

> PRESIDENT: "Well, you of course know, that I said at the time of the Hills' case—well, it is God-damned near impossible for a public figure to win a libel case any more."
> DEAN: "Yes sir. It is. To establish (1) malice, or reckless disregard of—no, they're both very difficult."
> PRESIDENT: "Yeah. Well, malice is impossible, virtually. This guy up there, 'Who, me?' Reckless disregard, you can, maybe."
> DEAN: "Tough. That's a bad decision, Mr. President. It really is. It was a bad decision."
> PRESIDENT: "What the hell happened? What's the name of that—I don't remember the case, but it was a horrible decision."
> DEAN: "New York Times v. Sullivan."
> PRESIDENT: "Sullivan case."
> DEAN: "And it came out of the South on a civil rights—"
> PRESIDENT: "Selma. It was talking about some, some guy that was—yeah, he was a police chief or something. Anyway, I remember reading it at the time when—that's when we were suing Life, you know, for the Hills. When Life was guilty as hell."
> DEAN: "Did they win it?"
> PRESIDENT: "Supreme Court—four to three. There were a couple of people who couldn't—no, five, five to four, five to three and a half."
> DEAN: (laughs).

A more sympathetic view of Nixon's role in the *Hill* case, and a convincing one, was presented by his former law partner and White House counsel, Leonard Garment, in an article in *The New Yorker* in 1989. Garment wrote that Nixon prepared for the first Supreme Court argument with exceptional care, and the justices thought he did a superior job. The morning after the argument Garment found on his desk a five-page, single-spaced memorandum dictated by Nixon that analyzed and criticized his own performance. Garment said it was "the most instructive example of Richard Nixon's tenacity and work habits that I've read in all the time I've known him." When the Court put the case down for reargument in October 1966, Nixon took three weeks off from campaigning for Republican congressional candidates in order to prepare. Garment telephoned Nixon with the news of the decision against Hill in January. Nixon said: "I always knew I wouldn't be permitted to win a big appeal against the press. Now, Len, get this absolutely clear: I never want to hear about the *Hill* case again."

Abe Fortas was at the other end of the spectrum from Nixon in partisan terms, but he shared the morbid view of the press reflected in Nixon's dark comment about the decision. In 1969 Fortas was forced to resign from the Court after *Life* disclosed that he had made an arrangement for continuing fees or honorariums from a man who was under investigation by the Securities and Exchange Commission. Garment said Fortas believed that *Life* had printed the article to punish him for his position in the *Hill* case. Garment also reported, with James Hill's permission, a tragic postlude to the case. In August 1971, Mrs. Hill committed suicide. Garment said he was not asserting "that the false and unwanted publicity of the *Life* article caused this tragedy. Suicide is among the darkest of human acts, the result of multiple influences. It is not unfair, however, to say that troubled persons, clinging to their psychological integrity in an invasive world, suffer with special acuteness when they are forced into the spotlight of negative community attention." At the least, knowledge of the suicide intensifies one's uneasiness about the way the Supreme Court decided the *Hill* case.

James Hill had not sued for libel, because the injury suffered by his family was not so much to its reputation as to its sense of self. Justice Brennan said in his opinion that the Court's application of the requirement for knowing or reckless falsehood in this privacy case did not determine what it would do in a libel case. But a few months later the Court did hold that the rule laid down in *Times v. Sullivan* applied in libel cases to plaintiffs other than officials like Commissioner Sullivan. The case was *Curtis Publishing Co. v. Butts*.

*The Saturday Evening Post*, a Curtis magazine, published a sensational article charging that football games had been rigged in the football-mad Southeastern Conference of college sports. It said that Wally Butts, athletic director of the University of Georgia, had given the Georgia team's secret plans to the Alabama coach, Bear Bryant, before their big game. The story was based on the strange experience of an Atlanta businessman who was trying to make a telephone call when, he said, he found himself connected to a conspiratorial conversation between Butts and Bryant. Butts sued Curtis Publishing for libel. A jury awarded him $60,000 in compensatory and $3 million in punitive damages, the latter reduced by the judge to $460,000. Reviewing that judgment, the Supreme Court focused on the question of Wally Butts's status. He was not an "official," because he was not on the state payroll; by special arrangement he was paid out of alumni funds. But he was a "public figure," someone well known to the public. Should he have to meet the same test of knowing or reckless falsehood as a public official? On that question, the Court divided four ways.

Justice Harlan, for himself and Justices Clark, Stewart and Fortas, said a public figure like Butts should be able to recover libel damages on proof less demanding than "reckless disregard" for the truth. It was enough, Justice Harlan said, if such a plaintiff showed that there had been "an extreme departure" from normal standards of investigation and reporting. There had been such a departure by *The Saturday Evening Post*, he said, so the judgment for Butts should be affirmed. Justices Brennan and White voted to apply the *Sullivan* reckless-disregard test in this case; they said the judgment should be reversed and the case sent back for a new trial. Justices Black and Douglas also voted to reverse, on their broader ground that the First Amendment gives absolute protection to speech and press. With four votes to affirm and four to reverse, the deciding vote was cast by Chief Justice Warren. He wrote an opinion agreeing with Justices Brennan and White that public figures must meet the same test as officials to win a libel case. He explained:

Increasingly in this country, the distinctions between governmental and private sectors are blurred. Since the depression of the 1930's and World War II there has been a rapid fusion of economic and political power, a merging of science, industry and government, and a high degree of interaction between the intellectual, governmental and business worlds. . . . In many situations, policy determinations which traditionally were channeled through formal political institutions are now originated and implemented through a complex array of boards, committees, commissions, corporations and associations, some only loosely connected with the Government. This blending of positions and power has also occurred in the case of individuals so that many who do not hold public office at the moment are nevertheless intimately involved in the resolution of important public questions. . . . Our citizenry has a legitimate and substantial interest in the conduct of such persons, and freedom of the press to engage in uninhibited debate about their involvement in public issues and events is as crucial as it is in the case of "public officials."

But on the facts Chief Justice Warren went against *The Saturday Evening Post*. He said the magazine's lawyers had deliberately chosen not to raise a constitutional defense at the trial, thus waiving it, and in any event he found in the record evidence of reckless disregard for the truth in publishing the article. His was therefore the fifth vote to uphold the damage award. Herbert Wechsler had argued the case for the Curtis Publishing Company, and it was agonizing to see his legal argument for extension of the *Sullivan* rule to public figures win but his client lose. "It was the only case in my fifty years," he said later, "where I won the opinion and lost the judgment: a disastrous experience." Two years later *The Saturday Evening Post* ended its long life as a weekly, a fall to which the *Butts* case may have contributed. (James Kirby, a law professor who observed the Butts libel trial on behalf of the Southeastern Conference, later published a book on the case, "Fumble: Bear Bryant, Wally Butts and the Great College Football Scandal." He concluded that *The Saturday Evening Post* had done a sloppy job but that the story about Butts and Bryant was probably true, and that a jury could not properly have found knowing or reckless falsification.)

After the *Butts* decision, the character of the plaintiff was critical in a libel case. If he was an official or public figure, he had to prove knowing or reckless falsehood. If he was a private citizen, the First Amendment did not affect the case; it was a matter for state law. Then, four years later, Justice Brennan offered another solution. He said that whether a potentially libelous statement was protected by the First Amendment should turn not on the type of person injured by the statement but on its subject matter. If the subject was "of public or general interest," then the statement was protected by the Constitution no matter who sued over it. The case was *Rosenbloom v. Metromedia*, decided in 1971. A Philadelphia radio station broadcast reports that a distributor of obscene magazines had been arrested. The distributor was acquitted of the obscenity charge in a criminal trial. Thereafter he sued the radio station for libel, claiming that its wrongful use of the word "obscene" to describe the magazines he distributed had hurt his reputation. The Supreme Court held by a vote of 5 to 3 that the broadcast was protected by the First Amendment and that the distributor could win damages only if he proved that there had been a knowing or reckless mistake. There was no majority opinion. Justice Brennan spoke for himself and two others, Chief Justice Warren E. Burger, who by then had replaced Chief Justice Warren, and Justice Harry A. Blackmun, who had succeeded Justice Fortas. Justice Brennan said the *Sullivan* libel test should apply in this case because the subject of the broadcast, a police drive against alleged obscenity, was a matter of public concern.

"If a matter is of public or general interest," Justice Brennan said, "it cannot suddenly become less so merely because a private individual is involved, or because in some sense the individual did not 'voluntarily' choose to become involved. The public's primary interest is in the event." How did Justice Brennan explain the departure from his earlier emphasis, starting in *Sullivan*, on the public character of the libel plaintiff? "Further reflection over the years," he said, had persuaded him "that the view of the 'public official' or 'public figure' as assuming the risk of defamation by voluntarily thrusting himself into the public eye bears little relationship either to the values protected by the First Amendment or to the nature of our society. . . . Voluntarily or not, we are all 'public' men to some degree. Conversely, some aspects of the lives of even the most public men fall outside the area of matters of public or general concern."

Justice Brennan's new view drew dissent from among others Justice Thurgood Marshall, who had replaced Justice Clark. Justice Marshall was very close to Justice Brennan on constitutional issues, and he shared in particular the commitment to freedom of speech and press. But he protested that the Brennan approach in the *Rosenbloom* case might end up by making all libel plaintiffs meet the *Sullivan* test, because "all human events are arguably within the area of 'public or general concern.' " To focus on the subject instead of the person hurt by a defamatory statement, Marshall said, would threaten "society's interest in protecting private individuals from being thrust into the public eye by the distorting light of defamation."

The Marshall dissent demonstrated that, with all the Court's concern for freedom of expression, there continued to be a sensitivity to reputation, the other value at stake in libel cases. Justice Brennan himself had never agreed with the argument of Justices Black and Douglas that the First Amendment completely overrode the ancient right to repair a wounded reputation by means of a libel suit. Early on, in the *Garrison* case, Brennan warned of the danger of "calculated falsehood" in the hands of the "unscrupulous." Other justices' opinions also emphasized the interest of reputation. One by Justice Stewart was often quoted: "The right of a man to the protection of his reputation from unjustified invasion and wrongful hurt reflects no more than our basic concept of the essential dignity and worth of every human being." Justice Stewart then referred to the days of Communist-hunting and character assassination: "The preventive effect of liability for defamation serves an important public purpose. For the rights and values of private personality far transcend mere personal interests. Surely if the Nineteen-Fifties taught us anything, they taught us that the poisonous atmosphere of the easy lie can infect and degrade a whole society." In his note to Justice Brennan during the

Court's consideration of *New York Times v. Sullivan* Justice Black had predicted that in time his belief in the supreme importance of free speech would prevail, and the Court would rule out libel suits altogether; but his view of libel never came near to persuading a majority of the Court.

The concern for reputation was no doubt one reason why Justice Brennan's attempt to apply the *Sullivan* rule to all libel cases on matters of public concern did not take hold. In 1974 a new majority of the Supreme Court definitively rejected it. The case was *Gertz v. Welch*, and it was a colorful example of the conflict between reputation and freedom of expression. Described from one point of view or another, it arouses very different reactions.

For advocates of press freedom, the story might go like this: In 1969 a magazine published an article critical of a Chicago lawyer, who sued for libel. As a result, the publisher and editors were embroiled in interminable litigation. In 1970 the lawyer won $50,000 from a jury. Two years later a federal Court of Appeals set the award aside, deciding that the lawyer had not met the constitutional libel test. He appealed to the Supreme Court, and in 1974 it gave him another chance, sending the case back for a new trial under new standards set by the Court. For unknown reasons the federal trial court dawdled, and it was not until 1981 that a second trial was held. This time the jury gave the lawyer $400,000. In order to appeal, the magazine had to pledge its headquarters building. When it finally lost, in 1983, it had to sell the building to pay the judgment. For one critical article, then, the magazine had to spend fourteen years and untold sums in lawyers' fees defending itself in the courts. And then it had to pay a judgment of $400,000—plus $81,808.09 in interest and court costs.

But now look at it from the viewpoint of the plaintiff, the lawyer who was attacked and wanted to redeem his reputation. The magazine that attacked him was *American Opinion*, a monthly published by the John Birch Society, the far-right organization founded by Robert Welch. Its article was about Elmer Gertz, a civil liberties lawyer who represented the family of a young man shot and killed by a Chicago policeman, Richard Nuccio. The State of Illinois prosecuted Nuccio and won a conviction for second-degree murder. *American Opinion* claimed that the prosecution was part of a Communist campaign to discredit the police. Although Gertz had nothing to do with the prosecution, the article said he was the architect of the "frame-up." It called Gertz a "Leninist" and a "Communist-fronter" and said the police file on him took "a big Irish cop to lift." Those statements were all false, and the editor of *American Opinion* had done nothing to check them. He testified that he had relied on the writer of the article, Alan Stang. Stang had written other articles describing people as Marxist, Communist or under Communist control, among them Richard Nixon.

When the Supreme Court decided the *Gertz* case, Justice Black had died. His successor, Lewis F. Powell Jr., wrote the Opinion of the Court. It was for a majority of only 5 to 4, but it set what turned out to be lasting rules. First, in a memorable passage, Justice Powell made clear that the Constitution does not allow punishment for the expression of beliefs or ideologies, however strange or dangerous the majority of people may believe them to be. He wrote: "Under the First Amendment there is no such thing as a false idea. However pernicious an opinion may seem, we depend for its correction not on the conscience of judges and juries but on the competition of other ideas." With those words, Justice Powell in effect wrote into law Holmes's principle that beliefs must be freely tested in the marketplace of ideas—the view that Holmes expressed in dissent in the *Abrams* case in 1919: "The best test of truth is the power of the thought to get itself accepted in the competition of the market." Justice Powell thus vindicated the Holmes and Brandeis dissents from decisions upholding the punishment of Anita Whitney, Benjamin Gitlow and others who advocated such unpopular ideas as pacifism and socialism.

But facts were different from beliefs, Justice Powell said: "There is no constitutional value in false statements of fact." They are protected only because error is "inevitable in free debate," and punishment of error might lead to "intolerable self-censorship." But if factual error had to be protected, Justice Powell continued, the law must balance the interest of free speech against that of reputation, and where the balance was struck depended on whether the person harmed was a public or a private figure. The public person was better able to command a forum for a reply, he said, as Justice Harlan had urged in *Time v. Hill*. Moreover, anyone who accepted public office or took a prominent role in society assumed the risk of controversy. (Harry Truman put it: "If you can't stand the heat, stay out of the kitchen.") Justice Powell defined two kinds of public figures. One is the person so prominent that he or she is always deemed a public figure. The other is the person who has thrust himself or herself to the forefront of a particular public issue, inviting comment in that context. (Justice Harlan had described the second type as those who thrust themselves into "the vortex" of particular controversies, and lawyers call them "vortex public figures.") Elmer Gertz was not a public figure of either kind, Justice Powell said, so he did not have to meet the *Sullivan* test.

But Justice Powell did not stop there. He went on to say that a private person who sues for libel must show something more than the bare fact that the defendant published a damaging falsehood about him; he must also show at least that the publisher acted negligently in doing so. This may seem a modest requirement, but in fact it was a substantial step for Justice Powell and the Court to take. The old common law of libel, which was still the law in most states when *Gertz* was decided in 1974, included no such requirement. Libel was a tort, a civil wrong, for which the wrongdoer had what lawyers call strict liability: If someone made a false statement damaging to reputation, he could be made to pay damages no matter how innocent the mistake had been. In superimposing a new federal requirement to prove that the mistake was negligent, the Supreme Court significantly extended the process it had started in *Times v. Sullivan*. Now private individuals who brought libel suits would have to meet a First Amendment test as well, albeit one of mere negligence rather than knowing or reckless falsehood. In a later case the Court held that in a private libel suit the plaintiff also had the burden of proving falsity. The decision reversed the common-law rule, which made a libel defendant prove a challenged statement true.

Justice White filed an outraged dissent from the decision to make private libel plaintiffs prove negligence. It was a step offensive to the principles of federalism, he said, the mutual respect of national and state governments; two hundred years of state law were being upset "in a few printed pages." Constitutional intrusion on state libel law, he said, should be limited to cases involving public officials and public figures. He wrote: "The central meaning of *New York Times*, and for me the First Amendment as it relates to libel laws, is that seditious libel—criticism of government and public officials—falls beyond the police power of the state."

What is the difference between "negligence" and "reckless disregard"? Those abstract lawyers' words do not have much meaning for the average person, but the Supreme Court had a real distinction in mind. In a 1968 case, the Court defined "reckless disregard" in a way that gave very great protection to the press even when it practiced dubious journalism. The opinion was by Justice White—oddly so, perhaps, considering his later reluctance to extend the application of *Times v. Sullivan*. He said a writer's or editor's failure to check a story before publishing it did not amount to reckless disregard for the truth; he was reckless only if he became aware that a story was probably false but went ahead and printed it anyway. Justice White put it: "Reckless conduct is not measured by whether a reasonably prudent man would have published, or would have investigated before publishing. There must be sufficient evidence to permit the conclusion that the defendant in fact entertained serious doubts as to the truth of his publication."

Justice White thus made the test of recklessness a subjective one: what a particular writer or editor actually knew before publishing. This is quite different from the usual test in tort cases, which is whether a reasonable or prudent person would have done what this defendant did—would have operated, say, as a surgeon accused of malpractice had operated. In the usual tort case "experts" are called to testify on what reasonable practice is, but there can be no expert testimony on the subjective question of what the author or publisher of a statement knew at the time he published. Justice White conceded that the lack of an obligation to check a story before publishing might be said to put "a premium on ignorance," but he said the rule was needed to assure open debate about public affairs. He did say that some stories were so suspicious that they had to be checked; for example, an editor would be reckless if he published an "inherently improbable" story or one based wholly on "an unverified anonymous telephone call." Justice Fortas alone dissented, saying that there should be "a duty to check" before publishing damaging statements about an official. In a tone reminiscent of his unpublished draft in *Time v. Hill* he added: "The occupation of public officeholder does not forfeit one's membership in the human race."

The duty to check is the difference between the two constitutional standards. An editor is negligent if he publishes a story without checking and it turns out to be false. He is reckless only if he is put on notice of likely falsity and still proceeds to publish.

The *Gertz* case finally settled where the line was to be drawn in libel law between the public and private spheres. Or almost finally. A few years later Justice Powell implied in another case that the First Amendment did not apply at all when a purely private person was defamed and the subject was of no public concern. The case involved a financial reporting service, Dun & Bradstreet, that had circulated false information about the plaintiff to just five subscribers: not a public matter, Justice Powell said.

In sum, the cases on the public-private issue left us with a complicated set of constitutional rules. If you are a private person, out of the public eye, and someone publishes a false and damaging statement about you on a subject of no general interest, you can recover libel damages in any way that state law provides; the Constitution does not apply to your case. If you are a private person attacked on a matter of public concern— like Elmer Gertz on the issue of Communists and the police—you must meet the requirements of state law and also, under the First Amendment, prove that a false statement was made about you at least negligently. If you are a public figure or a public official, you must meet the constitutional test of showing knowing or reckless publication of a falsehood. It is all much less straightforward, less neat, than it seemed when *New York Times v. Sullivan* was decided in 1964.

And of course the definitions of "public figure" are not exact and cannot be. In the years after *Gertz* the Supreme Court several times rejected arguments that a libel plaintiff was a public figure, making clear in the process that one cannot be made into a public figure merely by attracting involuntary notoriety. The Court held that Mary Alice Firestone, a society figure involved in a much publicized divorce proceeding, was not a public figure. Neither was a scientist researching the emotional responses of monkeys whose federal grants were ridiculed by Senator William Proxmire in what the senator called his Golden Fleece Award. Nor was a man who had pleaded guilty to contempt of court for failing to appear in response to a subpoena from a grand jury investigating Soviet espionage. But over the years lawyers and judges got used to the categories of public and private figures, and the new constitutional law of libel settled down on those terms.

All the same, intellectual doubts persist. There is undeniable force to Alexander Meiklejohn's view, and James Madison's, that the central concern of the First Amendment is freedom of debate about public affairs. The *Gertz* formula, in focusing on the fame of libel plaintiffs and subordinating the subject at issue, sometimes seems to turn that concern on its head. Carol Burnett, the entertainer, sued the *National Enquirer* over a gossip item saying that she had had a row with Henry Kissinger in a restaurant and implying that she was drunk. Ms. Burnett was undoubtedly a public figure. But what did the *Enquirer* item have to do with the uninhibited debate on public issues that the *Sullivan* case was meant to protect? Why should she have to meet a constitutional test in order to recover damages for a lie in a sleazy tabloid? (Ms. Burnett won $800,000, proving reckless or intentional falsehood on the *Enquirer*'s part.) Movie stars are among the most famous Americans and therefore qualify as public figures in law, yet they are not usually at the center of debate on public policy. Why should inaccurate gossip about their private lives deserve an especially high standard of First Amendment protection?

Consider the case of Wayne Newton, a highly popular entertainer in Las Vegas. In 1980 NBC broadcast in its *Nightly News* an investigative report on Newton suggesting that he had associations with a Mafia figure. Newton sued, and a jury in the federal court in Las Vegas awarded him more than $19 million in compensatory and punitive damages. (The trial judge reduced the total to $5,275,000.) On appeal, the U.S. Court of Appeals for the Ninth Circuit reversed the judgment, holding that there was "almost no evidence" of knowing or reckless falsehood on the part of the NBC journalists, much less the clear and convincing evidence required. The court's opinion began by quoting Madison's protest against the Sedition Act of 1798. Then it said: "In *New York Times Co. v. Sullivan*, the Supreme Court secured for the press the ability to write and publish freely without risking vindictive reprisals from local juries. The Court in *New York Times* . . . set aside a verdict of an all-white Alabama jury against a New York newspaper and several black civil rights leaders in favor of the local Commissioner of Public Affairs. Here, we consider the largest punitive damages verdict in American libel history returned against a different New York news organization by a Las Vegas jury in favor of a hometown hero."

What did Wayne Newton have to do with James Madison? Why did the First Amendment protect critics of an entertainer as Justice Brennan had said it protected the "citizen-critic of government"? Philosophically, cases like Wayne Newton's are a long way from the Alabama lawsuit that led the Supreme Court to bring libel within the First Amendment. If the *Sullivan* case had never arisen, would the Supreme Court have been persuaded to review the award of damages to Wayne Newton and impose constitutional limits on libel? Almost certainly not. By historical chance, a libel case that really did engage the central meaning of the First Amendment had come along. It called forth a transforming Supreme Court decision, and from this the constitutional doctrine spread to a much larger field.

There is a danger in the extension of First Amendment protection to most libel cases: The protection may be spread too thin. Judges tend to be readier to protect an interest that is narrowly and convincingly defined than they are to protect an indefinite class. If the constitutional libel defense covered only cases related to government and public policy, the protection might be firmer and more consistent. On the other hand, there is an argument that our social and cultural symbols, like our political leaders, must be fair game for criticism. It does say something about our society if a popular entertainer is involved with gangsters, and the press should be free to write or broadcast about such matters. But there may be a price to pay in the clarity and vigor of First Amendment protection.

In the cases that explored the implications of *Times v. Sullivan*, the justices struggled as they must when they apply to today's American society commands written into our fundamental law two hundred years ago. They were guided by their sense of the society: its traditions, its needs, its changing character. Interpreting the Constitution, they did their work much as English and American judges did in developing the common law over the centuries. In his book *The Common Law*, Justice Holmes wrote that in shaping the law those judges had been moved less by abstract logic than "by the felt necessities of the time, the prevalent moral and political theories, intuitions of public policy. . . ." The complex course of decision in the decades after *New York Times v. Sullivan* reflected just such a judicial process, as the Supreme Court struggled to make libel law conform to the command that there be "no law . . . abridging the freedom of speech, or of the press."

# 18

▣

# "THE DANCING HAS STOPPED"

WHEN *New York Times Co. v. Sullivan* was decided, Alexander Meiklejohn, the philosopher of free speech, said it was "an occasion for dancing in the streets." Twenty years later a conservative law professor, Richard A. Epstein, wrote: "A generation has now passed, and the dancing has stopped." A good many editors and writers would have agreed. For the prospect that they envisaged in 1964—a country where public debate went on uninhibited by the threat of heavy libel damages—had not come into being. On the contrary, libel suits seemed to be growing in number and size. Judge Robert Bork wrote in 1984: "In the past few years a remarkable upsurge in libel actions, accompanied by a startling inflation of damage awards, has threatened to impose a self-censorship on the press. . . ." Million-dollar libel verdicts, hitherto hardly imaginable, became an unexceptional occurrence. Justice Black had warned that James Hill's $30,000 judgment against Time Inc. would "frighten and punish the press so much that publishers will cease trying to report news in a lively and readable fashion." Now publishers had to think about the possibility of jury verdicts for five hundred times that amount.

At the time that Judge Bork made his alarmed comment, a jury had awarded $26.5 million to a former Miss Wyoming for a short story in *Penthouse* magazine—fiction—about a sexually prodigious character who she said resembled and insulted her. William Tavoulareas, the president of the Mobil Corporation, had won $2,050,000 from a jury for a report in *The Washington Post* that he had "set up his son" in a shipping-management firm that did business with Mobil. Both those judgments were eventually upset on appeal, but they put a heavy burden on the press defendants. In the Tavoulareas case, for example, several reporters and editors of the *Post* spent weeks preparing for and attending the trial. Tavoulareas estimated that by the end of the trial his lawyers' fees amounted to $1.8 million; the *Post*'s must also have been in that range, and the bills kept coming during appeals that took years to conclude. All of this was to defend a story that, in the end, was found by the U.S. Court of Appeals for the District of Columbia to be fundamentally correct.

The cost of defending against libel suits increased because of the *Sullivan* decision: an unintended consequence of the case. "Reckless disregard" for the truth was defined by the Supreme Court to mean that the publisher of a false statement could be made to pay damages only if he knew it was probably false when he published it. As libel plaintiffs tried to meet this difficult test, they inevitably sought to find out what the publisher knew at the time of publication—and who better to ask than the publisher himself? So lawyers began trying to discover what facts, say, a broadcaster may have had but not used in a disputed broadcast. Editors and reporters deeply resent intrusion into the editorial process by outsiders, not least by lawyers. Any print or broadcast report on a controversial subject necessarily involves choices of emphasis, of what facts or footage to use. Journalists believe, with reason, that they may be less than free if they conduct this process of choosing with the expectation that outsiders may later comb through the raw material and second-guess their judgments. But if a person criticized on the air or in print believes that the writer or broadcaster was aware of the truth and omitted it, how can he find out without exploring the editorial process?

The issue of journalists' rights to resist demands for details of their work was resolved in the case of *Herbert v. Lando*. Colonel Anthony Herbert was a Vietnam veteran who said he had been punished by the Army for trying to bring to its attention massacres by American forces. CBS Television did a program, *The Selling of Colonel Herbert*, that was skeptical of his claims. Colonel Herbert sued CBS, producer Barry Lando and others for libel. In discovery—the questioning and search for evidence that goes on before trial—Herbert's lawyer asked to look at CBS files and segments of filmed interviews that had been left on the cutting-room floor; he wanted to explore why some things were used and others left out. After answering up to a point, CBS resisted, arguing that exploring editorial decisions in this way would lead to fear on the part of editors, and thus to self-censorship of the very kind that *Times v. Sullivan* was supposed to prevent. But when CBS made this argument to the Supreme Court in 1978, the Court rejected it. Speaking for the Court, Justice White noted that public figures or officials had the burden under the *Sullivan* rule of proving that a publisher was aware of probable falsity; if they could not discover what the publisher knew, they might effectively be barred altogether from recovering libel damages—a step that the Court had consistently refused to take. The decision was, therefore, that libel defendants must provide material of the kind demanded by Colonel Herbert. Justice Brennan dissented in part, but he said later: "It would scarcely be fair to say that a plaintiff can only recover if he establishes intentional falsehood and at the same time to say that he cannot inquire into a defendant's intentions."

The *Herbert* decision became a significant factor in the rising cost of libel suits. If they could afford the cost of extensive discovery, plaintiffs now routinely explored the files and the minds of journalists. Not to be outdone, defendants subjected plaintiffs to probing discovery—to the point where some plaintiffs' lawyers complained of intimidation by large press enterprises. The *Herbert* case itself showed what a burden such discovery could be. It went on for twelve years, until finally in 1986 the U.S. Court of Appeals in New York ordered the colonel's libel claims dismissed and the Supreme Court declined to review the case a second time. By then producer Lando had been questioned at twenty-eight deposition sessions that produced almost three thousand pages of transcript and 240 exhibits; he also had to turn over all his files and videotapes of all the interviews done for the program. For their part CBS's lawyers demanded and got twelve thousand pages of documents from Colonel Herbert in discovery. In 1982, four years before the end, Mike Wallace of CBS, who took part in the program on Herbert and was a defendant in the libel case, estimated that CBS had spent between $3 million and $4 million in lawyers' fees on the case.

CBS and other media giants could afford to litigate libel claims. For smaller defendants the very process could be ruinous. *The Milkweed*, a monthly published in Madison, Wisconsin, had a circulation of 1,300 and a journalistic staff of one, Peter L. Hardin, editor and publisher; its field was milk marketing. In 1981 a large milk cooperative in Syracuse, New York, sued *The Milkweed* for $20 million over an article, based on government files obtained through the Freedom of Information Act, about the cooperative's application for a federal loan guarantee. Hardin was lucky. Only a year passed before a federal judge in Syracuse dismissed the suit. In that year, Hardin spent four months of his own time on the case; he had to go to Syracuse five times; he copied hundreds of pages of documents; he spent $20,000, mostly on lawyers' fees. The costs were modest, indeed almost laughable, compared with those of a big modern libel case, but they would have put *The Milkweed* out of business if readers had not responded to appeals for help.

Publications much richer than *The Milkweed* were driven to settle libel claims rather than undergo protracted and expensive litigation, with the ultimate risk of having to pay large damages as well. *The Wall Street Journal* had an announced policy of refusing to settle any libel case before trial, but in 1983 it paid $800,000 to settle one. That episode did not stop the *Journal* from continuing to do important investigative journalism. Other papers, with pockets not as deep as the *Journal*'s, may be moved by the punishment of a libel case to steer clear of controversy. This was the moral of the Alton *Telegraph* story.

Alton, in southern Illinois, is the town where an American press hero, the abolitionist editor Elijah Parish Lovejoy, was killed by a pro-slavery mob in 1837. The *Telegraph* had a tradition of uncovering official wrong; its stories once led to the resignation of two state supreme court justices. In 1969 two *Telegraph* reporters got a tip that underworld money was going to a local builder. In an effort to check, they sent a memo to a federal investigator; he passed it on to federal bank regulators, who in turn acted to cut off the builder's credit at a local savings institution. No story ever appeared in the newspaper, but the builder sued for libel over the memo. A jury awarded him $9.2 million. In order to appeal, the paper had to put up a bond of more than $10 million. Unable to raise this sum, the *Telegraph* sought protection in bankruptcy court, only to find that the bankruptcy filing prevented it from proceeding with its appeal of the libel judgment. The paper finally settled the case for $1.4 million; libel insurance covered $1 million, and the rest was borrowed. *The Wall Street Journal* told the story of the case under the headline "Chilling Effect: How Libel Suit Sapped the Crusading Spirit of a Small Newspaper." It said the Alton *Telegraph* had just about stopped looking into official wrongdoing. Reporters had to ask editors before writing letters, and destroyed notes to keep them from being used by possible future libel plaintiffs. When someone told the *Telegraph* about misconduct in a sheriff's office, the editor decided not to investigate, saying, "Let someone else stick their neck out this time."

The chilling power of a libel suit was demonstrated in an unusual way in a case involving the movie *Missing*, directed by Constantin Costa-Gavras. The movie was based on a book by Thomas Hauser, *The Execution of Charles Horman: An American Sacrifice*. Charles Horman was a young American writer who went to Chile in 1972 to write about the left-wing government of President Salvador Allende Gossens. The government was overthrown in a military coup, and a few days later Horman disappeared. His father, Edmund Horman, went down to Chile to look for his son. Gradually Edmund Horman came to suspect that American embassy officials were covering up the truth—because, he believed, his son had learned of a U.S. role in the coup. Charles Horman's body was found weeks later. The father sued American officials, including Secretary of State Henry Kissinger, over the death of his son, but he eventually dropped the suit. Hauser's book told the story through the eyes of Edmund Horman. The movie, starring Jack Lemmon and Sissy Spacek, made a powerful drama of it, with the documentary technique that Costa-Gavras had first used so effectively in his film about the Greek military junta, Z. When the movie came out, the State Department took the amazing step of issuing a white paper to denounce it. The U.S. Ambassador to Chile at the time of Charles Horman's disappearance, Nathaniel Davis, and two other American officials brought a $150 million libel suit against Hauser; Costa-Gavras; Universal Studios, which released the film; Harcourt Brace Jovanovich, publisher of the hardcover book; and the Hearst Corporation, which published the Avon paperback.

Nathaniel Davis said the movie made the "corrosive" suggestion that "we were complicit in telling the Chileans to murder Charles Horman." Professor Rodney Smolla, in his book *Suing the Press*, commented:

> "Corrosive" is exactly what it must seem to the Government, corrosive of the view that America never acts as a machismo imperialist power capable of collusion with foreign thugs. This is precisely the sort of corrosiveness, however, that the First Amendment requires the Government to endure. If the corrosive images of *Missing* are based on facts that the Government disputes, the Government may come forth with its own convincing evidence. But one of the essential points of the First Amendment is that citizens are not required to mutely take the Government's word for it.

Smolla added that Richard Nixon (President at the time of the Chilean coup), Kissinger, Davis and other U.S. officials had all denied any U.S. involvement in the coup. They might be telling the truth, he said; the version of Edmund Horman, Hauser and Costa-Gavras could be founded on paranoia. "Yet it is also at least theoretically possible that the likes of Nixon and Kissinger are lying about Chile. It is not as if they have never lied before."

Despite the strong First Amendment argument that Americans should be free to debate the role of their officials in a political event like the coup in Chile, the libel suit over *Missing* had a sting. The sting was in the tail. In 1982 Avon reissued Hauser's book, retitling it *Missing* to take advantage of the movie's release. It sold well. But when the libel action was filed in 1983, Avon decided not to print any more copies. Its lawyers advised that reprinting in order to meet demand for the book might hurt the publisher's position in the libel case. In 1985 the film was shown on network television. Ordinarily a publisher would promote a book to take advantage of such exposure, but Hauser's book was unmentioned and unobtainable. In frustration, Hauser asked the publishers to let the rights revert to him so that he could find someone else to republish it. They refused—and they held to this position even after judges threw out the libel claims. The publishers' lawyers explained that something could still go wrong on appeal, and that allowing more copies to be printed might complicate matters and mean more legal fees. And so a libel suit with little chance of succeeding—a frivolous suit, really—kept a serious book out of print for years. The *Missing* case showed how chilling the law of libel can be, especially when publishers are craven. Television is not noted for its courage, but it went ahead and showed the Costa-Gavras film. No court, no plaintiff, no insurance company asked to have the book suppressed. The publishers suppressed it.

The *Missing* libel tale ended with a whimper. After the libel claims were dismissed, a counterclaim by Hauser against Ambassador Davis and the other plaintiffs was still pending. On May 7, 1987, Davis's deposition was taken. (A deposition is testimony in a pretrial proceeding.) Hauser, who happened to be a lawyer himself, did the questioning. He asked Davis how many members of the C.I.A. were on the embassy roster when he was ambassador in Santiago. Davis was reluctant to answer. Suddenly he told his lawyer that he wanted to stop the deposition—and the case. He agreed to drop all appeals and promise never to sue over *Missing* again, in return for Hauser's giving up his counterclaim, and he and the other plaintiffs signed an agreement to this effect. Meanwhile, Hauser had sued Harcourt and Avon over their failure either to keep the book in print or to allow the rights to revert to him. A year later the two publishers settled, paying Hauser a substantial sum and letting him have his book back. Simon & Schuster then brought out a new edition.

Twenty years after *New York Times Co. v. Sullivan*, libel suits were a flourishing American industry. Not just entertainers and corporate executives but generals and governors and senators sued. General William Westmoreland, who had commanded U.S. forces in Vietnam, sued CBS. General Ariel Sharon of Israel sued *Time*. Judges of the Pennsylvania Supreme Court sued *The Philadelphia Inquirer* for libel over stories critical of them. The *Inquirer* spent the better part of two decades litigating over a 1973 story that questioned how a prosecutor, Richard A. Sprague, had handled a homicide case. (After a trial and extended appeals, a second trial jury in 1990 awarded Sprague $34 million, and the *Inquirer* appealed again.) Donald Trump, the real estate personality, sued the *Chicago Tribune* and its architecture critic for $500 million—unsuccessfully—over an article ridiculing his proposal to build a 150-story building in New York. Sooner or later, it seemed, someone would bring the first $1 billion libel suit.

Why the explosion in the number and size of libel suits? Why, especially, the many lawsuits by public figures and officials? The American tradition is the opposite. Harry Truman wrote his sister in 1948: "Every man in the White House was tortured and bedeviled by the so-called free press. They were lied about, misrepresented and actually libeled, and they had to take it and do nothing." Grant and other Civil War generals suffered criticism far more savage than anything dreamed of by William Westmoreland, but they did not sue. As recently as 1947 Professor Chafee, whose scholarship on the First Amendment had so impressed Justice Holmes, could write that "a libeled American prefers to vindicate himself by steadily pushing forward his career and not by hiring a lawyer to talk in a courtroom." What has happened to that tradition?

One explanation offered for the libel surge is that the press has subjected political figures to more wounding assaults since the *Sullivan* decision. President Nixon so argued in a radio address as Watergate was closing in on him in 1974. "People interested in running for public office," he said, should have "greater assurance of recourse against slanderous attacks on them or their families. . . . Unfortunately, some libel lawyers have interpreted recent Supreme Court decisions, particularly the decision in Sullivan v. New York Times, as being virtually a license to lie where a political candidate, a member of his family or one of his supporters or friends is involved. This is wrong."

A similar view was taken by some others whose judgment was not marred by the self-interest of an unraveling Richard Nixon. A distinguished state judge, Walter Schaefer of the Illinois Supreme Court, said in 1980 that the *Sullivan* decision had "sharply depreciated" the value of public service. But the notion that the press was harder on public servants after 1964 is contradicted by history. At the time of the First Amendment's adoption, and in the decades thereafter, political leaders were savaged by a press that was often in the pay of opposition parties. Jefferson was a celebrated advocate of the freedom of the press, one who said in 1787: "Were it left to me to decide whether we should have a government without newspapers, or newspapers without a government, I should not hesitate a moment to prefer the latter." But in 1807, after

he had been President for six years, he wrote to a friend: "Nothing can
now be believed which is seen in a newspaper. Truth itself becomes
suspicious by being put into that polluted vehicle." The yellow press at
the end of the nineteenth century was no better.

How, then, can one explain what Judge Bork called the "remarkable
upsurge" in libel? No doubt it reflected the general inflation in tort cases—
the huge verdicts won for medical malpractice, faulty products and the
like. Americans in the latter part of the twentieth century seem to believe
in the free-lunch theory of law; they are convinced that every misfortune
can be blamed on someone or something, and that lavish compensation
can be obtained. But there must be something more to the libel phenomenon, for it is even more extravagant than the situation in other torts.

The most convincing explanations, and the wittiest, were offered by
Professor Smolla. First there is what he described as "the general thinning
of the American skin." In and around the Me Generation, Smolla said,
people cared more about themselves. They spent time and money on
narcissistic self-improvement, first finding and then nurturing the inner
self. Smolla concluded: "One does not pay thousands of dollars to an
analyst to resurrect a self-image, and then sit idly by as that work is
publicly undone by 60 Minutes or The National Enquirer." Then the
character of the press has changed. Reporters used to be low-paid, ill-
educated types who sat around seedy press rooms, as in the play *The
Front Page*, drinking whiskey and making up colorful stories. Who cared
what a scoundrel like that said about you? But now they are journalists,
college graduates, and they drink white wine. Moreover, there were lots
of papers in the old days; what *The World* said might be contradicted
by *The Tribune*. Now there are fewer papers, weightier and more self-
important. "The establishment press takes itself so seriously," Smolla
wrote. It "seems to dispense not merely news but Truth, and juries may
be reflecting a general public backlash against that oracular role."

Television is even more of an oracle. Its pervasive reach has made
national eminences of the network anchor men and women and the top
reporters. To the public, that looks like power—and power sometimes
exercised in an unaccountable, even arrogant way. The networks, big
newspapers and magazines ask questions and demand answers, but when
anyone wants to know about their business, they wrap themselves in the
First Amendment and refuse to answer. So it often appears to the public.
The press sees it very differently. Journalists know how little power they
have to penetrate the secrecy of government. When Dan Rather tried to
get answers to important questions about George Bush's role in the Iran-
contra affair, Bush could so easily stonewall him—and in the process
paint Rather as a brute for trying. But the public perception is of a

powerful press. So libel suits have become a way of getting even with the high and mighty, Smolla said: a way of challenging a new power in American society.

The impression of arrogance has been deepened by the reluctance of much of the press to admit mistakes. A good many people who brought libel suits say they would not have done so if the publisher of an offending statement had been willing to retract it, or even discuss it. A painful example of stiff-necked press behavior was the performance of *Time* magazine in the case of Ariel Sharon. As Defense Minister of Israel in 1982, General Sharon directed the Israeli invasion of Lebanon, which turned out disastrously for both countries. In violation of a promise to the United States, he sent Israeli troops into Moslem West Beirut. After them came the Phalangist Christian forces, who entered Palestinian refugee camps and slaughtered hundreds of people, most of them women and children. Protests in Israel forced the appointment of a judicial commission, which found that General Sharon bore "indirect responsibility" for the massacre. *Time* was not content to report the commission's severe indictment of Sharon. "Time has learned," it added portentously, that a secret Appendix B to the commission report said Sharon had discussed with Phalangist leaders "the need for the Phalangists to take revenge." Sharon sued for $50 million. In extended discovery proceedings and a trial that lasted two months, *Time* relied on unnamed sources for its story, refusing to disclose their names. Eventually Israel allowed a guarded look by lawyers at Appendix B, and there was nothing in it about such a Sharon discussion with the Phalangists. *Time* then argued that this was a "relatively minor inaccuracy." But the reference to Appendix B had given *Time*'s tale an air of credibility. The truth was that *Time* had published an inaccurate story based on unreliable sources, if any, and it did not have the grace to admit its fault. Or the common sense either, because Sharon would have settled for a brief retraction long before the end of the expensive litigation. After eleven days of deliberations, the jury found that the story was false, but not recklessly so. As a result, Sharon lost his claim for damages. But *Time* suffered a loss of credibility, a wound inflicted by its own arrogance.

The press sometimes aggravates the public perception of arrogance by the way that it speaks of its constitutional rights. Phrases such as "freedom of the press" or "First Amendment rights" have taken on the air of dogma, and exclusivist dogma at that. Some editors and publishers act as if the press clause of the First Amendment were designed to protect journalism alone, and to make that protection superior to other rights in the Constitution—propositions that have no support in logic or history. The whole concept of press freedom was first sonorously argued by John

Milton at a time when there were no regular newspapers. Milton was concerned about the censorship of books and pamphlets, and it was in this tradition that the free press clauses of the American state constitutions and then the First Amendment arose. No one can seriously argue that the Framers of the First Amendment meant to assure freedom to newspapers and not to books. The combination of the speech and press clauses indicates that they were intended to protect expression in all forms, oral and printed. Nor is there a hint of preference for journalism, or the press generally, above other guarantees in the Constitution—the Sixth Amendment's assurances that criminal defendants will have a fair trial, for example.

When the Supreme Court decides a case against a claimed press interest, editors and publishers too often act as if the Constitution were gone. When the Court in the *Herbert* case decided that press defendants must answer questions about their editorial process in libel cases, the *Los Angeles Times* called the decision "Orwellian." An editor of the *St. Louis Post-Dispatch* said it had "the potential of totally inhibiting the press to a degree seldom seen outside a dictatorial or Fascist country." As stalwart a friend of free expression as Justice Brennan cautioned against such rhetorical overkill. In the *Herbert* case, he said, "the injury done the press was simply not of the magnitude to justify the resulting firestorm of acrimonious criticism." He added that the issues faced by the Court in that and other cases were ones on which reasonable judges could differ, and that the press would be well advised to make careful, credible arguments. Justice Brennan concluded: "This may involve a certain loss of innocence, a certain recognition that the press, like other institutions, must accommodate a variety of important social interests."

On one legal issue especially many journalists have argued for a special constitutional position. This is the claim of a privilege for journalists not to answer questions about confidential sources of information. In three cases decided by the Supreme Court in 1972, reporters who had information about possible crimes were subpoenaed by prosecutors to appear before grand juries. They refused to testify, saying that to do so would compromise their relationship with informants to whom they had promised anonymity. By a vote of 5 to 4, the Supreme Court rejected the claim that the freedom of the press guaranteed by the First Amendment entitled the reporters to a privilege against having to testify. Later cases in the lower courts involved a similar claim of privilege when reporters were subpoenaed by the *defendant* in a criminal case, or by someone suing for libel who wanted to know the names of unidentified sources of damaging quotations in a published story.

That reporters need to use confidential sources on occasion is certainly true. It would not have been possible for *The Washington Post* to expose the Watergate cover-up without leads from "Deep Throat" and other sources to whom its reporters promised confidentiality. Reporters and editors have to keep such promises or destroy their own credibility. But it does not follow that a right to withhold the names in legal proceedings can be found in the First Amendment, or that it trumps all other constitutional rights. A defendant in a criminal trial, for example, is constitutionally entitled to summon witnesses on his behalf. If a reporter has information that would prove the defendant innocent, does the Constitution really protect him if he refuses to testify? Occasionally—very occasionally—a journalist may be held in contempt for keeping his promise of confidentiality, and may go to jail. That is a painful price for the journalist to pay, but it happens seldom and may be less distorting to our system of law than a blanket privilege for journalists would be.

Or consider the libel situation. Suppose a newspaper or magazine, without naming sources, calls someone a terrorist. Is there a compelling interest—a constitutional interest—in denying the accused person the right to know the basis for this damaging accusation? In a South African libel case a news magazine reported that a black minister secretly called for violence against the apartheid system while publicly speaking of peace. The minister demanded to know the source of the charge. When the editor refused to disclose the name, a court awarded damages to the minister. Later it turned out that the magazine was funded by the government, and that the story was planted by the secret police. Those facts put a different cast on the claim for a journalist's privilege. And there were situations of a kind not so different in the United States during the McCarthy years: publications that smeared citizens as pro-Communist on the basis of alleged anonymous sources. The press can be destructive, too. It is not always the good guy.

Press exceptionalism—the idea that journalism has a different and superior status in the Constitution—is not only an unconvincing but a dangerous doctrine. Ordinary citizens find it hard to understand why the press should have more rights than they do. Moreover, in the long run, rights depend on public understanding and support. Judge Bork put it: "To the degree that the press is alone in the enjoyment of freedom, to that degree is its freedom imperiled."

The press draws its constitutional support from a First Amendment whose central purpose is to ensure robust debate on public affairs, but this purpose is not served by journalists alone. From the beginning, America has been a country where aroused citizens made a difference on crucial issues. From the abolitionists before the Civil War to the environmentalists of today, citizen campaigns have had an imprint on our history.

The phenomenon of libel suits shows that citizens may have as much of a stake in the central meaning of the First Amendment as the press does. For the surge of libel suits that so alarmed the press in the 1980s hit private citizens as well, and was if anything more chilling to those who spoke out on public issues.

Alan La Pointe of Richmond, California, campaigned against a trash incinerator proposed by the West Contra Costa Sanitary District. The state attorney general ruled that construction funds for the plant had been misspent, and La Pointe brought a taxpayer's suit. The Sanitary District countersued, demanding $42 million from La Pointe on the ground that his speeches and writings had blocked the incinerator. Eventually California courts dismissed the Sanitary District's claim, but La Pointe said he now wondered whether it was "worth the toll" to speak out as a citizen. Squaw Valley, California, has been the subject of much public debate and litigation over development plans, and the Squaw Valley Property Owners Association joined the Sierra Club in opposing one project. But the next time the developer, Alexander Cushing, had a talk with the directors of the Association, they decided not to oppose him. One of them said afterward: "Cushing's attitude was, you sue me, I sue you—it's as simple as that. . . . I have a small business and a second child on the way. I was nervous."

Two professors at the University of Denver, George W. Pring and Penelope Canan, studied what they called "strategic lawsuits against public participation." These were suits against individuals or groups for circulating a petition, testifying or otherwise taking part in some governmental process on an issue of public concern. In 1989 Pring and Canan wrote: "Every year, hundreds, perhaps thousands, of civil lawsuits are filed in the United States whose sole purpose is to prevent citizens from exercising their political rights or to punish those who have done so."

Letters to the editor, that most traditional way for individuals to have a voice on public issues, have also attracted growing numbers of libel suits. What may well have been the single most outrageous libel case— the worst abuse of the legal process—began with a letter to the editor of the *Journal of Medical Primatology*. The magazine, a specialist journal for students of apes and other primates, had a circulation of three hundred. The letter, published in 1983, was from Dr. Shirley McGreal, chairwoman of the International Primate Protection League. It criticized a plan by Immuno A.G., a multinational corporation based in Austria, to use captured chimpanzees for hepatitis research in Sierra Leone. McGreal charged that (1) Immuno was trying to avoid international restrictions on the importation of chimpanzees by building a facility in Sierra Leone; (2) the plan might decimate the wild chimpanzee population, because chimpanzees were generally captured by killing their mothers; and (3) any captured animals returned to the wild after experiments could spread hepatitis to other chimpanzees. Immuno brought a libel suit against eight defendants, including Dr. McGreal and Dr. Jan Moor-Jankowski, editor of the magazine and a professor at the New York University Medical School who directed its Laboratory for Experimental Medicine and Surgery in Primates. Immuno's complaint cited the McGreal letter and also comments by Dr. Moor-Jankowski, quoted in the British magazine *New Scientist*, calling the Immuno plan "scientific imperialism" and warning that it would "backfire on people like me involved in the bona fide use of chimpanzees" for research.

Immuno's suit was filed in 1984. Over the next few years all of the defendants except Dr. Moor-Jankowski settled because the cost of litigating against a large company was prohibitive. They paid Immuno what a judge called "substantial sums" to get out of the lawsuit, and most of them disavowed any intention to criticize the Sierra Leone plan. Dr. McGreal's insurance company settled for $100,000 on her behalf, having already spent $250,000 on the case; but Dr. McGreal herself never retracted anything. That left Dr. Moor-Jankowski as the lone defendant, with Immuno demanding $4 million in damages from him. He asked the trial judge, Beatrice Shainswit of the New York Supreme Court, to grant summary judgment for him, throwing out the suit. Summary judgment is a device used to dispose of lawsuits without a full trial when they present no substantial issues of fact—that is, when one side is entitled to win even on the facts stated by the other side. Summary judgment is crucial for defendants in libel cases, for otherwise they face expensive years of discovery and then a trial. But Judge Shainswit refused to grant summary judgment for Dr. Moor-Jankowski, saying that a jury must decide whether Dr. McGreal's letter to the editor was accurate and, if not, whether it was knowingly or recklessly false. The decision was appealed on up to New York's highest court, the Court of Appeals, which unanimously held that summary judgment should have been granted in Dr. Moor-Jankowski's favor.

Judge Judith Kaye wrote a memorable opinion for the Court of Appeals, saying: "For many members of the public a letter to the editor may be the only available opportunity to air concerns about issues affecting them." Quoting an English case, she said that a citizen "troubled by things going wrong" should feel free to write to the newspaper, and the paper to publish the letter: "It is often the only way to get things put right." She went on: "The availability of such a forum is important not only because it allows persons or groups with views on a subject of public

interest to reach and persuade the broader community but also because
it allows the readership to learn about grievances, both from the original
writers and from those who respond, that perhaps had previously circulated only as rumor; such a forum can advance an issue beyond invective. . . . The public forum function of letters to the editor is closely
related in spirit to the 'marketplace of ideas.' . . ."

Judge Kaye also stressed the importance of summary judgment in libel
cases. This case, she said, had "already engendered thousands of pages
of a litigation record and 'substantial' settlements from all other defendants." It exemplified, she said, quoting from an earlier case, the fact
that having to litigate a libel suit all the way through a trial "may be as
chilling to the exercise of First Amendment freedoms as fear of the outcome of the lawsuit itself."

The Court of Appeals decision was a famous victory for Dr. Moor-
Jankowski and for freedom of letters to the editor. But it was not, alas,
the end of the case. Judge Kaye based her judgment on both state and
federal law. She found that Dr. McGreal's letter taken as a whole was
an expression of opinion. And long-standing New York law, like the
common law of libel in most states, said that opinion could not be the
subject of libel suits—because, unlike facts, it could not be proved true
or false. But Judge Kaye also relied on Justice Powell's statement in the
*Gertz* case that "under the First Amendment there is no such thing as a
false idea. However pernicious an opinion may seem, we depend for its
correction not on the conscience of judges and juries but on the competition of other ideas." Many lower courts had understood this passage
to mean that any statement that could be characterized overall as an
expression of opinion was constitutionally immune from libel suits. But
a few months after the New York court decided the *Immuno* case, the
Supreme Court held that there was no such sweeping federal constitutional rule. Even though a statement overall was an expression of opinion,
the Court said, if it implied facts that could be proved false, it was subject
to libel. After that decision the Supreme Court, acting on a petition for
review of the *Immuno* case, sent it back to New York for another look
in light of the new definition of federal law. The Court of Appeals looked
again—and held to its judgment. Judge Kaye for the Court said Dr.
McGreal's letter to the editor was protected by the First Amendment
even in light of the recent Supreme Court decision. Judge Kaye went on
to make even clearer that, in any event, this libel suit was forbidden by
the New York State constitution, which she read as giving special protection to commentary such as letters to the editor. Dr. Moor-Jankowski,
legally ahead but severely bruised, wrote a letter to the editor of *The
New York Times* describing himself ironically as "the 'victorious' de-

fendant" and going on to describe what he called "the real-life effects of this suit." He said:

> I am a full-time research professor at the New York University School of Medicine and the unpaid editor of the small, international Journal of Medical Primatology. For the last seven years (10 percent of life expectancy of an American male) I have been sued. . . . So far, my legal expenses exceed $1 million. I underwent fourteen days of depositions over a year and a half in this country and was ordered by the lower court to participate in extremely costly depositions in Austria and Sierra Leone. . . . The seven years of proceedings consumed most of my time, curtailing my scientific activities. The court victory may still not effectively protect me or other editors of small professional journals from the chilling effect of suits by wealthy corporations using our legal system to discourage criticism of their activities. We need a legal deterrent to prohibitively costly, meritless libel suits that misuse the court system to undermine our First Amendment rights.

The saga of the *Immuno* case showed a number of things about the state of libel law twenty-five years after *Times v. Sullivan*. It showed that, unless judges are alert to the need for summary judgment, a large and ruthless corporation can bring a meritless libel suit and extract money from the defendants by threatening to bankrupt those who resist. It showed that libel can be as real a concern for a scholarly journal with a tiny circulation as for *The New York Times*. It showed that the Madisonian function of public criticism may be performed by a citizen writing a letter to the editor, and that she may be punished for performing it. It showed that if the marketplace of ideas is to work, someone like Dr. McGreal must be as free to express her views as is a columnist for the *Times*. Spokesmen for groups like Dr. McGreal's International Primate Protection League are important sources for the press; but even if the press were not involved at all, the Madisonian imperative would be no different. If Dr. McGreal had chosen to express her concerns by speaking out at a public meeting or circulating a petition instead of writing a letter to the editor, she should have been just as entitled to air her views without the intimidating fear of a libel suit.

Curiously, the constitutional law of libel did not quickly follow the logic of Madison and the marketplace of ideas. Formally, at least, the Supreme Court left open the question whether the *Sullivan* decision protected individuals who were sued for libel as it protected the press. In the *Gertz* case in 1974 Justice Powell, in holding that public figures like governmental officials must prove knowing or reckless falsehood to recover libel damages, kept referring to the press and the news media; evidently he had in mind the special need of the press for protective rules. In later cases several members of the Court, including Justice Brennan, raised the specific question of the rights of individuals who were sued for libel, and said they should be in the same constitutional position as the press; but a generation after *Sullivan*, a majority had not given a definitive answer.

Yet the facts of the *Sullivan* case itself would seem to settle the question. After all, not only *The New York Times* but the four Alabama ministers were defendants in Commissioner Sullivan's libel suit. Justice Brennan applied his newly fashioned constitutional rule to the four, holding that the case against them was "without constitutional support." At the argument of the case, there were these exchanges between Justice Goldberg and Professor Wechsler, representing the *Times*:

> JUSTICE GOLDBERG: "This [Wechsler's argument on seditious libel] applies not only to newspapers but to anybody?"
> WECHSLER: "Exactly; of course."
> JUSTICE GOLDBERG: "In other words, you are not arguing here for a special rule that applies to newspapers?"
> WECHSLER: "Certainly not."

Justice Brennan began his opinion in *Sullivan* by saying that the Court was required to determine the extent to which "the constitutional protections for speech and press" applied in libel cases: speech *and* press, not the press alone. He spoke of the need to protect "the citizen-critic of government": the citizen, not the press. A year later, on the strength of the *Sullivan* case, the Court summarily set aside libel damages awarded to a Mississippi police chief against a civil rights leader who, when he was arrested, issued a public statement saying that his arrest was "a diabolical plot." Though the Court did not specifically address the point, it applied the *Sullivan* rule to a statement by an individual.

If and when one of the hundreds or thousands of citizens sued for libel every year for expressing a view on a public issue takes the case to the Supreme Court, it is hard to believe that the Court will deny First Amendment protection to him or her. And the press will not object: On this issue, at least, it has taken an intelligently unselfish position, agreeing that the lone pamphleteer is as entitled to the protection of the First Amendment as a television network. A leading editor, Eugene L. Roberts Jr. of *The Philadelphia Inquirer*, spoke in 1989 about the danger of libel suits against citizens. He said: "Freedom of the press has not survived and thrived this long in America because it is a right reserved exclusively for the powerful press. It has survived, and thrived, because citizens rightly see press freedom as merely an extension of their own freedom. They are free to question, challenge and accuse the lawmakers they elect, so they are comfortable when the press is extended that same freedom."

If *Immuno A.G. v. Moor-Jankowski* was one extreme of the modern libel suit—a sledgehammer to crack the tiny nut of a letter to the editor read by a few hundred people—the other extreme was *Westmoreland v. CBS*. Here was a clash between a famous general and a giant television network about a broadcast seen by millions. But the moral of the case was really the same: the failure of the legal process in a libel action to serve legitimate social interests.

On January 23, 1982, CBS broadcast a ninety-minute documentary film charging that there had been "a conspiracy at the highest levels of American military intelligence" in the Vietnam war "to suppress and alter critical intelligence on the enemy." The program, called *The Uncounted Enemy: A Vietnam Deception*, said General Westmoreland, the commander of U.S. forces, had ordered that the number of North Vietnamese troops infiltrating into the South before the Tet offensive in 1968 be understated in reports to Washington. (In the Tet offensive the Viet Cong and North Vietnamese attacked many cities in South Vietnam and actually got inside the perimeter of the U.S. embassy in Saigon. The attacks were ultimately unsuccessful in military terms. But American public opinion, seeing that the other side was not as badly damaged as President Johnson and his military had been saying, moved against the war.) According to the broadcast, the true intelligence figures on North Vietnamese forces in the South were far higher than previous projections would have made plausible, and intelligence officers were ordered to make arbitrary cuts to avoid an angry reaction from the President.

General Westmoreland denounced the program, and the magazine *TV Guide* gave him powerful support in a long article called "Anatomy of a Smear." It said the producers of the program had violated CBS's own rules, for example by using a paid consultant as an on-air witness. CBS then did its own investigation, finding that its rules had indeed been violated but standing by the broadcast's conclusions. The network offered General Westmoreland fifteen minutes of unedited air time—a huge amount by television standards—but his lawyer said such a reply would only "dignify a lie." Instead the general sued CBS for $120 million.

The discovery phase of the case produced 400,000 pages of documents. When CBS's lawyers moved for summary judgment in 1984, their motion and supporting briefs ran to 1,342 pages; Westmoreland's lawyer filed 1,380 pages in reply. The trial judge, Pierre N. Leval of the United States District Court for the Southern District of New York, denied summary judgment, and the case went to trial in October 1984. By then each side had spent roughly $2 million. The trial went on for nearly four months, with extended evidence and arguments on why the program had used certain materials and not others. Then General Westmoreland, evidently feeling that the jury was unlikely to find that he had produced the necessary proof of knowing or reckless falsehood by CBS, gave up and dropped the case.

For both sides the litigation was damaging. General Westmoreland looked like the grand old Duke of York in the English verse, who marched ten thousand men up the hill and then marched them down again. CBS, for its part, was shown to have made some dubious judgments—if not reckless enough to lose a libel case. The law itself looked more than a little foolish, too. For enormous resources had been devoted to proving something that was essentially beyond proof: the "truth" of an aspect of the Vietnam war. The case turned in part on whether certain local guerrilla forces should be included in the estimated numbers of soldiers that U.S. and South Vietnamese forces were facing. But that question in turn depended on a judgment of what kind of war it was. There could be no provable "truth" about such matters—at least not of a kind that juries can appropriately determine. Everything that happened in Vietnam was the subject of intense political debate. Its truths were political truths, to be settled in politics, not law.

The point about statistics in Vietnam was made perfectly in a novel by Ward Just, *In the City of Fear*, published before the Westmoreland lawsuit. (Just had been a correspondent in Vietnam during the war.) In one scene the President of the United States is being briefed on Vietnam, and he begins to worry about the figures he is getting. "Are they cooked?" he asks. An adviser replies: "Not *cooked* exactly. . . . All the statistics are accurate, I'm sure." Another says: "That is the point about them. They are accurate, of course. Beautiful, in their way. And so numerous."

When Judge Leval let the case go to trial, he would have done better to recall Justice Harlan's warning in the case of *Time Inc. v. Hill:* "In many areas which are at the center of public debate, 'truth' is not a readily identifiable concept, and putting to the pre-existing prejudices of a jury the determination of what is 'true' may effectively institute a system of censorship." General Westmoreland was obviously sincere in denouncing the program as false, but his proper remedy was the one he turned down: a rare chance to defend himself in time provided by the television network. As it was, the general did appear a good deal on television before and after the trial, and his public standing clearly improved. The marketplace worked.

When the trial suddenly ended, the jurors were disappointed that they were not going to have their chance to deliver a verdict. Judge Leval tried to ease what he called their "sense of disappointment" by making some remarkable comments to them. "Judgments of history are too subtle and too complex to be resolved satisfactorily with the simplicity of a jury's verdict. . . ." he said. "So I suggest to you that it may be for the best that the verdict will be left to history." True. But if so, the case should never have gone to trial. Judge Leval should have granted summary judgment for CBS.

The *Westmoreland* case was a highly publicized symbol of spreading discontent with the law of libel: the constitutional law that began with *New York Times v. Sullivan*. Both the press and public-spirited individual citizens found themselves battered by libel claims and litigation costs that punished their expression as the *Sullivan* case had seemed to promise it would not be punished. For plaintiffs, too—those who felt genuinely wounded by what they considered false criticism—the libel process was frustrating. The dancing had stopped.

## 19

# BACK TO THE DRAWING BOARD?

IN September 1964, six months after the decision in *New York Times v. Sullivan*, Herbert Wechsler had a troubled letter from a *Times* executive, Lester Markel. Markel was a strong minded, demanding editor who for many years had been in charge of the paper's Sunday sections; he was now associate editor. He worried, he said, that in winning the *Sullivan* case "we may be opening the way to complete irresponsibility in journalism." Would Wechsler argue, he asked, that an official should have "no recourse in the law" if a newspaper "knowingly publishes a false report" about him? In fact Wechsler *had* argued that in the Supreme Court—his broader claim—but a majority had not agreed. In reply, Wechsler noted that the Court had left it open for an official to recover damages for a story that was knowingly or recklessly false. But he defended his argument for absolute immunity. Whether an official should be able to get libel damages for a knowing falsehood, he said, was a question that came down "to the reliability of the ordinary jury trial as an instrument for adjudicating knowledge." In other words, could a newspaper count on a jury to decide accurately and fairly what it "knew" before publishing a story? Doubts on that score had led Madison to argue for a broader immunity, Wechsler said, and the point still had "both practical and theoretical weight today. . . . So long as the law of libel retains the punitive aspect that it still has, I think there is a solid basis for contending that it will impose a serious threat to public discussion of the conduct of public officials if a newspaper must run the gamut of a jury on the issues of falsity and knowledge. That was why I felt free to argue that point in our case."

Markel wrote back suggesting that "a decent jury system in the South" would obviate the problem. He asked whether it was right to erode principles of journalistic responsibility "because justice is lopsided in one area of the nation." Wechsler replied that he did not think the problem was limited to the South. In the long run, he said, "the sort of difficulty now dramatically presented in the South is one that is likely to arise anywhere throughout the country."

Time proved Wechsler correct in his gloomy prophecy. The "punitive aspect" of libel, heavy damages and high litigating costs, grew worse for defendants. Juries outside the South were as generous in awarding damages to well-known local plaintiffs as the jury in Montgomery, Alabama, had been with Commissioner Sullivan. A jury in Philadelphia awarded $34 million to Richard Sprague, one in Las Vegas $19 million to Wayne Newton. Juries across the country tended to decide in favor of people suing the press for libel. Of the cases that actually went to trial, juries over the years decided roughly three-quarters against the press. That was the finding in studies by the Libel Defense Resource Center, an organization whose very existence, as a research group serving press institutions that have been or may be sued, demonstrates the increased concern about libel actions. Juries not only favored libel plaintiffs on the whole but gave very large sums in damages. According to an LDRC survey, the average amount awarded by juries in libel actions against the press in the period between 1980 and 1983 was $2,174,633. This was more than triple the average award found in a survey of medical malpractice cases. In short, juries seemed to think that persons whose reputations were wrongfully injured by the press deserved three times the compensation of those whose bodies had been injured by incompetent doctors. Why did jurors feel such antagonism toward the press and sympathy for those who claimed to be its victims? One reason may be the size of some press defendants—the broadcast networks, major newspapers and magazines—and their perceived wealth and power. In a dispute between the wounded individual and the big corporation, Americans tend to root for the individual as the underdog, even though a rich entertainer or a high public official may not really be an underdog. Power is always suspect, and a press that boasts of bringing down a President is powerful even if the claim is exaggerated. There is also the feeling that corporations can pay, so why not *make* them pay?

Most of the jury awards against the press were reversed or substantially reduced by appellate courts, according to the LDRC—between 60 and

70 percent at various times. The close scrutiny by appellate courts was reinforced when in 1984 the Supreme Court reiterated its statement in the *Sullivan* decision that appellate judges must subject the facts as well as legal rulings in libel cases to independent review, in order to make sure that critical speech was not being chilled. Judges were similarly rigorous in pruning out bad cases before trial, granting about three fourths of the motions for summary judgment by press defendants and thus disposing of the suits. Again a Supreme Court decision helped. The Court held in 1986 that a trial judge should grant summary judgment for a libel defendant in a suit by an official or public figure if the plaintiff had not shown, in pre-trial proceedings, convincing evidence of knowing or reckless falsehood. But despite the press's success in disposing of suits before trial and reversing jury awards on appeal, the burden of defending against libel suits has remained heavy. Insurance companies that write libel policies for the press reported at one point that 80 percent of what they paid out to their insured in libel cases went for costs—mostly lawyers' fees—and only 20 percent for damage awards. Eugene Roberts, editor of the much sued *Philadelphia Inquirer*, said that *Sullivan* had led to a new form of suppression: "The modern way to silence criticism is to price it out of existence with protracted libel litigation."

Dissatisfaction with the way libel law has worked under the regime of the *Sullivan* decision has led some legal thinkers to question whether the decision was right in the first place. Serious critics recognized, as they had to, that the Supreme Court in 1964 faced a compelling occasion for the imposition of some constitutional restraints on state libel law. The jury in Montgomery, Alabama, had given $500,000 to Commissioner Sullivan for an advertisement that did not mention him, and millions of dollars more were likely to be awarded in other cases pending in the South. If the Court had allowed Sullivan's judgment to stand, the results would have been disastrous for the civil rights movement and the American press. Under the circumstances something had to be done. But some critics of the *Sullivan* decision argued that the something should have been more modest than what Justice Brennan did in requiring an official who sued for libel to prove knowing or reckless falsehood in a publication about him.

Professor Richard Epstein, for example, said the Court could have focused solely on the Alabama jury's finding that the advertisement was "of and concerning" Sullivan even though he was not mentioned in it. Epstein said the Supreme Court could have held that that finding was a distortion of the common law of libel, the judge-made law that governs libel in most states. It could have told the Alabama courts, "You did not follow your own rules." In effect this would have constitutionalized the part of the common law requiring a libel plaintiff to prove that a statement was "of and concerning" him. Doing it that way, Epstein and others argued, would have been a more limited intrusion on state law. But on reflection, the argument is unpersuasive. For the Supreme Court to have told the courts of Alabama that they had made a mistake in applying their own libel rules would have been more intrusive, not less. In effect the Supreme Court would have been saying, "We are going to oversee your application of state law, making ourselves the court of last resort on what your common law of libel means." Moreover, the overseeing could not have been limited to the "of and concerning" rule.

Before long another Southern court of that time would have awarded huge damages to someone who in fact *was* mentioned in a critical publication. An early possibility was the Birmingham police chief, Bull Connor, who had sued over Harrison Salisbury's *New York Times* articles on the racist atmosphere of Birmingham. After the *Sullivan* decision his suit was dismissed. If it had proceeded to trial, an all-white jury would undoubtedly have given him large damages—and confronted the Supreme Court again with the problem of libel law being used as a political instrument to suppress criticism of white supremacy. If the Court had chosen in the *Sullivan* case to constitutionalize only the "of and concerning" requirement, it would now have had to find that some other part of the common law had been misapplied. Imposing a new federal requirement to prove knowing or reckless falsehood may have been more immediately dramatic, but in the long run it was less intrusive than it would have been for the Supreme Court, in case after case, to find that a state decision on state law violated the Constitution.

The same point applies to another argument made by Epstein and others: that the Supreme Court should have used the issue of damages to dispose of the *Sullivan* case. It could have held, for example, that in libel cases the First Amendment barred punitive damages—damages intended not to compensate victims but to punish outrageous conduct and deter it in future. Because the $500,000 awarded to Sullivan may have included punitive damages, the judgment would have been reversed and the case sent back for a new trial. Or, it has been argued, the Court could have gone further and held that the First Amendment barred *any* damages for libel except what a plaintiff could prove was actual financial injury, such as loss of a job because of a libelous publication.

The idea that the Court should have imposed constitutional limits on libel damages is attractive in hindsight, because damage awards have since risen to such outlandish heights. But if Wechsler or anyone else had tried to make such an argument in 1964, he would have faced formidable odds. The Supreme Court early in its history had rejected a general attack on punitive damages. Requiring libel plaintiffs to prove specific monetary injury would have meant upsetting as much common-law history as the Court actually upset in its decision. For centuries libel damages had been awarded without proof of loss, because injury to reputation was thought to be so subtle and insidious that it could not be quantified.

In his brief in the *Sullivan* case, Wechsler had attacked the $500,000 award as "monstrous" and mentioned the possibility of limiting libel damages. But he made little of the point; and when Justice Goldberg asked him at the argument whether he was making a constitutional attack on punitive damages as such, he answered no. Many years later Wechsler said: "As I've thought about the case over the years, I made only one judgment that I think was doubtful. The question was whether to attack the established doctrine on punitive and general damages—to argue that the Constitution limited libel damages to the amount of proved financial injury. I've often wondered whether if libel law had gone off on that point in the *Sullivan* case, people might not be happier today. But as a matter of the strategy of advocacy I think my judgment was right. The way of awarding damages was so well established throughout the English-speaking world that I decided it would be unwise to attack it. The judicial reaction would have been negative then."

The Supreme Court did try later to put First Amendment limits on libel damages, but its effort was confused and ineffective. In the case of *Rosenbloom v. Metromedia* in 1971, Justice Marshall put forward a proposal for constitutional restrictions on damages. That was the case in which a magazine distributor sued a radio station for describing him as a dealer in obscenity. The jury awarded the distributor $25,000 in compensatory and $725,000 in punitive damages. Justice Marshall said that punitive damages should be ruled out in libel cases. They were explained as having the same function as criminal penalties, he said—to punish and deter—but they were private fines, awardable by juries in uncontrolled amounts. He concluded: "Fear of the extensive awards that may be given . . . must necessarily produce the impingement on freedom of the press recognized in *New York Times*." In addition, Justice Marshall said the First Amendment should rule out the common-law doctrine that damage in libel cases is presumed. He said the Court should "restrict damages to actual losses," proved in the way that they are in tort cases of physical injury. But he added that such losses, though they must be "related to some proven harm," need not be direct financial injury. He evidently meant that there could be damages, as in other tort cases, for such things as pain and suffering. One other member of the Court, Justice Stewart, joined the Marshall opinion. But Justice Harlan offered a different suggestion. He said that presumed and punitive damages should be allowed—but only if the plaintiff, even if a private individual rather than an official or public figure, proved that there was a knowing or reckless falsehood. In other words, the Harlan proposal was that the *Sullivan* formula be applied also to the question of damages.

In 1974, in *Gertz v. Welch*, a majority of the Court addressed the question of damages. In the Opinion of the Court, Justice Powell established that public figures like officials must prove knowing or reckless falsehood in libel cases, and that private plaintiffs must prove at least negligence. He then went on to discuss the common-law rules that libel damages are presumed and that punitive damages may be awarded at the discretion of the jury. Presumed damages, Justice Powell said, were "an oddity of tort law." Allowing juries "to award damages where there is no loss unnecessarily compounds the potential of any system of liability for defamatory falsehood to inhibit the vigorous exercise of First Amendment freedoms." Further, he added, it "invites juries to punish unpopular opinion rather than to compensate individuals for injury sustained by the publication of a false fact." Punitive damages, even worse, allowed juries to award "wholly unpredictable amounts" as punishment for unwelcome opinions. All this sounded as though Justice Powell wanted to limit libel damages to financial losses proved by the plaintiff, eliminating presumed and punitive damages altogether. But that is not what he did. First he said that, to get compensatory damages, libel plaintiffs must offer proof of injury. But he added that the injury he meant was "not limited to out-of-pocket loss" but could include "impairment of reputation and standing in the community, personal humiliation and mental anguish and suffering." Those matters were so vague that they did not amount to any meaningful limitation on compensatory damages. And then, second, Justice Powell said that plaintiffs could win presumed damages, without proof of injury, and punitive damages, only if they proved knowing or reckless falsehood. He thus adopted Justice Harlan's suggestion in the *Rosenbloom* case, applying the *Sullivan* actual malice formula to damages.

The new rule looked as though it would do much to eliminate presumed and punitive damages, but it turned out to do little. Public figures and officials had to meet the standard of knowing or reckless falsehood anyway, under the *Sullivan* decision, so they had to do nothing further to pass the new *Gertz* test for presumed and punitive damages—and it was those public plaintiffs who won most of the inflated damage awards. Judged by what has happened in the real world of libel, Justice Powell's attempt to impose limits has had no measurable effect; if anything the big verdicts grew bigger. The juries that awarded $19 million to Wayne

Newton and $34 million to Richard Sprague were given no pause by the wishful niceties of *Gertz.*

"The legitimate function of libel law," Justice Harlan said in his *Rosenbloom* opinion, "must be understood as that of compensating individuals for actual, measurable harm. . . . A law that subjects publishers to jury verdicts for falsehoods that have done the plaintiff no harm . . . can only serve a purpose antithetical to the First Amendment." It was an admirable statement of what ought to be. In a country devoted to robust debate, libel should certainly be limited to compensation for harm, and not be allowed to become a stick to threaten the press or individual crusaders on public issues. But what ought to be is not what is. Libel is not confined to the compensatory function. Libel damages commonly—sometimes grossly—exceed any imaginable harm to the plaintiff.

A leading authority on the First Amendment, Professor David A. Anderson, made the nice point that some of the most famous libel plaintiffs were awarded large damages even though they had probably suffered no injury at all to their reputation. One was Commissioner Sullivan himself. His fellow Alabaman, Justice Black, reckoned that if any of Sullivan's friends in Montgomery believed he had ordered the repression of the civil rights movement described in the *New York Times* advertisement, his "political, social and financial prestige has likely been enhanced." Or take the *Gertz* case. Elmer Gertz, a civil liberties lawyer, won $400,000 from a jury because the John Birch Society magazine falsely labeled him a "Leninist." Gertz was a charming man who delighted in his damage award. He was seventy-six when he finally collected the money, and he used it to cruise around the world with his wife on the S.S. *Rotterdam.* Before embarking he said, "I think I should send a telegram to Mr. Welch from every port." (Robert Welch was the Birch Society's founder; his company, Robert Welch Inc., was the losing defendant in the libel case.) Gertz's pleasure was infectious, and it seems a shame to carp about his damages, but it is extremely unlikely that the magazine attack did his reputation as a lawyer or citizen any actual harm. Professor Anderson said Gertz "might have been harmed more if the Birch Society had praised him."

If a person has really been damaged by the intentional or reckless publication of a falsehood, there is a social interest in seeing him or her made whole. Judge Henry Friendly, of the U.S. Court of Appeals for the Second Circuit, wrote in 1967: "Newspapers, magazines and broadcasting companies are businesses conducted for profit and often make very large ones. Like other enterprises that inflict damage in the course of performing a service highly useful to the public, such as providers of food or shelter or manufacturers of drugs designed to ease or prolong life, they must pay the freight." But the unpredictable size of libel damages and their lack of connection with any actual harm make a businesslike approach to the problem difficult. Publishers can take out libel insurance. But with verdicts for sums like $19 million, awarded to plaintiffs who have proved no measurable harm to themselves, the insurance companies may raise their rates beyond what any but the most prosperous press organizations can pay.

In *New York Times v. Sullivan*, Justice Brennan wrote that "a succession of such judgments"—the $500,000 awarded to Commissioner Sullivan—would cast "a pall of fear and timidity" over a newspaper. A generation of experience with the *Sullivan* rule showed that the pall had not been dispelled. The decision made many valuable reforms in the law of libel. Among other things it ended the anomalous situation in which libel plaintiffs, unlike those in other torts, could recover damages for a wholly innocent mistake on the defendant's part. But another anomaly remained: allowing juries to award virtually unlimited damages without proof of meaningful harm. Correcting this oddity is the unfinished business of libel reform, the last necessary step to make libel law conform to the First Amendment. States can limit damages under their common law of libel, and some have done so, but constitutional limits have to come from the Supreme Court. A Court as alert as it was in 1964 to the way oppressive applications of the common law can chill speech would someday decide that the First Amendment limits all libel plaintiffs suing on matters of public concern to compensation for proved pecuniary injury—that is, out-of-pocket losses.

Limiting damages would no doubt make it more difficult to vindicate the interest of reputation in some cases. The multimillion-dollar libel claim has come to serve the function of expressing outrage at wounded reputation, whether the person suing wins in the end or not. A General Westmoreland who sues for $120 million is using the very size of the claim to show how angry he is at what was said about him. A plaintiff's libel lawyer put it, "If I don't sue for at least a million, people will think my client doesn't really care." Moreover, the hope of large damages at the end of the trail, faint as that hope is, leads lawyers to represent libel plaintiffs on a contingency basis, for a percentage of any final award— a system that allows people of modest means to bring civil suits for libel or other torts. In any event the interest of reputation is already compromised by the *Sullivan* rule. Some public figures and officials who have been the subject of a false and damaging publication have no way to hold the publisher legally responsible, or expose the error, because they cannot prove knowing or reckless falsification. *Sullivan* can frustrate not only a libel plaintiff who wants to chill public debate but one who wants only to rescue his or her good name from vicious, lying attacks. A case of the latter kind was in fact an early casualty of the *Sullivan* rule. It was the case of John Goldmark.

John Goldmark was a member of the Washington State Legislature from a remote county, Okanogan, where he was a rancher. After three terms in the House he was the chairman of the Ways and Means Committee. Then, in 1962, opponents in the Democratic primary ran a red-baiting campaign against him, saying among other things that he was a member of the American Civil Liberties Union, "an organization closely affiliated with the Communist movement." The campaign worked; Goldmark finished fourth in the primary. He decided to sue those who had impugned his patriotism. In January 1964, after a two-month trial, a jury found that they had libeled Goldmark and awarded him substantial damages. The verdict was praised around the country. An editorial in the *Oregonian* of Portland said: "A few more verdicts like the one in Okanogan might restore the nation to the tolerant level where the constitutional freedoms could be exercised as they should be in a free country." But two months later the Supreme Court decided the *Sullivan* case, and that cost Goldmark his judgment. Because the Okanogan jury had not been instructed that it must find proof of knowing or reckless falsehood in order to bring in a verdict for Goldmark, Judge Theodore Turner set the verdict aside. It was an ironic result, as Goldmark's lawyer, William L. Dwyer, observed in a book on the case. The figures of the radical right who had poisoned Goldmark's good name "would have applauded the Alabama verdict against the liberal *Times*," Dwyer said, "but now embraced the opinion reversing it." He noted the further irony that the American Civil Liberties Union, "the far right's bete noire," had urged the Supreme Court to reverse the Alabama judgment.

But Judge Turner did something more. He made some observations—findings, really—on the facts of the case. He said the jury's verdict "established that the plaintiff John Goldmark was not a Communist, nor a pro-Communist . . . and that the American Civil Liberties Union . . . was not a Communist front organization. . . . The court must take as established facts that the defendants made false charges that the plaintiff John Goldmark was a Communist or a Communist sympathizer . . . with intent to injure the plaintiff politically, and to cause his defeat."

In the years after *Times v. Sullivan*, a number of libel-reform proposals were discussed that would provide a regular way of doing what Judge Turner did informally in the *Goldmark* case: clear someone's name even though no damages were paid. These proposals were based on the view that Justice Brennan in *Sullivan* was concerned primarily with the chilling effect of damage judgments—judgments that might cast "a pall of fear and timidity" over publishers. If it was in order to stop menacing money judgments that the Court imposed the requirement of proving actual malice, then the requirement could be removed if no money was involved. The victim of a false statement could sue merely to have it found false, with no need to prove what the publisher knew.

Back in 1964, when Herbert Wechsler replied to the letter from Lester Markel of the *Times*, he raised one possibility. "If you believe that the official ought to have a legal remedy," he wrote Markel, it might be not a libel suit but a legal "right to reply, imposing on the newspaper a duty to print a defense of reasonable length." But in 1971 a state law creating a right to reply came before the Supreme Court and was held unconstitutional. The case was *Miami Herald v. Tornillo*. A Florida law gave political candidates who were criticized in the press a right to reply. A candidate attacked in a *Miami Herald* editorial demanded space for a reply. But the Supreme Court held that the First Amendment was violated when any government—Florida, in this case—told the press what it must print. The Court was unanimous on that conclusion. But Justice Brennan suggested another possibility in a brief concurring opinion that was joined by Justice William H. Rehnquist, Justice Harlan's successor. They said it might be constitutional to make the press publish a court's finding that an earlier story was false.

In 1983 Professor Marc A. Franklin put forward a variant on the Brennan-Rehnquist idea. His proposal was to let the victim of an allegedly false statement sue for a legal declaration that it was false and damaging to reputation. In such a suit the plaintiff would get no damages, but in exchange for giving up hope of a monetary award he would be spared the requirement of proving recklessness, negligence or any other kind of fault on the publisher's part; he would merely have to prove falsity. The winning party in such a suit for a declaratory judgment would generally be awarded his lawyer's fees. Professor Franklin did not include a requirement that the publisher of the offending statement publish a judicial finding of falsity, perhaps because of doubts that such a requirement would be constitutional in light of the *Tornillo* case.

In 1985 Representative Charles Schumer of Brooklyn, New York, introduced federal libel legislation. It applied only to cases brought by public figures or officials and involving statements carried by the print or broadcast press. It used the device of suits for a declaration of falsity, without any proof of fault by the publisher. But the Schumer bill also allowed any print or broadcast defendant to convert an ordinary libel suit for damages into one for a declaration of falsity without damages.

A third reform proposal was made in 1988 by a study group for the

Annenberg Washington Program. It suggested a model Libel Reform Act
for adoption by a state. The act required anyone planning a libel suit to
ask, first, for a retraction or an opportunity to reply. If the publisher
retracted or carried a reply in print or on the air, that would be the end
of the matter. If not, the offended person could bring either a suit for
damages or one for a declaration of falsity, the latter without damages
and without the need to prove fault. But if the plaintiff sought damages,
the defendant could convert the suit to one for a declaration. The Annenberg proposal included other reforms of libel law. One was to create
a presumption that letters to the editor are statements of opinion not
subject to libel suits—a rule that would have kept Immuno A.G. from
bringing its punitive and interminable suit over Dr. Shirley McGreal's
letter to the *Journal of Medical Primatology*.

Finally, there was a reform proposal from Judge Pierre N. Leval, who
had presided at the trial of General Westmoreland's libel suit. He suggested that, without any new legislation, libel plaintiffs could avoid the
*Sullivan* requirement by suing for a declaration of falsity and saying that
they wanted no damages. In all these ways, American reformers sought
to arrive at something like the system used in a number of European
countries. They deal with the problem of defamation by providing for
lawsuits to determine the truth, with awards of only symbolic damages
or none at all.

There was no rush to carry out any of the reform proposals. No state
quickly experimented with legislation on either the Annenberg model or
Professor Franklin's, and the Schumer bill got nowhere in Congress. But
the unrest over current libel law did erupt in the Supreme Court, in an
extraordinary opinion by Justice White. In the 1985 case of *Dun &
Bradstreet v. Greenmoss Builders*, he proposed to do nothing less than
overthrow the entire constitutional structure erected on the *Sullivan* case
and the decisions that followed it.

Justice White's record on libel has been puzzlingly inconsistent. He
joined Justice Brennan's opinion in *Times v. Sullivan*. Three years later,
in 1967, he was with Justice Brennan in *Curtis Publishing v. Butts*,
extending the *Sullivan* rule from officials to public figures. The next year
he wrote the Opinion of the Court in *St. Amant v. Thompson*, which
gave further protection to the press by saying that even a failure to check
did not ordinarily constitute recklessness. In 1979, in *Herbert v. Lando*,
the case holding that the press must answer libel plaintiffs' questions
about the editorial process of a disputed story, Justice White remarked
that the rules laid down by *Times v. Sullivan* had been "repeatedly affirmed" by the Court "as the appropriate First Amendment standard."
But six years later, in his separate concurring opinion in *Dun & Brad-*

*street*, he took it all back. He had become convinced, he said, "that the Court struck an improvident balance in the *New York Times* case between the public's interest in being fully informed about public officials and public affairs and the competing interest of those who have been defamed in vindicating their reputation." Justice White said the Court had "engaged in severe overkill. . . . Instead of escalating the plaintiff's burden of proof to an almost impossible level, we could have achieved our stated goal by limiting the recoverable damages to a level that would not unduly threaten the press."

In short, Justice White now proposed to abandon *New York Times v. Sullivan* and to substitute for it some kind of constitutional limit on damages. If this was done, a public figure or official could win a libel suit without having to show that a falsehood about him was published knowingly or recklessly. "His reputation would then be vindicated," Justice White said, "and to the extent possible, the misinformation circulated would have been countered. He might have also recovered a modest amount, enough perhaps to pay his litigation expenses." But White offered no clear constitutional formula to limit damages; nor did he explain how the Court could define "a modest amount" of damages, or an amount "that would not unduly threaten the press." He did not say how the Court would approach the question of construing the First Amendment to apply such limits. He did comment that the Court could limit or even forbid presumed and punitive damages, but this was the step that Justice Powell had attempted in the *Gertz* case—over White's dissent—and the attempt had failed. In sum, Justice White raised more questions than he offered solutions.

The White opinion in *Dun & Bradstreet v. Greenmoss Builders* was plainly distressing to Justice Brennan. In his own opinion in the case he said ironically: "Justice White also ventures some modest proposals for restructuring the First Amendment protections currently afforded defendants in defamation actions." The irony did not conceal Brennan's concern about what might be happening to a constitutional doctrine that he had fashioned and that he greatly prized. Chief Justice Burger also had an opinion in *Dun & Bradstreet*, and he agreed with Justice White that the *Sullivan* case "should be reexamined." Justice Rehnquist seemed likely to be another skeptic about the *Sullivan* rule; he had generally taken a narrow view of the freedom of speech and press protected by the First Amendment.

If Justice Brennan was concerned about the apparent vulnerability of *Times v. Sullivan*—the chance that after twenty years it might be overthrown by the Court—so were the press and its lawyers. To them the *Sullivan* case was the charter of freedom, the key to the modern press's willingness to differ with government and to investigate wrongdoing. It was not merely the specific rule laid down by Justice Brennan—the protection for factual errors unless they were deliberate or reckless—that mattered to the press. It was the wider understanding of how hard it is to avoid error, how much breathing space freedom needs. To trade all this in for a vague, hypothetical limit on libel damages would be a disaster, many editors and press lawyers believed.

When Justice Rehnquist succeeded Warren Burger as Chief Justice in 1986, the prospects for *Times v. Sullivan* looked even gloomier. To replace Rehnquist as an associate justice, President Reagan chose another conservative judge, Antonin Scalia. Then, two years later, the Supreme Court had before it the case of *Hustler Magazine v. Falwell*. It was a wonderful case and an important one. In a ludicrous context it posed serious questions about how much freedom of expression American society will tolerate.

*Hustler*, a magazine devoted largely to sex, published in 1983 what it called a "parody" of an advertisement for Campari bitters. Campari had run a number of advertisements consisting of interviews with celebrities about their "first times." The suggestive implication was of first sexual experiences, but each interview turned out to concern when the subject first tried Campari. The *Hustler* parody purported to be an interview with Jerry Falwell, a minister famous for his nationally televised sermons and his leadership of the Moral Majority, a right-wing lobbying group. The advertisement was headlined, "Jerry Falwell talks about his first time." At the bottom, in small type, it said, "Ad parody—not to be taken seriously." In the "interview" Falwell said, as the Supreme Court decorously put it in stating the facts, "that his 'first time' was during a drunken incestuous rendezvous with his mother in an outhouse." Falwell sued for libel and for another tort recognized in some states, "intentional infliction of emotional distress." The jury threw out the libel claim, on the ground that the parody could not reasonably be understood to make factual charges against Falwell. But it awarded $100,000 in compensatory and $100,000 in punitive damages to Falwell on his emotional-distress claim, and the U.S. Court of Appeals for the Fourth Circuit affirmed the judgment.

The argument of the case in the Supreme Court was an amusing occasion—but again, a serious one also. Alan L. Isaacman was arguing for *Hustler* when Justice Scalia made this observation: "To contradict Vince Lombardi, the First Amendment is not everything. It's a very important value, but it's not the only value in our society, certainly. . . . The rule you give us says that if you stand for public office, or become a public figure in any way, you cannot protect yourself or, indeed, your mother, against a parody of your committing incest with your mother in an outhouse. . . . Do you think George Washington would have stood for public office if that was the consequence?" Isaacman answered that a cartoon of Washington's day had portrayed him as an ass. Justice Scalia replied: "I can handle that. I think George could handle that. But that's a far cry from committing incest with your mother in an outhouse." Isaacman said: "What we're really talking about here is, well, is this tasteful or not tasteful? That's what you're talking about, because nobody believed that Jerry Falwell was being accused of committing incest." And it was in the oldest American tradition—the tradition of political cartooning, among other things—to hold public figures up to ridicule.

Norman Roy Grutman, representing Falwell, began by saying, "Deliberate, malicious character assassination is not protected by the First Amendment." Justice Sandra Day O'Connor, the first woman on the Court, appointed by President Reagan when Justice Stewart retired in 1981, asked, "Do you think a vicious cartoon should subject the drawer of that cartoon to potential liability?" Only, Grutman replied, if the cartoon "would be regarded by the average member of the community as so intolerable that no civilized person should have to bear it." Various members of the Court questioned whether words like "intolerable" drew a line that juries could understand. Justice Scalia said: "Maybe you haven't looked at the same political cartoons that I have, but some of them . . . back into English history—I mean, politicians depicted as horrible-looking beasts—and you talk about portraying someone as committing some immoral act? I would be very surprised if there were not a number of cartoons depicting one or another political figure as at least the *piano player* in a bordello."

The Supreme Court unanimously reversed Falwell's $200,000 judgment. Chief Justice Rehnquist wrote the Opinion of the Court. He began by quoting some of the classic arguments for freedom of expression, among them Justice Holmes's statement in his 1919 dissent in *Abrams v. United States* that "the best test of truth is the power of the thought to get itself accepted in the competition of the market." Falwell argued, the Chief Justice said, that there should be no First Amendment protection for outrageous, intentional infliction of emotional hurt. "But in the world of debate about public affairs, many things done with motives that are less than admirable are protected by the First Amendment." If this were not so, he added, political cartoonists and satirists would be hobbled. He went on to describe some notable cartoons in American history, including the one of Washington as an ass and Thomas Nast's devastating cartoons of the Tweed Ring that ran New York City politics after the Civil War. (A friend-of-the-court brief including nineteen historic car-

toons had been filed in the case on behalf of American Editorial Cartoonists, the Authors League of America and Mark Russell, a political
satirist. Evidently it was a most effective brief.) To argue as Grutman
had that only "outrageous" material should be subject to lawsuits did
not help, Chief Justice Rehnquist said, because "outrageousness" was
such a subjective thing when it came to politics or social issues that it
"would allow a jury to impose liability on the basis of the jurors' tastes
or views, or perhaps on the basis of their dislike of a particular
expression." The opinion concluded that a person who was savaged in
something like *Hustler*'s Campari-ad parody could not recover damages
for mere ridicule, however unpleasant. He had to show that the publication contained a false statement of fact about him, and that the falsehood was knowing or reckless. Since there were no statements about
Falwell in the *Hustler* parody that readers would take as factual charges,
he lost.

The decision in *Hustler v. Falwell* was important for freedom of speech
generally. It showed that the Supreme Court, including judges considered
conservative, had an expansive sense of the kind of speech about public
matters that the Constitution requires American society to tolerate—not
just George Washington as an ass but Jerry Falwell with his mother in
an outhouse.

But the *Hustler* case was also important for what it specifically signified
for libel and the *Sullivan* decision. Chief Justice Rehnquist applied the
*Sullivan* rule—the requirement of knowing or reckless falsification—to
this case of emotional assault, and did so emphatically. He analyzed the
values of free speech as Justice Brennan had, quoting from the opinion
in *Sullivan* the statements that public persons must endure "vehement,
caustic and sometimes unpleasantly sharp attacks" and that freedom of
expression needs "breathing space." He quoted half a dozen other libel
decisions that followed *Sullivan*, including two from which he himself
as an associate justice had dissented. It was as if he were saying: I am
the Chief Justice now, and I am rallying the Court behind this landmark
of our jurisprudence. Every member of the Court joined the Rehnquist
opinion except Justice White, who concurred separately. The message
was clear: For the foreseeable future, the constitutional law of libel would
rest on *New York Times Co. v. Sullivan*.

# 20

# ENVOI

A popular Government, without popular information, or the means of acquiring it, is but a prologue to a Farce or a Tragedy; or, perhaps both. Knowledge will forever govern ignorance: And a people who mean to be their own Governors, must arm themselves with the power which knowledge gives.

—JAMES MADISON, 1822.

WITH the decision in *New York Times v. Sullivan*, a sea change began in the law of the First Amendment. The Supreme Court increasingly gave the amendment's bold words their full meaning. For more than a century after the amendment was added to the Constitution in 1791, its guarantees for speech and press had lain dormant. When the state and federal governments adopted repressive legislation during and after World War I, the Supreme Court took a cramped view of freedom, allowing the punishment of pacifist and radical speech. Over the next forty years the Court gradually started to apply the speech and press clauses in a meaningful way, to protect unorthodox or dissenting views. But the justices remained reluctant to include within the protective shelter of the First Amendment expression that shocked or really challenged the existing order.

Then, in the years following the *Sullivan* decision, the Court resoundingly vindicated the promise of the First Amendment that in the United States there shall be "no law . . . abridging the freedom of speech, or of the press." The Court did not build specifically on Justice Brennan's historical analysis in *Sullivan*, which found the central purpose of the First Amendment revealed in the successful Jeffersonian struggle against the Sedition Act of 1798. But the justices did read the amendment in the way that Jefferson and Madison had, as assuring the right to criticize government—the right to disagree in robust, uninhibited terms.

The Vietnam war provided a striking example of judicial change. Julian Bond, a young black leader of the civil rights movement in the South, was elected to the Georgia House of Representatives in 1964. But the House refused to let him take his seat, on the ground that his opposition to the Vietnam war prevented him from conscientiously swearing to "support the Constitution." Bond had endorsed a statement by the Student Non-violent Coordinating Committee that said, "We are in sympathy with, and support, the men in this country who are unwilling to respond to a military draft." Bond said, "I like to think of myself as a pacifist and one who opposes that war and any other war and eager and anxious to encourage people not to participate in it for any reason that they choose." When members of the Georgia House asked him at a hearing how he felt about those who burned their draft cards, he said he admired their courage. Asked to explain, he said: "I have never suggested or counseled or advocated that any one other person burn their draft card. In fact, I have mine in my pocket and will produce it if you wish. I do not advocate that people should break laws. What I simply [wanted] to say was that I admired the courage of someone who could act on his convictions knowing that he faces pretty stiff consequences."

For words not so different from Bond's, Eugene Debs in World War I was convicted of obstructing military recruitment and sentenced to ten years in prison. The Supreme Court upheld the conviction, in an opinion by Justice Holmes that brushed aside First Amendment objections. But in 1966 the Supreme Court held unanimously that the Georgia House had violated the First Amendment in refusing to seat Julian Bond. Chief Justice Warren said Bond could not have been constitutionally convicted under a federal statute that makes it a crime to counsel or aid draft evasion—a later version of the law that sent Debs to prison. The Chief Justice wrote: "The central commitment of the First Amendment, as summarized in the Opinion of the Court in *New York Times Co. v. Sullivan*, is that 'debate on public issues should be uninhibited, robust and wide-open.' We think the rationale of the *New York Times* case disposes of the claim that Bond's statements fell outside the range of constitutional protection. . . . The interest of the public in hearing all sides of a public issue is hardly advanced by extending more protection to citizen-critics than to legislators."

In *Whitney v. California* in 1927—the case that evoked Justice Brandeis's classic statement of the reasons for freedom of speech—the Supreme Court upheld the constitutionality of California's Criminal Syndicalism Act. It was one of many state laws passed between 1917 and 1920 that made it a crime to teach or advocate the necessity or propriety of violence as a means of social change. In 1969 the Court overruled its decision in *Whitney v. California*, holding the typical criminal syndicalism law unconstitutional and establishing a strict new rule to judge speech that advocates violent or unlawful action. The case was *Brandenburg v. Ohio*. It involved not a radical like Anita Whitney, or most of the principals in the early cases, but a member of the Ku Klux Klan. At a Klan rally in Hamilton County, Ohio, a hooded figure said, among other things, "I believe the nigger should be returned to Africa, the Jew returned to Israel." The speaker was identified by the authorities, prosecuted and convicted of violating Ohio's Criminal Syndicalism Act by advocating the necessity of terrorism or lawlessness. In an unsigned opinion, the Supreme Court abandoned the "clear and present danger" test for judging advocacy of violence, which had been urged by Holmes and Brandeis as a formula to protect speech but then had been used by the Court in 1951 to sustain the conviction of the leaders of the Communist party. Instead the Court now laid down what became a new rule: "The constitutional guarantees of free speech and free press do not permit a State to forbid or proscribe advocacy of the use of force or of law violation except where such advocacy is directed to inciting or producing imminent lawless action and is likely to incite or produce such action."

The requirement that the speech be "directed to inciting or producing imminent lawless action" was seen by Professor Gerald Gunther, Judge Learned Hand's biographer, as focusing on the character of the actual words used—and hence as essentially like the test that Judge Hand tried unsuccessfully to establish in the *Masses* case in 1917. The new rule protected speech, however opposed to existing society or policy, unless it urged *immediate* lawlessness. The rest of the *Brandenburg* test, requiring a likelihood that lawlessness would actually occur, added a stronger version of the predictive element in the clear and present danger formula. Altogether, *Brandenburg v. Ohio* gave the greatest protection to what could be called subversive speech that it has ever had in the United States, and almost certainly greater than such speech has in any other country. The decision fully reflected Madison's view of the First Amendment, and the political philosophy that Jefferson articulated in his first inaugural address: "If there be any among us who wish to dissolve this Union or to change its republican form, let them stand undisturbed as monuments of the safety with which error of opinion may be tolerated where reason is left free to combat it."

In 1971 the Court dealt with the problem of offensive speech. The question was whether the First Amendment protected someone who delivered a political message in language that would offend the audience. The case was *Cohen v. California.* When it was argued in the Supreme Court, Chief Justice Burger was afraid that the facts would offend some in the courtroom. Before Cohen's counsel, Professor Melville B. Nimmer, began his argument, the Chief Justice told him: "The Court is thoroughly familiar with the factual setting of this case, and it will not be necessary for you, I'm sure, to dwell on the facts." Professor Nimmer replied, "I certainly will keep very brief the statement of facts." Cohen, he said, had been convicted of violating the California law against disturbing the peace. Then he added: "What this young man did was to walk through a courthouse corridor in Los Angeles County . . . wearing a jacket upon which were inscribed the words, 'Fuck the Draft.' "

Professor Nimmer was brave to speak as he did, because of course Chief Justice Burger had been trying to keep the four-letter word from being uttered in the courtroom. But it was essential that he do so. For if he had been intimidated into suppressing the word at issue, he would in a sense have accepted that it could be suppressed. He would have undermined his own argument, which was that even offensive language may have a place in the marketplace of ideas protected by the First Amendment.

The Supreme Court reversed Cohen's conviction by a vote of 5 to 4. The Opinion of the Court was by Justice Harlan, and it was a remarkable opinion. John Harlan was a New York gentleman of the old school. But he was able to detach himself from personal feelings, as judges are meant to—from his own standards of behavior—and see that in the context of the Vietnam war "this unseemly expletive" was a form of political speech. "While the particular four-letter word being litigated here is perhaps more distasteful than most others of its genre," Justice Harlan said, "it is nevertheless often true that one man's vulgarity is another's lyric." And here the vulgarity engaged the values of the First Amendment:

> The constitutional right of free expression is powerful medicine in a society as diverse and populous as ours. It is designed and intended to remove governmental restraints from the arena of public discussion, putting the decision as to what views shall be voiced largely into the hands of each of us, in the hope that use of such freedom will ultimately produce a more capable citizenry

and more perfect polity and in the belief that no other approach
would comport with the premise of individual dignity and choice
upon which our political system rests. . . . To many, the immediate consequence of this freedom may often appear to be
only verbal tumult, discord and even offensive utterance. These
are, however, within established limits, in truth necessary side
effects of the broader enduring values which the process of open
debate permits us to achieve. That the air may at times seem
filled with verbal cacophony is, in this sense not a sign of weak-
ness but of strength.

The Supreme Court's most controversial decisions in the area of offensive expression were those on flag-burning. In *Texas v. Johnson* in
1989, the Court held unconstitutional a Texas law that made it a crime
to "desecrate" the flag in a way that "will seriously offend" people. A
flag was burned during a political demonstration to express disagreement
with government policy. Justice Brennan, writing for a majority of five,
said the act was a form of communication, expressing political views.
"If there is a bedrock principle underlying the First Amendment," he
wrote, "it is that the Government may not prohibit the expression of an
idea simply because society finds the idea itself offensive or disagreeable."
The decision caused a political uproar, with President Bush calling for a
constitutional amendment to protect the flag. After angry debate Congress instead passed a Flag Protection Act, which sought to avoid the
Court's ruling in the *Johnson* case by making it a crime to burn the flag
regardless of whether onlookers were offended (the condition in the Texas
law).

A prosecution under the new law quickly made its way up to the
Supreme Court, and in 1990 a majority held that it, too, conflicted with
the First Amendment. Again Justice Brennan wrote the Opinion of the
Court: one of his last before retiring that summer. Congress was trying
to protect the flag as a symbol, he said, and in doing so it was just as
much suppressing critical expression. He added that burning a particular
flag "does not diminish or otherwise affect the symbol itself in any way."
He ended his opinion with a fitting last word about American principles:
"We are aware that desecration of the flag is deeply offensive to many.
But the same might be said, for example, of . . . vulgar repudiations of
the draft, see *Cohen v. California*, and scurrilous caricatures, see *Hustler
Magazine v. Falwell*. . . . Punishing desecration of the flag dilutes the
very freedom that makes this emblem so revered, and worth revering."

The Court also continued to disapprove almost all prior restraints on
expression: the legal position established by Chief Justice Hughes in 1931

in *Near v. Minnesota.* In the 1970s a number of lower courts issued restraining orders to protect a defendant's right to a fair trial—for example ordering the press not to publish stories about an alleged confession before the trial. In 1976 the Supreme Court dealt with a case that seemed to present an especially grave risk of unfairness to the defendant, who was charged with the necrophiliac murders of six members of a family in the small town of Sutherland, Nebraska. The Nebraska courts prohibited reporting of a confession or other matters "strongly implicative" of the defendant, so that a future jury would not be prejudiced against him. But the Supreme Court set aside that order. Writing for the Court, Chief Justice Burger said "prior restraints on speech and publication are the most serious and the least tolerable infringement on First Amendment rights." They should not be imposed, he said, unless "alternative measures" such as moving the trial to a distant court or delaying it were shown to be unavailable or ineffectual.

The decision in the Nebraska case settled the issue of restraints for the purpose of fair trial—or did, at least, until 1990, when the Cable News Network acted in a way that served to reopen the question. CNN broadcast a report about the case of General Manuel Noriega, the former Panamanian dictator, who was seized by U.S. forces when they invaded Panama and was being held in a Florida prison awaiting trial on federal drug charges. CNN said that Noriega's telephone calls from the prison, including conversations with his lawyers, had been taped—and that it had some of the tapes. The report was a significant journalistic exposure of possibly unfair government tactics against a criminal defendant, but CNN went a step further and played one of the tapes on the air. Noriega's lawyers promptly moved for an order prohibiting CNN from broadcasting any more tapes, arguing that they might disclose defense strategy, and a federal judge issued the order. CNN appealed to the U.S. Court of Appeals, which agreed to consider the case at once. Then, the night before the argument, CNN broadcast a tape in apparent violation of the order. This was a defiance almost certain to antagonize judges. Thereafter the Court of Appeals refused to lift the restraining order, and the Supreme Court quickly declined to consider the case. Then the trial judge had a magistrate listen to the disputed tapes, and it turned out that there was nothing of interest on them. The judge lifted his restraining order, but CNN made no further broadcasts (no doubt because the tapes were not worth playing). By challenging the courts, CNN had diverted attention from its real point, which was to focus on the government's behavior in taping the Noriega conversations. Moreover, it had set a precedent that weakened the protection against prior restraints. Other judges now could say that at least they had the power to issue temporary restraints while looking into the substance of what someone proposed to broadcast or print in order to determine whether a longer ban was needed and was allowed by the First Amendment.

But the great prior restraint case was a clash over the right to publish alleged national security secrets. In the spring of 1971 *The New York Times* obtained forty-three volumes of a secret official history of the Vietnam war, put together by the Defense Department while the war was going on. The Pentagon Papers, as they came to be called, bore such high classifications as Top Secret. In June 1971 the *Times* began to publish excerpts from the documents and extended articles on what they showed about the origins of the war. The government went to court and asked for an injunction against continued publication.

By chance, the case went to a new federal judge on his first day on the job, Murray Gurfein. Judge Gurfein had been a military intelligence officer in World War II, and some expected him to be sympathetic to the government's claim that publishing the Pentagon Papers would hurt the American war effort in Vietnam, which was still going on, and would obstruct attempts to arrange a peace settlement. Judge Gurfein did issue a temporary restraining order. But three days later, after hearing government witnesses and trying unsuccessfully to get them to point out specific items in the Papers that might be dangerous if published, he refused to issue an injunction. In his opinion Judge Gurfein wrote: "The security of the nation is not at the ramparts alone. Security also lies in the value of our free institutions. A cantankerous press, an obstinate press, a ubiquitous press must be suffered by those in authority in order to preserve the even greater values of freedom of expression and the right of the people to know."

The case did not end there. The Court of Appeals extended the temporary restraint and told Judge Gurfein to hear more evidence from the government about the potential harm from publication. Meanwhile, *The Washington Post* had acquired copies of the Papers, began publishing stories on them and was also temporarily restrained. The cases went quickly to the Supreme Court. There the Solicitor General, Erwin N. Griswold, told the Court that publication would "affect lives . . . the process of the termination of the war . . . the process of recovering prisoners of war."

Two weeks after the controversy began, by a vote of 6 to 3, the Supreme Court rejected the government's claim for an injunction. There were two distinct themes in the various opinions for the majority. First, Congress had not passed any statute giving the courts specific authority to stop publication of this kind of material. Second, in order to overcome the First Amendment presumption against prior restraints the government had to show that disclosure would, as Justice Stewart put it, "surely result in direct, immediate and irreparable damage to our Nation or its people," and the government had not done so.

The Pentagon Papers case was a famous victory for the press, and for the Madisonian principle that the public must know what its government is doing. Or so it seemed at the time. Later decisions showed that it was not much of a victory. For in subsequent years the Supreme Court was increasingly deferential to the executive branch of the government whenever it claimed that national security was at risk. The deference reached an extreme in the case of *Snepp v. United States*.

Frank Snepp was a Central Intelligence Agency official who served in Vietnam. When the war ended in 1975 with the victory of North Vietnam and the hasty departure of Americans from Saigon, he was distressed by what he saw as abandonment of the South Vietnamese who had helped the United States, especially intelligence sources. Not only were they left behind; so were intelligence files containing their names, thus ensuring that they would be badly treated. Snepp wrote a book, *Decent Interval*, and published it without first submitting it to the C.I.A. for clearance, as he had promised to do. The government sued him for violation of the promise, which it argued was a contract. The Supreme Court agreed that it was, and granted the extraordinary relief sought by the government. First, it enjoined Snepp—for the rest of his life—from ever again writing or speaking without prior C.I.A. approval about intelligence matters that he learned while an agency employee. Moreover, the C.I.A. was to be the judge of whether he had learned something as an employee, so he had to submit for clearance anything that touched on subjects he had dealt with while there—for example, anything on Vietnam. (In subsequent years Snepp had to submit book reviews, film scripts and even fiction for approval.) It was the first time the Supreme Court had approved a prior restraint on writing or speaking about matters of government policy. Second, the Court imposed what it called a "constructive trust" on Snepp's earnings from *Decent Interval*, meaning that he had to turn over to the Treasury his advance from the publisher and all royalties. In time the amount exceeded $180,000, more than the maximum fine for many heinous crimes.

Neither of the two requirements mentioned in the Pentagon Papers case was met in the *Snepp* case. There was no statute that authorized an injunction against Snepp or the seizure of his royalties, and there was no finding that his book would result in "direct, immediate, irreparable" or any other kind of harm to the nation. In fact, for purposes of argument the government had conceded that the book contained no classified information. The Court did not even mention *Near v. Minnesota*, the presumption against prior restraints or any First Amendment law. It acted summarily, without briefs or argument, in an unsigned opinion from which Justices Stevens, Brennan and Marshall dissented. The claim of threats to the operation of the C.I.A. evidently moved the majority not to apply the Court's usual skeptical eye to assertions that some publication must be blocked for the good of society.

In other cases, too, the Court has deferred to C.I.A. and national security claims, carving out what amounts to an exception to the First Amendment. This is in spite of the belief of just about everyone who has been inside the national security system that its claimed needs for secrecy are grossly exaggerated. Erwin Griswold, who argued the Pentagon Papers case for the government, said later that he had "never seen any trace of a threat to national security" arising from publication of the Papers. He made this comment in an article he wrote for *The Washington Post* in 1989, when the government was arguing that release of classified documents in the trial of Oliver North for offenses in the Iran-contra affair would imperil national security. Griswold said: "It quickly becomes apparent to any person who has considerable experience with classified material that there is massive overclassification and that the principal concern of the classifiers is not with national security, but rather with governmental embarrassment of one sort or another. There may be some basis for short-term classification while plans are being made, or negotiations are going on, but apart from details of weapons systems, there is very rarely any real risk to current national security from the publication of facts relating to transactions in the past, even the fairly recent past. This is the lesson of the Pentagon Papers experience."

No doubt the Supreme Court's deference to Presidents on issues of national security is a reflection of the general growth of presidential power in the twentieth century. In the age of nuclear weapons and instant global communication it is inevitable that the public in this and other countries will look to the President of the United States for leadership on issues of war and peace. Presidents have used the needs of national security in such an age to justify cloaking more and more of the vital business of government in secrecy. The intelligence agencies spend billions of dollars every year, but the public is not allowed to know the amount or the justifications for it. There are vast secret budgets for weapons. The price of all this secrecy is one that Madison understood: the growth of autocracy, and the inefficiency that results from the lack of open debate and public control.

Here as elsewhere the First Amendment's guarantees of free speech and press are not merely for the benefit of the individual; they are the necessities of wise government. When a policy fails as dismally as it did in the Vietnam war, the public must know how the wrong decisions were made. When a war ends as badly as Vietnam did, the public should hear criticism from an insider like Frank Snepp. The one area of First Amendment law that most needs attention is the exception that the courts have implicitly created for anything arguably related to the national security. To put it another way, on this issue the Supreme Court needs to recover the courage of its First Amendment convictions.

Apart from the national security problem, speech and press enjoy extraordinary freedom a generation after *New York Times v. Sullivan.* Whether the Supreme Court will continue to enforce the guarantees of the First Amendment so rigorously is of course an uncertainty. There are justices who think it has gone too far. In the first flag-burning case, for example, Chief Justice Rehnquist said in dissent: "Surely one of the high purposes of a democratic society is to legislate against conduct that is regarded as evil and profoundly offensive to the majority of people— whether it be murder, embezzlement, pollution or flag-burning."

Freedom of expression depends not only on law and the courts but on public attitudes, and on that score the First Amendment appears to be in moderately good health. Americans are far too bewitched by the presidency and its ever-growing claims that national security demands secret government. The public tends to resent the press when it tries to hold the President accountable on issues of war and peace, as Madison and his colleagues intended the press to do. On the other hand, Americans at the end of the twentieth century are much more tolerant of dissent than they used to be. Cincinnati jurors who were undoubtedly shocked at the homoerotic photographs of Robert Mapplethorpe nevertheless acquitted a museum director charged with criminal offenses for showing the pictures. A Fort Lauderdale, Florida, jury acquitted the rap group 2 Live Crew of obscenity charges. Most significantly, the demand for a constitutional amendment to protect the American flag died away. After the second Supreme Court flag decision the proposed amendment got nowhere in Congress. Perhaps Americans, or enough of them, came to agree with Justice Holmes that "we should be eternally vigilant against attempts to check the expression of opinions that we loathe and believe to be fraught with death."

If there is a doubt about the many Supreme Court decisions beginning with *Times v. Sullivan* that gave legal force to the First Amendment, it is a wariness about the amount of law and legalism in American society. The grandeur and the vitality of the First Amendment can be obscured when it is turned over to lawyers, when judges begin drawing lines between permitted and forbidden expression. Something like that happened in the Pentagon Papers case. The moment the Nixon administration sued to stop publication and the lawyers and judges took over, the public's attention turned to "the meaning of the First Amendment" instead of staying on the message of the Pentagon Papers, which was the corruption of the political process that had embroiled us in Vietnam.

Professor Alexander M. Bickel, who represented the *Times*, wrote afterward:

> Law can never make us as secure as we are when we do not need it. Those freedoms which are neither challenged nor defined are the most secure. In this sense, for example, it is true that the American press was freer before it won its battle with the Government [over the Pentagon Papers] in 1971 than after its victory. Before June 15, 1971, through the troubles of 1798, through one civil and two world wars, and other wars, there had never been an effort by the federal government to censor a newspaper by attempting to impose a restraint prior to publication, directly or in litigation. That spell was broken, and in a sense freedom was thus diminished.

*Times v. Sullivan* started a process of steeping the press in law, and the process has gone further in libel than anywhere else in the field of expression. Before 1964 virtually no American newspaper had lawyers on its staff to worry about libel, and there was no press law to speak of. When libel suits came along, as they occasionally did, they were dealt with as matters of modest importance. Today all major newspapers, magazines and broadcasters have lawyers on hand and must be concerned about libel. The subject has become immensely sophisticated, with layers of federal constitutional law overlying state libel law. Justice Brennan's *Sullivan* test establishing that officials can recover libel damages only if they prove "actual malice"—knowing or reckless falsehood—has even made it into the movies, in the film *Absence of Malice*.

The complexity of modern libel law follows inexorably from the Supreme Court's choice in *Times v. Sullivan* to respect two interests, reputation and freedom of expression. If the Court had taken Justice Black's advice and found that the First Amendment prohibited libel suits altogether, the law would be simple. The accommodation of conflicting interests is always complicated. It requires judges to draw nice lines, it requires lawyers to argue, it requires academics to reflect. All of this is a burden, but there is no reason to think that Americans would prefer Justice Black's solution of forgetting reputation altogether. Herbert

Wechsler saw the inevitable complexity as early as 1964, when he replied to Lester Markel's doubts about the *Sullivan* decision. He ended his letter to Markel by saying: "These are fascinating questions, and I wish I could go further toward proposing an entirely satisfactory solution. It would not be unusual in life if no solution can be found that does not offer difficulties of some kind."

The complexities of libel law are the price of a decision that has greatly enlarged the freedom of the press and of all Americans. Without *New York Times v. Sullivan*, it is questionable whether the press could have done as much as it has to penetrate the power and secrecy of modern government, or to confront the public with the realities of policy issues. In the immediate context of the *Sullivan* case, the racial issue in the South, the decision made all the difference. Eric Embry, who represented the *Times* in the trial of Sullivan's libel suit, was asked at the twentieth anniversary of the Supreme Court decision what would have happened if the decision had gone the other way. He replied, "The answer is that CBS, which I represented, would not have gone on doing programs on the South." The ultimate beneficiary was not the press but the public, which was able to hear criticism and exercise its voice. A leading constitutional law teacher, Professor A. E. Dick Howard of the University of Virginia, said of *Times v. Sullivan*, "I can think of no case that in practical terms matters more to the exchange of ideas in this country."

Decades after the *Sullivan* decision, those who were directly involved in the litigation seemed content with the outcome. Roland Nachman, who represented Commissioner Sullivan and lost the case, viewed it with a certain ironic amusement. "I was the regular lawyer for the Montgomery *Advertiser* and the *Alabama Journal* at the time," he said, "defending them against libel suits. I had to get permission from them to represent the plaintiff in a libel case. They are still my clients, and they think the greatest thing I ever did for them was to lose that case!" Herbert Wechsler noted that despite all the complaints about the *Sullivan* rule and all the proposals for legislative reform, the constitutional law of libel was still on the foundation where the Supreme Court had placed it in 1964. He said: "I think one reason why the *Sullivan* decision has withstood the hostility to it in so many different quarters is that there is this historical material—the Jeffersonian and Madisonian material produced by Republican hostility to the Sedition Act—which the decision reflects and in a sense truly implements. Anybody who undertakes to read what Madison said, the idea that the citizen is the critic and not the government—my heavens, that's a powerful argument! And to find that this idea was accepted by Congress and accepted by the dominant political party so early in the country's history seems to me to give a legitimacy to that conclusion that is very consoling to people who are concerned about the judicial function in constitutional decisions."

The American idea of free expression that was embraced in *New York Times v. Sullivan* and other First Amendment decisions also has increasing appeal elsewhere in the world. The struggle against totalitarian government, that terrible twentieth-century phenomenon, brought wider understanding of the connection—the Madisonian connection—between democracy and freedom of speech and press. Liu Binyan, a courageous Chinese journalist who was in exile from his homeland while it was ruled by tyrants, wrote of his own gradual learning, in China, of the nature of representative government. He said: "Democracy means the power to choose, and choice is an illusion without information." The sentence might have been written by James Madison.

In Britain the press remains tightly confined compared with its American colleagues. Prior restraints kept the British press, for years, from quoting from a book by a former British counterspy, Peter Wright, while it was published all over the world. A supposed "reform" of the Official Secrets Act by Margaret Thatcher's government forbade all former intelligence officers ever to write a word about their work—a silence far more complete than the *Snepp* decision's requirement that former intelligence officials submit their writings for clearance before publication. But proposals to open up what has in many ways been a closed system of government have been gaining strength, inspired in good part by the American example.

European countries adhered after World War II to a European Convention on Human Rights that guaranteed freedom of expression, among other things, and that is enforced by a European Commission and a European Court of Human Rights. And the court to some extent has reflected American ideas of freedom in interpreting the convention. In 1979 it found that Britain had violated the convention in restraining publication of newspaper articles about the victims of a damaging drug, thalidomide. The British courts said the articles would amount to contempt of court because they might influence pending suits for damages over the drug. But the European Court said "the families of numerous victims of the tragedy . . . had a vital interest in knowing all the underlying facts." After the decision, Britain changed its law of contempt to accord with the decision.

The European Court of Human Rights in 1986 decided a libel case in a way that Americans would understand and applaud. In 1975 an Austrian journalist, Peter Michel Lingens, had published articles highly critical of Bruno Kreisky, then the Austrian Chancellor, charging him with the "basest opportunism." Kreisky sued, and the Austrian courts awarded him damages for libel. The European Court found that the Austrian proceedings violated the European Convention on Human Rights, and ordered compensation to Lingens for his damage judgment and costs. The court said "freedom of expression . . . constitutes one of the essential foundations of a democratic society and one of the basic conditions for its progress. . . . It is applicable not only to 'information' or 'ideas' that are favorably received or regarded as inoffensive or as a matter of indifference, but also to those that offend, shock or disturb. Such are the demands of that pluralism, tolerance and broadmindedness without which there is no 'democratic society.' " The Court went on to say:

> Freedom of the press furthermore affords the public one of the best means of discovering and forming an opinion of the ideas and attitudes of political leaders. More generally, freedom of political debate is at the very core of the concept of a democratic society. . . . The limits of acceptable criticism are accordingly wider as regards a politician as such than as regards a private individual. Unlike the latter, the former inevitably and knowingly lays himself open to close scrutiny of his every word and deed by both journalists and the public at large, and he must consequently display a greater degree of tolerance.

The European Court's language was reminiscent of Justice Brennan's comment that officials must be "men of fortitude, able to thrive in a hardy climate," and reflective generally of *Times v. Sullivan* and other American libel decisions, on which the Court had been briefed.

Not that Europe or other parts of the world are ready to follow the American theory of free speech to the end of protecting even the most hateful speech. Perhaps Europeans have suffered too much, firsthand, from hateful ideas that gained power on their continent. A distinguished French constitutional lawyer, Roger Errera, writing about the influence of the United States Constitution in the world, rejected for other countries the American willingness to tolerate such "extreme forms of political speech" as the proposed Nazi march in Skokie, Illinois. Americans, he suggested, have a quality that, given their experience, Europeans cannot have—"an inveterate social and historical optimism."

Errera was right; Americans *are* optimists. Madison had to be an optimist to believe that democracy would work in a sprawling new federation if only the people had "the right of freely examining public characters and measures." Martin Luther King Jr. had to be an optimist to believe that speech, appealing to conscience, could undo generations of racial discrimination. And optimism was the unstated premise when the Supreme Court looked to Madison's vision to resolve the case of *New York Times Co. v. Sullivan.*

# APPENDIX 1

**First Draft of
Justice Brennan's Opinion
in *New York Times Co. v. Sullivan***

Following is the first draft of Justice Brennan's opinion, as set in type by the Supreme Court's printer and found in Justice Brennan's files in the Library of Congress Manuscript Division.

# SUPREME COURT OF THE UNITED STATES

### Nos. 39 and 40.—October Term, 1963.

The New York Times Company,
    Petitioner,
39           *v.*
    L. B. Sullivan.

Ralph D. Abernathy et al.,
    Petitioners,
40           *v.*
    L. B. Sullivan.

On Writs of Certiorari to the Supreme Court of Alabama.

[February —, 1964.]

Mr. Justice Brennan delivered the opinion of the Court.

We decide for the first time in this case the question of the extent that the protections for speech and press of the First and Fourteenth Amendments delimit a State's power to apply its law of civil libel in an action in its courts brought by a public official against critics of his official conduct.[1]

Respondent is the Commissioner of the City of Montgomery, Alabama, in charge of the Police Department. A jury in the Circuit Court of Montgomery County awarded him damages of $500,000 in a civil libel action brought by him against the four individual petitioners, who are Negroes and Alabama clergymen, and against petitioner The New York Times Company. His complaint alleged that he was libeled by statements in the third and sixth paragraphs of a 10 paragraph appeal for

---

[1] The issue was presented but not decided in *Schenectady Union Publishing Co.* v. *Sweeney*, 316 U. S. 642, where an equally divided Court affirmed the judgment below.

## 2    NEW YORK TIMES CO. *v.* SULLIVAN.

contributions which was carried as an advertisement in
the New York Times on March 29, 1960.[2]

The advertisement was inserted by the "Committee to
Defend Martin Luther King and the Struggle for Freedom in the South." Its appeal was for contributions to
support the "non-violence" movement of Southern Negro
students in the struggle of Negroes for civil rights, and
to finance the defense of Reverend Dr. Martin Luther
King, Jr., leader of the movement, against perjury indictments pending in Montgomery.[3] The names of the four
individual petitioners appeared at the foot of the advertisement among the names of persons, primarily clergymen, who endorsed the appeal.

The appeal asserted that the Negro students were
courageous "protagonists of democracy" whose efforts
were being "met by an unprecedented wave of terror"
illustrated by specific occurrences in named southern communities. The third paragraph and the first five sentences of the sixth paragraph described occurrences which
the respondent alleged libeled him in his capacity as
Montgomery's Police Commissioner. They were:

Third paragraph:

"In Montgomery, Alabama, after students sang
'My Country 'Tis of Thee' on the State Capitol
steps, their leaders were expelled from school, and
truckloads of police armed with shotguns and tear-
gas ringed the Alabama State College Campus.
When the entire student body protested to state
authorities by refusing to re-register, their dining hall
was padlocked in an attempt to starve them into
submission."

---

[2] The full text of the advertisement is in the Appendix.
[3] Dr. King was acquitted of the charges.

The Sixth paragraph:

"Again and again the Southern violators have answered Dr. King's peaceful protests with intimidation and violence. They have bombed his home almost killing his wife and child. They have assaulted his person. They have arrested him seven times—for 'speeding,' 'loitering' and similar 'offenses.' And now they have charged him with 'perjury'—a *felony* under which they would imprison him for *ten years.*"

None of the statements mentions the respondent by name nor is he elsewhere mentioned by name in the advertisement. However, the respondent contended that the references in the third paragraph to "police" and in the sixth paragraph to "arrests" would lead a reader reasonably to impute to him as the official in charge of the Police Department, not only the conduct that the "police . . . ringed . . . the . . . campus" and "arrested . . . [Rev. Dr. King] . . . seven times," but also as charging that it was he who brought it about that the students' "leaders were expelled from school" and "their dining hall was padlocked in an attempt to starve them into submission," and also as identifying him with the "Southern violators" and the "They" who "answered Dr. King's peaceful protests with intimidation and violence" "bombed his home almost killing his wife and child," "assaulted his person," and "charged him with 'perjury.' " The respondent and six local Montgomery residents testified that they read the paragraphs as referring to the respondent as Police Commissioner.

Respondent also introduced evidence to show the falsity of the statements. That evidence was that no disciplinary action had in fact been taken against any student leaders for the demonstration on the State Cap-

4    NEW YORK TIMES CO. v. SULLIVAN.

itol steps: nine student leaders expelled by the State
Board of Education were expelled for demanding service
at a lunch counter in the Montgomery County Court
House on another day.  A student strike in sympathy
with the expelled leaders occurred later but it ended after
a day and virtually all of the students re-registered.  The
campus dining hall was never padlocked and the only
students who may have been barred from eating there
were those properly excluded for reasons wholly unrelated to the student demonstrations.  The occasion for
the presence of the police on the campus was not the
demonstration on the Capitol steps but another student
demonstration at a church near the campus, at which
time and on two more occasions, the police did not "ring"
the campus, but were "deployed" nearby in large numbers.  Reverend Dr. King's home was bombed twice
when his wife and child were at home but respondent's
evidence was that the police not only were not involved
but did everything they could to apprehend the perpe-
trators.  Reverend Dr. King had been arrested not seven
but four times.  Although Dr. King claimed to have
been assaulted some four years earlier for loitering outside a courtroom, one of the participating officers testified
and denied the charge.  The respondent testified himself
that the police had not bombed the King home or
assaulted Dr. King or condoned the bombing or assaulting.  He also testified that he had nothing to do with
procuring the perjury indictment against Dr. King.

Alabama law denies a public officer recovery of punitive damages in a libel action brought on account of a
publication concerning his official conduct or actions
unless the officer makes a written demand for a public
retraction within five days before bringing suit and the
defendant fails or refuses to publish an appropriate
retraction.  Alabama Code, Title 7, § 914.  The respondent made a demand upon each of the petitioners for a

retraction. None of the individual petitioners responded to the demand, primarily because the position of each of them, supported by his testimony at the trial, was that he had not authorized the use of his name as an endorser of the appeal and therefore had not published anything of or concerning the respondent.[4] The petitioner, The New York Times Company, did not publish a retraction but respondend to the demand by a letter in which it was stated, among other things, that "we . . . are somewhat puzzled as to how you think the statements in any

---

[4] Since we reverse the decision of the Alabama Supreme Court on the grounds urged by all petitioners under the free speech and free press provisions of the First Amendment as applied to the States by the Fourteenth Amendment, we do not decide the questions presented of alleged violations of the Fourteenth Amendment either (1) those presented by the individual petitioners: that due process of law was violated by the award for claimed libel upon a record alleged to be entirely devoid of evidence of any authorization, consent or publication by any of them of the alleged libel; that they were deprived of equal protection and due process in that the suit brought against them by a white public official was tried in a courtroom wherein racial segregation of whites and Negroes was enforced and which allegedly was permeated with an atmosphere of racial bias, passion and hostile community pressures; and that they were denied due process and a fair and impartial trial by a trial before an all-white jury resulting from the intentional and systematic exclusion of Negro citizens, and before a trial judge not properly qualified and biased against them because they were Negroes: or (2) that presented by the petitioner, The New York Times Company: that the assumption of jurisdiction in a libel action against a foreign corporation publishing a newspaper in another State, allegedly based upon sporadic news-gathering activities by correspondents, occasional solicitation of advertising and minuscule distribution of the newspaper within the forum State, transcended the territorial limitations of due process, imposed a forbidden burden on interstate commerce or abridged the freedom of the press. The Alabama Supreme Court's ruling that the petitioner, The New York Times Company, entered a general appearance in the action constitutes an adequate and independent ground of decision supporting the trial court's jurisdiction of the person.

6   NEW YORK TIMES CO. *v.* SULLIVAN.

way reflect on you," and ". . . you might if you desire, let us know in what respect you claim that the statements in the advertisement reflect on you."[5] The respondent filed this suit a few days later without answering the letter. In the trial court all the petitioners, by demurrers and various motions, invoked the protections for speech and press of the First and Fourteenth Amendments.

The trial judge overruled all of the petitioners' constitutional and other objections and submitted the case to the jury under instructions that, on the issue of liability, they were to determine only whether the statements were to be read as having been made of and concerning the respondent. The jury was further instructed that if they found that the statements were made of and concerning the respondent, the statements were "libelous *per se*," that "the law implies legal injury from the bare fact of the publication itself"; that "falsity and malice are presumed"; that "general damages need not be alleged or proved but are presumed"; and that "punitive damages may be awarded by the jury even though the amount of actual damages is neither found nor shown."

The Supreme Court of Alabama affirmed. It sustained the trial judge's rulings and instructions in all respects and rejected the petitioner's free speech and free press contentions with the statement that the "First Amendment of the United States Constitution does not protect libelous publications." 273 Ala. 656,——, 144 So. 2d 25, ——.[6] Because of the importance of the constitu-

---

[5] Governor John Patterson of Alabama also demanded a retraction from the petitioner, The New York Times Company, so far as the advertisement related to him and to his conduct as Governor and Ex-Officio Chairman of the State Board of Education of Alabama. The petitioner published a retraction and an apology in the issue of The Times of May 16, 1960.

[6] The court also stated that "The Fourteenth Amendment is directed against State action and not private action," 273 Ala., at ——,

tional issues involved we granted the separate petitions for certiorari of the individual petitioners and of the
petitioner The New York Times Company, 371 U. S. 946.[7]

## I.

The statements from our opinions [8] which imply that
the Constitution is not offended by a State's law of libel
do not decide the question presented in this case. That
question, we repeat, is whether the Alabama libel law, as
applied to these petitioners, encroaches upon the constitutionally protected freedoms of the people and the press
to discuss and criticize the official conduct of public
officers. The general proposition that freedom of expression upon public questions is secured against state action
by the First Amendment through the Fourteenth Amendment has long been settled by our decisions.[9] In applying that constitutional principle, we have said that the
First Amendment "was fashioned to assure the unfettered
interchange of ideas for the bringing about of political
and social changes desired by the people," *Roth* v. *United
States,* 354 U. S. 476, 484; that "the maintenance of the
opportunity for free political discussions to the end that

---

144 So. 2d ——. However, the action of the Alabama courts was
state action within the meaning of the Fourteenth Amendment.
*Shelley* v. *Kraemer,* 334 U. S. 1; *Barrows* v. *Jackson,* 346 U. S. 249;
*AFL* v. *Swing,* 312 U. S. 321.

[7] The respondent sued the five petitioners in a single action which
was tried before a jury which returned a verdict against all of them.
The four individual petitioners and the petitioner, The New York
Times Company, proceeded separately in the Alabama Supreme
Court and in this Court.

[8] See, for example, *Konigsberg* v. *State Bar of California.* 366 U. S.
36, 49 (1961); *Times Film Corp.* v. *City of Chicago,* 365 U. S. 43,
48 (1961); *Roth* v. *United States,* 354 U. S. 476, 486 (1957); *Beauharnais* v. *Illinois.* 343 U. S. 250, 266 (1952); *Pennekamp* v. *Florida,*
328 U. S. 331, 348–349 (1946); *Chaplinsky* v. *New Hampshire.* 315
U. S. 568, 572 (1942); *Near* v. *Minnesota.* 283 U. S. 697, 715 (1931).

[9] See *Gitlow* v. *New York,* 268 U. S. 652.

government may be responsive to the will of the people and that changes may be obtained by lawful means, an opportunity essential to the security of the republic, is a fundamental principle of our constitutional system." *Stromberg* v. *California,* 283 U. S. 359, 369; see also *DeJonge* v. *Oregon,* 299 U. S. 353, 365; that the "prized American privilege to speak one's mind, although not always with perfect good taste" applies at least to speech "on all public institutions," *Bridges* v. *California,* 314 U. S. 252, 270; that this opportunity is to be afforded for "vigorous advocacy" no less than "abstract" disquisition, *NAACP* v. *Button,* 371 U. S. 415, 429; that the constitutional protection does not turn upon the "truth, popularity, or social utility, of the ideas and beliefs which are offered." *NAACP* v. *Button, supra,* at 445; and that constitutional freedom of expression "needs breathing space to survive." *NAACP* v. *Button, supra,* at 433. The First Amendment, said Judge Learned Hand, "presupposes that right conclusions are more likely to be gathered out of a multitude of tongues, than through any kind of authoritative selection. To many this is, and always will be folly; but we have staked upon it our all." *United States* v. *Associated Press,* 52 F. Supp. 362, 372. And Mr. Justice Brandeis, in his oft-cited concurring opinion in *Whitney* v. *California,* 274 U. S. 357, 375–376, said:

"Those who won our independence believed . . . that public discussion is a political duty; and that this should be a fundamental principle of the American government. They recognized the risks to which all human institutions are subject. But they knew that order cannot be secured merely through fear of punishment for its infraction; that it is hazardous to discourage thought, hope and imagination; that fear breeds repression; that repression breeds hate; that hate menaces stable government; that the path of safety lies in the opportunity to discuss freely supposed grievances and proposes remedies; and that the fitting remedy for evil counsels is good ones. Believing in the power of reason as applied through public discussion, they eschewed silence coerced by law—the argument of force in its worst form. Recognizing the occasional tyrannies of governing majorities, they amended the Constitution so that free speech and assembly should be guaranteed."

This concept of the basic objective of the First Amendment draws powerful support from James Madison, the Architect of the Bill of Rights. His agreement with this view was made clear in his uncompromising opposition to the ill-starred Sedition Act of 1798, 1 Stat. 596, which provided heavy penalties for writing, publishing, or speaking anything "false, scandalous, and malicious, against the Administration, Congress or the President, with intent to defame or to bring them . . . into contempt or disrepute . . . or to stir up sedition within the United States." On December 21, 1798, the General Assembly of Virginia adopted a resolution, among others, "that the General Assembly doth particularly protest against the palpable and alarming infractions of the Constitution . . . [the Sedition Act exercises] a power not delegated by the Constitution, but, on the contrary, expressly and positively forbidden by [the First Amendment]—a power which, more than any other, ought to provide universal alarm, because it is levelled against the right of freely examining public characters and measures, and of free communication among the people thereon, which has ever been justly deemed the only effectual guardian of every other right." 4 Elliot's Debates on the Federal Constitution, pp. 553, 554. Madison prepared the report in support of this protest. *Id.,* pp. 569–576. His major premise was that the form of government created by our Constitution was "altogether different"

10   NEW YORK TIMES CO. *v.* SULLIVAN.

from the British form where the Crown was sovereign, and the people the subjects; in contrast. he said. in the United States. "the people, not the government, possess the absolute sovereignty," and the officials of government were therefore responsible to the people. "Is it not natural and necessary, under such different circumstances," he asked, that "a different degree of freedom in the use of the press should be contemplated?" *Id.,* p. 569. Earlier, in a debate in the House of Representatives, he had said: "If we advert to the nature of Republican government, we shall find that the censorial power is in the people over the government, and not in the government over the people." 4 Annals of Congress. p. 934.[10] Of the exercise of that power by the press. the report says: "in every state, probably, in the Union, the press has exerted a freedom in canvassing the merits and measures of public men, of every description, which has not been confined to the strict limits of the common law. On this footing the freedom of the press has stood; on this foundation it yet stands. . . ." Elliot's Debates, *supra,* 570.[11]

---

[10] This view was also implicit in the letter of 1774 of the Continental Congress to the inhabitants of Quebec:

"The last right we shall mention, regards the freedom of the press. The importance of this consists, besides the advancement of truth, science, morality, and arts in general, in its diffusion of liberal sentiments on the administration of the Government, its ready communication of thoughts between subjects, and its consequential promotion of union among them, whereby oppressive officers are shamed or intimidated, into more honorable and just modes of conducting affairs." 1 Journal of the Continental Congress (1774) 108.

[11] Thomas Jefferson shared Madison's views. The Act expired by its own terms in 180—, and only a few prosecutions had been brought under it. Jefferson, as President, pardoned those who had been convicted and sentenced and remitted their fines. He said, "I discharged every person under punishment or prosecution under the Sedition law because I considered, and now consider, that law to

The First Amendment, concludes Madison, was expressly added to the Constitution to secure this freedom of the people freely to discuss public affairs and the conduct of public officers, and is necessarily violated by a law which punishes them for exercising that right.[12]

---

be a nullity as absolute and palpable as if Congress had ordered us to fall down and worship a golden image." —— —— —— ——. The constitutionality of the Act was not tested in the courts. Agreement with the views of Madison and Jefferson has been expressed by Justices of this Court. See *Abrams* v. *United States*, 250 U. S. 616, 630 (Holmes and Brandeis dissenting); *Beauharnais* v. *Illinois*, 343 U. S. 250, 289 (Jackson, J., dissenting); and see Cooley, Const. Lim. (7th ed.), pp. 613–614.

[12] Madison said: ". . . it is manifestly impossible to punish the intent to bring those who administer the government into disrepute or contempt, without striking at the right of freely discussing public characters and measures; because those who engage in such discussions must expect and intend to excite these unfavorable sentiments, so far as they may be thought to be deserved. To prohibit the intent to excite those unfavorable sentiments against those who administer the government, is equivalent to a prohibition of the actual excitement of them; and to prohibit the actual excitement of them is equivalent to a prohibition of discussions having that tendency and effect: which, again, is equivalent to a protection of those who administer the government, if they should at any time deserve the contempt or hatred of the people, against being exposed to it, by free animadversions on their characters and conduct. Nor can there be a doubt, if those in public trust be shielded by penal laws from such strictures of the press as may expose them to contempt, or disrepute, or hatred, where they may deserve it, that, in exact proportion as they may deserve to be exposed, will be the certainty and criminality of the intent to expose them, and the vigilance of prosecuting and punishing it: nor a doubt that a government thus intrenched in penal statutes against the just and natural effects of a culpable adminisration, will easily evade the responsibility which is essential to a faithful discharge of its duty.

"Let it be recollected, lastly that the right of electing the members of the government constitutes more particularly the essence of a free and responsible government. The value and efficacy of this right de-

12    NEW YORK TIMES CO. *v.* SULLIVAN.

It was suggested on oral argument of the instant case that, under Madison's view, the First Amendment bars sanctions against defamatory criticism of public officials reflecting upon their official conduct even when tainted with express malice. We do not think that the Amendment reaches so far. We have recognized, to be sure, that ". . . public men, are, as it were, public property," *Beauharnais* v. *Illinois,* 343 U. S. 250, 263, n. 18, and "men of fortitude, able to thrive in a hardy climate." *Craig* v. *Harney,* 331 U. S. 367, 376. Some error in statement reflecting upon official conduct is to be expected [13] and, consistently with the First Amendment, must be tolerated. We agree with the views stated by Judge Edgerton for the Court of Appeals of the District of Columbia in affirming the dismissal of a Congressman's libel suit based upon a newspaper article charging him with anti-Semitism in opposing the appointment of a district judge. Judge Edgerton said, *Sweeney* v. *Patterson,* 128 F. 2d 457, 458:

"Cases which impose liability for erroneous reports of the political conduct of officials reflect the obsolete doctrine that the governed must not criticize their governors. Since Congress governs the country, all inhabitants, and not merely the constituents of particular members, are vitally concerned in the political conduct and views of every member of Congress. Everyone, including appellees and their readers, has an interest to defend, any any one may find means

---

pends on the knowledge of the comparative merits and demerits of the candidates for public trust, and on the equal freedom, consequently, of examining and discussing these merits and demerits of the candidates respectively." Elliot's Debates, p. 575.

[13] It has been said: "Charges of gross incompetence, disregard of the public interest, communist sympathies and the like, usually have filled the air; and hints of bribery, embezzlement and other criminal conduct are not infrequent." Noel, Defamation of Public Officers and Candidates, 49 Col. L. Rev. 879 (1949).

of defending it.   The interest of the public here outweighs the interest of appellant or any other individual.   The protection of the public requires not
merely discussion, but information.   Political conduct and views which some respectable people approve, and others condemn, are constantly imputed
to Congressmen.   Errors of fact, particularly in regard to a man's mental states and processes, are
inevitable.   Information and discussion will be discouraged, and the public interest in public knowledge of important facts will be poorly defended, if
error subjects its author to a libel suit without even
a showing of economic loss.   Whatever is added to
the field of libel is taken from the field of free
debate." [14]

But the line may surely be drawn to exclude from constitutional protection the statement which is not criticism, or intended as such, but, in the guise of criticism,
is deliberate, malevent and knowing falsity, or utterance
reckless of the truth, voiced from vindictive motives to
destroy the reputation of a public official. [15]   We have

---

[14] See also *Coleman* v. *MacLennan,* 78 Kan. Rep. 711, 724:
". . . it is of the utmost consequence that the people should discuss
the character and qualifications of candidates for their suffrages.
The importance to the state and to society of such discussions is so
vast, and the advantages derived are so great, that they more than
counterbalance the inconvenience of private persons whose conduct
may be involved, and occasional injury to the reputations of individuals must yield to the public welfare, although at times such injury may be great.   The public benefit from publicity is so great, and
the chance of injury to private character so small, that such discussion must be privileged."

[15] Compare Cooley, Const. Lim. (7th ed.), 603, 604:
"The evils to be prevented were not the censorship of the press
merely, but any action of the government by means of which it might
prevent such free and general discussion of public matters as seems
absolutely essential to prepare the people for an intelligent exercise of
their rights as citizens.   The constitutional liberty of speech and of

## 14 NEW YORK TIMES CO. *v.* SULLIVAN.

held that obscene speech has no constitutional protection because it is "utterly without redeeming social importance." *Roth* v. *United States, supra,* 484. This may be also said of the utterance of the unscrupulous defames and traduces of reputation.

However, here again. "The line between speech unconditionally guaranteed and speech which may be regulated . . . is finely drawn . . . [and] the separation of legitimate from illegitimate speech calls for . . . sensitive tools. . . ." *Speiser* v. *Randall,* 357 U. S. 513, 525. Libel, like obscenity, is only another "special instance of the larger principle that the freedoms of expression must be ringed about with adequate bulwarks." *Bantam Books* v. *Sullivan,* 372 U. S. 58, 66. State regulations of obscenity do not satisfy the command of the Fourteenth Amendment unless the state enforces them under procedures that guard against the curtailment of protected nonobscene expression, which is often separated from obscenity only by a dim and uncertain line. *Marcus* v. *Search Warrant,* 367 U. S. 717, 730–731; *Smith* v. *California,* 361 U. S. 147; *Bantam Books* v. *Sullivan, supra.* The Fourteenth Amendment also demands that the States apply their law in a civil libel action with safeguards evolved to prevent the invasion of the freedom to discuss public affairs and to criticize the official conduct of public officers.

### II.

Safeguards have already been devised by state courts to guard against the risk that the civil action for libel

the press, as we understand it, implies a right to freely utter and publish whatever the citizen may please, and to be protected against any responsibility for so doing, except so far as such publications, from their blasphemy, obscenity, or scandalous character, may be a public offense, or as by their falsehood and malice they may injuriously affect the standing, reputation or pecuniary interests of individuals."

## NEW YORK TIMES CO. *v.* SULLIVAN.    15.

might be a vehicle for the suppression of protected. comment. These safeguards allow the defenses of privilege and fair comment to defeat a public official's libel action, even for imputations which might otherwise constitute actionable libel, unless he proves express malice. We think that these safeguards satisfy the requirements of the Fourteenth Amendment. They are well defined in an opinion of the Kansas Supreme Court in *Coleman* v. *MacLennan*, 78 Kan. 711. The Attorney General of Kansas, a candidate for re-election and a member of a state commission charged with the management and control of the state fund. sued the owner and publisher of the Topeka State Journal for alleged libel in an article published by the paper which reflected upon his official conduct in connection with a school fund transaction. The defendant pleaded privilege and the trial judge, over the objection of the Attorney General, instructed the jury that "where an article is published and circulated among voters for the sole purpose of giving what the defendant believes to be truthful information concerning a candidate for public office and for the purpose of enabling such voters to cast their ballot more intelligently, and the whole thing is done in good faith and without malice, the article is privileged, although the principal matters contained in the article may be untrue in fact and derogatory to the character of the plaintiff; and in such a case the burden is on the plaintiff to show actual malice in the publication of the article." The jury, in answer to a special question. found that the Attorney General had not proved express malice. The Supreme Court of Kansas sustained the instruction as a correct statement of the law, saying:

"In such a case the occasion gives rise to a privilege, qualified to this extent: anyone claiming to be de-

16    NEW YORK TIMES CO. *v.* SULLIVAN.

famed by the communication must show actual
malice or go remediless. This privilege extends to
a great variety of subject, and includes matters of
public concern, public men, and candidates for
office." 78 Kan. 723–724.[16]

The Kansas court rejected as an insufficient safeguard
the rule followed in *King* v. *Root,* 4 Wend. (N. Y.) 114,
and in *Post Publishing Co.* v. *Hallam,* 59 F. 530, which
denied a defense for statements untrue in fact, although
made in good faith, without malice and under the honest
belief that they were true. 78 Kan. 729–742. This limitation of the defendant to the defense of truth was said
to be necessary because "the danger that honorable or
worthy men may be driven from politics and public service by allowing too great latitude in attacks upon their

---

[16] Accord: *Gough* v. *Tribune-Journal Co.,* 75 Idaho 502, 510
(1954); *Salinger* v. *Cowles.* 195 Iowa 873, 890–891 (1923); *Bradford*
v. *Clark,* 90 Me. 298, 302 (1897); *Lawrence* v. *Fox.* 357 Mich. 134,
142 (1959); *Ponder* v. *Cobb.* 257 N. C. 281, 293 (1962); *Moore* v.
*Davis.* 16 S. W. 2d 380, 384 (Tex. Civ. App. 1929). Applying the
same rule to candidates for public office, see *Phoenix Newspapers* v.
*Choisser.* 82 Ariz. 271, 277 (1957); *Friedell* v. *Blakeley Printing Co.,*
163 Minn. 226, 231 (1925); *Boucher* v. *Clark Pub Co.,* 14 S. D. 72,
82 (1900). And cf. *Charles Parker Co.* v. *Silver City Crystal Co.,*
142 Conn. 605, 614 (1955) (same privilege against private corporation allegedly libeled in political broadcast). See also *Chagnon* v.
*Union Leader Corp.,* 103 N. H. 426 (1961): *Stice* v. *Beacon Newspaper Corp.,* 185 Kan. 61, 340 P. 2d 396 (1959); *Friedell* v. *Blakeley
Printing Co.,* 163 Minn. 226, 203 N. W. 974 (1925); *Moore* v. *Davis,*
16 S. W. 2d 380 (1929); *Lafferty* v. *Houlihan.* 81 N. H. 67, 121 A.
92 (1923); *Salinger* v. *Cowles.* 195 Iowa 873, 191 N. W. 167 (1922);
*McLean* v. *Merriman.* 42 S. C. 394, 175 N. W. 878 (1920); *Boucher*
v. *Clark Pub. Co.,* 14 S. D. 72, 84 N. W. 237 (1900). Scholarly
opinion favors this requirement that a plaintiff officer or candidate
prove actual malice. See, *e. g.,* 1 Harper and James, The Law of
Torts (1956), pp. 449–450: Noel, Defamation of Public Officers and
Candidates, 49 Col. L. Rev. 875, 891–895 (1949); cf. Developments
in the Law: Defamation, 69 Harv. L. Rev. 875, 928 (1956).

character outweighs any benefit that might occasionally
accrue to the public from charges that are true in fact
but are incapable of legal proof." *Post Publishing Co.* v.
*Hallam, supra,* 652.  We may doubt, but need not take
issue with, the accuracy of the premise.  It is in any event
beside the point.  The First Amendment expresses the
highest public concern that people freely discuss public
matters and the official conduct of public officers.  Erroneous statement is inevitable in the give-and-take of free
discussion.  To limit the speaker to the defense of truth
must often mean that while his statements are true in
fact, his defense must fail.  Even *Hallam* recognizes the
difficulties attending proof of the defense, and those difficulties are measurably enhanced when the alleged defamatory matter is in part statement of facts and in part
statements of judgment or opinion.[17]  These considerations demonstrate that defendants must be armed with
more than the defense of truth if they are not to be made
timid about discussing public matters and the conduct
of public officials from fear of being mulcted in heavy
damages.  State procedures cannot satisfy the Fourteenth Amendment without recognizing a privilege for
erroneous statement honestly made.  What we said in
*Smith* v. *California,* 361 U. S. 147, in holding that the
Fourteenth Amendment requires proof of *scienter* to sustain a conviction for possessing obscene writings for sale
is pertinent.  We said:

> "For if the bookseller is criminally libel without
> knowledge of the contents . . . he will tend to
> restrict the books he sells to those he has inspected;
> and thus the state will have imposed a restriction
> upon the distribution of constitutionally protected
> as well as obscene literature . . . and the book-
> seller's burden would become the public's burden,

---

[17] See Harper and James, The Law of Torts, § 5.20, pp. 418–419.

for by restricting him the public's access to reading
matter would be restricted . . . his timidity in the
face of his absolute criminal liability, thus would
tend to restrict the public's access to forms of the
printed word which the State could not constitutionally suppress directly. The bookseller's self-
censorship, compelled by the state, would be a censorship affecting the whole public hardly less virulent
for being privately administered. Through it, the
distribution of all books, both obscene and not obscene, would be impeded. [361 U. S. 147, 153–154.]
Similarly a rule which makes the critic of the official
conduct of a public officer the guarantor of the truth
of the facts underlying his criticism might operate to
inhibit discussion vital to the public interest, or at
least have the also undesirable result of inducing excessive caution to make only statements which 'steer
far wider of the unlawful zone.' " *Speiser* v. *Randall,
supra,* 357 U. S., at 526.[18]

Moreover, in an action which intertwines the "web of
freedoms which make up free speech," "the procedures
by which the facts of the case are determined assume an
importance fully as great as the validity of the substantive rule of law to be applied." *Speiser* v. *Randall, supra,*

---

[18] The privilege immunizing honest misstatements of fact is often
referred to as "conditional privilege" to distinguish it from the "absolute privilege" recognized in judicial, legislative, administrative and
executive proceedings. See, *e. g.,* Harper and James, The Law of
Torts, §§ 5.22–5.24, pp. 421–435; §§ 5.25–5.27, pp. 435–456. The
principle of fair comment is reserved for honest expression of opinion.
§ 5.28, pp. 456–462. Since we hold that the Fourteenth Amendment
requires recognition of the conditional privilege for honest misstatements of fact, it follows that a defense of fair comment must also
be afforded for honest expression of opinion based upon privileged,
as well as true, statements of fact. Both defenses are of course
defeasible if the public official proves actual malice.

357 U. S., at 520.    State procedures uniformly leave to
the court the determinations whether the publication
complained of is capable of bearing a defamatory meaning, and on the issue of privilege, the determination
whether the occasion for the publication is one which
gives rise to the privilege.[19]   These procedures are consistent with the constitutional requirements.   However,
the rule employed in Alabama in this case, which attaches
a presumption of malice to a holding that the publication
is capable of a defamatory meaning, and dispenses with
affirmative proof of actual malice, does not meet the constitutional standard.   "Broad prophylactic rules in the
area of free expression are suspect . . . . Precision of
regulation must be the touchstone in an area so closely
touching our most precious freedoms."   *NAACP* v. *Button, supra,* 371 U. S., at 435.   The Alabama rule plainly
cannot meet the required standard in the fact of the
defenses of privilege or fair comment.   There is in such
case a "constitutional restriction" against allowing the
public official a recovery in the absence of affirmative
proof of express malice.   In addition, since the freedoms
at stake "are delicate and vulnerable as well as supremely
precious in our society," *NAACP* v. *Button, supra,* 371
U. S., at 433, they call for "placing upon [the plaintiff]
the burden of persuading the trier of fact by clear, convincing and unequivocal evidence," *Nishikawa* v. *Dulles,*
356 U. S. 129, 135, as to every element necessary to establish his cause of action within the principles we have
announced.   Otherwise, the fear of a large damage award,
doubtless greater than the fear which attends the possibility of a prosecution for criminal libel, *City of Chicago*
v. *Tribune,* 307 Ill. 595, 607, might constitute the
action for civil libel a repressive measure of significant
proportions.

---

[19] See Harper and James, *supra,* note 17, § 5.29, p. 463.

## III.

It is apparent from what we have said that the judgment of the Alabama Court must be reversed. The petitioners seasonably raised their claim under the First and Fourteenth Amendments and, upon the proofs, were entitled to a judgment that the respondent had not made out a case for liability.

*First.* The respondent argues that the findings of the jury are insulated from this Court's review by the provision of the Seventh Amendment that "no fact tried by a jury, shall be otherwise re-examined in any court of the United States, than according to the rules of the common law." *Justices* v. *United States ex rel. Murray,* 9 Wall. 274; *Chicago B. & Q.* v. *Chicago,* 166 U. S. 226, 242, 243. That provision and the cited cases do not foreclose us from examining the proofs to determine whether the Constitution forbids the State from basing the judgment upon them. "This Court will review the finding of facts by a state court . . . where a conclusion of law as to a federal right and a finding of fact are so intermingled as to make it necessary, in order to pass upon the federal question, to analyze the facts." *Fiske* v. *Kansas,* 274 U. S. 380, 385, 386.

*Second.* The threshold question is whether the statements in the advertisement complained of can be reasonably said to be capable of a defamatory meaning. The Alabama Supreme Court sustained the trial court's holding that the statements were defamatory ("libelous per se") under the doctrine that "where the words published tend to injure a person libeled by them in his reputation, profession, trade or business, or charge him with an indictable offense, or tends to bring the individual into public contempt . . ." they are defamatory. 273 Ala. ——, 144 So. 2d ——. Alabama therefore fails to distinguish between public officials and private individuals in determining whether the statements complained of constitute actionable libel.  Since that distinction has constitutional significance, we proceed to our own judgment whether the statements complained of by the respondent are capable of bearing a defamatory meaning.  Cf. *Manual Enterprises* v. *Day,* 370 U. S. 478, 488.

The question cannot be answered except in the context of the entire advertisement.  The core of the message to the public in the advertisement is in the opening sentences that "The whole world knows by now" that Negroes in the United States are struggling for their civil rights by means of "non-violent demonstrations" of "Southern Negro students" and that these efforts "are being met by an unprecedented wave of terror" in the South.  Then follows descriptions of alleged events constituting the alleged "wave of terror."  Among these are those described in the statements which the respondent alleged had libeled him.  Following these, the message continues that the "strategy is to behead this affirmative movement and thus to demoralize Negro Americans and weaken their will to struggle."  Funds are sought with the plea that to "Heed Their Rising Voices" is not enough, that the "defense of Martin Luther King, spiritual leader of the student sit-in movement, clearly, therefore, is an integral part of the total struggle for freedom in the South."

The respondent does not deny that the advertisement describes with substantial accuracy a state of affairs in the South of great public interest and concern.  A part of the scene in contemporary America is the struggle of Negroes to secure their constitutional rights and their use of the demonstrations described to achieve that end.  The opposition engendered to this movement is also a fact familiar to every citizen.  This Court said in *NAACP* v. *Button, supra,* at 435, that "We cannot close our eyes to the fact that the militant Negro civil rights movement has engendered the intense resentment and opposition of the politically dominant white communities of Virginia." Similarly, we cannot close our eyes to the like situation in Alabama. The statements respondent complains of appear in a recitation of abuses which are emphasized to bring home to readers the necessity for funds to carry on the struggle for civil rights. None of the abuses is attributable to any particular person or persons but to impersonal "Southern violators of the Constitution" and "they." Respondent's proofs showed that abuses of this nature had in fact occurred in Montgomery. His evidence showed that Dr. King's home was bombed while his wife and child were in the house, that Dr. King had been arrested and that he was awaiting trial on perjury charges. There also had been a student demonstration on the State Capitol steps, student leaders had been expelled from Alabama State College, and demonstrations had been staged at or near the campus requiring the deploying of police nearby. The discrepancies in the description of those events in the advertisement could hardly be said to be serious: the students sang the National Anthem and not My Country 'Tis of Thee on the Capitol steps; leaders were expelled not for leading that demonstration but for conduct in a courthouse cafeteria in demanding food service; the students had not refused to re-register after their strike in protest of the expulsion of their leaders, and their dining hall had not been padlocked; Dr. King had been arrested only four times and not seven; the police had not "ringed" the campus but had been "deployed" there; Dr. King claimed to have been assaulted but the police officer involved denied the assault. We hold that the statements complained of by respondent are not capable of bearing a defamatory meaning either on their face or when read in the light of the proofs. The statements as part of the advertisement fall well within constitutionally protected commentary upon a serious contemporary domestic problem.

*Third.* The respondent's name was nowhere mentioned in the statements nor anywhere in the advertisement. Neither the complaint nor the trial judge specified what statements of the two paragraphs might be read as referring to the respondent. The Supreme Court of Alabama held that the reference to "police" in the third paragraph might be read as referring to the respondent. "We think it common knowledge that the average person knows that municipal agents, such as policemen, firemen, and others are under the control and direction of the city governing board. and more particularly under the direction and control of a single Commissioner. In measuring the performance or deficiencies of such groups, praise or criticism is usually attached to the official in complete control of the body." 273 Ala. ——, 144 So. 2d ——.

Even if the reference to "police," or as respondent urges in this Court, also the reference to "arrest," might reasonably justify readers to think that those references referred to the respondent,[20] they would not in our view rationally support a reading of "Southern Violators of the Constitution" and "they" as imputing to the respondent the bombing of Dr. King's home, the alleged assault upon him, or that respondent brought about the prosecution of Dr. King for perjury. Plainly, the respondent's own testimony and that of his six witnesses that they read the

---

[20] "A person may be defamed by language which is defamatory of a small group of which he is a member if the circumstances are such as to enable others reasonably to conclude that the plaintiff was the person to whom the defamatory communication was applicable." Harper and James, *supra.* § 5.7, p. 367. It was stipulated that the Montgomery Police Department consisted of 175 full time officers and 24 special traffic officers. In light of our conclusion we express no view whether this was a sufficiently small group to justify the respondent's reliance upon the quoted principle.

# 24 NEW YORK TIMES CO. *v.* SULLIVAN.

statement as meaning him, does not satisfy the standard of clear, convincing, and unequivocal evidence of that fact. If those proofs are weighty support that the references to "police" and "arrests" imputed to the respondent as Police Commissioner the conduct of "ringing" the campus and arresting Dr. King seven times, respondent's own proofs established that these statements were not defamatory matter.

*Fourth.* The proofs were utterly barren of any evidence that the statements were made by the petitioners with actual malice, that is in bad faith, deliberately, maliciously, and knowing of, or reckless of, their falsity, and out of ill-will toward the respondent, from vindictive motives unrelated to comment upon public affairs or criticism of the conduct of public business. The trial judge refused to instruct the jury, as requested by the petitioner, The New York Times Company, that punitive damages might be awarded only if the publication "was motivated by personal ill-will, that is actual intent to do the plaintiff harm, or that the defendant, The New York Times Co., was guilty of gross negligence and recklessness and not of just ordinary negligence or carelessness in publishing the matter complained of so as to indicate a wanton disregard of plaintiff's rights." The trial court's view, sustained by the Alabama Supreme Court, was that since the matter complained of was defamatory on its face, malice was "presumed." For reasons which we have stated, the respondent could not be relieved of the burden of proving actual malice by attaching a presumption of malice to the holding that the statements constituted defamatory matter.

*Reversed.*

# APPENDIX 2

### Opinions in *New York Times Co. v. Sullivan* by Justices Brennan, Black and Goldberg

Following are the texts of the Opinion of the Court by Justice Brennan and the concurring opinions by Justices Black and Goldberg, as they appear in the volumes of Supreme Court decisions, the *United States Reports*.

# NEW YORK TIMES CO. *v.* SULLIVAN.

CERTIORARI TO THE SUPREME COURT OF ALABAMA.

No. 39. Argued January 6, 1964.—Decided March 9, 1964.*

Respondent, an elected official in Montgomery, Alabama, brought this civil action in a state court alleging that he had been libeled by an advertisement in corporate petitioner's newspaper, the text of which appeared over the names of the four individual petitioners and many others. The advertisement included statements, some of which were false, about police action allegedly directed against students who participated in a civil rights demonstration and against a leader of the civil rights movement; respondent claimed the statements were imputable to him because his duties included supervision of the police department. The trial judge instructed the jury that such statements were "libelous per se," legal injury being implied without proof of actual damages, and that for the purpose of compensatory damages malice was presumed, so that such damages could be awarded against petitioners if the statements were found to have been published by them and to have related to respondent. As to punitive damages, the judge instructed that mere negligence was not evidence of actual malice and would not justify an award of punitive damages; he refused to instruct that actual intent to harm or recklessness had to be found before punitive damages could be awarded, or that a verdict for respondent should differentiate between compensatory and punitive damages. The jury found for respondent and the State Supreme Court affirmed. *Held:* A State cannot under the First and Fourteenth Amendments award damages to a public official for defamatory falsehood relating to his official conduct unless he proves "actual malice"—that the statement was made with knowledge of its falsity or with reckless disregard of whether it was true or false.

(a) Application by state courts of a rule of law, whether statutory or not, to award a judgment in a civil action, is "state action" under the Fourteenth Amendment. P. 265.

(b) Expression does not lose constitutional protection to which it would otherwise be entitled because it appears in the form of a paid advertisement. Pp. 265–266.

___

*Together with No. 40, *Abernathy et al.* v. *Sullivan,* also on certiorari to the same court, argued January 7, 1964.

(c) Factual error, content defamatory of official reputation, or both, are insufficient to warrant curbing free expression unless actual malice is alleged and proved. Pp. 272–273.

(d) State court judgment entered upon a general verdict which does not differentiate between punitive damages, as to which under state law actual malice must be proved, and general damages, as to which it is "presumed," precludes any determination as to the basis of the verdict and requires reversal, where presumption of malice is inconsistent with federal constitutional requirements. P. 284.

(e) The evidence was constitutionally insufficient to support the judgment for respondent, since it failed to support a finding that the statements were made with actual malice or that they related to respondent. Pp. 285–292.

273 Ala. 656, 144 So. 2d 25, reversed and remanded.

*Herbert Wechsler* argued the cause for petitioner in No. 39. With him on the brief were *Herbert Brownell, Thomas F. Daly, Louis M. Loeb, T. Eric Embry, Marvin E. Frankel, Ronald S. Diana* and *Doris Wechsler.*

*William P. Rogers* and *Samuel R. Pierce, Jr.* argued the cause for petitioners in No. 40. With *Mr. Pierce* on the brief were *I. H. Wachtel, Charles S. Conley, Benjamin Spiegel, Raymond S. Harris, Harry H. Wachtel, Joseph B. Russell, David N. Brainin, Stephen J. Jelin* and *Charles B. Markham.*

*M. Roland Nachman, Jr.* argued the cause for respondent in both cases. With him on the brief were *Sam Rice Baker* and *Calvin Whitesell.*

Briefs of *amici curiae,* urging reversal, were filed in No. 39 by *William P. Rogers, Gerald W. Siegel* and *Stanley Godofsky* for the Washington Post Company, and by *Howard Ellis, Keith Masters* and *Don H. Reuben* for the Tribune Company. Brief of *amici curiae,* urging reversal, was filed in both cases by *Edward S. Greenbaum, Harriet F. Pilpel, Melvin L. Wulf, Nanette Dembitz* and *Nancy F. Wechsler* for the American Civil Liberties Union et al.

MR. JUSTICE BRENNAN delivered the opinion of the Court.

We are required in this case to determine for the first time the extent to which the constitutional protections for speech and press limit a State's power to award damages in a libel action brought by a public official against critics of his official conduct.

Respondent L. B. Sullivan is one of the three elected Commissioners of the City of Montgomery, Alabama. He testified that he was "Commissioner of Public Affairs and the duties are supervision of the Police Department, Fire Department, Department of Cemetery and Department of Scales." He brought this civil libel action against the four individual petitioners, who are Negroes and Alabama clergymen, and against petitioner the New York Times Company, a New York corporation which publishes the New York Times, a daily newspaper. A jury in the Circuit Court of Montgomery County awarded him damages of $500,000, the full amount claimed, against all the petitioners, and the Supreme Court of Alabama affirmed. 273 Ala. 656, 144 So. 2d 25.

Respondent's complaint alleged that he had been libeled by statements in a full-page advertisement that was carried in the New York Times on March 29, 1960.[1] Entitled "Heed Their Rising Voices," the advertisement began by stating that "As the whole world knows by now, thousands of Southern Negro students are engaged in widespread non-violent demonstrations in positive affirmation of the right to live in human dignity as guaranteed by the U. S. Constitution and the Bill of Rights." It went on to charge that "in their efforts to uphold these guarantees, they are being met by an unprecedented wave of terror by those who would deny and negate that document which the whole world looks upon as setting the pattern for modern freedom. . . ." Succeeding

---

[1] A copy of the advertisement is printed in the Appendix.

paragraphs purported to illustrate the "wave of terror" by describing certain alleged events. The text concluded with an appeal for funds for three purposes: support of the student movement, "the struggle for the right-to-vote," and the legal defense of Dr. Martin Luther King, Jr., leader of the movement, against a perjury indictment then pending in Montgomery.

The text appeared over the names of 64 persons, many widely known for their activities in public affairs, religion, trade unions, and the performing arts. Below these names, and under a line reading "We in the south who are struggling daily for dignity and freedom warmly endorse this appeal," appeared the names of the four individual petitioners and of 16 other persons, all but two of whom were identified as clergymen in various Southern cities. The advertisement was signed at the bottom of the page by the "Committee to Defend Martin Luther King and the Struggle for Freedom in the South," and the officers of the Committee were listed.

Of the 10 paragraphs of text in the advertisement, the third and a portion of the sixth were the basis of respondent's claim of libel. They read as follows:

Third paragraph:

> "In Montgomery, Alabama, after students sang 'My Country, 'Tis of Thee' on the State Capitol steps, their leaders were expelled from school, and truckloads of police armed with shotguns and tear-gas ringed the Alabama State College Campus. When the entire student body protested to state authorities by refusing to re-register, their dining hall was padlocked in an attempt to starve them into submission."

Sixth paragraph:

> "Again and again the Southern violators have answered Dr. King's peaceful protests with intimidation and violence. They have bombed his home almost killing his wife and child. They have

assaulted his person.   They have arrested him seven
times—for 'speeding,' 'loitering' and similar 'offenses.'
And now they have charged him with 'perjury'—a
*felony* under which they could imprison him for
*ten years. . . .*"

Although neither of these statements mentions respondent by name, he contended that the word "police"
in the third paragraph referred to him as the Montgomery
Commissioner who supervised the Police Department, so
that he was being accused of "ringing" the campus with
police.   He further claimed that the paragraph would be
read as imputing to the police, and hence to him, the padlocking of the dining hall in order to starve the students
into submission.[2]   As to the sixth paragraph, he contended that since arrests are ordinarily made by the
police, the statement "They have arrested [Dr. King]
seven times" would be read as referring to him; he further contended that the "They" who did the arresting
would be equated with the "They" who committed the
other described acts and with the "Southern violators."
Thus, he argued, the paragraph would be read as accusing
the Montgomery police, and hence him, of answering
Dr. King's protests with "intimidation and violence,"
bombing his home, assaulting his person, and charging
him with perjury.   Respondent and six other Montgomery residents testified that they read some or all of
the statements as referring to him in his capacity as
Commissioner.

It is uncontroverted that some of the statements contained in the two paragraphs were not accurate descriptions of events which occurred in Montgomery.   Although
Negro students staged a demonstration on the State Capitol steps, they sang the National Anthem and not "My

---

[2] Respondent did not consider the charge of expelling the students
to be applicable to him, since "that responsibility rests with the State
Department of Education."

Country, 'Tis of Thee." Although nine students were
expelled by the State Board of Education, this was not
for leading the demonstration at the Capitol, but for
demanding service at a lunch counter in the Montgomery
County Courthouse on another day. Not the entire
student body, but most of it, had protested the expulsion,
not by refusing to register, but by boycotting classes on
a single day; virtually all the students did register for
the ensuing semester. The campus dining hall was not
padlocked on any occasion, and the only students who
may have been barred from eating there were the few
who had neither signed a preregistration application nor
requested temporary meal tickets. Although the police
were deployed near the campus in large numbers on three
occasions, they did not at any time "ring" the campus,
and they were not called to the campus in connection with
the demonstration on the State Capitol steps, as the third
paragraph implied. Dr. King had not been arrested
seven times, but only four; and although he claimed to
have been assaulted some years earlier in connection with
his arrest for loitering outside a courtroom, one of the
officers who made the arrest denied that there was such
an assault.

On the premise that the charges in the sixth paragraph
could be read as referring to him, respondent was allowed
to prove that he had not participated in the events
described. Although Dr. King's home had in fact been
bombed twice when his wife and child were there, both of
these occasions antedated respondent's tenure as Commissioner, and the police were not only not implicated in
the bombings, but had made every effort to apprehend
those who were. Three of Dr. King's four arrests took
place before respondent became Commissioner. Although Dr. King had in fact been indicted (he was subsequently acquitted) on two counts of perjury, each of
which carried a possible five-year sentence, respondent
had nothing to do with procuring the indictment.

Respondent made no effort to prove that he suffered actual pecuniary loss as a result of the alleged libel.[3] One of his witnesses, a former employer, testified that if he had believed the statements, he doubted whether he "would want to be associated with anybody who would be a party to such things that are stated in that ad," and that he would not re-employ respondent if he believed "that he allowed the Police Department to do the things that the paper say he did." But neither this witness nor any of the others testified that he had actually believed the statements in their supposed reference to respondent.

The cost of the advertisement was approximately $4800, and it was published by the Times upon an order from a New York advertising agency acting for the signatory Committee. The agency submitted the advertisement with a letter from A. Philip Randolph, Chairman of the Committee, certifying that the persons whose names appeared on the advertisement had given their permission. Mr. Randolph was known to the Times' Advertising Acceptability Department as a responsible person, and in accepting the letter as sufficient proof of authorization it followed its established practice. There was testimony that the copy of the advertisement which accompanied the letter listed only the 64 names appearing under the text, and that the statement, "We in the south . . . warmly endorse this appeal," and the list of names thereunder, which included those of the individual petitioners, were subsequently added when the first proof of the advertisement was received. Each of the individual petitioners testified that he had not authorized the use of his name, and that he had been unaware of its use until receipt of respondent's demand for a retraction. The manager of the Advertising Ac-

---

[3] Approximately 394 copies of the edition of the Times containing the advertisement were circulated in Alabama. Of these, about 35 copies were distributed in Montgomery County. The total circulation of the Times for that day was approximately 650,000 copies.

ceptability Department testified that he had approved
the advertisement for publication because he knew nothing to cause him to believe that anything in it was false,
and because it bore the endorsement of "a number of
people who are well known and whose reputation" he
"had no reason to question." Neither he nor anyone
else at the Times made an effort to confirm the accuracy of the advertisement, either by checking it against
recent Times news stories relating to some of the described
events or by any other means.

Alabama law denies a public officer recovery of punitive damages in a libel action brought on account of a
publication concerning his official conduct unless he first
makes a written demand for a public retraction and the
defendant fails or refuses to comply. Alabama Code,
Tit. 7, § 914. Respondent served such a demand upon
each of the petitioners. None of the individual petitioners responded to the demand, primarily because each
took the position that he had not authorized the use of
his name on the advertisement and therefore had not
published the statements that respondent alleged had
libeled him. The Times did not publish a retraction in
response to the demand, but wrote respondent a letter
stating, among other things, that "we . . . are somewhat
puzzled as to how you think the statements in any way
reflect on you," and "you might, if you desire, let us know
in what respect you claim that the statements in the
advertisement reflect on you." Respondent filed this
suit a few days later without answering the letter. The
Times did, however, subsequently publish a retraction of
the advertisement upon the demand of Governor John
Patterson of Alabama, who asserted that the publication
charged him with "grave misconduct and . . . improper
actions and omissions as Governor of Alabama and
Ex-Officio Chairman of the State Board of Education of
Alabama." When asked to explain why there had been
a retraction for the Governor but not for respondent, the

Secretary of the Times testified: "We did that because we didn't want anything that was published by The Times to be a reflection on the State of Alabama and the Governor was, as far as we could see, the embodiment of the State of Alabama and the proper representative of the State and, furthermore, we had by that time learned more of the actual facts which the ad purported to recite and, finally, the ad did refer to the action of the State authorities and the Board of Education presumably of which the Governor is the ex-officio chairman . . . ." On the other hand, he testified that he did not think that "any of the language in there referred to Mr. Sullivan."

The trial judge submitted the case to the jury under instructions that the statements in the advertisement were "libelous per se" and were not privileged, so that petitioners might be held liable if the jury found that they had published the advertisement and that the statements were made "of and concerning" respondent. The jury was instructed that, because the statements were libelous per se, "the law . . . implies legal injury from the bare fact of publication itself," "falsity and malice are presumed," "general damages need not be alleged or proved but are presumed," and "punitive damages may be awarded by the jury even though the amount of actual damages is neither found nor shown." An award of punitive damages—as distinguished from "general" damages, which are compensatory in nature—apparently requires proof of actual malice under Alabama law, and the judge charged that "mere negligence or carelessness is not evidence of actual malice or malice in fact, and does not justify an award of exemplary or punitive damages." He refused to charge, however, that the jury must be "convinced" of malice, in the sense of "actual intent" to harm or "gross negligence and recklessness," to make such an award, and he also refused to require that a verdict for respondent differentiate between compensatory and punitive damages. The judge rejected petitioners' contention that his rulings abridged the freedoms of speech and of the press that are guaranteed by the First and Fourteenth Amendments.

In affirming the judgment, the Supreme Court of Alabama sustained the trial judge's rulings and instructions in all respects. 273 Ala. 656, 144 So. 2d 25. It held that "where the words published tend to injure a person libeled by them in his reputation, profession, trade or business, or charge him with an indictable offense, or tend to bring the individual into public contempt," they are "libelous per se"; that "the matter complained of is, under the above doctrine, libelous per se, if it was published of and concerning the plaintiff"; and that it was actionable without "proof of pecuniary injury . . . , such injury being implied." *Id.*, at 673, 676, 144 So. 2d, at 37, 41. It approved the trial court's ruling that the jury could find the statements to have been made "of and concerning" respondent, stating: "We think it common knowledge that the average person knows that municipal agents, such as police and firemen, and others, are under the control and direction of the city governing body, and more particularly under the direction and control of a single commissioner. In measuring the performance or deficiencies of such groups, praise or criticism is usually attached to the official in complete control of the body." *Id.*, at 674–675, 144 So. 2d, at 39. In sustaining the trial court's determination that the verdict was not excessive, the court said that malice could be inferred from the Times' "irresponsibility" in printing the advertisement while "the Times in its own files had articles already published which would have demonstrated the falsity of the allegations in the advertisement"; from the Times' failure to retract for respondent while retracting for the Governor, whereas the falsity of some of the allegations was then known to the Times and "the matter contained in the advertisement was equally false as to both parties"; and from the testimony of the Times' Secretary that,

apart from the statement that the dining hall was padlocked, he thought the two paragraphs were "substantially
correct." *Id.,* at 686–687, 144 So. 2d, at 50–51. The
court reaffirmed a statement in an earlier opinion that
"There is no legal measure of damages in cases of this
character." *Id.,* at 686, 144 So. 2d, at 50. It rejected
petitioners' constitutional contentions with the brief
statements that "The First Amendment of the U. S. Constitution does not protect libelous publications" and
"The Fourteenth Amendment is directed against State
action and not private action." *Id.,* at 676, 144 So. 2d,
at 40.

Because of the importance of the constitutional issues
involved, we granted the separate petitions for certiorari
of the individual petitioners and of the Times. 371 U. S.
946. We reverse the judgment. We hold that the rule
of law applied by the Alabama courts is constitutionally
deficient for failure to provide the safeguards for freedom
of speech and of the press that are required by the First
and Fourteenth Amendments in a libel action brought by
a public official against critics of his official conduct.[4]  We

---

[4] Since we sustain the contentions of all the petitioners under the
First Amendment's guarantees of freedom of speech and of the press
as applied to the States by the Fourteenth Amendment, we do not
decide the questions presented by the other claims of violation of the
Fourteenth Amendment. The individual petitioners contend that
the judgment against them offends the Due Process Clause because
there was no evidence to show that they had published or authorized
the publication of the alleged libel, and that the Due Process and
Equal Protection Clauses were violated by racial segregation and
racial bias in the courtroom. The Times contends that the assumption of jurisdiction over its corporate person by the Alabama courts
overreaches the territorial limits of the Due Process Clause. The
latter claim is foreclosed from our review by the ruling of the Alabama courts that the Times entered a general appearance in the
action and thus waived its jurisdictional objection; we cannot say
that this ruling lacks "fair or substantial support" in prior Alabama
decisions. See *Thompson* v. *Wilson,* 224 Ala. 299, 140 So. 439 (1932);
compare *N. A. A. C. P.* v. *Alabama,* 357 U. S. 449, 454–458.

further hold that under the proper safeguards the evidence presented in this case is constitutionally insufficient to support the judgment for respondent.

### I.

We may dispose at the outset of two grounds asserted to insulate the judgment of the Alabama courts from constitutional scrutiny. The first is the proposition relied on by the State Supreme Court—that "The Fourteenth Amendment is directed against State action and not private action." That proposition has no application to this case. Although this is a civil lawsuit between private parties, the Alabama courts have applied a state rule of law which petitioners claim to impose invalid restrictions on their constitutional freedoms of speech and press. It matters not that that law has been applied in a civil action and that it is common law only, though supplemented by statute. See, *e. g.*, Alabama Code, Tit. 7, §§ 908–917. The test is not the form in which state power has been applied but, whatever the form, whether such power has in fact been exercised. See *Ex parte Virginia*, 100 U. S. 339, 346–347; *American Federation of Labor* v. *Swing*, 312 U. S. 321.

The second contention is that the constitutional guarantees of freedom of speech and of the press are inapplicable here, at least so far as the Times is concerned, because the allegedly libelous statements were published as part of a paid, "commercial" advertisement. The argument relies on *Valentine* v. *Chrestensen*, 316 U. S. 52, where the Court held that a city ordinance forbidding street distribution of commercial and business advertising matter did not abridge the First Amendment freedoms, even as applied to a handbill having a commercial message on one side but a protest against certain official action on the other. The reliance is wholly misplaced. The Court in *Chrestensen* reaffirmed the constitutional protection for "the freedom of communicating information and disseminating opinion"; its holding was based upon the factual conclusions that the handbill was "purely commercial advertising" and that the protest against official action had been added only to evade the ordinance.

The publication here was not a "commercial" advertisement in the sense in which the word was used in *Chrestensen.* It communicated information, expressed opinion, recited grievances, protested claimed abuses, and sought financial support on behalf of a movement whose existence and objectives are matters of the highest public interest and concern. See *N. A. A. C. P.* v. *Button,* 371 U. S. 415, 435. That the Times was paid for publishing the advertisement is as immaterial in this connection as is the fact that newspapers and books are sold. *Smith* v. *California,* 361 U. S. 147, 150; cf. *Bantam Books, Inc.,* v. *Sullivan,* 372 U. S. 58, 64, n. 6. Any other conclusion would discourage newspapers from carrying "editorial advertisements" of this type, and so might shut off an important outlet for the promulgation of information and ideas by persons who do not themselves have access to publishing facilities—who wish to exercise their freedom of speech even though they are not members of the press. Cf. *Lovell* v. *Griffin,* 303 U. S. 444, 452; *Schneider* v. *State,* 308 U. S. 147, 164. The effect would be to shackle the First Amendment in its attempt to secure "the widest possible dissemination of information from diverse and antagonistic sources." *Associated Press* v. *United States,* 326 U. S. 1, 20. To avoid placing such a handicap upon the freedoms of expression, we hold that if the allegedly libelous statements would otherwise be constitutionally protected from the present judgment, they do not forfeit that protection because they were published in the form of a paid advertisement.[5]

---

[5] See American Law Institute, Restatement of Torts, § 593, Comment b (1938).

## II.

Under Alabama law as applied in this case, a publication is "libelous per se" if the words "tend to injure a person . . . in his reputation" or to "bring [him] into public contempt"; the trial court stated that the standard was met if the words are such as to "injure him in his public office, or impute misconduct to him in his office, or want of official integrity, or want of fidelity to a public trust . . . ." The jury must find that the words were published "of and concerning" the plaintiff, but where the plaintiff is a public official his place in the governmental hierarchy is sufficient evidence to support a finding that his reputation has been affected by statements that reflect upon the agency of which he is in charge. Once "libel per se" has been established, the defendant has no defense as to stated facts unless he can persuade the jury that they were true in all their particulars. *Alabama Ride Co.* v. *Vance,* 235 Ala. 263, 178 So. 438 (1938); *Johnson Publishing Co.* v. *Davis,* 271 Ala. 474, 494–495, 124 So. 2d 441, 457–458 (1960). His privilege of "fair comment" for expressions of opinion depends on the truth of the facts upon which the comment is based. *Parsons* v. *Age-Herald Publishing Co.,* 181 Ala. 439, 450, 61 So. 345, 350 (1913). Unless he can discharge the burden of proving truth, general damages are presumed, and may be awarded without proof of pecuniary injury. A showing of actual malice is apparently a prerequisite to recovery of punitive damages, and the defendant may in any event forestall a punitive award by a retraction meeting the statutory requirements. Good motives and belief in truth do not negate an inference of malice, but are relevant only in mitigation of punitive damages if the jury chooses to accord them weight. *Johnson Publishing Co.* v. *Davis, supra,* 271 Ala., at 495, 124 So. 2d, at 458.

The question before us is whether this rule of liability, as applied to an action brought by a public official against critics of his official conduct, abridges the freedom of speech and of the press that is guaranteed by the First and Fourteenth Amendments.

Respondent relies heavily, as did the Alabama courts, on statements of this Court to the effect that the Constitution does not protect libelous publications.[6] Those statements do not foreclose our inquiry here. None of the cases sustained the use of libel laws to impose sanctions upon expression critical of the official conduct of public officials. The dictum in *Pennekamp* v. *Florida*, 328 U. S. 331, 348–349, that "when the statements amount to defamation, a judge has such remedy in damages for libel as do other public servants," implied no view as to what remedy might constitutionally be afforded to public officials. In *Beauharnais* v. *Illinois*, 343 U. S. 250, the Court sustained an Illinois criminal libel statute as applied to a publication held to be both defamatory of a racial group and "liable to cause violence and disorder." But the Court was careful to note that it "retains and exercises authority to nullify action which encroaches on freedom of utterance under the guise of punishing libel"; for "public men, are, as it were, public property," and "discussion cannot be denied and the right, as well as the duty, of criticism must not be stifled." *Id.*, at 263–264, and n. 18. In the only previous case that did present the question of constitutional limitations upon the power to award damages for libel of a public official, the Court was equally divided and the question was not decided. *Schenectady Union Pub. Co.* v. *Sweeney*, 316 U. S. 642.

---

[6] *Konigsberg* v. *State Bar of California*, 366 U. S. 36, 49, and n. 10; *Times Film Corp.* v. *City of Chicago*, 365 U. S. 43, 48; *Roth* v. *United States*, 354 U. S. 476, 486–487; *Beauharnais* v. *Illinois*, 343 U. S. 250, 266; *Pennekamp* v. *Florida*, 328 U. S. 331, 348–349; *Chaplinsky* v. *New Hampshire*, 315 U. S. 568, 572; *Near* v. *Minnesota*, 283 U. S. 697, 715.

In deciding the question now, we are compelled by neither precedent nor policy to give any more weight to the epithet "libel" than we have to other "mere labels" of state law. *N. A. A. C. P.* v. *Button,* 371 U. S. 415, 429. Like "insurrection," [7] contempt,[8] advocacy of unlawful acts,[9] breach of the peace,[10] obscenity,[11] solicitation of legal business,[12] and the various other formulae for the repression of expression that have been challenged in this Court, libel can claim no talismanic immunity from constitutional limitations. It must be measured by standards that satisfy the First Amendment.

The general proposition that freedom of expression upon public questions is secured by the First Amendment has long been settled by our decisions. The constitutional safeguard, we have said, "was fashioned to assure unfettered interchange of ideas for the bringing about of political and social changes desired by the people." *Roth* v. *United States,* 354 U. S. 476, 484. "The maintenance of the opportunity for free political discussion to the end that government may be responsive to the will of the people and that changes may be obtained by lawful means, an opportunity essential to the security of the Republic, is a fundamental principle of our constitutional system." *Stromberg* v. *California,* 283 U. S. 359, 369. "[I]t is a prized American privilege to speak one's mind, although not always with perfect good taste, on all public institutions," *Bridges* v. *California,* 314 U. S. 252, 270, and this opportunity is to be afforded for "vigorous advocacy" no less than "abstract discussion." *N. A. A. C. P.* v. *Button,* 371 U. S. 415, 429.

---

[7] *Herndon* v. *Lowry,* 301 U. S. 242.

[8] *Bridges* v. *California,* 314 U. S. 252; *Pennekamp* v. *Florida,* 328 U. S. 331.

[9] *De Jonge* v. *Oregon,* 299 U. S. 353.

[10] *Edwards* v. *South Carolina,* 372 U. S. 229.

[11] *Roth* v. *United States,* 354 U. S. 476.

[12] *N. A. A. C. P.* v. *Button,* 371 U. S. 415.

The First Amendment, said Judge Learned Hand, "presupposes that right conclusions are more likely to be gathered out of a multitude of tongues, than through any kind of authoritative selection. To many this is, and always will be, folly; but we have staked upon it our all." *United States* v. *Associated Press,* 52 F. Supp. 362, 372 (D. C. S. D. N. Y. 1943). Mr. Justice Brandeis, in his concurring opinion in *Whitney* v. *California,* 274 U. S. 357, 375–376, gave the principle its classic formulation:

> "Those who won our independence believed . . . that public discussion is a political duty; and that this should be a fundamental principle of the American government. They recognized the risks to which all human institutions are subject. But they knew that order cannot be secured merely through fear of punishment for its infraction; that it is hazardous to discourage thought, hope and imagination; that fear breeds repression; that repression breeds hate; that hate menaces stable government; that the path of safety lies in the opportunity to discuss freely supposed grievances and proposed remedies; and that the fitting remedy for evil counsels is good ones. Believing in the power of reason as applied through public discussion, they eschewed silence coerced by law—the argument of force in its worst form. Recognizing the occasional tyrannies of governing majorities, they amended the Constitution so that free speech and assembly should be guaranteed."

Thus we consider this case against the background of a profound national commitment to the principle that debate on public issues should be uninhibited, robust, and wide-open, and that it may well include vehement, caustic, and sometimes unpleasantly sharp attacks on government and public officials. See *Terminiello* v. *Chicago,* 337 U. S. 1, 4; *De Jonge* v. *Oregon,* 299 U. S. 353,

365. The present advertisement, as an expression of grievance and protest on one of the major public issues of our time, would seem clearly to qualify for the constitutional protection. The question is whether it forfeits that protection by the falsity of some of its factual statements and by its alleged defamation of respondent.

Authoritative interpretations of the First Amendment guarantees have consistently refused to recognize an exception for any test of truth, whether administered by judges, juries, or administrative officials—and especially not one that puts the burden of proving truth on the speaker. Cf. *Speiser* v. *Randall,* 357 U. S. 513, 525–526. The constitutional protection does not turn upon "the truth, popularity, or social utility of the ideas and beliefs which are offered." *N. A. A. C. P.* v. *Button,* 371 U. S. 415, 445. As Madison said, "Some degree of abuse is inseparable from the proper use of every thing; and in no instance is this more true than in that of the press." 4 Elliot's Debates on the Federal Constitution (1876), p. 571. In *Cantwell* v. *Connecticut,* 310 U. S. 296, 310, the Court declared:

> "In the realm of religious faith, and in that of political belief, sharp differences arise. In both fields the tenets of one man may seem the rankest error to his neighbor. To persuade others to his own point of view, the pleader, as we know, at times, resorts to exaggeration, to vilification of men who have been, or are, prominent in church or state, and even to false statement. But the people of this nation have ordained in the light of history, that, in spite of the probability of excesses and abuses, these liberties are, in the long view, essential to enlightened opinion and right conduct on the part of the citizens of a democracy."

That erroneous statement is inevitable in free debate, and that it must be protected if the freedoms of ex-

pression are to have the "breathing space" that they
"need . . . to survive," *N. A. A. C. P.* v. *Button,* 371
U. S. 415, 433, was also recognized by the Court of Appeals for the District of Columbia Circuit in *Sweeney* v.
*Patterson,* 76 U. S. App. D. C. 23, 24, 128 F. 2d 457, 458
(1942). Judge Edgerton spoke for a unanimous court
which affirmed the dismissal of a Congressman's libel suit
based upon a newspaper article charging him with anti-
Semitism in opposing a judicial appointment. He said:

> "Cases which impose liability for erroneous re-
> ports of the political conduct of officials reflect the
> obsolete doctrine that the governed must not criti-
> cize their governors. . . . The interest of the pub-
> lic here outweighs the interest of appellant or any
> other individual. The protection of the public
> requires not merely discussion, but information.
> Political conduct and views which some respectable
> people approve, and others condemn, are constantly
> imputed to Congressmen. Errors of fact, particu-
> larly in regard to a man's mental states and processes,
> are inevitable. . . . Whatever is added to the field
> of libel is taken from the field of free debate." [13]

Just as factual error affords no warrant for repressing
speech that would otherwise be free, the same is true of
injury to official reputation. Where judicial officers are
involved, this Court has held that concern for the dignity
and reputation of the courts does not justify the punish-

---

[13] See also Mill, On Liberty (Oxford: Blackwell, 1947), at 47:
". . . [T]o argue sophistically, to suppress facts or arguments, to
misstate the elements of the case, or misrepresent the opposite opinion . . . all this, even to the most aggravated degree, is so continually
done in perfect good faith, by persons who are not considered, and
in many other respects may not deserve to be considered, ignorant or
incompetent, that it is rarely possible, on adequate grounds, conscientiously to stamp the misrepresentation as morally culpable; and
still less could law presume to interfere with this kind of controversial
misconduct."

ment as criminal contempt of criticism of the judge or his decision. *Bridges* v. *California,* 314 U. S. 252. This is true even though the utterance contains "half-truths" and "misinformation." *Pennekamp* v. *Florida,* 328 U. S. 331, 342, 343, n. 5, 345. Such repression can be justified, if at all, only by a clear and present danger of the obstruction of justice. See also *Craig* v. *Harney,* 331 U. S. 367; *Wood* v. *Georgia,* 370 U. S. 375. If judges are to be treated as "men of fortitude, able to thrive in a hardy climate," *Craig* v. *Harney, supra,* 331 U. S., at 376, surely the same must be true of other government officials, such as elected city commissioners.[14] Criticism of their official conduct does not lose its constitutional protection merely because it is effective criticism and hence diminishes their official reputations.

If neither factual error nor defamatory content suffices to remove the constitutional shield from criticism of official conduct, the combination of the two elements is no less inadequate. This is the lesson to be drawn from the great controversy over the Sedition Act of 1798, 1 Stat. 596, which first crystallized a national awareness of the central meaning of the First Amendment. See Levy, Legacy of Suppression (1960), at 258 *et seq.;* Smith, Freedom's Fetters (1956), at 426, 431, and *passim.* That statute made it a crime, punishable by a $5,000 fine and five years in prison, "if any person shall write, print, utter or publish . . . any false, scandalous and malicious

---

[14] The climate in which public officials operate, especially during a political campaign, has been described by one commentator in the following terms: "Charges of gross incompetence, disregard of the public interest, communist sympathies, and the like usually have filled the air; and hints of bribery, embezzlement, and other criminal conduct are not infrequent." Noel, Defamation of Public Officers and Candidates, 49 Col. L. Rev. 875 (1949).

For a similar description written 60 years earlier, see Chase, Criticism of Public Officers and Candidates for Office, 23 Am. L. Rev. 346 (1889).

writing or writings against the government of the United
States, or either house of the Congress . . . , or the President . . . , with intent to defame . . . or to bring them,
or either of them, into contempt or disrepute; or to
excite against them, or either or any of them, the hatred of
the good people of the United States." The Act allowed
the defendant the defense of truth, and provided that the
jury were to be judges both of the law and the facts. Despite these qualifications, the Act was vigorously condemned as unconstitutional in an attack joined in by
Jefferson and Madison. In the famous Virginia Resolutions of 1798, the General Assembly of Virginia resolved
that it

> "doth particularly protest against the palpable and
> alarming infractions of the Constitution, in the two
> late cases of the 'Alien and Sedition Acts,' passed at
> the last session of Congress . . . . [The Sedition
> Act] exercises . . . a power not delegated by the
> Constitution, but, on the contrary, expressly and
> positively forbidden by one of the amendments
> thereto—a power which, more than any other, ought
> to produce universal alarm, because it is levelled
> against the right of freely examining public char-
> acters and measures, and of free communication
> among the people thereon, which has ever been justly
> deemed the only effectual guardian of every other
> right." 4 Elliot's Debates, *supra*, pp. 553–554.

Madison prepared the Report in support of the protest.
His premise was that the Constitution created a form of
government under which "The people, not the government, possess the absolute sovereignty." The structure
of the government dispersed power in reflection of the
people's distrust of concentrated power, and of power
itself at all levels. This form of government was "altogether different" from the British form, under which the
Crown was sovereign and the people were subjects. "Is

it not natural and necessary, under such different circumstances," he asked, "that a different degree of freedom in the use of the press should be contemplated?" *Id.,* pp. 569–570. Earlier, in a debate in the House of Representatives, Madison had said: "If we advert to the nature of Republican Government, we shall find that the censorial power is in the people over the Government, and not in the Government over the people." 4 Annals of Congress, p. 934 (1794). Of the exercise of that power by the press, his Report said: "In every state, probably, in the Union, the press has exerted a freedom in canvassing the merits and measures of public men, of every description, which has not been confined to the strict limits of the common law. On this footing the freedom of the press has stood; on this foundation it yet stands . . . ." 4 Elliot's Debates, *supra,* p. 570. The right of free public discussion of the stewardship of public officials was thus, in Madison's view, a fundamental principle of the American form of government.[15]

---

[15] The Report on the Virginia Resolutions further stated:

"[I]t is manifestly impossible to punish the intent to bring those who administer the government into disrepute or contempt, without striking at the right of freely discussing public characters and measures; . . . which, again, is equivalent to a protection of those who administer the government, if they should at any time deserve the contempt or hatred of the people, against being exposed to it, by free animadversions on their characters and conduct. Nor can there be a doubt . . . that a government thus intrenched in penal statutes against the just and natural effects of a culpable administration, will easily evade the responsibility which is essential to a faithful discharge of its duty.

"Let it be recollected, lastly, that the right of electing the members of the government constitutes more particularly the essence of a free and responsible government. The value and efficacy of this right depends on the knowledge of the comparative merits and demerits of the candidates for public trust, and on the equal freedom, consequently, of examining and discussing these merits and demerits of the candidates respectively." 4 Elliot's Debates, *supra,* p. 575.

Although the Sedition Act was never tested in this Court,[16] the attack upon its validity has carried the day in the court of history. Fines levied in its prosecution were repaid by Act of Congress on the ground that it was unconstitutional. See, *e. g.*, Act of July 4, 1840, c. 45, 6 Stat. 802, accompanied by H. R. Rep. No. 86, 26th Cong., 1st Sess. (1840). Calhoun, reporting to the Senate on February 4, 1836, assumed that its invalidity was a matter "which no one now doubts." Report with Senate bill No. 122, 24th Cong., 1st Sess., p. 3. Jefferson, as President, pardoned those who had been convicted and sentenced under the Act and remitted their fines, stating: "I discharged every person under punishment or prosecution under the sedition law, because I considered, and now consider, that law to be a nullity, as absolute and as palpable as if Congress had ordered us to fall down and worship a golden image." Letter to Mrs. Adams, July 22, 1804, 4 Jefferson's Works (Washington ed.), pp. 555, 556. The invalidity of the Act has also been assumed by Justices of this Court. See Holmes, J., dissenting and joined by Brandeis, J., in *Abrams* v. *United States,* 250 U. S. 616, 630; Jackson, J., dissenting in *Beauharnais* v. *Illinois,* 343 U. S. 250, 288–289; Douglas, The Right of the People (1958), p. 47. See also Cooley, Constitutional Limitations (8th ed., Carrington, 1927), pp. 899–900; Chafee, Free Speech in the United States (1942), pp. 27–28. These views reflect a broad consensus that the Act, because of the restraint it imposed upon criticism of government and public officials, was inconsistent with the First Amendment.

There is no force in respondent's argument that the constitutional limitations implicit in the history of the Sedition Act apply only to Congress and not to the States. It is true that the First Amendment was originally addressed only to action by the Federal Government, and

---

[16] The Act expired by its terms in 1801.

that Jefferson, for one, while denying the power of Congress "to controul the freedom of the press," recognized such a power in the States. See the 1804 Letter to Abigail Adams quoted in *Dennis* v. *United States,* 341 U. S. 494, 522, n. 4 (concurring opinion). But this distinction was eliminated with the adoption of the Fourteenth Amendment and the application to the States of the First Amendment's restrictions. See, *e. g., Gitlow* v. *New York,* 268 U. S. 652, 666; *Schneider* v. *State,* 308 U. S. 147, 160; *Bridges* v. *California,* 314 U. S. 252, 268; *Edwards* v. *South Carolina,* 372 U. S. 229, 235.

What a State may not constitutionally bring about by means of a criminal statute is likewise beyond the reach of its civil law of libel.[17] The fear of damage awards under a rule such as that invoked by the Alabama courts here may be markedly more inhibiting than the fear of prosecution under a criminal statute. See *City of Chicago* v. *Tribune Co.,* 307 Ill. 595, 607, 139 N. E. 86, 90 (1923). Alabama, for example, has a criminal libel law which subjects to prosecution "any person who speaks, writes, or prints of and concerning another any accusation falsely and maliciously importing the commission by such person of a felony, or any other indictable offense involving moral turpitude," and which allows as punishment upon conviction a fine not exceeding $500 and a prison sentence of six months. Alabama Code, Tit. 14, § 350. Presumably a person charged with violation of this statute enjoys ordinary criminal-law safeguards such as the requirements of an indictment and of proof beyond a reasonable doubt. These safeguards are not available to the defendant in a civil action. The judgment awarded in this case—without the need for any proof of actual pecuniary loss—was one thousand times greater than the maximum fine provided by the Alabama criminal statute, and one hundred times greater than that provided by the Sedition Act.

---

[17] Cf. *Farmers Union* v. *WDAY,* 360 U. S. 525, 535.

And since there is no double-jeopardy limitation applicable to civil lawsuits, this is not the only judgment that may be awarded against petitioners for the same publication.[18] Whether or not a newspaper can survive a succession of such judgments, the pall of fear and timidity imposed upon those who would give voice to public criticism is an atmosphere in which the First Amendment freedoms cannot survive. Plainly the Alabama law of civil libel is "a form of regulation that creates hazards to protected freedoms markedly greater than those that attend reliance upon the criminal law." *Bantam Books, Inc.,* v. *Sullivan,* 372 U. S. 58, 70.

The state rule of law is not saved by its allowance of the defense of truth. A defense for erroneous statements honestly made is no less essential here than was the requirement of proof of guilty knowledge which, in *Smith* v. *California,* 361 U. S. 147, we held indispensable to a valid conviction of a bookseller for possessing obscene writings for sale. We said:

"For if the bookseller is criminally liable without knowledge of the contents, . . . he will tend to restrict the books he sells to those he has inspected; and thus the State will have imposed a restriction upon the distribution of constitutionally protected as well as obscene literature. . . . And the bookseller's burden would become the public's burden, for by restricting him the public's access to reading matter would be restricted . . . [H]is timidity in the face of his absolute criminal liability, thus would tend to restrict the public's access to forms of the printed word which the State could not constitu-

---

[18] The Times states that four other libel suits based on the advertisement have been filed against it by others who have served as Montgomery City Commissioners and by the Governor of Alabama; that another $500,000 verdict has been awarded in the only one of these cases that has yet gone to trial; and that the damages sought in the other three total $2,000,000.

tionally suppress directly. The bookseller's self-censorship, compelled by the State, would be a censorship affecting the whole public, hardly less virulent for being privately administered. Through it, the distribution of all books, both obscene and not obscene, would be impeded." (361 U. S. 147, 153–154.) A rule compelling the critic of official conduct to guarantee the truth of all his factual assertions—and to do so on pain of libel judgments virtually unlimited in amount—leads to a comparable "self-censorship." Allowance of the defense of truth, with the burden of proving it on the defendant, does not mean that only false speech will be deterred.[19] Even courts accepting this defense as an adequate safeguard have recognized the difficulties of adducing legal proofs that the alleged libel was true in all its factual particulars. See, *e. g., Post Publishing Co.* v. *Hallam,* 59 F. 530, 540 (C. A. 6th Cir. 1893); see also Noel, 49 Col. L. Rev. 875, 892 (1949). Under such a rule, would-be critics of official conduct may be deterred from voicing their criticism, even though it is believed to be true and even though it is in fact true, because of doubt whether it can be proved in court or fear of the expense of having to do so. They tend to make only statements which "steer far wider of the unlawful zone." *Speiser* v. *Randall, supra,* 357 U. S., at 526. The rule thus dampens the vigor and limits the variety of public debate. It is inconsistent with the First and Fourteenth Amendments.

The constitutional guarantees require, we think, a federal rule that prohibits a public official from recovering damages for a defamatory falsehood relating to his official conduct unless he proves that the statement was made with "actual malice"—that is, with knowledge that it was

---

[19] Even a false statement may be deemed to make a valuable contribution to public debate, since it brings about "the clearer perception and livelier impression of truth, produced by its collision with error." Mill, On Liberty (Oxford: Blackwell, 1947), at 15; see also Milton, Areopagitica, in Prose Works (Yale, 1959), Vol. II, at 561.

false or with reckless disregard of whether it was false or not. An oft-cited statement of a like rule, which has been adopted by a number of state courts,[20] is found in the Kansas case of *Coleman* v. *MacLennan*, 78 Kan. 711, 98 P. 281 (1908). The State Attorney General, a candidate for re-election and a member of the commission charged with the management and control of the state school fund, sued a newspaper publisher for alleged libel in an article purporting to state facts relating to his official conduct in connection with a school-fund transaction. The defendant pleaded privilege and the trial judge, over the plaintiff's objection, instructed the jury that

"where an article is published and circulated among voters for the sole purpose of giving what the de-

---

[20] *E. g., Ponder* v. *Cobb*, 257 N. C. 281, 299, 126 S. E. 2d 67, 80 (1962); *Lawrence* v. *Fox*, 357 Mich. 134, 146, 97 N. W. 2d 719, 725 (1959); *Stice* v. *Beacon Newspaper Corp.*, 185 Kan. 61, 65–67, 340 P. 2d 396, 400–401 (1959); *Bailey* v. *Charleston Mail Assn.*, 126 W. Va. 292, 307, 27 S. E. 2d 837, 844 (1943); *Salinger* v. *Cowles*, 195 Iowa 873, 889, 191 N. W. 167, 174 (1922); *Snively* v. *Record Publishing Co.*, 185 Cal. 565, 571–576, 198 P. 1 (1921); *McLean* v. *Merriman*, 42 S. D. 394, 175 N. W. 878 (1920). Applying the same rule to candidates for public office, see, *e. g., Phoenix Newspapers* v. *Choisser*, 82 Ariz. 271, 276–277, 312 P. 2d 150, 154 (1957); *Friedell* v. *Blakely Printing Co.*, 163 Minn. 226, 230, 203 N. W. 974, 975 (1925). And see *Chagnon* v. *Union-Leader Corp.*, 103 N. H. 426, 438, 174 A. 2d 825, 833 (1961), cert. denied, 369 U. S. 830.

The consensus of scholarly opinion apparently favors the rule that is here adopted. *E. g.*, 1 Harper and James, Torts, § 5.26, at 449–450 (1956); Noel, Defamation of Public Officers and Candidates, 49 Col. L. Rev. 875, 891–895, 897, 903 (1949); Hallen, Fair Comment, 8 Tex. L. Rev. 41, 61 (1929); Smith, Charges Against Candidates, 18 Mich. L. Rev. 1, 115 (1919); Chase, Criticism of Public Officers and Candidates for Office, 23 Am. L. Rev. 346, 367–371 (1889); Cooley, Constitutional Limitations (7th ed., Lane, 1903), at 604, 616–628. But see, *e. g.*, American Law Institute, Restatement of Torts, § 598, Comment a (1938) (reversing the position taken in Tentative Draft 13, § 1041 (2) (1936)); Veeder, Freedom of Public Discussion, 23 Harv. L. Rev. 413, 419 (1910).

fendant believes to be truthful information concerning a candidate for public office and for the purpose of enabling such voters to cast their ballot more intelligently, and the whole thing is done in good faith and without malice, the article is privileged, although the principal matters contained in the article may be untrue in fact and derogatory to the character of the plaintiff; and in such a case the burden is on the plaintiff to show actual malice in the publication of the article."

In answer to a special question, the jury found that the plaintiff had not proved actual malice, and a general verdict was returned for the defendant. On appeal the Supreme Court of Kansas, in an opinion by Justice Burch, reasoned as follows (78 Kan., at 724, 98 P., at 286):

"It is of the utmost consequence that the people should discuss the character and qualifications of candidates for their suffrages. The importance to the state and to society of such discussions is so vast, and the advantages derived are so great, that they more than counterbalance the inconvenience of private persons whose conduct may be involved, and occasional injury to the reputations of individuals must yield to the public welfare, although at times such injury may be great. The public benefit from publicity is so great, and the chance of injury to private character so small, that such discussion must be privileged."

The court thus sustained the trial court's instruction as a correct statement of the law, saying:

"In such a case the occasion gives rise to a privilege, qualified to this extent: any one claiming to be defamed by the communication must show actual malice or go remediless. This privilege extends to a great variety of subjects, and includes matters of

public concern, public men, and candidates for office."
78 Kan., at 723, 98 P., at 285.

Such a privilege for criticism of official conduct [21] is
appropriately analogous to the protection accorded a
public official when *he* is sued for libel by a private citizen.
In *Barr* v. *Matteo*, 360 U. S. 564, 575, this Court held the
utterance of a federal official to be absolutely privileged
if made "within the outer perimeter" of his duties. The
States accord the same immunity to statements of their
highest officers, although some differentiate their lesser
officials and qualify the privilege they enjoy.[22] But all
hold that all officials are protected unless actual malice
can be proved. The reason for the official privilege is said
to be that the threat of damage suits would otherwise
"inhibit the fearless, vigorous, and effective administration of policies of government" and "dampen the ardor
of all but the most resolute, or the most irresponsible, in
the unflinching discharge of their duties." *Barr* v.
*Matteo, supra,* 360 U. S., at 571. Analogous considerations support the privilege for the citizen-critic of gov
ernment. It is as much his duty to criticize as it is the
official's duty to administer. See *Whitney* v. *California,*
274 U. S. 357, 375 (concurring opinion of Mr. Justice
Brandeis), quoted *supra,* p. 270. As Madison said, see
*supra,* p. 275, "the censorial power is in the people over the
Government, and not in the Government over the people." It would give public servants an unjustified preference over the public they serve, if critics of official conduct

---

[21] The privilege immunizing honest misstatements of fact is often
referred to as a "conditional" privilege to distinguish it from the
"absolute" privilege recognized in judicial, legislative, administrative
and executive proceedings. See, *e. g.,* Prosser, Torts (2d ed., 1955),
§ 95.

[22] See 1 Harper and James, Torts, § 5.23, at 429–430 (1956);
Prosser, Torts (2d ed., 1955), at 612–613; American Law Institute,
Restatement of Torts (1938), § 591.

did not have a fair equivalent of the immunity granted to the officials themselves.

We conclude that such a privilege is required by the First and Fourteenth Amendments.

### III.

We hold today that the Constitution delimits a State's power to award damages for libel in actions brought by public officials against critics of their official conduct. Since this is such an action,[23] the rule requiring proof of actual malice is applicable. While Alabama law apparently requires proof of actual malice for an award of punitive damages,[24] where general damages are concerned malice is "presumed." Such a presumption is inconsistent

---

[23] We have no occasion here to determine how far down into the lower ranks of government employees the "public official" designation would extend for purposes of this rule, or otherwise to specify categories of persons who would or would not be included. Cf. *Barr v. Matteo,* 360 U. S. 564, 573–575. Nor need we here determine the boundaries of the "official conduct" concept. It is enough for the present case that respondent's position as an elected city commissioner clearly made him a public official, and that the allegations in the advertisement concerned what was allegedly his official conduct as Commissioner in charge of the Police Department. As to the statements alleging the assaulting of Dr. King and the bombing of his home, it is immaterial that they might not be considered to involve respondent's official conduct if he himself had been accused of perpetrating the assault and the bombing. Respondent does not claim that the statements charged him personally with these acts; his contention is that the advertisement connects him with them only in his official capacity as the Commissioner supervising the police, on the theory that the police might be equated with the "They" who did the bombing and assaulting. Thus, if these allegations can be read as referring to respondent at all, they must be read as describing his performance of his official duties.

[24] *Johnson Publishing Co.* v. *Davis,* 271 Ala. 474, 487, 124 So. 2d 441, 450 (1960). Thus, the trial judge here instructed the jury that "mere negligence or carelessness is not evidence of actual malice or malice in fact, and does not justify an award of exemplary or punitive damages in an action for libel." [*Footnote 24 continued on p. 284*]

with the federal rule. "The power to create presumptions is not a means of escape from constitutional restrictions," *Bailey* v. *Alabama,* 219 U. S. 219, 239; "the showing of malice required for the forfeiture of the privilege is not presumed but is a matter for proof by the plaintiff . . . ." *Lawrence* v. *Fox,* 357 Mich. 134, 146, 97 N. W. 2d 719, 725 (1959).[25] Since the trial judge did not instruct the jury to differentiate between general and punitive damages, it may be that the verdict was wholly an award of one or the other. But it is impossible to know, in view of the general verdict returned. Because of this uncertainty, the judgment must be reversed and the case remanded. *Stromberg* v. *California,* 283 U. S. 359, 367–368; *Williams* v. *North Carolina,* 317 U. S. 287, 291–292; see *Yates* v. *United States,* 354 U. S. 298, 311–312; *Cramor* v. *United States,* 325 U. S. 1, 36, n. 45.

Since respondent may seek a new trial, we deem that considerations of effective judicial administration require us to review the evidence in the present record to deter-

---

The court refused, however, to give the following instruction which had been requested by the Times:

"I charge you . . . that punitive damages, as the name indicates, are designed to punish the defendant, the New York Times Company, a corporation, and the other defendants in this case, . . . and I further charge you that such punitive damages may be awarded only in the event that you, the jury, are convinced by a fair preponderance of the evidence that the defendant . . . was motivated by personal ill will, that is actual intent to do the plaintiff harm, or that the defendant . . . was guilty of gross negligence and recklessness and not of just ordinary negligence or carelessness in publishing the matter complained of so as to indicate a wanton disregard of plaintiff's rights."

The trial court's error in failing to require any finding of actual malice for an award of general damages makes it unnecessary for us to consider the sufficiency under the federal standard of the instructions regarding actual malice that were given as to punitive damages.

[25] Accord, *Coleman* v. *MacLennan, supra,* 78 Kan., at 741, 98 P., at 292; *Gough* v. *Tribune-Journal Co.,* 75 Idaho 502, 510, 275 P. 2d 663, 668 (1954).

mine whether it could constitutionally support a judgment for respondent. This Court's duty is not limited to the elaboration of constitutional principles; we must also in proper cases review the evidence to make certain that those principles have been constitutionally applied. This is such a case, particularly since the question is one of alleged trespass across "the line between speech unconditionally guaranteed and speech which may legitimately be regulated." *Speiser* v. *Randall,* 357 U. S. 513, 525. In cases where that line must be drawn, the rule is that we "examine for ourselves the statements in issue and the circumstances under which they were made to see . . . whether they are of a character which the principles of the First Amendment, as adopted by the Due Process Clause of the Fourteenth Amendment, protect." *Pennekamp* v. *Florida,* 328 U. S. 331, 335; see also *One, Inc.,* v. *Olesen,* 355 U. S. 371; *Sunshine Book Co.* v. *Summerfield,* 355 U. S. 372. We must "make an independent examination of the whole record," *Edwards* v. *South Carolina,* 372 U. S. 229, 235, so as to assure ourselves that the judgment does not constitute a forbidden intrusion on the field of free expression.[26]

Applying these standards, we consider that the proof presented to show actual malice lacks the convincing

---

[26] The Seventh Amendment does not, as respondent contends, preclude such an examination by this Court. That Amendment, providing that "no fact tried by a jury, shall be otherwise reexamined in any Court of the United States, than according to the rules of the common law," is applicable to state cases coming here. *Chicago, B. & Q. R. Co.* v. *Chicago,* 166 U. S. 226, 242–243; cf. *The Justices* v. *Murray,* 9 Wall. 274. But its ban on re-examination of facts does not preclude us from determining whether governing rules of federal law have been properly applied to the facts. "[T]his Court will review the finding of facts by a State court . . . where a conclusion of law as to a Federal right and a finding of fact are so intermingled as to make it necessary, in order to pass upon the Federal question, to analyze the facts." *Fiske* v. *Kansas,* 274 U. S. 380, 385–386. See also *Haynes* v. *Washington,* 373 U. S. 503, 515–516.

clarity which the constitutional standard demands, and hence that it would not constitutionally sustain the judgment for respondent under the proper rule of law. The case of the individual petitioners requires little discussion. Even assuming that they could constitutionally be found to have authorized the use of their names on the advertisement, there was no evidence whatever that they were aware of any erroneous statements or were in any way reckless in that regard. The judgment against them is thus without constitutional support.

As to the Times, we similarly conclude that the facts do not support a finding of actual malice. The statement by the Times' Secretary that, apart from the padlocking allegation, he thought the advertisement was "substantially correct," affords no constitutional warrant for the Alabama Supreme Court's conclusion that it was a "cavalier ignoring of the falsity of the advertisement [from which] the jury could not have but been impressed with the bad faith of The Times, and its maliciousness inferable therefrom." The statement does not indicate malice at the time of the publication; even if the advertisement was not "substantially correct"—although respondent's own proofs tend to show that it was—that opinion was at least a reasonable one, and there was no evidence to impeach the witness' good faith in holding it. The Times' failure to retract upon respondent's demand, although it later retracted upon the demand of Governor Patterson, is likewise not adequate evidence of malice for constitutional purposes. Whether or not a failure to retract may ever constitute such evidence, there are two reasons why it does not here. *First,* the letter written by the Times reflected a reasonable doubt on its part as to whether the advertisement could reasonably be taken to refer to respondent at all. *Second,* it was not a final refusal, since it asked for an explanation on this point—a request that respondent chose to ignore. Nor does the retraction upon the demand of the Governor supply the necessary proof.  It may be doubted that a failure to retract which is not itself evidence of malice can retroactively become such by virtue of a retraction subsequently made to another party.  But in any event that did not happen here, since the explanation given by the Times' Secretary for the distinction drawn between respondent and the Governor was a reasonable one, the good faith of which was not impeached.

Finally, there is evidence that the Times published the advertisement without checking its accuracy against the news stories in the Times' own files.  The mere presence of the stories in the files does not, of course, establish that the Times "knew" the advertisement was false, since the state of mind required for actual malice would have to be brought home to the persons in the Times' organization having responsibility for the publication of the advertisement.  With respect to the failure of those persons to make the check, the record shows that they relied upon their knowledge of the good reputation of many of those whose names were listed as sponsors of the advertisement, and upon the letter from A. Philip Randolph, known to them as a responsible individual, certifying that the use of the names was authorized.  There was testimony that the persons handling the advertisement saw nothing in it that would render it unacceptable under the Times' policy of rejecting advertisements containing "attacks of a personal character"; [27] their failure to reject it on this ground was not unreasonable.  We think

---

[27] The Times has set forth in a booklet its "Advertising Acceptability Standards."  Listed among the classes of advertising that the newspaper does not accept are advertisements that are "fraudulent or deceptive," that are "ambiguous in wording and . . . may mislead," and that contain "attacks of a personal character."  In replying to respondent's interrogatories before the trial, the Secretary of the Times stated that "as the advertisement made no attacks of a personal character upon any individual and otherwise met the advertising acceptability standards promulgated," it had been approved for publication.

the evidence against the Times supports at most a finding of negligence in failing to discover the misstatements, and is constitutionally insufficient to show the recklessness that is required for a finding of actual malice. Cf. *Charles Parker Co.* v. *Silver City Crystal Co.*, 142 Conn. 605, 618, 116 A. 2d 440, 446 (1955); *Phoenix Newspapers, Inc.*, v. *Choisser*, 82 Ariz. 271, 277–278, 312 P. 2d 150, 154–155 (1957).

We also think the evidence was constitutionally defective in another respect: it was incapable of supporting the jury's finding that the allegedly libelous statements were made "of and concerning" respondent. Respondent relies on the words of the advertisement and the testimony of six witnesses to establish a connection between it and himself. Thus, in his brief to this Court, he states:

> "The reference to respondent as police commissioner is clear from the ad. In addition, the jury heard the testimony of a newspaper editor . . . ; a real estate and insurance man . . . ; the sales manager of a men's clothing store . . . ; a food equipment man . . . ; a service station operator . . . ; and the operator of a truck line for whom respondent had formerly worked . . . . Each of these witnesses stated that he associated the statements with respondent . . . ." (Citations to record omitted.)

There was no reference to respondent in the advertisement, either by name or official position. A number of the allegedly libelous statements—the charges that the dining hall was padlocked and that Dr. King's home was bombed, his person assaulted, and a perjury prosecution instituted against him—did not even concern the police; despite the ingenuity of the arguments which would attach this significance to the word "They," it is plain that these statements could not reasonably be read as accusing respondent of personal involvement in the acts in question.  The statements upon which respondent principally relies as referring to him are the two allegations that did concern the police or police functions: that "truckloads of police . . . ringed the Alabama State College Campus" after the demonstration on the State Capitol steps, and that Dr. King had been "arrested . . . seven times." These statements were false only in that the police had been "deployed near" the campus but had not actually "ringed" it and had not gone there in connection with the State Capitol demonstration, and in that Dr. King had been arrested only four times.  The ruling that these discrepancies between what was true and what was asserted were sufficient to injure respondent's reputation may itself raise constitutional problems, but we need not consider them here.  Although the statements may be taken as referring to the police, they did not on their face make even an oblique reference to respondent as an individual.  Support for the asserted reference must, therefore, be sought in the testimony of respondent's witnesses. But none of them suggested any basis for the belief that respondent himself was attacked in the advertisement beyond the bare fact that he was in overall charge of the Police Department and thus bore official responsibility for police conduct; to the extent that some of the witnesses thought respondent to have been charged with ordering or approving the conduct or otherwise being personally involved in it, they based this notion not on any statements in the advertisement, and not on any evidence that he had in fact been so involved, but solely on the unsupported assumption that, because of his official position, he must have been.[28]  This reliance on the bare

--------

[28] Respondent's own testimony was that "as Commissioner of Public Affairs it is part of my duty to supervise the Police Department and I certainly feel like it [a statement] is associated with me when it describes police activities."  He thought that "by virtue of being

fact of respondent's official position [29] was made explicit
by the Supreme Court of Alabama. That court, in holding that the trial court "did not err in overruling the
demurrer [of the Times] in the aspect that the libelous

---

Police Commissioner and Commissioner of Public Affairs," he was
charged with "any activity on the part of the Police Department."
"When it describes police action, certainly I feel it reflects on me
as an individual." He added that "It is my feeling that it reflects
not only on me but on the other Commissioners and the community."
  Grover C. Hall testified that to him the third paragraph of the
advertisement called to mind "the City government—the Commissioners," and that "now that you ask it I would naturally think a
little more about the police Commissioner because his responsibility
is exclusively with the constabulary." It was "the phrase about
starvation" that led to the association; "the other didn't hit me with
any particular force."
  Arnold D. Blackwell testified that the third paragraph was associated in his mind with "the Police Commissioner and the police force.
The people on the police force." If he had believed the statement
about the padlocking of the dining hall, he would have thought "that
the people on our police force or the heads of our police force were
acting without their jurisdiction and would not be competent for
the position." "I would assume that the Commissioner had ordered
the police force to do that and therefore it would be his responsibility."
  Harry W. Kaminsky associated the statement about "truckloads
of police" with respondent "because he is the Police Commissioner."
He thought that the reference to arrests in the sixth paragraph
"implicates the Police Department, I think, or the authorities that
would do that—arrest folks for speeding and loitering and such as
that." Asked whether he would associate with respondent a newspaper report that the police had "beat somebody up or assaulted
them on the streets of Montgomery," he replied: "I still say he is
the Police Commissioner and those men are working directly under
him and therefore I would think that he would have something to do
with it." In general, he said, "I look at Mr. Sullivan when I see the
Police Department."
  H. M. Price, Sr., testified that he associated the first sentence of
the third paragraph with respondent because: "I would just automatically consider that the Police Commissioner in Montgomery

[Footnote 29 is on p. 291]

matter was not of and concerning the plaintiffs," based its ruling on the proposition that:

"We think it common knowledge that the average person knows that municipal agents, such as police and firemen, and others, are under the control and direction of the city governing body, and more particularly under the direction and control of a single commissioner. In measuring the performance or deficiencies of such groups, praise or criticism is usually attached to the official in complete control of the body." 273 Ala., at 674–675, 144 So. 2d, at 39.

This proposition has disquieting implications for criticism of governmental conduct. For good reason, "no court of last resort in this country has ever held, or even suggested, that prosecutions for libel on government have any place in the American system of jurisprudence." *City of Chicago* v. *Tribune Co., 307 Ill. 595, 601, 139 N. E.*

---

would have to put his approval on those kind of things as an individual."

William M. Parker, Jr., testified that he associated the statements in the two paragraphs with "the Commissioners of the City of Montgomery," and since respondent "was the Police Commissioner," he "thought of him first." He told the examining counsel: "I think if you were the Police Commissioner I would have thought it was speaking of you."

Horace W. White, respondent's former employer, testified that the statement about "truck-loads of police" made him think of respondent "as being the head of the Police Department." Asked whether he read the statement as charging respondent himself with ringing the campus or having shotguns and tear-gas, he replied: "Well, I thought of his department being charged with it, yes, sir. He is the head of the Police Department as I understand it." He further said that the reason he would have been unwilling to re-employ respondent if he had believed the advertisement was "the fact that he allowed the Police Department to do the things that the paper say he did."

[29] Compare *Ponder* v. *Cobb,* 257 N. C. 281, 126 S. E. 2d 67 (1962).

86, 88 (1923). The present proposition would sidestep this obstacle by transmuting criticism of government, however impersonal it may seem on its face, into personal criticism, and hence potential libel, of the officials of whom the government is composed. There is no legal alchemy by which a State may thus create the cause of action that would otherwise be denied for a publication which, as respondent himself said of the advertisement, "reflects not only on me but on the other Commissioners and the community." Raising as it does the possibility that a good-faith critic of government will be penalized for his criticism, the proposition relied on by the Alabama courts strikes at the very center of the constitutionally protected area of free expression.[30] We hold that such a proposition may not constitutionally be utilized to establish that an otherwise impersonal attack on governmental operations was a libel of an official responsible for those operations. Since it was relied on exclusively here, and there was no other evidence to connect the statements with respondent, the evidence was constitutionally insufficient to support a finding that the statements referred to respondent.

The judgment of the Supreme Court of Alabama is reversed and the case is remanded to that court for further proceedings not inconsistent with this opinion.

*Reversed and remanded.*

---

[30] Insofar as the proposition means only that the statements about police conduct libeled respondent by implicitly criticizing his ability to run the Police Department, recovery is also precluded in this case by the doctrine of fair comment. See American Law Institute, Restatement of Torts (1938), § 607. Since the Fourteenth Amendment requires recognition of the conditional privilege for honest misstatements of fact, it follows that a defense of fair comment must be afforded for honest expression of opinion based upon privileged, as well as true, statements of fact. Both defenses are of course defeasible if the public official proves actual malice, as was not done here.

MR. JUSTICE BLACK, with whom MR. JUSTICE DOUGLAS joins, concurring.

I concur in reversing this half-million-dollar judgment against the *New York Times* and the four individual defendants. In reversing the Court holds that "the Constitution delimits a State's power to award damages for libel in actions brought by public officials against critics of their official conduct." *Ante,* p. 283. I base my vote to reverse on the belief that the First and Fourteenth Amendments not merely "delimit" a State's power to award damages to "public officials against critics of their official conduct" but completely prohibit a State from exercising such a power. The Court goes on to hold that a State can subject such critics to damages if "actual malice" can be proved against them. "Malice," even as defined by the Court, is an elusive, abstract concept, hard to prove and hard to disprove. The requirement that malice be proved provides at best an evanescent protection for the right critically to discuss public affairs and certainly does not measure up to the sturdy safeguard embodied in the First Amendment. Unlike the Court, therefore, I vote to reverse exclusively on the ground that the *Times* and the individual defendants had an absolute, unconditional constitutional right to publish in the *Times* advertisement their criticisms of the Montgomery agencies and officials. I do not base my vote to reverse on any failure to prove that these individual defendants signed the advertisement or that their criticism of the Police Department was aimed at the plaintiff Sullivan, who was then the Montgomery City Commissioner having supervision of the city's police; for present purposes I assume these things were proved. Nor is my reason for reversal the size of the half-million-dollar judgment, large as it is. If Alabama has constitutional power to use its civil libel law to impose damages on the press for criticizing the way public officials perform or fail to perform their duties, I know of no provision in the Federal Constitution which either expressly or impliedly bars the State from fixing the amount of damages.

The half-million-dollar verdict does give dramatic proof, however, that state libel laws threaten the very existence of an American press virile enough to publish unpopular views on public affairs and bold enough to criticize the conduct of public officials. The factual background of this case emphasizes the imminence and enormity of that threat. One of the acute and highly emotional issues in this country arises out of efforts of many people, even including some public officials, to continue state-commanded segregation of races in the public schools and other public places, despite our several holdings that such a state practice is forbidden by the Fourteenth Amendment. Montgomery is one of the localities in which widespread hostility to desegregation has been manifested. This hostility has sometimes extended itself to persons who favor desegregation, particularly to so-called "outside agitators," a term which can be made to fit papers like the *Times*, which is published in New York. The scarcity of testimony to show that Commissioner Sullivan suffered any actual damages at all suggests that these feelings of hostility had at least as much to do with rendition of this half-million-dollar verdict as did an appraisal of damages. Viewed realistically, this record lends support to an inference that instead of being damaged Commissioner Sullivan's political, social, and financial prestige has likely been enhanced by the *Times'* publication. Moreover, a second half-million-dollar libel verdict against the *Times* based on the same advertisement has already been awarded to another Commissioner. There a jury again gave the full amount claimed. There is no reason to believe that there are not more such huge verdicts lurking just around the corner for the *Times* or any other newspaper or broadcaster which

might dare to criticize public officials. In fact, briefs
before us show that in Alabama there are now pending
eleven libel suits by local and state officials against the
*Times* seeking $5,600,000, and five such suits against
the Columbia Broadcasting System seeking $1,700,000.
Moreover, this technique for harassing and punishing a
free press—now that it has been shown to be possible—is
by no means limited to cases with racial overtones; it can
be used in other fields where public feelings may make
local as well as out-of-state newspapers easy prey for libel
verdict seekers.

In my opinion the Federal Constitution has dealt with
this deadly danger to the press in the only way possible
without leaving the free press open to destruction—by
granting the press an absolute immunity for criticism of
the way public officials do their public duty. Compare
*Barr* v. *Matteo,* 360 U. S. 564. Stopgap measures like
those the Court adopts are in my judgment not enough.
This record certainly does not indicate that any different
verdict would have been rendered here whatever the Court
had charged the jury about "malice," "truth," "good
motives," "justifiable ends," or any other legal formulas
which in theory would protect the press. Nor does the
record indicate that any of these legalistic words would
have caused the courts below to set aside or to reduce the
half-million-dollar verdict in any amount.

I agree with the Court that the Fourteenth Amendment made the First applicable to the States.[1] This
means to me that since the adoption of the Fourteenth
Amendment a State has no more power than the Federal
Government to use a civil libel law or any other law to
impose damages for merely discussing public affairs and
criticizing public officials. The power of the United

---

[1] See cases collected in *Speiser* v. *Randall,* 357 U. S. 513, 530
(concurring opinion).

States to do that is, in my judgment, precisely nil. Such
was the general view held when the First Amendment was
adopted and ever since.[2] Congress never has sought to
challenge this viewpoint by passing any civil libel law.
It did pass the Sedition Act in 1798,[3] which made it a
crime—"seditious libel"—to criticize federal officials or
the Federal Government. As the Court's opinion correctly points out, however, *ante,* pp. 273–276, that Act
came to an ignominious end and by common consent has
generally been treated as having been a wholly unjus-
tifiable and much to be regretted violation of the First
Amendment. Since the First Amendment is now made
applicable to the States by the Fourteenth, it no more
permits the States to impose damages for libel than it
does the Federal Government.

We would, I think, more faithfully interpret the First
Amendment by holding that at the very least it leaves
the people and the press free to criticize officials and discuss public affairs with impunity. This Nation of ours
elects many of its important officials; so do the States,
the municipalities, the counties, and even many precincts.
These officials are responsible to the people for the way
they perform their duties. While our Court has held
that some kinds of speech and writings, such as "obscenity," *Roth* v. *United States,* 354 U. S. 476, and "fighting
words," *Chaplinsky* v. *New Hampshire,* 315 U. S. 568, are
not expression within the protection of the First Amendment,[4] freedom to discuss public affairs and public officials

---

[2] See, *e. g.,* 1 Tucker, Blackstone's Commentaries (1803), 297–299
(editor's appendix). St. George Tucker, a distinguished Virginia
jurist, took part in the Annapolis Convention of 1786, sat on both
state and federal courts, and was widely known for his writings on
judicial and constitutional subjects.

[3] Act of July 14, 1798, 1 Stat. 596.

[4] But see *Smith* v. *California,* 361 U. S. 147, 155 (concurring opinion); *Roth* v. *United States,* 354 U. S. 476, 508 (dissenting opinion).

is unquestionably, as the Court today holds, the kind of speech the First Amendment was primarily designed to keep within the area of free discussion. To punish the exercise of this right to discuss public affairs or to penalize it through libel judgments is to abridge or shut off discussion of the very kind most needed. This Nation, I suspect, can live in peace without libel suits based on public discussions of public affairs and public officials. But I doubt that a country can live in freedom where its people can be made to suffer physically or financially for criticizing their government, its actions, or its officials. "For a representative democracy ceases to exist the moment that the public functionaries are by any means absolved from their responsibility to their constituents; and this happens whenever the constituent can be restrained in any manner from speaking, writing, or publishing his opinions upon any public measure, or upon the conduct of those who may advise or execute it." [5] An unconditional right to say what one pleases about public affairs is what I consider to be the minimum guarantee of the First Amendment.[6]

I regret that the Court has stopped short of this holding indispensable to preserve our free press from destruction.

MR. JUSTICE GOLDBERG, with whom MR. JUSTICE DOUGLAS joins, concurring in the result.

The Court today announces a constitutional standard which prohibits "a public official from recovering damages for a defamatory falsehood relating to his official conduct unless he proves that the statement was made with

---

[5] 1 Tucker, Blackstone's Commentaries (1803), 297 (editor's appendix); cf. Brant, Seditious Libel: Myth and Reality, 39 N. Y. U. L. Rev. 1.

[6] Cf. Meiklejohn, Free Speech and Its Relation to Self-Government (1948).

'actual malice'—that is, with knowledge that it was false or with reckless disregard of whether it was false or not." *Ante,* at 279–280. The Court thus rules that the Constitution gives citizens and newspapers a "conditional privilege" immunizing nonmalicious misstatements of fact regarding the official conduct of a government officer. The impressive array of history [1] and precedent marshaled by the Court, however, confirms my belief that the Constitution affords greater protection than that provided by the Court's standard to citizen and press in exercising the right of public criticism.

In my view, the First and Fourteenth Amendments to the Constitution afford to the citizen and to the press an absolute, unconditional privilege to criticize official conduct despite the harm which may flow from excesses and abuses. The prized American right "to speak one's mind," cf. *Bridges* v. *California,* 314 U. S. 252, 270, about public officials and affairs needs "breathing space to survive," *N. A. A. C. P.* v. *Button,* 371 U. S. 415, 433. The right should not depend upon a probing by the jury of the motivation [2] of the citizen or press. The theory

---

[1] I fully agree with the Court that the attack upon the validity of the Sedition Act of 1798, 1 Stat. 596, "has carried the day in the court of history," *ante,* at 276, and that the Act would today be declared unconstitutional. It should be pointed out, however, that the Sedition Act proscribed writings which were "false, scandalous *and malicious.*" (Emphasis added.) For prosecutions under the Sedition Act charging malice, see, *e. g.,* Trial of Matthew Lyon (1798), in Wharton, State Trials of the United States (1849), p. 333; Trial of Thomas Cooper (1800), in *id.,* at 659; Trial of Anthony Haswell (1800), in *id.,* at 684; Trial of James Thompson Callender (1800), in *id.,* at 688.

[2] The requirement of proving actual malice or reckless disregard may, in the mind of the jury, add little to the requirement of proving falsity, a requirement which the Court recognizes not to be an adequate safeguard. The thought suggested by Mr. Justice Jackson in *United States* v. *Ballard,* 322 U. S. 78, 92–93, is relevant here: "[A]s a matter of either practice or philosophy I do not see how

of our Constitution is that every citizen may speak
his mind and every newspaper express its view on matters of public concern and may not be barred from
speaking or publishing because those in control of government think that what is said or written is unwise,
unfair, false, or malicious.   In a democratic society, one
who assumes to act for the citizens in an executive, legislative, or judicial capacity must expect that his official
acts will be commented upon and criticized.   Such criticism cannot, in my opinion, be muzzled or deterred by
the courts at the instance of public officials under the
label of libel.

It has been recognized that "prosecutions for libel on
government have [no] place in the American system of
jurisprudence." *City of Chicago* v. *Tribune Co.*, 307 Ill.
595, 601, 139 N. E. 86, 88.   I fully agree.   Government,
however, is not an abstraction; it is made up of individuals—of governors responsible to the governed.   In
a democratic society where men are free by ballots to
remove those in power, any statement critical of governmental action is necessarily "of and concerning" the
governors and any statement critical of the governors'
official conduct is necessarily "of and concerning" the
government.   If the rule that libel on government has
no place in our Constitution is to have real meaning, then
libel on the official conduct of the governors likewise can
have no place in our Constitution.

We must recognize that we are writing upon a clean
slate.[3]   As the Court notes, although there have been

we can separate an issue as to what is believed from considerations
as to what is believable.  The most convincing proof that one believes
his statements is to show that they have been true in his experience.
Likewise, that one knowingly falsified is best proved by showing that
what he said happened never did happen."  See note 4, *infra.*

[3] It was not until *Gitlow* v. *New York*, 268 U. S. 652, decided in
1925, that it was intimated that the freedom of speech guaranteed by

"statements of this Court to the effect that the Constitution does not protect libelous publications . . . [n]one of the cases sustained the use of libel laws to impose sanctions upon expression critical of the official conduct of public officials." *Ante,* at 268. We should be particularly careful, therefore, adequately to protect the liberties which are embodied in the First and Fourteenth Amendments. It may be urged that deliberately and maliciously false statements have no conceivable value as free speech. That argument, however, is not responsive to the real issue presented by this case, which is whether that freedom of speech which all agree is constitutionally protected can be effectively safeguarded by a rule allowing the imposition of liability upon a jury's evaluation of the speaker's state of mind. If individual citizens may be held liable in damages for strong words, which a jury finds false and maliciously motivated, there can be little doubt that public debate and advocacy will be constrained. And if newspapers, publishing advertisements dealing with public issues, thereby risk liability, there can also be little doubt that the ability of minority groups to secure publication of their views on public affairs and to seek support for their causes will be greatly diminished. Cf. *Farmers Educational & Coop. Union* v. *WDAY, Inc.,* 360 U. S. 525, 530. The opinion of the Court conclusively demonstrates the chilling effect of the Alabama libel laws on First Amendment freedoms

the First Amendment was applicable to the States by reason of the Fourteenth Amendment. Other intimations followed. See *Whitney* v. *California,* 274 U. S. 357; *Fiske* v. *Kansas,* 274 U. S. 380. In 1931 Chief Justice Hughes speaking for the Court in *Stromberg* v. *California,* 283 U. S. 359, 368, declared: "It has been determined that the conception of liberty under the due process clause of the Fourteenth Amendment embraces the right of free speech." Thus we deal with a constitutional principle enunciated less than four decades ago, and consider for the first time the application of that principle to issues arising in libel cases brought by state officials.

in the area of race relations. The American Colonists were not willing, nor should we be, to take the risk that "[m]en who injure and oppress the people under their administration [and] provoke them to cry out and complain" will also be empowered to "make that very complaint the foundation for new oppressions and prosecutions." The Trial of John Peter Zenger, 17 Howell's St. Tr. 675, 721–722 (1735) (argument of counsel to the jury). To impose liability for critical, albeit erroneous or even malicious, comments on official conduct would effectively resurrect "the obsolete doctrine that the governed must not criticize their governors." Cf. *Sweeney* v. *Patterson,* 76 U. S. App. D. C. 23, 24, 128 F. 2d 457, 458.

Our national experience teaches that repressions breed hate and "that hate menaces stable government." *Whitney* v. *California,* 274 U. S. 357, 375 (Brandeis, J., concurring). We should be ever mindful of the wise counsel of Chief Justice Hughes:

> "[I]mperative is the need to preserve inviolate the constitutional rights of free speech, free press and free assembly in order to maintain the opportunity for free political discussion, to the end that government may be responsive to the will of the people and that changes, if desired, may be obtained by peaceful means. Therein lies the security of the Republic, the very foundation of constitutional government." *De Jonge* v. *Oregon,* 299 U. S. 353, 365.

This is not to say that the Constitution protects defamatory statements directed against the private conduct of a public official or private citizen. Freedom of press and of speech insure that government will respond to the will of the people and that changes may be obtained by peaceful means. Purely private defamation has little to do with the political ends of a self-governing society. The imposition of liability for private defamation does not abridge the freedom of public speech.[4]  This, of course, cannot be said "where public officials are concerned or where public matters are involved. . . .  [O]ne main function of the First Amendment is to ensure ample opportunity for the people to determine and resolve public issues.  Where public matters are involved, the doubts should be resolved in favor of freedom of expression rather than against it."  Douglas, The Right of the People (1958), p. 41.

In many jurisdictions, legislators, judges and executive officers are clothed with absolute immunity against liability for defamatory words uttered in the discharge of their public duties.  See, e. g., Barr v. Matteo, 360 U. S. 564; City of Chicago v. Tribune Co., 307 Ill., at 610; 139 N. E., at 91.  Judge Learned Hand ably summarized the policies underlying the rule:

> "It does indeed go without saying that an official, who is in fact guilty of using his powers to vent his spleen upon others, or for any other personal motive not connected with the public good, should not escape liability for the injuries he may so cause; and, if it were possible in practice to confine such complaints to the guilty, it would be monstrous to deny recovery. The justification for doing so is that it is impossible to know whether the claim is well founded until the

---

[4] In most cases, as in the case at bar, there will be little difficulty in distinguishing defamatory speech relating to private conduct from that relating to official conduct.  I recognize, of course, that there will be a gray area.  The difficulties of applying a public-private standard are, however, certainly of a different genre from those attending the differentiation between a malicious and nonmalicious state of mind.  If the constitutional standard is to be shaped by a concept of malice, the speaker takes the risk not only that the jury will inaccurately determine his state of mind but also that the jury will fail properly to apply the constitutional standard set by the elusive concept of malice.  See note 2, supra.

case has been tried, and that to submit all officials, the innocent as well as the guilty, to the burden of a trial and to the inevitable danger of its outcome, would dampen the ardor of all but the most resolute, or the most irresponsible, in the unflinching discharge of their duties. Again and again the public interest calls for action which may turn out to be founded on a mistake, in the face of which an official may later find himself hard put to it to satisfy a jury of his good faith. There must indeed be means of punishing public officers who have been truant to their duties; but that is quite another matter from exposing such as have been honestly mistaken to suit by anyone who has suffered from their errors. As is so often the case, the answer must be found in a balance between the evils inevitable in either alternative. In this instance it has been thought in the end better to leave unredressed the wrongs done by dishonest officers than to subject those who try to do their duty to the constant dread of retaliation. . . .

"The decisions have, indeed, always imposed as a limitation upon the immunity that the official's act must have been within the scope of his powers; and it can be argued that official powers, since they exist only for the public good, never cover occasions where the public good is not their aim, and hence that to exercise a power dishonestly is necessarily to overstep its bounds. A moment's reflection shows, however, that that cannot be the meaning of the limitation without defeating the whole doctrine. What is meant by saying that the officer must be acting within his power cannot be more than that the occasion must be such as would have justified the act, if he had been using his power for any of the purposes on whose account it was vested in him. . . ." *Gregoire* v. *Biddle*, 177 F. 2d 579, 581.

If the government official should be immune from libel actions so that his ardor to serve the public will not be dampened and "fearless, vigorous, and effective administration of policies of government" not be inhibited, *Barr* v. *Matteo, supra,* at 571, then the citizen and the press should likewise be immune from libel actions for their criticism of official conduct. Their ardor as citizens will thus not be dampened and they will be free "to applaud or to criticize the way public employees do their jobs, from the least to the most important." [5]  If liability can attach to political criticism because it damages the reputation of a public official as a public official, then no critical citizen can safely utter anything but faint praise about the government or its officials. The vigorous criticism by press and citizen of the conduct of the government of the day by the officials of the day will soon yield to silence if officials in control of government agencies, instead of answering criticisms, can resort to friendly juries to forestall criticism of their official conduct.[6]

The conclusion that the Constitution affords the citizen and the press an absolute privilege for criticism of official conduct does not leave the public official without defenses against unsubstantiated opinions or deliberate misstatements. "Under our system of government, counterargument and education are the weapons available to expose these matters, not abridgment . . . of free speech . . . ." *Wood* v. *Georgia,* 370 U. S. 375, 389. The public

---

[5] MR. JUSTICE BLACK concurring in *Barr* v. *Matteo,* 360 U. S. 564, 577, observed that: "The effective functioning of a free government like ours depends largely on the force of an informed public opinion. This calls for the widest possible understanding of the quality of government service rendered by all elective or appointed public officials or employees. Such an informed understanding depends, of course, on the freedom people have to applaud or to criticize the way public employees do their jobs, from the least to the most important."

[6] See notes 2, 4, *supra.*

official certainly has equal if not greater access than most private citizens to media of communication.  In any event, despite the possibility that some excesses and abuses may go unremedied, we must recognize that "the people of this nation have ordained in the light of history, that, in spite of the probability of excesses and abuses, [certain] liberties are, in the long view, essential to enlightened opinion and right conduct on the part of the citizens of a democracy." *Cantwell* v. *Connecticut,* 310 U. S. 296, 310.  As Mr. Justice Brandeis correctly observed, "sunlight is the most powerful of all disinfectants." [7]

For these reasons, I strongly believe that the Constitution accords citizens and press an unconditional freedom to criticize official conduct.  It necessarily follows that in a case such as this, where all agree that the allegedly defamatory statements related to official conduct, the judgments for libel cannot constitutionally be sustained.

---

[7] See Freund, The Supreme Court of the United States (1949), p. 61.

# NOTES

These notes generally follow legal methods of citation. For example: *New York Times Co. v. Sullivan*, 376 U.S. 254, 270 (1964) means that the Supreme Court decided the case in 1964 and that the opinions can be found starting at page 254 of volume 376 of the *United States Reports*, the official volumes of the Court's decisions; the particular passage quoted or referred to in the text is on page 270. Books and articles give the name of the author first, then the title, the volume number and title of a periodical if one is being cited, page number and year. For example: Rabban, *The First Amendment in Its Forgotten Years*, 90 Yale Law Journal 514, 542 (1981). When a book is part of a multivolume set, the volume number is given first: 4 *Elliot's Debates on the Federal Constitution* 546.

## Chapter 1

PAGE

7    The results of the advertisement are described in Taylor Branch's *Parting the Waters: America in the King Years 1954–63* 289 (1988).

8    The First Amendment reads in full: "Congress shall make no law respecting an establishment of religion, or prohibiting the free exercise thereof; or abridging the freedom of speech, or of the press; or the right of the people peaceably to assemble, and to petition the Government for a redress of grievances."

## Chapter 2

9 Ray Jenkins's recollections were in a letter to the author.

10 Grover Hall, Sullivan and the bat incident: *Parting the Waters* 281–82.

Sullivan and the Freedom Riders: *Parting the Waters* 444, 448–49.

## Chapter 3

15 "Letter from Birmingham Jail," quoted in *Parting the Waters* 739.

16 The provision for counting three fifths of slaves in apportioning House seats is in Article I, Section 2 of the Constitution. The provision that the slave trade may not be stopped before 1808: Article I, Section 9. The Dred Scott case: *Scott v. Sandford*, 60 U.S. (19 How.) 393, 404–5 (1857).

17 *Strauder v. West Virginia*, 100 U.S. 303, 307–8 (1880).

18 *Plessy v. Ferguson*, 163 U.S. 537, 551, 560, 562 (1896).

19 *Brown v. Board of Education*, 347 U.S. 483, 492, 495 (1954).

20 The Montgomery bus boycott is described in Anthony Lewis, *Portrait of a Decade* 70–84 (1964). Dr. King's words are quoted on page 74.

21 Governor Patterson: in *Portrait of a Decade* 88.

## Chapter 4

24 Embry's recollections: conversation with the author.

26 Judge Jones on courtroom segregation: reported in the *Alabama Journal*, February 1, 1961.

## Chapter 5

36 The estimate of $300 million in Southern libel suits: Harrison E. Salisbury, *Without Fear or Favor* 388 (1980).

37 Sitton's report from Sasser, Georgia, is printed in full in *Portrait of a Decade* 141–47.

39 Sitton on the Mack Charles Parker case: *Portrait of a Decade* 210–14.

Mayor Hanes: *Portrait* 186.

40 Sitton on Mrs. Gabrielle: *Portrait* 162–63.

41    Professor Bickel's comment is in Bickel, *The Least Dangerous Branch* 267 (1962).
      The Kennedy speech is printed in part in *Portrait* 192–95.
42    Madison: 4 *Elliot's Debates on the Federal Constitution* 571.
      *Beauharnais v. Illinois*, 343 U.S. 250, 251, 266 (1952).
      *Times Talk*: the issue of March 1961, p. 1.
43    Impounding Abernathy's car: see the *Alabama Journal*, February 4, 1961. Selling his land: see "Pastor's Land Sold in Libel Judgment," New York Times, March 22, 1961, p. 34, col. 5.
44    The Supreme Court's three decisions in *N.A.A.C.P. v. Alabama*: 357 U.S. 449 (1958), 360 U.S. 240 (1959), 377 U.S. 288, 310 (1964). The Alabama Supreme Court decision: 273 Ala. 656, 674–76, 686, 144 So. 2d 25, 39, 40, 50 (1962).


      *Chapter 6*


48    *Marbury v. Madison*, 1 Cranch 137, 177 (1803). (Supreme Court volumes were at first called by the name of the reporter of decisions, for example William Cranch.)
      Jefferson on the "despotic" judiciary: in a letter to Abigail Adams, September 11, 1804, 7 The Writings of Thomas Jefferson (Ford ed. 1897) 310.
      Jefferson on judicial enforcement of a Bill of Rights: letter to Madison, March 15, 1789, in 5 *Documentary History of the Constitution* 161–63, published by the State Department (1901–05).
49    President Washington's request for advice was conveyed to the Supreme Court by Secretary of State Jefferson. The letter and the justices' reply are printed in *Hart and Wechsler's The Federal Courts and the Federal System* 65–67 (Bator, Mishkin, Shapiro & Wechsler 3d ed. 1988).
      Marshall on the Constitution: in *McCulloch v. Maryland*, 4 Wheat. 316, 415 (1819).
51    Professor Anderson's comments are in his important article, *The Origins of the Press Clause*, 30 UCLA Law Review 455, 491, 535 (1983). Professor Levy's revised edition is entitled *Emergence of a Free Press*.
52    Chief Justice Holt: in *Rex v. Tutchin*, 3 Anne 1704, reprinted in Howell, ed., *State Trials*, vol. 14, 1095, 1128 (1812).
      Professor Kalven on seditious libel: Kalven, *A Worthy Tradition* 63 (1988).
54    Croswell's case: *People v. Croswell*, 3 Johnson's Cases 337 (New York) (1804), reprinted in N.Y. Common Law Rep. App. 717–41 (1883). The case is discussed in Forkosch, *Freedom of the Press: Croswell's Case*, 33 Fordham Law Review 415, 417, 448 (1965).
55    The Philadelphia *Aurora*, quoted in Nevins, *American Press Opinion: Washington to Coolidge* 21 (1928).

## Chapter 7

56    Madison's comment to Jefferson is printed in Saul Padover, *The Complete Madison* 257–58 (1953).

57    Abigail Adams's comment is found in a book indispensable to an understanding of the Sedition Act and its history: James Morton Smith, *Freedom's Fetters: The Alien and Sedition Laws and American Civil Liberties* 96 (1956).

58    On how judges applied the Sedition Act, see John D. Stevens, *Congressional History of the 1798 Sedition Law,* Journalism Quarterly, Summer 1966, pp. 247–48. Professor Stevens's article is a superb brief account of the passage and application of the act.

59    John Allen: in *Freedom's Fetters* 113–14.

Gallatin: *Freedom's Fetters* 122–23.

60    Gallatin: in Levy, *Emergence of a Free Press* 302–3 (1985).

Nicholas: *Emergence* 301–2.

Nicholas: *Emergence* 310.

Jefferson and Madison acting in secret: See Stevens, *Congressional History* 249.

61    The Virginia Resolutions and Madison's Report on them are found in 4 *Elliot's Debates on the Federal Constitution* 546–80. The passages quoted in the text are at pages 553, 554, 569, 570.

The text of the minority address on the Virginia Resolutions was printed as a pamphlet, *Address of the Minority,* Richmond, 1798. Substantial excerpts appear in Brief for the United States in Reply to Brief of Gilbert E. Roe, in *Debs v. United States,* No. 714, Supreme Court, October Term 1918, pp. 12–16. The identification of Marshall as the author is in 2 Beveridge, *The Life of John Marshall* 401–6 (1919). That attribution is persuasively challenged in 3 *The Papers of John Marshall* 499 (1979), in an editorial note that says the content of the minority address suggests that Henry Lee was the author.

63    The Lyon prosecution: *Freedom's Fetters* 226 et seq.

64    The Brown case: *Freedom's Fetters* 257 et seq.

The Callender case: *Freedom's Fetters* 334 et seq.

65    The letter to Abigail Adams: 1 *The Adams-Jefferson Letters: The Complete Correspondence Between Thomas Jefferson and Abigail and John Adams* (Capon, ed.) 274–76 (1959).

66    On Congressional refund of fines: see Stevens 255.

## Chapter 8

68     The 1833 decision on the scope of the Bill of Rights was *Barron v. Baltimore*, 7 Pet. 243.
       The decision against maximum-hour laws: *Lochner v. New York*, 198 U.S. 45 (1905).
       On child labor: *Hammer v. Dagenhart*, 247 U.S. 251 (1918).
       The 1897 decision: *Robertson v. Baldwin*, 165 U.S. 275, 281.
       *Patterson v. Colorado*, 205 U.S. 454, 462 (1907).

69     Rabban, *The First Amendment in Its Forgotten Years*, 90 Yale Law Journal 514, 542 (1981). (Cited hereafter as Rabban Yale.)
       Schofield: in Rabban Yale 560, 565, 570, 571.
       Schofield's statement that one object of the American Revolution was to get rid of the English common law on speech and press is quoted in Chafee, *Freedom of Speech* 21 (1920).

70     *Masses Publishing Co. v. Patten*, 244 F. 535, 539–40 (S.D.N.Y. 1917).

71     Blasi, *Learned Hand and the Self-Government Theory of the First Amendment*: Masses Publishing Co. v. Patten, 61 University of Colorado Law Review 1 (1990).
       *Schenck v. United States*, 249 U.S. 47, 51–52 (1919).

72     Holmes pointing to *The Common Law*: see Rabban, *The Emergence of Modern First Amendment Doctrine*, 50 University of Chicago Law Review 1205, 1265–66, 1271 (1983). (Cited hereafter as Rabban Chicago.)
       *Debs v. United States*, 249 U.S. 211, 212–14 (1919).

74     Holmes on child labor: in *Hammer v. Dagenhart*, 247 U.S. at 280 (1918).
       Ernst Freund's critical comment on *Debs* is discussed in Rabban Chicago 1281–83. See also Polenberg, *Fighting Faiths* 219–21 (1987).
       Gunther on the Hand-Holmes correspondence: Gunther, *Learned Hand and the Origins of Modern First Amendment Doctrine: Some Fragments of History*, 27 Stanford Law Review 719, 732, 755, 757–59 (1975).

75     Chafee, *Freedom of Speech in War Time*, 32 Harvard Law Review 932, 934, 947–8, 963, 967–8 (1919).

76     *Abrams v. United States*, 250 U.S. 616, 621, 627–31 (1919).

## Chapter 9

81     The letters to Croly and Laski: *Fighting Faiths* 221–22. On Chafee's article, see *Fighting Faiths* 22–23. See also Rabban Chicago 1315, Rabban Yale 581 n.364. The 1922 Holmes letter to Chafee: See Rabban Chicago 1265–66, 1271.

Holmes's reading: *Fighting Faiths* 224–27.

Chafee, *Freedom of Speech* 155.

Kalven, *A Worthy Tradition* 146.

82      The further Espionage Act cases in which Brandeis wrote the dissent for Holmes and himself: *Schaefer v. United States*, 251 U.S. 466 (1920), and *Pierce v. United States*, 252 U.S. 239 (1920). The case in which Holmes and Brandeis wrote separate dissenting opinions: *United States ex rel Milwaukee Social Democratic Publishing Co. v. Burleson*, 255 U.S. 407 (1921).

83      *Gitlow v. New York*, 268 U.S. 652, 666, 672–73 (1925).

84      *Whitney v. California*, 274 U.S. 357, 374–77 (1927).

     For a moving commentary on Brandeis's opinion, see Blasi, *The First Amendment and the Ideal of Civic Courage: The Brandeis Opinion in* Whitney v. California, 29 William & Mary Law Review 653 (1988).

87      Freund, *Mr. Justice Brandeis: A Centennial Memoir*, 70 Harvard Law Review 769, 789 (1957).

     Strum, *Louis D. Brandeis: Justice for the People* 237 (1984). For an illuminating discussion of Brandeis's feelings about ancient Greece and the influence of Zimmern's book, see Blasi's William & Mary article at 686–89.

     Governor Young's pardon is described in Blasi, William & Mary at 696–97.

     *United States v. Schwimmer*, 279 U.S. 644, 653–55 (1929).

     Holmes on war as "inevitable and rational": See 2 *Holmes-Pollock Letters* 230 (Howe editor, 1941). A brilliant discussion of war in the pyschology of Holmes can be found in Zobel, *The Three Civil Wars of Oliver Wendell Holmes: Notes for an Odyssey*, Boston Bar Journal, December 1982, p. 13; January 1983, p. 18; February 1983, p. 18.

89      The case in which the Court held the income tax unconstitutional was *Pollock v. Farmers' Loan and Trust Co.*, 157 U.S. 429 (1895). It was overruled in 1913 by the Sixteenth Amendment to the Constitution.

## Chapter 10

90      *Near v. Minnesota*, 283 U.S. 697, 702, 704, 713–20 (1931).

     *Bridges v. California*, 314 U.S. 252, 263 (1941).

     Friendly, *Minnesota Rag* (1981).

91      The Minnesota Supreme Court decision: *State ex rel. Olson v. Guilford*, 174 Minn. 457, 463, 219 N.W. 770, 772 (1928). Howard A. Guilford was Near's partner.

95      The Pentagon Papers Case: *New York Times v. United States*, 403 U.S. 713, 717 (1971).

96–97      The Louisiana newspaper tax case: *Grosjean v. American Press Co. Inc.*, 297 U.S. 233, 247–48, 250 (1936).

98      The description of what happened in the Supreme Court before the
        decision of the *Bridges* case is based on Justice Black's papers in the
        manuscript collection of the Library of Congress and on Justice
        Frankfurter's in the Harvard Law Library. See also Lewis, *Justice
        Black and the First Amendment*, 38 Alabama Law Review 289, 291–
        92, 295–97 (1987).

99      Chief Justice Hughes's comment to the other members of the Court
        was related by one of them, Justice William O. Douglas.

100     *Stromberg v. California*, 283 U.S. 359, 361 (1931).
        *De Jonge v. Oregon*, 299 U.S. 353 (1937).
        The Herndon case: *Herndon v. Lowry*, 301 U.S. 242, 263–64
        (1937).

101     The case of the Communist party leaders: *Dennis v. United States*,
        341 U.S. 494, 510, 581 (1951).


### Chapter 11

104     The Wechsler lecture is in his *Principles, Politics, and Fundamental
        Law* 3 (1961).
        *United States v. Classic*, 313 U.S. 299 (1941).

111     *Alabama Public Service Commission v. Southern Railway Co.*, 341
        U.S. 341 (1951).
        Roland Nachman went on to a distinguished career as an Alabama
        lawyer. Among other things he served for eight years on the American
        Bar Association's Committee on the Federal Judiciary, which com-
        ments on the qualifications of nominees to all federal courts, in-
        cluding the Supreme Court.


### Chapter 12

116     *Cantwell v. Connecticut*, 310 U.S. 296, 310 (1940).

118     The Chicago Tribune case: *City of Chicago v. Tribune Co.*, 307 Ill.
        595, 601, 139 N.E. 86, 88 (1923).
        The official immunity case: *Barr v. Matteo*, 360 U.S. 564, 571, 575
        (1959).

120     The decision of the U.S. Court of Appeals for the District of Columbia
        Circuit: *Sweeney v. Patterson*, 128 F.2d 457, 458 (1942).
        *Coleman v. MacLennan*, 78 Kan. 711, 723 (1908).

121     *Fiske v. Kansas*, 274 U.S. 380 (1927).

124     Chafee, Book Review, 62 Harvard Law Review 891, 897 (1949).

125     *Smith v. California*, 361 U.S. 147 (1959).

## Chapter 13

134      The Skokie case: *Collin v. Smith*, 578 F.2d 1197 (7th Cir 1978), cert. denied 439 U.S. 916 (1978).

136      The obscenity case: *Roth v. United States*, 354 U.S. 476 (1957).

## Chapter 14

144      The N.A.A.C.P. case: *N.A.A.C.P. v. Button*, 371 U.S. 415, 423–24 n.7, 433, 445 (1963).
The subsequent contempt case: *Craig v. Harney*, 331 U.S. 367, 376 (1947).

## Chapter 15

154      Kalven on Meiklejohn: *A Worthy Tradition* 67.
Dancing in the streets: Kalven, *The New York Times Case: A Note on "The Central Meaning of the First Amendment,"* 1964 Supreme Court Review 191, 221 n.125.
Judge Leventhal: in *Afro-American Publishing Co., Inc. v. Jaffe*, 366 F.2d 649, 660 (D.C. Cir. 1966).
*Garrison v. Louisiana*, 379 U.S. 64, 66, 74–75 (1964).

155      Justice Brennan's Meiklejohn Lecture was published in 79 Harvard Law Review 1, 18 (1965).

158      Judge Gurfein's statement: in *United States v. New York Times Co.*, 328 F. Supp. 324, 331 (S.D.N.Y. 1971).

160      The South African case: *South Africa Associated Newspapers Limited and Another v. Estate Pelser*, [1975] 4 So. Afr.L.R. 797, 800 (App. Div.)

162      *Parting the Waters* 580.
Lowery's comments: conversation with the author.
*Shuttlesworth v. Birmingham*, 376 U.S. 339 (1964), reversing 42 Ala. App. 1, 2, 149 So.2d 921, 923 (1962).

163      The 1955 decision: *Williams v. Georgia*, 349 U.S. 375. The 1948 decision: *Cole v. Arkansas*, 333 U.S. 196.

## Chapter 16

165      *Nishikawa v. Dulles*, 356 U.S. 129, 133 (1958).
166      *Baker v. Carr*, 369 U.S. 186 (1962).

172       Justice Jackson's comment: in Jackson, *The Supreme Court in the American System of Government* 16 (1955).

174       *Martin v. Hunter's Lessee*, 1 Wheat 304 (1816).
          *Cohens v. Virginia*, 6 Wheat. 264 (1821).

175       The story about Justices Black and Harlan in their last days is told in Hugo Black Jr., *My Father: A Remembrance* 260–61 (1975).

181       The other opinions that used variants of the phrase "effective judicial administration" were *United States v. Barnett*, 376 U.S 681, 694– 95 n.12 (1964) ("effective administration of justice") and *Aro Mfg. Co. Inc. v. Convertible Top Replacement Co. Inc.*, 377 U.S. 476, 502 (1964) ("efficient judicial administration").


## Chapter *17*

183       Meiklejohn, *The First Amendment Is an Absolute*, 1961 Supreme Court Review 245, 259.

184       *Time Inc. v. Hill*, 385 U.S. 374, 388–89 (1967).

188       Garment, "Annals of Law: The Hill Case," *The New Yorker*, April 17, 1989, pp. 90, 98, 104, 109.

189       *Curtis Publishing Co. v. Butts*, 388 U.S. 130, 155, 163–64 (1967).

191       *Rosenbloom v. Metromedia*, 403 U.S. 29, 43, 47–48, 79 (1971).

192       The Stewart passage is in *Rosenblatt v. Baer*, 383 U.S. 75, 91, 92– 93 (1966).

193       *Gertz v. Robert Welch, Inc.*, 418 U.S. 323, 339–40, 370, 387 (1974).

195       The 1968 case defining "reckless disregard": *St. Amant v. Thompson*, 390 U.S. 727, 731–32, 734 (1968).

197       The Firestone case: *Time, Inc. v. Firestone*, 424 U.S. 448 (1976).
          The case of the researcher: *Hutchinson v. Proxmire*, 443 U.S. 111 (1979).
          The contempt case: *Wolston v. Reader's Digest Ass., Inc.*, 443 U.S. 157 (1979).
          *Newton v. National Broadcasting Co.*, 930 F.2d 662 (9th Cir. 1990).


## Chapter *18*

200       Epstein, *Was* New York Times v. Sullivan *Wrong?*, 53 University of Chicago Law Review 782, 783 (1986).
          Judge Bork's comment: in *Ollman v. Evans*, 750 F.2d 970, 996 (C.A.D.C. en banc 1984).
          The Miss Wyoming case: *Pring v. Penthouse International, Ltd.*, 695 F.2d 438 (10th Cir. 1982).
          The Tavoulareas case: *Tavoulareas v. Piro*, 817 F.2d 762 (C.A.D.C. en banc 1987).

201       *Herbert v. Lando*, 441 U.S. 153 (1979).

202   The later Court of Appeals decision in the Herbert case is *Herbert v. Lando*, 781 F.2d 298 (C.A.2 1986), cert. denied 476 U.S. 1182 (1986).

The Milkweed case is described in the Columbia Journalism Review, January/February 1983, pp. 42–43.

203   *Wall Street Journal* libel settlement: See "Journal Settles Libel Suit for $800,000," *New York Times*, June 9, 1984, p. 8, col. 4.

The Alton Telegraph story: *Wall Street Journal*, September 29, 1983, p. 1, col. 1.

The story of *Missing* and the litigation over it is evocatively described in Smolla, *Suing the Press* 148–59 (1986).

206   The jury award to Sprague: See Hinds, "Philadelphia Inquirer Loses Libel Suit," *New York Times*, May 4, 1990, p. A16, col. 1.

Donald Trump's lawsuit: initiated, see "N.Y. Developer Brings Libel Suit," *Washington Post*, September 26, 1984, p. D6, col. 4; described and analyzed, see Goldberger, "Architecture View: Can a Critic Really Control the Marketplace?," *New York Times*, October 14, 1984, sec. 2, p. 31, col. 4; dismissed, see "Trump's Suit vs. Tribune Is Dismissed," *Chicago Tribune*, September 9, 1985, business section, p. 4.

Chafee, 1 *Government and Mass Communications* 106–7 (1947).

Schaefer, *Defamation and the First Amendment*, 52 University of Colorado Law Review 1, 8 (1980).

Jefferson in 1787: see Saul Padover, *Thomas Jefferson on Democracy* 92 (Mentor Edition).

Jefferson in 1807: Padover 97.

207   Smolla on the surge in libel suits: *Suing the Press* 9–19.

209   Justice Brennan on the press's rhetorical overkill: Brennan, *Address*, 32 Rutgers Law Review 173, 179, 181 (1979).

The three privilege cases were decided together by the Supreme Court as *Branzburg v. Hayes*, 408 U.S. 665 (1972).

210   The South African libel case: *Buthelezi v. Poorter and Others*, [1975] 4 So. Afr.L.R. 608.

Judge Bork's comment: Bork, "Freedom, the Courts and the Media," *Center* magazine, March/April 1979, p. 34.

211   The La Pointe case: See Eve Pell, "The High Cost of Speaking Out," *California* magazine, November 1988, p. 88.

Squaw Valley: See *California* magazine, September 1989, p. 18.

Canan and Pring, *Strategic Lawsuits Against Public Participation*, 35 Social Problems 506 (1988). See also Bishop, "Developers and Others Use New Tool to Quell Protests by Private Citizens," *New York Times*, April 26, 1991, p. B9, col. 1.

211–14   The Immuno case: *Immuno A.G. v. Moor-Jankowski*, 549 N.Y.S.2d 938, 940–44 (1989), vacated and remanded, 110 Sup. Ct. 3266 (1990), decided again by the New York Court of Appeals, 77 N.Y. 2d 235 (1991), cert. denied 59 U.S. Law Week 3810 (June 3, 1991). Dr. Moor-Jankowski's letter: See "View From Inside a Landmark Libel Case," *New York Times*, January 25, 1991, p. A28, col. 3.

215     The Roberts speech: see *A Supreme Court Decision Fosters Litiga-
        tion*, Nieman Reports, Spring 1990, p. 4.

216     A detailed description of the Westmoreland case is in *Suing the Press*
        198–237.


## Chapter 19

221     The 1984 Supreme Court decision: *Bose Corporation v. Consumers
        Union*, 466 U.S. 485.
        The 1986 decision: *Anderson v. Liberty Lobby, Inc.*, 477 U.S. 242
        (1986).
        The insurance figures: see Henry R. Kaufman, *Trends in Libel*, chap-
        ter 1 in *The Cost of Libel: Economic and Policy Implications* (Dennis
        and Noam, editors) 7 (1989).
        Roberts: Nieman Reports, Spring 1990, p. 4.
        Epstein, *Was* New York Times v. Sullivan *Wrong?*, 53 University of
        Chicago Law Review 782, 792 (1986).

222–23  In its 1990 term the Supreme Court considered a claim that unlimited
        jury discretion to award punitive damages in civil cases (all kinds of
        cases, not just libel) could be so unfair to defendants that they would
        be deprived of property without the "due process of law" guaranteed
        by the Fourteenth Amendment. On the facts of the case before it,
        the Court rejected the argument. *Pacific Mutual Life Insurance Co.
        v. Haslip*, 111 Sup. Ct. 1032 (1991).

225     Anderson, *Reputation, Compensation, and Proof*, 25 William &
        Mary Law Review 747, 755 (1984).
        Judge Friendly: in *Buckley v. New York Post*, 373 F.2d 175, 182
        (1967).

227     Dwyer, *The Goldmark Case* 273, 279–80 (1984).

228     *Miami Herald v. Tornillo*, 418 U.S. 241 (1974).
        The Franklin reform proposal: Franklin, *Good Names and Bad Law:
        A Critique of Libel Law and a Proposal*, 18 U. of San Francisco
        Law Review 1 (1983).

229     The Leval proposal: Leval, *The No-Money, No-Fault Libel Suit:
        Keeping* Sullivan *in Its Proper Place*, 101 Harvard Law Review 1287
        (1988).
        *Dun & Bradstreet, Inc. v. Greenmoss Builders, Inc.*, 472 U.S. 749,
        764, 767, 771, 775 n.1 (1985).
        *St. Amant v. Thompson*, 390 U.S. 727 (1968).

231     *Hustler Magazine Inc. v. Falwell*, 485 U.S. 46, 48, 51–55 (1988).


## Chapter 20

234     Madison: in a letter to W. T. Barry, August 4, 1822, quoted in
        Padover, *The Complete Madison* 346 (1953).

235    The Julian Bond case: *Bond v. Floyd*, 385 U.S. 116, 120–21, 124, 135–36 (1966).

236    *Brandenburg v. Ohio*, 395 U.S. 444 (1969).

237    *Cohen v. California*, 403 U.S. 15, 23–25 (1971).

238    *Texas v. Johnson*, 491 U.S. 397, 414 (1989).
       The second flag-burning case: *United States v. Eichman*, 110 Sup. Ct. 2404, 2408, 2410 (1990).

239    For a detailed and informative description of how the CNN conflict developed, see Singer, "How Prior Restraint Came to America," *The American Lawyer*, January-February 1991, p. 88.

240    Judge Gurfein: *United States v. New York Times Co.*, 328 F.Supp. 324, 331 (S.D.N.Y. 1971).
       The Pentagon Papers decision in the Supreme Court: *New York Times Co. v. United States*, 403 U.S. 713, 730 (1971).

241    *Snepp v. United States*, 444 U.S. 507 (1980).

242    Griswold, "Secrets Not Worth Keeping," *Washington Post*, February 15, 1989, p. A25.

243    The Cincinnati verdict: See Wilkerson, "Cincinnati Jury Acquits Museum in Mapplethorpe Obscenity Case," *New York Times*, October 6, 1990, p. 1, col. 1.
       The Fort Lauderdale verdict: See Rimer, "Rap Band Members Found Not Guilty in Obscenity Trial," *New York Times*, October 21, 1990, section 1, p. 1, col. 1.

244    Bickel, *The Morality of Consent* 60–61 (1975).

245    Professor Howard, in *The Brennan Legacy: A Roundtable Discussion*, 77 American Bar Association Journal 52, 58 (1991).

246    Liu Binyan: "The Price China Has Paid: An Interview with Liu Binyan," *New York Review of Books*, January 19, 1989, p. 31.
       The Thalidomide Case: *Sunday Times v. United Kingdom*, 2 E.H.R.R. 245, 281 (1979).
       The libel case: *Lingens v. Austria*, 8 E.H.R.R. 407, 409, 418–19 (1986). A significant brief as a friend of the court, explaining the *Sullivan* rule to the European Court and arguing for its adoption, was filed by Floyd Abrams, a leading First Amendment lawyer, on behalf of the International Centre for the Protection of Human Rights.

# TABLE OF CASES

Abrams v. U.S., 76–79, 80–82, 87, 89, 108, 145, 154, 157, 194, 232
Afro-American v. Jaffe, 154n.
Alabama P.S.C. v. Southern, 111
Anderson v. Liberty Lobby, 221n.
Aro v. Convertible, 181n.
Baker v. Carr, 166
Barr v. Matteo, 118n., 147
Barron v. Baltimore, 68n.
Beauharnais v. Illinois, 42, 109, 134, 142
Bond v. Floyd, 235
Bose v. Consumers Union, 221n.
Brandenburg v. Ohio, 236
Branzburg v. Hayes, 209n.
Bridges v. Calif., 90, 97–102, 106, 132, 135, 143, 156
Brown v. Board of Education, 19, 36, 104, 110, 139, 150
Buckley v. N.Y. Post, 225n.
Buthelezi v. Poorter, 210n.
Cantwell v. Connecticut, 116, 144
City of Chicago v. Tribune, 118, 125, 149, 170
Cohen v. California, 237
Cohens v. Virginia, 174
Cole v. Arkansas, 163n.
Coleman v. MacLennan, 120, 147, 167
Collin v. Smith, 134n.
Craig v. Harney, 144n.
Curtis Publishing v. Butts, 189, 229

Debs v. U.S., 61n, 72, 81, 118, 235
DeJonge v. Oregon, 100, 108
Dennis v. U.S., 101n.
Dred Scott v. Sandford, 16
Dun & Bradstreet v. Greenmoss, 229
Fiske v. Kansas, 121, 132, 167
Garrison v. Louisiana, 154, 167, 184, 192
Gertz v. Welch, 193, 213–15, 224, 230
Gitlow v. New York, 83, 87, 90, 145
Grosjean v. American Press, 96n.
Hammer v. Dagenhart, 68n., 74n.
Herbert v. Lando, 201, 209, 229
Herndon v. Lowry, 100n., 104, 142
Hustler v. Falwell, 231–33, 238
Hutchinson v. Proxmire, 197n.
Immuno v. Moor-Jankowski, 211, 216
Lingens v. Austria, 246n.
Lochner v. New York, 68n.
Marbury v. Madison, 48
Martin v. Hunter's Lessee, 174
The Masses, 70, 71, 75, 87, 236
McCulloch v. Maryland, 49n.
Miami Herald v. Tornillo, 228
Milwaukee Publishing v. Burleson, 82n.
N.A.A.C.P. v. Alabama, 44n.
N.A.A.C.P. v. Button, 144n.
Near v. Minnesota, 90–97, 109, 142, 156, 239, 241
Newton v. NBC, 197
Nishikawa v. Dulles, 165, 167, 170

Ollman v. Evans, 200n.
Pacific Mutual v. Haslip, 222n.
Patterson v. Colorado, 68, 71, 93
Pentagon Papers Case, 95, 158, 240,
    242
People v. Croswell, 54n.
Pierce v. U.S., 82n.
Plessy v. Ferguson, 18
Pring v. Penthouse, 200n.
Rex v. Tutchin, 52n.
Robertson v. Baldwin, 68n.
Rosenblatt v. Baer, 192n.
Rosenbloom v. Metromedia, 191, 223
Roth v. U.S., 136n.
St. Amant v. Thompson, 195n., 229
Schaefer v. U.S., 82n.
Schenck v. U.S., 71, 74–76, 81
Shuttlesworth v. Birmingham, 162n.
Smith v. California, 125, 146

Snepp v. U.S., 241, 246
S.A. Associated Newspapers v. Pelser,
    160n.
Strauder v. West Virginia, 17
Stromberg v. California, 100, 143
Sunday Times v. U.K., 246n.
Sweeney v. Patterson, 120n.
Tavoulareas v. Piro, 200n.
Texas v. Johnson, 238, 243
Time Inc. v. Firestone, 197n.
Time Inc. v. Hill, 184, 217
U.S. v. Barnett, 181n.
U.S. v. Classic, 104
U.S. v. Eichman, 238n.
U.S. v. Schwimmer, 87, 89, 92, 158
Whitney v. California, 84, 100, 119,
    143, 147, 236
Williams v. Georgia, 163n.
Wolston v. Reader's Digest, 197n.

# INDEX

Abernathy, Ralph D., 11–12, 32, 43,
    162
*Abernathy et al. v. Sullivan:*
    and Brennan's *Sullivan* opinion, 141,
        148, 215
    brief in opposition in, 112
    four ministers named in, 11–12
    ministers' lawyers in, 27, 109–10,
        138
    ministers' Supreme Court brief in, 123
    oral arguments in, 137–39
    petition for certiorari in, 109–12
    *see also New York Times Co. v.
        Sullivan*
abolitionists, 11, 34, 203, 210
Abrams, Floyd, 156
Abrams, Jacob, 77, 78
*Abrams v. United States*, 76–79
    Clarke's decision in, 77
    dissent of Holmes and Brandeis in,
        77–79, 80–82, 108, 154, 158, 194,
        232
    events of, 76–77, 157–58
actual malice, 159
    Black on, 151, 177
    in Brennan's *Sullivan* opinion, 147,
        148, 149, 166–67, 168, 172–73,
        244
    Court of Appeals' formulation of, 120
    definitions of reckless disregard and,
        147, 201

malice compared with, 147
Powell's application of, 214–15,
    224
Adams, Abigail, 57, 65, 67, 73, 112,
    145
Adams, John, 54, 57, 63, 64, 65
    Sedition Act signed by, 58
advertisements, editorial, 5, 159–60
Alabama:
    black voter registration in, 21, 26
    libel law in, 12, 32–33, 106, 116,
        117–18, 120, 137, 138, 141, 146,
        180
    N.A.A.C.P. barred from, 44
    *New York Times* circulation in, 9, 23,
        111
    political change in, 44
    school segregation in, 21, 110
Alabama, University of, 21
Alabama Court of Appeals, 163
*Alabama Journal*, 9–10, 27, 34, 111,
    245
*Alabama Pleading and Practice at Law*
    (Jones), 25, 26, 132
*Alabama Public Service Commission v.
    Southern Railway*, 111
Alabama State College, 7, 10, 28, 29,
    31, 130
Alabama Supreme Court, 163
    on criticism of government body, 44–
        45, 108, 118, 130, 149

Alabama Supreme Court (cont'd)
  Sullivan and, 44–45, 103, 105, 108,
  132–33
Allen, John, 59
Alton Telegraph, 202
American Civil Liberties Union
  (A.C.L.U.), 92, 126, 227
American Law Institute, 114
American Nazi Party, 134, 247
American Newspaper Publishers Associ-
  ation, 92
American Opinion, 193, 225
amici curiae briefs, definition of, 124
"Anatomy of a Smear," 216
Anderson, David, 51, 225
Annenberg Washington Program, 229
anticommunism, 59, 83, 87, 112, 114,
  185, 193
  see also McCarthy era
anti-Semitism, 82, 90
appearances, general vs. special, 25, 26
Areopagitica (Milton), 51–52
armed forces, segregation in, 16
Aronson, Gershon, 5, 6, 7, 31
Authority in the Modern State (Laski),
  81
Avon, 204, 205

bad tendency, free speech and, 68, 70,
  74, 75–76
Baker, Sam Rice, 123
Baker v. Carr, 166
Bancroft, Harding, 31, 127, 128
Barnett, Stephen R. Sullivan decision-
  making report of, 165–82
Barr v. Matteo, 147
Beard, Charles, 87
Beauharnais v. Illinois, 42–43, 109,
  134, 142
Beddow, Roderick, 24
Bettman, Alfred, 73
Beveridge, Albert J., 61
Bickel, Alexander M., 40–41, 95, 128,
  244
Bill of Rights, U.S., 47, 48, 50, 59, 68,
  83
Birmingham, Ala.:
  racial incidents in, 39–40, 41, 162–
  63
  Salisbury's stories on, 21–22, 24, 35,
  105, 161, 222
Black, Hugo L., Jr., 99, 150
Black, Hugo L., Sr.:
  Alabama reputation of, 150
  Brennan's notes from, 152, 174–75,
  192–93
  Bridges opinion of, 99–102, 108,
  116, 143, 144
  on "clear and present danger," 101
  death of, 175, 194

on First Amendment, 96, 97–98, 99,
  100, 101, 129, 185–86, 190, 192,
  193, 244
Harlan and, 175
in Pentagon Papers case, 96
private papers of, 99
in Sullivan oral argument, 133–34,
  138
Sullivan separate concurring opinion
  by, 150–52, 159, 160, 171, 177,
  225
Supreme Court appointment of, 97,
  129
Time Inc. v. Hill and, 185–86, 200
Black Codes, 17, 18
Blackmun, Harry A., 191
blacks:
  excluded from juries, 17, 105, 110
  in political office, 42
  voting registration by, 19, 21, 26, 36,
  110
  see also civil rights movement;
  segregation
Blackstone, Sir William:
  on prior restraint, 53–54, 60, 68, 70,
  71, 93, 94
  Roe on, 74
  on seditious libel, 53–54, 60, 68, 69
Blackwell, Arnold D., 29
Blasi, Vincent, 71, 86
Bond, Julian, 235
Bork, Robert, 200, 207, 210
Branch, Taylor, 162
Brandeis, Louis D., 80–89, 114, 169,
  236
  background of, 82
  on "clear and present danger," 85,
  101
  on federalism, 171
  on free speech, 85–87
  Holmes compared with, 82
  Holmes's Abram dissent joined by, 77,
  82, 145
  Near v. Minnesota and, 92, 94
  on privacy, 184
  on stare decisis, 155
  Whitney dissent of, 84–87, 89, 100,
  101, 119, 143, 147, 194, 236
Brandenburg v. Ohio, 236
Brennan, William J., Jr., 190, 215, 242,
  247
  actual malice formula of, 147, 148–
  49, 151, 159, 166–67, 168, 172–
  73, 177
  Black's notes to, 152, 174–75, 192–
  93
  "convincing clarity" phrase of, 148,
  159, 167, 173
  Dun & Bradstreet v. Greenmoss
  Builders and, 230–31

flag-burning cases and, 238
*Herbert v. Lando* and, 202, 209
*Miami Herald v. Tornillo* and, 228
on obscenity, 136, 146, 167
on privacy, 186, 189
on public or general interest statements, 191–92
in *Sullivan* decision-making process,
   164–82
*Sullivan* evidence examined by, 147–
   49
*Sullivan* majority opinion by, 140–50,
   153–82, 226, 233, 235
in *Sullivan* oral arguments, 130, 131,
   132, 136, 139
Supreme Court appointment of, 127,
   129
as Warren's choice for opinion writer,
   166
Bridges, Harry, 98, 102, 132
*Bridges v. California*, 90, 97–102, 106,
   132, 135
   Black-Frankfurter conflict caused by,
   97, 98–100
   Black's opinion in, 99–102, 108, 116,
   143, 144
   events of, 98
   briefs in opposition, 111–12
Brown, David, 64
Brown, Henry, 18
Brownell, Herbert, Jr., 113, 122, 127,
   128
*Brown v. Board of Education*, 19 20,
   36, 89, 104, 110, 139, 150, 179
Bryan, William Jennings, 187
Bryant, Paul "Bear," 189, 191
burden of proof, 156–57, 165–66
Burger, Warren E., 191, 230, 231, 237,
   239
Burleson, Albert, 69–70
Burnett, Carol, 197
Bush, George, 207, 238
Butler, Pierce, 94
Butts, Wally, 189–90, 191
Byrnes, James F., 99

Cable News Network (CNN), 239
Callender, James T., 54, 64–65
Canan, Penelope, 211
*Cantwell v. Connecticut*, 116, 144
*Cato's Letters*, 51
CBS:
   *Herbert v. Lando* and, 201–2
   Southern libel suits against, 36, 151,
   245
   Westmoreland's libel suit against, 205,
   216–18, 226
Central Intelligence Agency (C.I.A.),
   205, 241–42
certiorari, definition of, 105

Chafee, Zechariah, Jr.:
   on "clear and present danger," 75–76
   conservative attacks on, 83–84
   on First Amendment, 75, 108, 145
   Holmes influenced by, 81, 87, 206
   on libel suits, 206
   on press freedom, 124
   on Sedition Act, 75
Chase, Samuel, 64–65
*Chicago Tribune*, 118, 124–25, 206
child labor laws, 68
Chile, Horman case and, 203–5
Cincinnati, Ohio, 243
Circuit Court of Montgomery County,
   12
citizenship, Constitution on, 17
*City of Chicago v. Tribune Company*,
   118, 125, 149, 170
Civil Rights Act (1866), 17
Civil Rights Act (1957), 20–21
Civil Rights Act (1964), 42
Civil Rights Commission, 20
civil rights laws, revival of, 105
civil rights movement, 5–6
   Freedom Riders and, 10–11, 21, 26,
   129, 162–63
   growth of, 19–20
   sit-ins and, 5–6, 10, 39
   Southern politics transformed by, 42
   white resistance to, 21, 26, 39–40,
   150
Civil War, U.S., 11, 16–17, 25, 81
Clark, Tom C., 134, 187, 190, 192
   in *Sullivan* decision-making process,
   171, 178–79, 180, 181
   Supreme Court appointment of, 129
Clarke, John H., 77
"clear and present danger," 82, 84, 114
   Black on, 100
   Brandeis on, 85, 101
   Chafee on, 75–76, 81
   in Holmes's *Abrams* dissent, 77, 81
   in Holmes's *Schenck* decision, 72, 80,
   83
   Supreme Court's abandonment of,
   236
*Cohens v. Virginia*, 174, 175
*Cohen v. California*, 237–38
*Coleman v. MacLennan*, 120, 147, 167
*Commentaries on the Laws of England*
   (Blackstone), 53–54
Committee to Defend Martin Luther
   King and the Struggle for Freedom
   in the South, 5, 6, 7, 9, 32, 109
common law:
   Blackstone as authority on, 53
   English tradition of, 48, 69
   Holmes on, 48, 198–99
   on libel, 116, 119–20, 195, 213, 221,
   223–24

common law (*cont'd*)
  on seditious libel, 52
  Seventh Amendment and, 135
  Supreme Court's use of, 48–49
*Common Law, The* (Holmes), 48, 72,
  82, 198
Communist Labor party, 85
Communist party, 100, 101, 114, 158,
  236
*Confederate Creed, The* (Jones), 25
Confederate States of America, 16–17,
  19, 25
Congress, U.S.:
  anticommunism and, 59
  civil rights legislation passed by, 17,
    19, 20–21, 42
  Federalist control of, 58, 65
  flag-burning and, 238, 243
  jurisdictional statutes passed by, 13
  Southern Manifesto and, 19–20
  Supreme Court and, 89
  *see also* House of Representatives,
    U.S.; Senate, U.S.
Connor, Eugene "Bull," 39, 222
Constitution, U.S., 8, 13, 46–51
  centralized power prevented by, 46–
    47
  on citizenship, 17
  common law and, 48–49
  drafting of, 46–47
  Electoral College and, 57
  endurability of, 49–50
  federalism and, 61, 171
  international influence of, 247
  ratification of, 47
  separation of powers in, 47
  slavery and, 16
  Supreme Court as interpreter of, 48–
    50
  *see also* Bill of Rights, U.S.; *specific
    amendments*
Constitutional Convention, 16, 42, 46,
  · 50, 57
constructive trusts, 241
contempt of court:
  *Bridges v. California* and, 97–102,
    106, 108, 132, 135, 144, 156
  in Great Britain, 97, 156, 246
  "convincing clarity," libel and, 148,
    159, 167, 173
Cooper, Thomas, 66
Costa-Gavras, Constantin, 203, 204,
  205
Court of Appeals, U.S., 101, 129
  in CNN case, 239
  in *Gertz v. Welch*, 193
  in *Herbert v. Lando*, 202
  in *Hustler Magazine v. Falwell*, 231
  in *Masses* case, 70
  in Newton case, 197–98

in Pentagon Papers case, 240
in Skokie case, 134
on special damages, 120
in Tavoulareas case, 201
Crawford, Vernon Z., 27, 28–29
criminal syndicalism, 84–85, 100, 108,
  121, 167, 236
Croly, Herbert, 81
Croswell, Harry, 54, 64
Crymes, Theotis, 35–36
*Curse of Bigness, The* (Brandeis), 82
*Curtis Publishing Co. v. Butts*, 189–92,
  229
Cushing, Alexander, 211

Dale, Sebe, 39
Daly, Thomas F., 122
Darrow, Clarence, 187
Davis, Jefferson, 26
Davis, Nathaniel, 204, 205
Debs, Eugene V., 72–73, 74, 76, 80–
  81, 118, 235
*Decent Interval* (Snepp), 241
Declaration of Independence, U.S., 57
declarations of falsity, 228–29
"Deep Throat," 126, 210
Defense Department, U.S., 240
*DeJonge v. Oregon*, 100, 108
Democratic Republican party (Jefferso-
  nian Republican party), 57–58, 59,
  60, 63, 64, 65, 66, 145
depositions, definition of, 205
*Desperate Hours, The* (Hayes), 184
Diana, Ronald, 43, 113, 122
discovery, in libel suits, 201, 202
double jeopardy, 118, 146
Douglas, William O.:
  absolute immunity favored by, 150,
    179, 190, 192
  Black's *Sullivan* opinion joined by,
    150, 179
  *Bridges* dissent of, 98
  in *Sullivan* oral arguments, 134
  Supreme Court appointment of, 129
*Dred Scott v. Sandford*, 16, 17
Dryfoos, Orvil, 13, 107, 127, 163
due process of law, 17, 68, 83, 109
*Duluth Rip-saw*, 91
Dun & Bradstreet, 196
*Dun & Bradstreet v. Greenmoss Build-
  ers*, 229–31
Dwyer, William L., 227

editorial advertisements, 5, 159–60
education:
  desegregation in, 19–21, 40, 41, 89,
    110, 139
  segregation in, 16, 19–20, 21
effective judicial administration, 180–81
Eisenhower, Dwight D., 21, 129

election of 1796, 57
election of 1800, 63, 64, 65, 73
election of 1876, 18
Electoral College, 57
Emancipation Proclamation, 17
Embry, T. Eric, 122, 161, 163, 245
  election to Alabama Supreme Court,
    44
  in *Sullivan* trial, 24, 25, 26, 27, 29,
    30, 31, 32, 43
Epstein, Richard A., 200, 221, 222
Errera, Roger, 247
Espionage Act (1917), 69–74, 76–79,
  80, 82
Espy, Mike, 42
Europe, libel law in, 229, 246–47
European Convention on Human Rights,
  246, 247
European Court of Human Rights, 246,
  247
*Execution of Charles Horman, The*
  (Hauser), 203–5

Falwell, Jerry, 231–33
Faulk, John Henry, 112
fault, in libel law, 156–57
Federal Bureau of Investigation (F.B.I.),
  36, 39, 101
*Federal Courts and the Federal System,
  The* (Wechsler and Hart), 104
federal government:
  branches of, 47
  Constitutional powers of, 47
  increased power of, 171
federalism, 61, 104, 121, 171, 175, 195
Federalist Papers, 57
Federalist party, 57–59, 60, 61, 64, 65,
  92
*Fighting Faiths* (Polenberg), 77
Firestone, Mary Alice, 197
First Amendment:
  adoption of, 50
  advertisements protected by, 159–60
  bad tendency and, 68, 70, 74, 75–76
  Black on, 96, 97–98, 99, 100, 101,
    129, 185–86, 190, 192, 193, 244
  Brandeis and Holmes's influence in
    interpretation of, 80–89
  Chafee on, 75, 108, 145
  contempt of court and, 98–99
  English tradition and, 98, 100, 102
  Espionage Act and, 69–74, 76–79,
    80, 82
  Frankfurter on, 100
  as fundamental protection, 83
  Hand on, 116
  journalistic privilege and, 131, 208–
    10, 215–16
  Marshall on, 62
  offensive speech protected by, 237–38

religion clause of, 62–63
Sedition Act and, 59–60, 62, 106,
  117, 137
seditious libel and, 55, 80, 108, 131,
  154, 195
state-level application of, 83–84, 85,
  90, 145, 169
Supreme Court as interpreter of, 48–
  50
Supreme Court's pre–World War I
  view of, 67–69, 73, 234
text of, 8, 47
*see also* freedom of speech; freedom of
  the press; libel, libel law
*Fiske v. Kansas*, 121, 132, 167
flag-burning cases, 238, 243
Fortas, Abe, 185–86, 187, 189, 190,
  191, 196
Fourteenth Amendment, 26, 91, 97,
  135, 142
  citizenship and, 17
  *Dred Scott* decision overruled by, 17
  due process of law and, 17, 68, 83
  equal protection clause of, 17, 18, 49
  First Amendment applied to states
    through, 83, 145, 169
Frankel, Marvin E., 104, 105–6, 113,
  114, 115, 122
Frankfurter, Felix, 53, 99, 111, 129
  English tradition revered by, 53, 98,
    100
  on freedom of speech, 97, 98, 100
  personal attacks in opinions of, 181
  on state power, 171
  Supreme Court appointment of, 97,
    98
Franklin, Marc A., 228, 229
freedom of speech:
  Brandeis on, 85–87
  meaning of, 47–50
  offensive speech and, 237–38
  opinions and, 213
  in Pennsylvania Declaration of Rights,
    51
  *see also* contempt of court; First
    Amendment; freedom of the press;
    libel, libel law
"Freedom of Speech in Wartime" (Chafee), 75, 81, 87
freedom of the press, 47, 50–55, 59,
  80–89
  comprehensive freedom and, 51
  federalism and, 61
  investigative journalism and, 158,
    202–3
  libel suits as threat to, 200–218
  licensing and, 51–52, 93
  Madison Report and, 61
  *Masses* case and, 69–70, 71
  privacy and, 183–89

348

freedom of the press (cont'd)
  in state constitutions, 50–51
  Supreme Court's growing recognition
    of, 93–94, 97
  see also contempt of court; First
    Amendment; freedom of speech; li-
    bel, libel law; media; prior restraint;
    Sedition Act
Freedom of the Press in the United
  States (Schofield), 69
Freedom Riders, 10–11, 21, 26, 129,
  162–63
Freedom's Fetters (Smith), 63
Freund, Ernst, 74, 81
Freund, Paul A., 87
Friedman, Stephen J., 180
Friendly, Fred W., 90–91
Friendly, Hugh, 225–26
Fumble (Kirby), 191

Gallatin, Albert, 59, 60, 117, 145
Gandhi, Mohandas K., 20, 36
Garment, Leonard, 188–89
Garrison, Jim, 154–55
Garrison v. Louisiana, 154–55, 184,
  192
general appearances, 25, 26
Georgia:
  black voter registration in, 37–39
  school segregation in, 21
Georgia House of Representatives, 235
Gertz, Elmer, 193, 196, 225
Gertz v. Welch, 193–97, 213, 214–15,
  224, 225, 230
Gitlow, Benjamin, 84, 194
Gitlow v. New York, 83–84, 85, 90,
  145
Goldberg, Arthur:
  absolute immunity favored by, 150,
    179
  in Sullivan decision-making process,
    150, 179, 180
  in Sullivan oral arguments, 131–32,
    135–36, 138, 215, 223
  Supreme Court appointment of, 129
  United Nations ambassador appoint-
    ment of, 185
Golden Fleece Award, 197
Goldmark, John, 227
Goodale, James, 35
government, see federal government;
  state governments
Gray, Fred, 27, 32
Great Britain, 56
  common-law tradition of, 48, 69
  contempt of court in, 97, 156, 246
  House of Lords of, 128
  libel law in, 157
  licensing of press in, 51–52, 93
  Official Secrets Act of, 246

prior restraint in, 96, 247
seditious libel in, 52–54, 60, 61, 69,
  125
Greek Commonwealth, The (Zimmern),
  87
Greensboro, N.C., 5–6
Griswold, Erwin, 240, 242
Grutman, Norman Roy, 232, 233
Gunther, Gerald, 70, 74, 236
Gurfein, Murray, 95, 158, 240

Hall, Grover C., Jr.:
  editorial response to "Heed Their Ris-
    ing Voices" by, 11, 22, 29
  libel suit meaning and, 26
  racial views of, 10–11
  Sullivan and, 10–11, 29
  trial testimony of, 29
Hall, Grover C., Sr., 10
Hamilton, Alexander, 46, 57, 89
Hancock, John, 47
Hand, Learned, 143, 169
  First Amendment views of, 70–71,
    72, 74–75, 76, 101, 116, 119
  Holmes's correspondence with, 74–
    75, 81
  Masses decision of, 70–71, 87, 236
Hanes, Arthur J., 39–40
Harcourt Brace Jovanovich, 204, 205
Hardin, Peter L., 202–3
Harlan, John Marshall (d. 1911), 18–19
Harlan, John Marshall (d. 1971), 228
  Black and, 175
  Curtis Publishing Co. v. Butts and,
    190
  in N.A.A.C.P. case, 44
  on offensive speech, 237–38
  Rosenbloom v. Metromedia and,
    223–24, 225
  in Sullivan decision-making process,
    164, 171–78, 180–82
  in Sullivan oral arguments, 130, 132,
    138
  Supreme Court appointment of, 127,
    129
  Time Inc. v. Hill dissent of, 187, 194,
    217
Hart, Henry M., Jr., 104
Harvard Law Review, 75, 81, 184
Harvard Law School, 82, 83
Hauser, Thomas, 203, 205
Hayes, Joseph, 184
Hayes, Rutherford B., 18
Hearst Corporation, 204
"Heed Their Rising Voices" (advertise-
  ment), 5–8
  Alabama Journal's story on, 9–10
  cost of, 6, 111
  inaccuracies in, 31, 32, 33, 121, 130,
    132–33, 137, 141, 143, 150, 159

libel suits as result of, 12, 13–14,
    146, 151; *see also Abernathy et al.
    v. Sullivan; New York Times Co. v.
    Sullivan*
McKee's report on, 12, 31
ministers named without consent in,
    11–12, 138
money raised by, 7
Montgomery *Advertiser's* editorial re-
    sponse to, 11, 22, 29
*New York Times* editorial quoted in,
    6
*New York Times* retraction and, 12–
    13, 31
as political document, 117, 130
publication of, 5–7
signatories of, 7, 9, 149
sponsoring committee for, 5, 6, 7, 9,
    32, 109
in *Sullivan* opinion, 141, 143, 149,
    150, 169
Sullivan's reputation and, 29, 30, 121,
    132, 133–34, 143, 149, 151, 170,
    221, 225
in *Sullivan* Supreme Court oral argu-
    ment, 130–38
in *Sullivan* trial, 28, 29, 30–33
text of, 6–7, 9–10, 28
Henry, Patrick, 47
Herbert, Anthony, 201–2
*Herbert v. Lando*, 201–2, 209, 229
Herndon, Angelo, 100, 142–43
*Herndon v. Lowry*, 100, 104, 142–43
Hill, Elizabeth, 184, 189
Hill, James, 184, 186, 187, 189, 200
Hofstadter, Richard, 59
Holmes, Oliver Wendell, Jr., 68–89, 94,
    119, 206, 243
    *Abrams* dissent of, 77–79, 80–82,
        108, 145, 154, 158, 194, 233
    background of, 82
    "clear and present danger" phrase of,
        72, 75–76, 77, 80, 81, 82–83, 84,
        85, 100–101, 114, 236
    on common law, 48, 198–99
    *Debs* decision of, 72–74, 235
    *Gitlow* dissent of, 83–84
    *Patterson v. Colorado* decision of,
        68–69, 71, 93, 94
    *Schenck* opinion of, 71, 72, 74, 75,
        76, 81
    *Schwimmer* dissent of, 87–89, 92,
        158
    on Sedition Act, 117
    "shouting fire in a theater" phrase of,
        71, 74
Holt, Charles, 63
Holt, John, 52
Horman, Charles, 203–4
Horman, Edmund, 204

House of Lords, Great Britain, 128
House of Representatives, U.S., 16
    First Amendment and, 50, 67
    Sedition Act and, 58
Howard, A. E. Dick, 245
Hughes, Charles Evans, 98, 99
    Chief Justice appointment of, 83
    free speech views of, 100, 108, 143
    *Near v. Minnesota* opinion of, 93–94,
        96, 238–39
*Hustler Magazine v. Falwell*, 231–33,
    238

Illinois Supreme Court, 118, 149
Immuno A.G., 211, 229
*Immuno A.G. v. Moor-Jankowski*,
    212–14, 216, 229
Industrial Workers of the World (Wob-
    blies), 85, 121
*in personam* jurisdiction, 24–25, 26
insurance, for libel suits, 221, 226
*In the City of Fear* (Just), 217
investigative journalism, libel suits as
    threat to, 202–3
Isaacman, Alan L., 231–32

Jackson, Robert H., 99, 172
James, Earl, *New York Times* sued by,
    13, 35, 146, 151
Jefferson, Thomas, 54, 63
    Adams's friendship with, 65
    death of, 65
    on democracy, 62
    election of, 64, 65, 73, 81
    in Federalist-Republican battle, 57
    inaugural address of, 66, 236–37
    on judiciary, 48
    Madison's state-level free speech
        amendment opposed by, 67–68
    omitted from Sedition Act, 58
    on press freedom, 67–68, 100, 145,
        206–7
    Sedition Act opposed by, 60–61, 112,
        130, 144, 235, 243
    Sedition Act victims pardoned by, 64,
        65, 73, 145
    on state libel power, 67–68, 112
Jehovah's Witnesses, 49, 116
Jenkins, Ray, 9–10
John Birch Society, 193, 225
Johnson, Lyndon B., 42, 185, 216
Jones, Thomas Goode, 25
Jones, Walter Burgwyn, 44
    background of, 25–26
    libel law as applied by, 32–33, 34–
        35
    in *Sullivan* trial, 25, 26, 27, 30, 32–
        33, 43, 45, 109, 123, 132
*Journal of Medical Primatology*, 211,
    214, 229

juries:
  anti-media bias of, 220
  blacks excluded from, 17, 105, 110
  in Espionage Act cases, 69, 74, 75, 76
  in libel cases, 106, 118, 122, 148,
    217–18, 219–20, 222, 224, 226,
    232
  reversal of awards by, 220–21
  in seditious libel cases, 52, 58
  Seventh Amendment and, 135, 167
  in *Sullivan*, 27, 130, 134–35
jurisdiction:
  federal vs. state, 13–14
  *in personam*, 24–25, 26
  statutes on, 13
  in *Sullivan*, 13–14, 24–26, 109, 122,
    132, 142
Just, Ward 217
Justice Department, U.S., 20–21, 26, 73

Kalven, Harry, Jr., 52, 81, 84, 154
Kaminsky, Harry W., 29
Kansas Supreme Court, 120
Kaye, Judith, 212–13
Kennedy, John F., 129
  assassination of, 42
  civil rights and, 39, 41–42
Kennedy, Robert F., 11, 40, 129
Kennedy administration, 21
Kentucky Legislature, 61
King, A. D., 39
King, Martin Luther, Jr., 248
  Alabama tax-evasion charges against,
    6, 9, 26–27
  Hall praised by, 11
  Hanes on, 39–40
  in "Heed Their Rising Voices," 5–7,
    12, 28, 30, 31, 121, 130, 141, 159
  Montgomery bus boycott and, 20
  Montgomery mob and, 21
  nonviolence urged by, 20, 36
  Patterson's libel suit filed against, 13
  on segregation, 15
Kirby, James, 191
Kirkland, Weymouth, 92
Kissinger, Henry, 197, 204
Kreisky, Bruno, 247
Ku Klux Klan, 10, 17, 236

Lachowsky, Hyman, 77
Lando, Barry, 201–2
La Pointe, Alan, 211
Laski, Harold, 81
*Legacy of Suppression* (Levy), 51
"Letter from Birmingham Jail" (King),
  15
letters to the editor, libel suits and, 211–
  14, 229
Leval, Pierre N., 216–17, 218, 229
Leventhal, Harold, 154

Levy, Leonard W., 51, 54
libel, libel law:
  absolute immunity and, 130–32, 146,
    166–67, 219
  in Alabama, 12, 32–33, 106, 116,
    117–18, 120, 137, 138, 141, 146,
    180
  burden of proof in, 156–57, 165–66
  common law on, 116, 119–20, 195,
    213, 221, 223–24
  "convincing clarity" and, 148, 159,
    167, 173
  as corporate weapon, 211–14
  criteria for, 28, 106
  declarations of falsity and, 228–29
  defense costs in lawsuits for, 201,
    220, 221
  discovery in, 201, 202
  in Europe, 229, 246–47
  fault and, 156–57
  federal vs. state jurisdiction in, 13–14
  government officials' immunity from
    suits for, 118–19, 147
  government officials' suits for, 118–
    19, 130–32, 183–99,
    204
  in Great Britain, 157
  growth of damage awards for, 200–
    201, 206, 220, 224–25
  insurance for, 221, 226
  juries and, 106, 118, 122, 148, 217–
    18, 219–20, 222, 224, 226, 232
  letters to the editor as lawsuit targets
    in, 211–14, 229
  malice and, 141, 147, 167
  opinion and, 213, 229
  public participation and, 211
  public vs. private spheres and, 183–
    99
  punitive damages in, 121–22, 134–
    35, 180, 220–30
  recent surge in lawsuits for, 200–218
  reforms proposed for, 219–33
  retractions and, 12, 229
  reversal of jury awards and, 220–21
  right to reply and, 228, 229
  Southern wave of lawsuits for, 36,
    161
  special damages for, 119–20
  state jurisdiction over, 13–14, 67–68,
    103, 112, 120
  statements of public or general interest
    and, 191–92
  as state political weapon, 34–36, 42,
    44–45, 118, 153, 222
  strict liability and, 195
  summary judgment and, 212, 213,
    214, 216, 218, 221
  truth and, 30, 32–33, 52, 54, 68–69,
    106, 116–17, 119, 120, 131–35,

143–44, 146, 157–60, 165, 167,
  168, 187, 217
*see also* actual malice; "clear and
  present danger"; First Amendment;
  Sedition Act; seditious libel
Libel Defense Resource Center, 220
liberty of contract, 68
Library of Congress, 99, 164
*Life*, 184, 185, 187, 189
Lincoln, Abraham, 17, 81
Lingens, Peter Michel, 246–47
Lipman, Samuel, 77
Little Rock, Ark., 41
Liu Binyan, 246
Locke, John, 81
Loeb, Louis M., 26, 107, 109, 127
  Birmingham lawyers retained by, 24
  ministers and, 43–44
  as *New York Times*'s chief lawyer,
    23–24
  *Sullivan* Supreme Court brief and,
    113, 122
  Wechsler retained by, 105
Long, Huey, 96–97
Lord, Day & Lord, 12, 24, 43, 105, 128
*Los Angeles Times*, 98, 102, 132, 209
Louisiana, school desegregation in, 21,
  40
Lovejoy, Elijah Parish, 203
Lowell, A. Lawrence, 83–84
Lowery, J. E., 12, 162
  *see also Abernathy et al. v. Sullivan*
Lucy, Autherine, 21
lynchings, 19, 39
Lyon, Matthew, 63–64, 66, 117, 145

McCarthy, Joseph, 87, 155
McCarthy era, 87, 112, 167, 185, 192,
  210
McCormick, Robert Rutherford, 92, 96
McGreal, Shirley, 211–12, 213, 214,
  229
McKee, Don, 12, 23, 31
McReynolds, James C., 94, 98, 99
Madison, James, 97, 236
  absolute immunity favored by, 131,
    146, 166–67, 219
  on democracy and free expression, 65,
    145, 153–54, 246, 247–48
  in drafting of Constitution, 46, 47, 48
  First Amendment drafted by, 42, 50
  on freedom of the press, 61, 93, 146
  on governmental secrecy, 242
  on people's sovereignty, 61, 62, 71,
    119, 145, 147, 153–54, 234
  political affiliation of, 57
  Report on the Virginia Resolutions by,
    61, 71, 73, 93, 115, 117, 130,
    144–45, 157, 169

state-level free speech amendment of,
  67
on suppression of freedom, 56
malice:
  actual malice compared with, 147
  in *Sullivan*, 141, 167
Mapplethorpe, Robert, 243
*Marbury v. Madison*, 48
Markel, Lester, 219–20, 228, 245
Markham, James E., 92–93, 94
Marshall, John, 48, 49–50, 61–63, 68,
  73
Marshall, Thurgood, 192, 223, 242
*Martin v. Hunter's Lessee*, 174
Mason, George, 47
Mason, Stevens T., 64
Massachusetts, 75
  Constitution ratified in, 47
*Masses*, 69–70, 71, 87, 236
media:
  confidential sources used by, 208,
    209–10
  jury bias against, 220
  Northern racial tensions ignored by,
    11
  public perception of, 207–8, 220, 243
  *St. Amant v. Thompson* and, 229
  self-censorship by, 200, 202
  as tool for political change, 36–37,
    40–41
  *see also* First Amendment; freedom of
    the press; television
medical malpractice, 220
Meiklejohn, Alexander, 154, 155, 183,
  197, 200
*Miami Herald*, 228
*Miami Herald v. Tornillo*, 228
*Milkweed*, 202–3
Mill, John Stuart, 53, 80
Milton, John, 51–52, 53, 93, 208–9
Minnesota, Public Nuisance Law of, 91,
  92, 93
*Minnesota Rag* (Friendly), 90
Minnesota Supreme Court, 91–92
*Missing* (Hauser), 205
*Missing* (movie), 203–5
Mississippi, 21, 42
Montgomery, Ala:
  black voter registration in, 36
  bus boycott in, 20
  racial incidents in, 10–11, 21, 150
Montgomery *Advertiser*, 9, 10, 11, 22,
  23, 29, 35, 111, 245
Moor-Jankowski, Jan, 212–14
Murphy, Frank, 98, 99
Murray, John, 5, 6, 7, 32

Nachman, M. Roland, Jr., 111, 161,
  245

Nachman, M. Roland, Jr. (cont'd)
  Sullivan Supreme Court brief by,
    123–24
  Sullivan Supreme Court oral argument
    of, 135–37, 138–39, 145, 167
  in Sullivan trial, 27, 29, 30
National Association for the Advance-
  ment of Colored People
  (N.A.A.C.P.), 26, 44, 144
National Enquirer, 197
national security cases, 240–43
NBC Nightly News, 197–98
Near, Jay M., 90–91, 92, 94, 96
Near v. Minnesota, 90–95, 97, 109,
    142, 156, 239, 242
Nebraska, 239
neutral principles, 104
New Orleans, La., school desegregation
    in, 40, 41
New Republic, 74, 80–81
New Scientist, 212
Newton, Wayne, 197–98, 220, 224–25
New York:
  Constitution ratified in, 47
  public commentary protected in, 213
  seditious libel in, 54
New York Civil Liberties Union, 126
New York Court of Appeals, 212–13
New Yorker, 188
New York State Legislature, 83
New York Supreme Court, 212
New York Times:
  advertising acceptability department
    of, 6, 31, 111
  advertising revenue of, 25
  Birmingham libel suits filed against,
    22, 222
  circulation figures of, 9, 25, 111
  editorial advertisements policy of, 5
  on Faulk's libel suit, 112
  "Heed Their Rising Voices" ad pub-
    lished by, 5–8
  house organ of, 43, 113
  James's libel suit against, 13, 14, 35,
    146, 151
  lawyers for, see Loeb, Louis M.; Lord,
    Day & Lord; Wechsler, Herbert
  libel policy of, 23, 107
  libel suit over Salisbury's Birmingham
    stories in, 22, 24, 35, 105
  libel suits as threat to survival of, 35,
    146
  McKee as stringer for, 12, 23
  Moor-Jankowski's letter to, 213–14
  other Southern libel suits against, 151
  Parks's libel suit filed against, 13
  Patterson's apology from, 12–13, 31,
    45, 137, 141, 148
  Patterson's libel suit filed against, 13

  Pentagon Papers and, 95–96, 128,
    240
  Sellers's libel suit filed against, 13, 14
  Sitton's Southern coverage in, 37–40
  Sullivan's demand of retraction from,
    11–12, 31, 45, 137, 141, 148
  Tweed exposed by, 92
  see also New York Times Co. v.
    Sullivan
New York Times Co. v. Sullivan, 5–45,
    67, 103–248
  Alabama Journal's editorial response
    to, 34
  Alabama jurisdiction and, 13–14, 24–
    26, 109, 122, 132, 142
  Alabama Supreme Court appeal de-
    nied in, 44
  amici curiae briefs in, 124–26, 138,
    146, 158
  Black's separate concurring opinion
    in, 150–52, 159, 160, 171, 177
  Brennan's majority opinion in, 140–
    50, 153–64, 226, 233, 235
  Bridges v. California and, 102
  brief in opposition in, 111–12
  damage award in, 33, 34, 35, 43, 45,
    121–22, 132, 141, 146, 161, 221
  Hall's trial testimony in, 29
  Jones's charge to jury in, 32–33,
    134–35
  jury in, 27, 130, 134–35
  legal legacy of, 7–8, 153–64, 234–
    48
  new trial denied in, 43–44, 168, 170,
    172–81
  New York Times Co. lawyers in, 24,
    26, 103
  New York Times Co. Supreme Court
    brief in, 113–22, 156
  oral arguments in, 127–39, 144, 146,
    165, 167, 215
  other trial witnesses in, 29–30, 31
  petition for certiorari in, 103–9, 112
  service of process in, 23, 25
  subsequent applications of, 183–99
  Sullivan's lawyers in, 27, 111, 123
  Sullivan's Supreme Court brief in,
    123–24
  Sullivan's trial testimony in, 28–29
  Supreme Court's decision-making pro-
    cess in, 164–82
  Supreme Court's decision on, 7–8, 36,
    140–82
  trial in, 23–33, 43, 123
  trial verdict in, 33
  see also Abernathy et al. v. Sullivan
Nicholas, John, 60, 61, 117, 145, 146
Nimmer, Melville B., 237
Nishikawa v. Dulles, 165–66, 167, 170

Nixon, Richard M., 187–89, 194, 206
  Chilean coup and, 204
  Watergate affair and, 126, 188
Nixon administration, 128, 244
Noriega, Manuel, 239
North, Oliver, 242

O'Brian, John Lord, 73
obscenity, 136, 146, 167, 191, 223, 243
O'Connor, Sandra Day, 232
offensive speech, Supreme Court on,
  237–38
Olson, Floyd B., 91
On Liberty (Mill), 53
opinion, libel and, 213
oral argument, 128
Oregon, 100, 108

Palmer, A. Mitchell, 83
Parker, Mack Charles, 39
Parker, William M., Jr., 29–30
Parks, Frank, 13
Parks, Rosa, 20
Parting the Waters (Branch), 162
Paterson, William, 63, 65
Patterson, John, 21, 35
  libel suit filed by, 13
  New York Times's apology to, 12–13,
    31, 45, 137, 141, 148
Patterson v. Colorado, 68–69, 71, 93,
  94
Pennsylvania, Declaration of Rights of,
  51
Pennsylvania Supreme Court, 205
Pentagon Papers, 95–96, 128, 158,
  240–41, 242, 244
Penthouse, 200
Philadelphia Inquirer, 205–6, 215, 221
Pickering, Timothy, 63
Pierce, Samuel R., Jr., 138
Plessy, Homer, 18
Plessy v. Ferguson, 18–19
Polenberg, Richard, 77, 81
political parties, rise of, 57
Portland Oregonian, 227
Powell, Lewis F., Jr., 194–95, 196, 213,
  214–15, 224, 230
presidential/vice-presidential tickets, in-
  troduction of, 57
press, see freedom of the press; media
Price, H. M., Sr., 29
Pring, George W., 211
prior restraint, 51
  Blackstone on, 53–54, 60, 68, 70, 71,
    93, 94
  First Amendment and prevention of,
    94, 97
  Hand on, 70
  Holmes on, 71, 93, 94

national security cases and, 241–43
Near v. Minnesota and, 93, 94–95,
  238–39, 242
subsequent punishment and, 51, 54,
  60, 70, 95, 97
privacy, free press and, 183–89
Proxmire, William, 197
public figures and officials:
  in Alabama Supreme Court's libel
    interpretation, 44–45, 108, 118,
    130, 149
  definitions of, 197
  as immune from libel suits, 118–19,
    147
  libel suits from, 118–19, 130–32,
    183–99, 204
  vortex, 194
Public Nuisance Law, 91, 92, 93
public participation, lawsuits against,
  211
Pulitzer Prize, of Hall, 10

Rabban, David M., 69, 72
Randolph, A. Philip, 6, 149
Rather, Dan, 207
Reagan, Ronald, 231, 232
reckless falsehood, see actual malice
Red Channels, 112
Redding, D. Vincent, 6, 31
Reed, Stanley, 98
Rehnquist, William H., 228, 232, 233
  Chief Justice appointment of, 231
  on flag-burning, 243
religion, First Amendment and, 62–63
reply, right to, 228, 229
Republican party, 18
retractions, libel law and, 12
returns, 170–71
"Right to Privacy, The" (Brandeis and
  Warren), 184
right to reply, 228, 229
Roberts, Eugene L., 215–16, 221
Roberts, Owen, 94, 98, 100–101, 116,
  144
Roe, Gilbert E., 73–74, 81
Rogers, William P., 125, 138, 159
Roosevelt, Franklin D., 97, 98, 99, 129,
  171
Roosevelt, Theodore, 82
Rosenbloom v. Metromedia, 191–92,
  223–24, 225
Roth v. United States, 167
Rushin, Judith, 27
Rustin, Bayard, 32

Salisbury, Harrison E., 21–22, 24, 35,
  105, 161, 222
Sanford, Edward T., 83, 85, 87

Sasser, Ga., voter-registration rally in, 37–39
*Saturday Evening Post,* 189, 190, 191
*Saturday Press,* 90–91, 92
Scalia, Antonin, 231–32
Schaefer, Walter, 206
*Schenck v. United States,* 71–72, 74, 75, 76, 81
Schofield, Henry, 69, 76
school desegregation, 19–21, 40, 41, 89, 110, 139
see also *Brown v. Board of Education*
Schumer, Charles, 228, 229
Schwartz, Bernard, 185
Schwimmer, Rosika, 87, 158
Scopes, John T., 187
Seay, S. S., Jr., 27
Seay, S. S., Sr., 12, 32
see also *Abernathy et al. v. Sullivan*
section 2106, 173, 174, 175
Sedition Act (1798), 56–66, 69, 92, 118
in Black's *Sullivan* opinion, 151
in Brennan's *Sullivan* opinion, 144–45, 181
constitutionality of, 59–60, 65, 67–68, 73, 81, 106, 112, 130, 144–45, 146, 151, 153
enacting of, 58
expiration of, 58, 65
First Amendment and, 59–60, 62, 106, 117, 137
Jefferson not protected by, 58
Jefferson's opposition to, 60–61, 67–68, 112, 130, 144, 235, 245
Madison's Report in protest of, 61, 71, 73, 93, 115, 117, 130, 144–45, 157, 169
Marshall's report in support of, 61–63
in New York Times Co. Supreme Court brief, 115, 117
pardoning of victims of, 64, 65, 73, 145
political background of, 56–58, 59
political criticisms of, 59–61
popular outrage against, 65, 115, 117, 144, 156
prosecutions brought under, 63–65
provisions of, 55, 58
restitution to victims of, 66, 73, 117, 145
see also libel, libel law; seditious libel
seditious libel, 52–55, 64, 106
Blackstone on, 53–54, 60, 68, 69
definition of, 52
First Amendment and, 55, 80, 108, 131, 154, 195
in Great Britain, 52–54, 60, 61, 69, 125
juries and, 52, 58

state laws on, 54, 55
truth and, 52, 54, 58, 60
see also libel, libel law; Sedition Act
segregation, 5, 15–22, 150
history of, 16–19
legal extent of, 15–16, 18
neutral principles and, 104
self-censorship, 146, 157, 194, 200, 202
Sellers, Clyde, 13
*Selling of Colonel Herbert, The,* 201
Senate, U.S., 42
First Amendment and, 50, 67
Sedition Act and, 58
service of process, 23, 25
Seventh Amendment, 135, 167, 168
Shainswit, Beatrice, 212
Shapiro, Irving, 91
Shapiro, Sam, 91
Sharon, Ariel, 205, 208
"shouting fire in a theater," 71, 74
Shuttlesworth, Fred. L., 12, 162–63
see also *Abernathy et al. v. Sullivan*
Simon & Schuster, 205
sit-ins, 5–6, 10, 39
Sitton, Claude, 31
Southern reporting by, 37–40
Sixth Amendment, 209
Skokie, Ill., 134, 247
slavery, 16–17
Smith, James Morton, 63
*Smith v. California,* 125, 146
Smolla, Rodney, 204, 207, 208
Snepp, Frank, 241, 243
*Snepp v. United States,* 241–42, 246
Socialist party, 72, 83–84
South Africa, Republic of, 160, 210
South Carolina, 21
Southern Christian Leadership Conference (S.C.L.C.), 32
Southern Manifesto, 19–20
Soviet Union, seditious libel in, 52
speech, freedom of, see freedom of speech
Sprague, Richard A., 206, 220, 225
*Spycatcher* (Wright), 96, 246
Squaw Valley Property Owners Association, 211
*St. Amant v. Thompson,* 229
*St. Louis Post-Dispatch,* 209
Stang, Alan, 193–94
*stare decisis,* 155–56
State Department, U.S., 204
state governments:
child labor laws and, 74
common law followed by, 54
Constitutional powers of, 47
decreased power of, 171
First Amendment applied to, 83–84, 85, 90, 145, 169

freedom of the press in constitutions
    of, 50–51
libel in jurisdiction of, 103
Madison's free speech amendment
    and, 67–68
seditious libel laws of, 54, 55
Supreme Court and, 173–74
Stedman, Seymour, 73
Steimer, Mollie, 76
Steiner, Robert E., III, 27, 32, 123
Stevens, John P., 242
Stewart, Potter, 192, 223, 241
    retirement of, 232
    in *Sullivan* decision-making process,
        171, 178, 179, 181
    in *Sullivan* oral arguments, 131,
        137
    Supreme Court appointment of, 129
Stone, Harlan F., 94, 98, 99, 104
*Strauder v. West Virginia*, 17, 18
*Stride Toward Freedom* (King), 11
*Stromberg v. California*, 100, 143
Strong, William, 17
Strum, Philippa, 87
Student Nonviolent Coordinating Com-
    mittee (S.N.C.C.), 235
*Suing the Press* (Smolla), 204
Sullivan, L. B.:
    effect of "Heed Their Rising Voices"
        on reputation of, 29, 30, 121, 132,
        133–34, 143, 149, 151, 170, 221,
        225
    Freedom Riders incident and, 10–11
    Hall and, 10–11, 29
    libel suit filed by, 12, 13, 23
    in others' trial testimony, 29, 30
    political aim of, 35, 42
    retraction demanded by, 11–12, 31,
        45, 137, 141, 148
    trial testimony of, 28–29
    see also *Abernathy et al. v. Sullivan;
        New York Times Co. v. Sullivan*
*Sullivan* case, see *New York Times Co.
    v. Sullivan*
Sulzberger, Arthur Hays, 24, 43, 107,
    163
summary judgment, 212, 213, 214, 216,
    218, 221
*Sunday Times* (London), 97
Supreme Court, U.S.:
    advisory opinions and, 49
    appraisals of facts by, 120–21, 132,
        135, 136, 167–68
    Bond case and, 235
    Chief Justice's assignment power in,
        166
    common law and, 48–49
    conferences of, 98, 99, 165, 172
    Congress and, 89
    Constitution interpreted by, 48–50

"effective judicial administration"
    phrase used by, 180–81
influence of Brandeis and Holmes on,
    80, 89
neutral principles and, 104
as nine separate offices, 172
oral argument before, 128
persuasive power of, 89
pre–World War I First Amendment
    view of, 67–69, 73
returns and, 170–71
and revival of civil rights laws, 105
on right to reply, 228
seating arrangement of, 128–29
*stare decisis* and, 155–56
state courts and, 173–74
*Sullivan*-era members of, 129
trial duty by members of, 63
on waiving of state court procedural
    rules, 163
Sutherland, George, 94, 97


Taney, Roger B., 16, 17
Tavoulareas, William, 200–201
television:
    *Missing* shown on, 205
    public opinion influenced by, 40–41
    public perception of, 207
Terrell County, Ga., black voter regis-
    tration in, 37–39
*Texas v. Johnson*, 238
thalidomide, 97, 246
Thatcher, Margaret, 246
Thirteenth Amendment, 17
Thompson, William A., 36
Thompson, William Hale, 125
*Time*, 205, 208
*Time Inc. v. Hill*, 184–89, 194, 196,
    200, 217
*Times Talk*, 43, 113
tort law, 195, 196, 207, 224, 226, 231
"Toward Neutral Principles of Constitu-
    tional Law" (Wechsler), 104
Truman, Harry S., 16, 119, 194, 206
Trump, Donald, 206
Turner, Theodore, 227
*TV Guide*, 216
Tweed, William M. "Boss," 92, 232
Twelfth Amendment, 57
2 Live Crew, 243
*Two Treatises on Civil Government*
    (Locke), 81


*Uncounted Enemy: A Vietnam Decep-
    tion, The*, 216
*United States v. Classic*, 104–5
*United States v. Schwimmer*, 87–89, 92,
    158
Universal Studios, 204

*Unpublished Opinions of the Warren Court, The* (Schwartz), 185

vaccination, compulsory, 75
Van Devanter, Willis, 94
Vermont *Journal*, 63
Vietnam War:
  Bond's opposition to, 235
  free expression of opposition to, 73, 158
  Pentagon Papers and, 95–96, 128, 158, 241, 242, 244
  *Westmoreland v. CBS* and, 205, 216–17
Virginia, 16, 42, 47, 50–51
  House of Delegates of, 61, 73
  N.A.A.C.P. and, 144
Virginia Court of Appeals, 173–74
Virginia Resolutions, Madison's Report on, 61, 71, 73, 93, 115, 117, 130, 144–45, 157, 169
vortex public figures, 194
voter registration, by blacks, 19, 21, 26, 36, 110
Voting Rights Act (1965), 42

Wachtel, I. H., 109, 123
Wallace, Mike, 202
*Wall Street Journal*, 203
Warren, Earl, 139, 165–66, 185, 190–91
  Bond case and, 235–36
  *Brown v. Board of Education* and, 19, 139, 179
  in *Sullivan* decision-making process, 166, 171, 178, 179, 181, 182
  Supreme Court appointment of, 127, 129
Warren, Samuel, 184
Washington, Bushrod, 65
Washington, D.C., segregation in, 16
Washington, George, 46, 49, 54, 55, 57, 232, 233
*Washington Post*, 242
  Pentagon Papers and, 95–96, 240
  *Sullivan amicus curiae* brief of, 125–26, 138, 146, 158
  Tavoulareas's libel suit against, 200–201
  Watergate affair coverage by, 126, 158, 210
*Wasp, The*, 54
Watergate affair, 126, 158, 188, 210
Webster, Daniel, 128

Wechsler, Doris, 113, 114, 115, 122, 139, 142
Wechsler, Herbert, 157, 163, 223, 228
  absolute immunity favored by, 130–32, 146, 167, 219
  as American Law Institute executive director, 114
  background of, 103–4
  *Curtis Publishing Co. v. Butts* and, 191
  federalist expertise of, 121, 182
  on libel law's complexity, 183, 244–45
  *Sullivan* petition of certiorari written by, 103, 105–9, 112
  *Sullivan* Supreme Court brief written by, 113–22, 156
  *Sullivan* Supreme Court decision received by, 140
  *Sullivan* Supreme Court oral argument by, 127–35, 144, 146, 165, 167, 215
Wechsler, Nancy F., 126
Welch, Robert, 193, 225
"We Shall Overcome," 38, 39
Westmoreland, William, 205, 206, 216–17, 226
*Westmoreland v. CBS*, 205, 216–18, 226
West Virginia, blacks barred from juries in, 17
White, Byron R., 190, 202, 233
  *Gertz v. Welch* dissent of, 195–96
  libel voting record of, 229–30
  in *Sullivan* decision-making process, 150, 171, 178, 179, 181, 229
  in *Sullivan* oral arguments, 130, 131, 133, 134, 136, 137
  Supreme Court appointment of, 129
White, Horace W., 30
Whitesell, Calvin, 27, 123
Whitney, Anita, 84–85, 87, 194, 236
*Whitney v. California*, 84–87, 100, 101, 119, 143, 147, 194, 236
Wilder, Douglas, 42
Wilson, Woodrow, 76, 81, 82, 157–58
Woolworth's, Greensboro sit-in at, 5–6
Wright, Peter, 246

XYZ affair, 56–57

Young, C. C., 87

Zimmerman, Alfred, 87